THE "MYSTERIES" OF QUMRAN

Society of Biblical Literature

Early Judaism and Its Literature

Judith H. Newman, Series Editor

Number 25

THE "MYSTERIES" OF QUMRAN
Mystery, Secrecy, and Esotericism
in the Dead Sea Scrolls

THE "MYSTERIES" OF QUMRAN
Mystery, Secrecy, and Esotericism in the Dead Sea Scrolls

Samuel I. Thomas

Society of Biblical Literature
Atlanta

THE "MYSTERIES" OF QUMRAN
Mystery, Secrecy, and Esotericism
in the Dead Sea Scrolls

Library of Congress Cataloging-in-Publication Data

Thomas, Samuel I. (Samuel Isaac)
   The "mysteries" of Qumran : mystery, secrecy, and esotericism in the Dead Sea scrolls / Samuel I. Thomas.
      p. cm. — (Early Judaism and its literature ; no. 25)
   Includes bibliographical references and index.
   ISBN 978-1-58983-413-2 (paper binding : alk. paper)
   1. Dead Sea scrolls. 2. Qumran community. 3. Judaism—History—Post-exilic period, 586 B.C.–210 A.D. Title.
   BM487.T47   2009b
   296.1'55—dc22
                                        2009043890

Printed in the United States of America on acid-free, recycled paper conforming to ANSI/NISO Z39.48-1992 (R1997) and ISO 9706:1994 standards for paper permanence.

For Christiana,
Eleanor,
and Cosmo

CONTENTS

ABBREVIATIONS

In general this study follows the conventions of the *SBL Handbook of Style*, edited by Patrick H. Alexander, John F. Kutsko, James D. Ernest, Shirley A. Decker-Lucke, and David L. Petersen (Peabody, Mass.: Hendrickson, 1999).

GENERAL

AB	Anchor Bible
ABD	*Anchor Bible Dictionary*. Edited by David Noel Freedman. 6 vols. New York: Doubleday, 1992.
ABRL	Anchor Bible Reference Library
ANRW	*Aufstieg und Niedergang der römischen Welt: Geschichte und Kultur Roms im Spiegel der neueren Forschung*. Edited by H. Temporini and W. Haase. Berlin, 1972–
AOAT	Alter Orient und Altes Testament
ATD	Acta Theologica Danica
BBB	Bonner biblische Beiträge
BDB	Brown, F., S. R. Driver, and C. A. Briggs. *A Hebrew and English Lexicon of the Old Testament*. Oxford, 1907
BEATAJ	Beiträge zur Erforschung des Alten Testaments und des antiken Judentum
BETL	Bibliotheca ephemeridum theologicarum lovaniensium
BN	*Biblische Notizen*
BJS	Brown Judaic Studies
BZAW	Beihefte zur Zeitschrift für die alttestamentliche Wissenschaft
CBC	Cambridge Bible Commentary
CBQ	*Catholic Biblical Quarterly*
CBQMS	Catholic Biblical Quarterly Monograph Series
CRINT	Compendia rerum iudaicarum ad Novum Testamentum
CSR	Contributions to the Study of Religion
DAWBSSA	Deutsche Akademie der Wissenschaften zu Berlin. Schriften der Sektion für Altertumswissenschaft
DDD	*Dictionary of Deities and Demons in the Bible*. Edited by K. van der Toorn, B. Becking, and P. W. van der Horst. Leiden, 1995
DJD	Discoveries in the Judaean Desert
DSD	*Dead Sea Discoveries*
DSSR	Dead Sea Scrolls Reader
EDSS	*Encyclopedia of the Dead Sea Scrolls*. Edited by Lawrence Schiffman and James C. VanderKam. 2 vols. Oxford, 2000
EncJud	*Encyclopaedia Judaica*. 16 vols. New York: Macmillan, 1972

FAT	Forschungen zum Alten Testament
FO	*Folia orientalia*
GMS	Grazer Morgenländischen Symposion
GTI	Gnostica: Text and Interpretations
HBT	*Horizons in Biblical Theology*
HDR	Harvard Dissertations in Religion
HR	*History of Religions*
HSM	Harvard Semitic Monographs
HSS	Harvard Semitic Studies
HUCA	*Hebrew Union College Annual*
ICC	International Critical Commentary
JAAR	*Journal of the American Academy of Religion*
JAOS	*Journal of the American Oriental Society*
JANESCU	*Journal of the Ancient Near Eastern Society of Columbia University*
JBL	*Journal of Biblical Literature*
JCS	*Journal of Cuneiform Studies*
JJS	*Journal of Jewish Studies*
JNES	*Journal of Near Eastern Studies*
JQR	*Jewish Quarterly Review*
JR	*Journal of Religion*
JSJ	*Journal for the Study of Judaism in the Persian, Hellenistic, and Roman Periods*
JSJSup	Journal for the Study of Judaism: Supplement Series
JSOTSup	Journal for the Study of the Old Testament: Supplement Series
JSP	*Journal for the Study of the Pseudepigrapha*
JSPSup	Journal for the Study of the Pseudepigrapha: Supplement Series
JSS	*Journal of Semitic Studies*
JTS	*Journal of Theological Studies*
KAT	Kommentar zum Alten Testament
LCL	Loeb Classical Library
LHBOTS	Library of Hebrew Bible / Old Testament Studies
LSTS	Library of Second Temple Studies
NTS	*New Testament Studies*
OBO	Orbis biblicus et orientalis
OIS	Oriental Institute Seminars
OTL	Old Testament Library
OTP	*Old Testament Pseudepigrapha.* Edited by James H. Charlesworth. 2 vols. New York: Doubleday, 1983
OtSt	*Oudtestamentische Studiën*
RB	*Revue Biblique*
RevQ	*Revue de Qumrân*

RHPR	*Revue d'histoire et de philosophie religieuses*
RI	Recherches Intertestamentaires
RO	*Rocznik Orientalistyczny*
RQ	*Revue de Qumran*
RSR	*Recherches de science religieuse*
RVV	Religionsgeschichtliche Versuche und Vorarbeiten
SBLDS	Society of Biblical Literature Dissertation Series
SBLEJL	Society of Biblical Literature Early Judaism and Its Literature
SBLSCS	Society of Biblical Literature Septuagint and Cognate Studies
SBLSP	*Society of Biblical Literature Seminar Papers*
SBLSS	Society of Biblical Literature Symposium Series
SBLTT	Society of Biblical Literature Texts and Translations
SBM	Stuttgarter biblische Monographien
SBT(h)	Studies in Biblical Theology
SCI	*Scripta Classica Israelica*
SDSSRL	Studies on the Dead Sea Scrolls and Related Literature
SHR	Studies in the History of Religions (Supplement to *Numen*)
SJLA	Studies in Judaism in Late Antiquity
ST	*Studia theologica*
STAC	Studien und Texte zu Antike und Christentum
STDJ	Studies on the Texts of the Desert of Judah
StPB	Studia post-biblica
SUNT	Studien zur Umwelt des Neuen Testaments
SVTP	Studia in Veteris Testamenti pseudepigraphica
TBL	Themes in Biblical Narrative
TCBAI	Transactions of the Casco Bay Assyriological Institute
TDOT	*Theological Dictionary of the Old Testament.* Edited by G. J. Botterweck and H. Ringgren. Translated by J. T. Willis, G. W. Bromiley, and D. E. Green. 14 vols. Grand Rapids, 1974–
TLOT	*Theological Lexicon of the Old Testament.* Edited by E. Jenni, with assistance from C. Westermann. Translated by M. E. Biddle. 3 vols. Peabody, Mass., 1997.
TSAJ	Texte und Studien zum antiken Judentum
UF	*Ugarit-Forschungen*
VTSup	Vetus Testamentum: Supplement Series
WMANT	Wissenschaftliche Monographien zum Alten und Neuen Testament
WUNT	Wissenschaftliche Untersuchungen zum Neuen Testament
YNER	Yale Near Eastern Researches
ZAVA	*Zeitschrift für Assyriologie und Vorderasiatische Archäologie*
ZAW	*Zeitschrift für die alttestamentliche Wissenschaft*
ZT(h)K	*Zeitschrift für Theologie und Kirche*

DEAD SEA SCROLLS

Throughout this book all texts and translations of the Qumran Scrolls are from the Discoveries in the Judaean Desert series unless otherwise noted.

DJD 1   Barthélemy, D. and J. T. Milik. *Qumran Cave 1*. Discoveries in the Judaean Desert 1. Oxford: Clarendon Press, 1955.

DJD 5   Allegro, J. M. *Qumran Cave 4.I (4Q158–186)*. Discoveries in the Judaean Desert 5. Oxford: Clarendon Press, 1968.

DJD 7   Baillet, M. *Qumrân Grotte 4.III (4Q282–5Q520)*. Discoveries in the Judaean Desert 7. Oxford: Clarendon Press, 1982.

DJD 10   Qimron, E., and J. Strugnell. *Qumran Cave 4.V: Miqsat Ma'ase ha-Torah*. Discoveries in the Judaean Desert 10. Oxford: Clarendon Press, 1994.

DJD 11   Eshel, E., H. Eshel, C. Newsom, B. Nitzan, E. Schuller, and A. Yardeni in consultation with J. VanderKam and M. Brady. *Qumran Cave 4.VI: Poetical and Liturgical Texts, Part 1*. Discoveries in the Judaean Desert 11. Oxford: Clarendon Press, 1997.

DJD 20   Elgvin, T. et al in consultation with J. A. Fitzmyer, S.J. *Qumran Cave 4.XV: Sapiential Texts, Part 1*. Discoveries in the Judaean Desert 20. Oxford: Clarendon Press, 1997.

DJD 21   Talmon, S., J. Ben Dov, and U. Glessmer. *Qumran Cave 4.XVI: Calendrical Texts*. Discoveries in the Judaean Desert 21. Oxford: Clarendon Press, 2001.

DJD 26   Alexander, P. and G. Vermes. *Qumran Cave 4.XIX: 4QSerekh ha-Yahad and Two Related Texts*. Discoveries in the Judaean Desert 26. Oxford: Clarendon Press, 1998.

DJD 29   Chazon, E., T. Elgvin, E. Eshel, D. Falk, B. Nitzan, E. Qimron, E. Schuller, D. Seely, E. Tigchelaar, and M. Weinfeld in consultation with J. VanderKam and M. Brady. *Qumran Cave 4.XX: Poetical and Liturgical Texts, Part 2*. Discoveries in the Judaean Desert 29. Oxford: Clarendon Press, 1999

DJD 31   Puech, É. *Qumrân Grotte 4.XXII: Textes Araméens, Première Partie, 4Q529–549*. Discoveries in the Judaean Desert 31. Oxford: Clarendon Press, 2001.

DJD 34   Strugnell, J., D. J. Harrington, and T. Elgvin in consultation with J. A. Fitzmyer, S.J. *Qumran Cave 4.XXIV: Sapiential Texts, Part 2, 4QInstruction: 4Q415ff*. Discoveries in the Judaean Desert 34. Oxford: Clarendon Press, 1999.

DJD 36   Pfann, S. J., P. Alexander, M. Broshi, E. Chazon, H. Cotton, F. M. Cross, T. Elgvin, D. Ernst, E. Eshel, H. Eshel, J. Fitzmyer, F. García Martínez, J. C. Greenfield, M. Kister, A. Lange, E. Larson, A. Lemaire, T. Lim, J. Naveh, D. Pike, M. Sokoloff, H. Stegemann, A. Steudel, M. Stone, L. Stuckenbruck, S. Talmon,S. Tanzer, E. J. C. Tigchelaar, E. Tov, G. Vermes, and A. Yardeni. *Qumran Cave 4.XXVI: Cryptic Texts and Miscellanea, Part 1.* Discoveries in the Judaean Desert 36. Oxford: Clarendon Press, 2000.

DJD 37   Puech, É. *Grotte 4.XXVII: Textes Araméens, Deuxième Partie, 4Q550–75, 580–82.* Discoveries in the Judaean Desert 37. Oxford: Clarendon Press, 2008.

DJD 40   Newsom, C., H. Stegemann, and E. Schuller. *Qumran Cave 1.III: 1QHodayot^a with Incorporation of 4QHodayot^{a-f} and 1QHodayot^b.* Discoveries in the Judaean Desert 40. Oxford: Clarendon Press, 2008.

PREFACE

In its earlier life this book was a doctoral dissertation written under the direction of James C. VanderKam at the University of Notre Dame. Jim has always been a reliable guide, and I continue to learn from his model of patient, steady, and excellent scholarship. As many people will readily attest (though with his characteristic humility, Jim would surely protest), his kindness and generosity are apparently without limit. I am exceedingly fortunate to have had him as a mentor and friend.

I am indebted to the other members of my dissertation committee, who have also been exemplary teachers. Gary Anderson has been a reliable source of information and inspiration, and I continue to marvel at the depth and range of his intellectual pursuits. John Meier helped me sharpen my scholarly work considerably by his keen and incisive reading and his encyclopedic knowledge of the relevant primary and secondary literature. And Gene Ulrich has always been quick to offer his time and attention, and if I had his mind for fragment recall and textual reasoning this project would have been completed long ago and with greater acuity.

I would also like to thank Hindy Najman of the University of Toronto, who encouraged me at an early stage to pursue the project and continued to help me through the various aporias of graduate student life. Joe Blenkinsopp has also shaped my thinking in important ways. His many writings have guided several generations of biblical scholars, and there is scarcely an aspect of the discipline to which he has not made a genuine and important—and often humane—contribution. It goes without saying that the people who have given their attention to my scholarly work are not responsible for any of its deficiences.

While I was at Notre Dame I was fortunate to receive a dissertation fellowship from the University. Additionally, the Catholic Biblical Association awarded me the Memorial Stipend for four years, which provided extra monetary support and made it possible to conduct my research under considerably less financial pressure.

Jarvis Streeter, as Chair of the Religion department at California Lutheran University, has consistently supported my teaching and scholarship and has extended himself in every way as a colleague and friend. I have been extraordinarily privileged to have wonderful colleagues in the Religion Department as a whole, people who cultivate the spirit of "learned and leisurely hospitality" that Ivan Illich once identified as "the only antidote to the stance of deadly cleverness that is acquired in the professional pursuit of objectively secured knowledge."

California Lutheran University—through the Provost's Office and the Hewlett Grant committee—has provided additional research support for which I am grateful. Kathy Horneck of the Pearson Library has been a resourceful and dependable partner in my research, making the Interlibrary Loan service as efficient as possible. If there are questions about whether I have done my research, she can testify that at least I checked out many books. Sue Bauer of Information Systems and Services graciously lent her expertise to the formatting of the manuscript.

I had the benefit of having many people read drafts of the various sections that make up this book, several of which were freshly written or heavily revised from the dissertation. Julia Fogg, Paul Hanson, Alex Lemon, Dan Machiela, Alison Schofield, Michael Stone, Jim VanderKam, and Molly Zahn all generously read chapters and provided helpful criticism. My students Caitlin Ellrott, Micah Peterson, Katey Wade, and Amy Wayne hunted down errors and assisted with the indexes, and I look forward to seeing how these young scholars develop their academic and professional pursuits into their very bright futures. Art Coppel— ever the sleuth even into his retirement—has been an exemplary proofreader and index-maker.

I am grateful to Judith Newman and Billie Jean Collins for accepting this book for publication in the Early Judaism and Its Literature series, and for all their help along the way. Judith provided both encouragement and helpful criticism to make this a better book than it might have been. Bob Buller provided much needed and much appreciated technical assistance as I formatted the manuscript. I would also like to thank Leigh Andersen, managing editor of SBL publications, for her solid and efficient support (and her patience) throughout the duration of the revision and publication process.

Many of the revisions to this manuscript took place in the children's section at the Foster Public Library in Ventura, California—a place where myth and reality are often difficult to distinguish from one another. Remarkably, this was one of the quieter areas of the library, and as I worked I kept my own daughter Eleanor close to mind. She learned more words than I wrote during the summer of 2008. While I was in the process of finishing the book, Eleanor was joined by Cosmo James who became the youngest member of the family. However the scholarly reviews come in, this book pales in comparison to their brilliance, and I am far more proud of them than of anything I have produced here.

Finally, my deepest gratitude goes to my wife Christiana. Without her this book would not have been written, a situation that has put her in a bit of a bind. She is patient and generous beyond all measure, and has taught me a thing or two about the value of perseverance and good humor.

CHAPTER ONE

INTRODUCTION

> Of course, we must keep in mind that two of the most
> famous discoveries of the [twentieth] century brought
> to light a number of documents emanating from
> secret or esoteric groups. I am referring to the Gnostic
> library of Nag Hammadi and to the manuscripts
> found in the Dead Sea caves.
>
> Mircea Eliade

To investigate the topic of mystery language in the Dead Sea Scrolls is to
venture into a hazardous proposition. The term "mystery" itself entails a
denial of access to its meaning; it often denotes things not understandable by human imagination, things—in Elliot Wolfson's words—
that are beyond "the spot where intellect falters before its own limit."[1]
Even if they are comprehensible, the contents of mysteries are often not

---

The epigraph for this chapter is from Mircea Eliade, *Occultism, Witchcraft,
and Cultural Fashions: Essays in Comparative Religions* (Chicago: University of
Chicago Press, 1978), 54.

[1] Elliot Wolfson, "The Seven Mysteries of Knowledge: Qumran
E/Sotericism Recovered," in *The Idea of Biblical Interpretation: Essays in Honor of
James L. Kugel* (ed. Hindy Najman and Judith Newman; JSJSup 83; Leiden: Brill,
2003), 179. At the beginning of his article "Religious Secrets and Secrecy in
Classical Greece" (in *Secrecy and Concealment: Studies in the History of
Mediterranean and Near Eastern Religions* [ed. Hans Kippenberg and Guy
Stroumsa; SHR 65; Leiden: Brill, 1995]), Jan Bremmer issues a similar statement:
"It is of course trivial to stress that by their nature secret acts in antiquity are
often difficult to discover, let alone study. There are few records of interrogation
left and few documents allow a more extended analysis." (61). But already here
we might make an important distinction between Wolfson's "mystery" as
epistemological limit or conundrum and Bremmer's understanding of secrecy as
a social phenomenon.

meant for *public* exposition, and the dynamics of their revelation and concealment complicate any effort to sort out their epistemological and social dimensions. Nevertheless, I attempt in this book to describe how Jewish texts from the Second Temple period employ mystery language, and how Qumran texts in particular express concepts of mystery in a way that encompasses sectarian knowledge and the different modes of religious authority in which it operates. Instead of focusing the discussion only on the contents of such knowledge,[2] this book investigates the use of mystery language in terms of its functions within the Qumran texts, and within the discourse(s) of the community/-ies responsible for their composition and preservation.[3]

Of course, mysteries often have an element of secrecy—in the social and political sense—and secret knowledge bestows certain advantages upon the knower, especially if it is a theological kind of knowledge that ties its legitimacy to divine provenance and to notions of special revelation. Hugh Urban, one of the recent authorities on the social functions of secrecy, describes it this way: "secrecy is better understood … not in terms of its content or substance—which is ultimately unknowable, if there even is one—but rather in terms of its *forms* or *strategies*—the tactics by which social agents conceal or reveal, hoard or exchange, certain valued information."[4] In this way, the category of "mystery" has as much to do with authority and power—and with strategies for claiming, expressing, and asserting authority and power—as it does with the special knowledge that falls within the esoteric domain.

With respect to the social dimensions of mysteries, there are several important and related issues. In recent years there has been a growing body of work dedicated to sorting out the complicated nature of Jewish sectarianism during the Second Temple period, one that has increasingly

---

[2] As Guy Stroumsa has pointed out, "we witness a weakened emphasis on the 'objective' secret. When what counts most is the identity of those who know the divine secrets and the protection of their special status, the secrets themselves seem to loose [*sic*] some of their importance" (*Hidden Wisdom: Esoteric Traditions and the Roots of Christian Mysticism* [Numen 70; Leiden: Brill, 1996], 5).

[3] See pages 23–30 for discussion of the social history of the group(s) associated with the site of Khirbet Qumran.

[4] Hugh B. Urban, "The Torment of Secrecy: Ethical and Epistemological Problems in the Study of Esoteric Traditions," *HR* 37 (1998): 210. Urban continues: "In this sense secrecy is a discursive strategy that transforms a given piece of knowledge into a scarce and precious resource, a valuable commodity, the possession of which bestows status, prestige, or symbolic capital on its owner."

incorporated a wider and more sophisticated range of methodologies to tackle that difficult problem.[5] In order to discuss early Jewish mystery language in terms of social-historical analysis, one must address the broad trend of sectarian formations in early Judaism, and the specific sectarianism of the group(s) associated with the Qumran Scrolls.[6] An allied but methodologically somewhat distinct dimension is that of "esotericism," which, as we will see in more detail in chapter 2, includes the concrete social exempla of sectarian group-formation but also incorporates the crucial aspect of special, and often secret, knowledge, which becomes, at least in part, both a justification for and a product of sectarianism.

MYSTERY AND SECRECY IN EARLY JUDAISM AND IN QUMRAN TEXTS

In Second Temple Judaism there are essentially two levels at which notions of mystery and secrecy appear to operate: the theological (or even mythological), which has to do with divine revelation and concealment; and the social or political, which has to do with the way certain persons or groups characterize, organize, and withhold or reveal certain kinds of knowledge (often of the theological or mythological kind) from other persons or groups. The present study is concerned with

---

[5] Important gains have been made with the use of social-scientific models and methods for understanding sectarian group-formation. Early studies include Bryan R. Wilson, *Magic and the Millennium: A Sociological Study of Religious Movements of Protest among Tribal and Third-World Peoples* (London: Heinemann, 1973); idem, *Religion in Sociological Perspective* (Oxford: Oxford University Press, 1982); idem, *The Social Dimensions of Sectarianism* (Oxford: Clarendon, 1990); Rodney Stark and William S. Bainbridge, *The Future of Religion: Secularization, Revival and Cult Formation* (Berkeley: University of California Press, 1985); Roy Wallis, ed., *Sectarianism: Analyses of Religious and Non-Religious Sects* (London: Owen, 1975). For discussion of more recent works, see below pages 61–66.

[6] The term "Dead Sea Scrolls" properly refers to the manuscripts found at numerous sites around the Dead Sea region, including Wadi Daliyeh, Ketef Jericho, Khirbet Mird, Wadi Murabbaʿat, Wadi Sdeir (Naḥal David), Naḥal Ḥever, Naḥal Mishmar, Naḥal Ṣeʾelim, and Masada, and not just those found near the Khirbet Qumran site. I will usually use the term "Qumran Scrolls" to refer to the manuscripts recovered from the Qumran caves, even if some copies of those texts were also found elsewhere (e.g. the *Songs of the Sabbath Sacrifice* at Masada; *Aramaic Levi* and the *Damascus Document* in the Cairo Genizah, etc.). See Emanuel Tov, ed., *The Texts from the Judaean Desert: Indices and an Introduction to the Discoveries in the Judaean Desert Series* (DJD 39; Oxford: Clarendon Press, 2002).

both aspects: the theological dimensions of special knowledge; and the social dimensions of secrecy and esotericism. An investigation of both of these aspects of the problem can help us to understand much about the Qumran Scrolls and the self-presentation of the group(s) affiliated with many of those texts.[7]

The main object of inquiry here will be the word רז *raz*—a Persian word borrowed into Aramaic and later into Hebrew,[8] and usually translated into Greek as μυστήριον, from which the English "mystery" is derived via the Latin *mysterium*. In addition to the word רז in its various forms, certain Hebrew words like סוד *sod* and נסתרות / סתר *nistarot / s-t-r*, are relevant to this study, though they have distinct valences within the broader sphere of secrecy and secret knowledge. While these terms have overlapping semantic ranges to some degree, they also have specific applications in the Qumran Scrolls. Though they have often been treated as pure synonyms in earlier studies, one should not assume that they are interchangeable even if there is some conceptual overlap. Because of its importance in the Qumran Scrolls, the primary task here is to elucidate the uses of רז and to tie Qumran notions of "mystery" into the larger framework of sectarianism, esotericism, and discourses of authority.

The word רז is intriguing not only for what it signifies—or sometimes fails to signify—but also for where it appears in ancient Jewish texts: in extant manuscripts from the Second Temple period, it occurs in Aramaic in the book of Daniel,[9] *1 Enoch* (*Book of the Watchers* [4Q201 1 iv 5]; *Birth of Noah* pericope, chapters 106-107 [4Q204 5 ii 26]), the *Book of Giants* (4Q203 9 3; possibly 1Q23), the *Visions of Amram* (4Q545 4 16; 4Q546 12 4), the *Genesis Apocryphon* (1Q20, passim), and the so-called "Elect of God" text (4Q534 1 i 7-8; 4Q536 2i+3 9, 12). In Hebrew it is witnessed in 4QInstruction (4Q415–18, 423; 1Q26),[10] *Mysteries*

---

[7] Guy Stroumsa's *Hidden Wisdom* is an attempt to provide a similar analysis for early Christianity in its various forms (Gnostic, Manichean, Orthodox, etc.). As a way to orient his Introduction he aptly quotes 1 Cor 2:6–7: "Yet among the mature we do speak wisdom, though it is not a wisdom of this age or of the rulers of this age, who are doomed to perish. But we speak God's wisdom, secret and hidden [θεοῦ σοφίαν ἐν μυστηρίῳ τὴν ἀποκεκρυμμένην], which God decreed before the ages for our glory" (NRSV translation).

[8] See the Appendix below for an extended etymological discussion.

[9] In fact, there are no extant manuscripts for the relevant portions of Daniel, but we may assume with some confidence that רז is attested there in its earliest stages of composition and transmission.

[10] This work was first known as 4QSapiential Work A, or 4QSapA, and is also referred to as *Musar-le-Mevin*; since the publication of the official edition, it is now customarily called 4QInstruction.

(1Q27/4Q299–300 [301?]), the *Songs of the Sabbath Sacrifice* (4Q401–407; 11Q17; Mas1k), and many of the central Qumran sectarian texts (*Community Rule, War Rule, Hodayot,* and others). It is also probable that the word is attested in Isa 24:16b (part of the so-called "Isaian Apocalypse"), though this is a long-disputed identification, a somewhat notorious *crux interpretum* of biblical translation and scholarship.

The word רז has received a significant amount of attention in recent years, due in no small part to the publication of the important Qumran wisdom composition 4QInstruction (4Q415–18, 423; 1Q26).[11] The use in that text of the highly enigmatic phrase רז נהיה ("the mystery that is to be") has been a source of great interest, and often frustration, for scholars throughout the last decade.[12] This renewed interest picks up a latent fascination with Qumran "mystery" since the earliest stages of scholarship on the Qumran Scrolls.

In the first two decades of Scrolls publication, the word רז received considerable attention, and commentators were quick to see it as an important link between many of the newly discovered texts. With the publication of the first scrolls from cave 1, namely the *Community Rule* (1QS), the *Hodayot* (1QHᵃ), the *War Rule* (1QM), *Pesher Habakkuk* (1QpHab) and the fragments known early on as "un apocryphe" (1Q26)[13] and "Livre des mystères" (1Q27),[14] scholars were confronted with what appeared to be an unusually high frequency of attestation in these Hebrew texts, especially given the relative paucity of "mystery" in non-Qumran texts of the Second Temple period and earlier.[15]

One of the first scholars to treat the use of רז in the Scrolls was J. T. Milik in the first volume of the Discoveries in the Judaean Desert series. Commenting on the justification for the title *Mysteries* selected for 1Q27, a "texte pseudépigraphique," Milik wrote, "en s'inspirant de la fréquence du mot רז, on peut donner à cette composition le titre

---

[11] For the *editio princeps* of 4QInstruction see John Strugnell, Daniel Harrington and Torleif Elgvin, DJD 34. 1Q26, another fragmentary manuscript of the same composition, was first published in DJD 1 by J. T. Milik (see below, n. 17).

[12] The phrase occurs over twenty times in 4QInstruction; see below for further discussion.

[13] It later became clear that this text was a manuscript of the same text as 4QInstruction (4Q415–18, 23). See DJD 34:535–39.

[14] This manuscript was later associated with the composition now usually called *Mysteries* (1Q27; 4Q299–300 [301?]).

[15] The word רז occurs only in the book of Daniel (2:18, 19, 27, 28, 29, 30, 47; 4:6), Sirach (8:18; 12:12), and as I argue below, in Isaiah (24:16).

'Livre/Apocalypse des Mystères.'"[16] Milik went on to identify the similar uses of רז in other cave 1 texts, but did not remark at any length about mystery language in Qumran writings generally.

In his 1956 article in Latin, E. Vogt took note of the fact that mystery language, though relatively rare in early Second Temple texts, seemed to play a significant role in key non-biblical texts from Qumran.[17] Of course, only the cave 1 materials were available for discussion at that point.[18] In his eclectic approach Vogt surveyed all the Hebrew, Aramaic, and Greek evidence for mystery language in early Jewish texts.[19] In all, however, this article lacked any major conclusions apart from the idea that all these texts formed the "background" for Christian ideas about "mystery" expressed in the New Testament. Despite its understandable limitations, Vogt's study has been used primarily for its catalog of relevant literature and for his description of how mystery language enters into Aramaic and Hebrew usage during the Second Temple period.

In a handful of works still cited often,[20] Raymond Brown redoubled Vogt's effort to link early Jewish mystery language to ancient Near Eastern traditions about the divine assembly and attendant notions of secrecy (i.e. סוד), and took the extra step of placing the various references to mystery into helpful categories: (1) evil mysteries; (2) cosmic

---

[16] D. Barthélemy, O.P. and J. T. Milik, eds., DJD 1:103. A manuscript of the text that later came to be called 4QInstruction was also discovered in Cave 1, and was initially named "un apocryphe" (1Q26) in the DJD edition. Parts of 1Q27 had been previously published by Roland de Vaux in "La Grotte des manuscrits hébreux," *Revue Biblique* 56 (1949): 605–609 (cf. J. T. Milik, *Verbum Domini* 39 [1952]: 42), and commented on by I. Rabinowitz, "The Authorship, Audience, and Date of the de Vaux Fragment of an Unknown Work," *JBL* 71 (1952): 19–32.

[17] E. Vogt, "Mysteria in Textibus Qumrân," *Biblica* 37 (1956): 247–57.

[18] "Vox *rāz* = 'secretum, mysterium' in manuscriptis Qumrân plus quam 40^ies occurrit" (Vogt, "Mysteria," 247). We now know that the word is attested over 140 times in as many as twenty-nine different compositions, and new attestations are still trickling out from new readings of fragmentary manuscripts.

[19] In addition to the cave 1 texts he also adduced the Cairo Geniza *Damascus Document*, Daniel, Sirach, Wisdom of Solomon, Tobit, and *1 Enoch*.

[20] Brown wrote his Johns Hopkins dissertation on "The Semitic Background of the Pauline *Mystērion*" (Ph.D. diss., Johns Hopkins University, 1958), which was followed by several short publications on the topic: "The Pre-Christian Semitic Concept of 'Mystery,'" *CBQ* 20 (1958): 417–43; "The Semitic Background of the New Testament *Mysterion*," *Biblica* 39 (1958): 426–48 and *Biblica* 40 (1959): 70–87 (both republished together in *The Semitic Background of the Term "Mystery" in the New Testament* [Biblical Series 21; Philadelphia: Fortress, 1968]).

mysteries; (3) mysteries of God's will and human action; (4) mysteries of the last times; (5) mysteries of divine providence; (6) mysteries of the Qumran sect's interpretation of the Law. Brown's work, though useful and insightful in many respects, is also rather incomplete and limited in its overall interpretive potential for gaining more depth of insight into important Qumran viewpoints. Brown's studies were also undertaken with the aim of throwing light once again on early Christian mystery language, a tendency that can be found in nearly all early investigations of mystery language in the Qumran Scrolls.[21] In any case, with the full publication of the cave 4 (and other) material in recent years, we are now in a better position to gain a more comprehensive and nuanced understanding of mystery language in the Scrolls.[22]

More than twenty years elapsed between Brown's work and the next significant study of mystery language in early Jewish texts. In 1982 Christopher Rowland published his widely read book, *The Open Heaven*,[23] in which he attempted a comprehensive re-evaluation of the nature of "apocalyptic"[24] in early Judaism and Christianity by drawing

---

[21] See also B. Rigaux, "Révélation des Mystères et Perfection a Qumran et dans le Nouveau Testament," *NTS* 4 (1958): 237–62; J. M. C. Ramírez, "El Tema 'Misterio' divino en la 'Regla de la Comunidad de Qumran," *ST* 7 (1975): 481–97; idem, "Los 'Himnos' de Qumran y el 'Misterio' paulino," *ST* 8 (1976): 9–56; idem, "El 'Misterio' divino en los escritos posteriors de Qumran," *ST* 8 (1976): 445–75.

[22] The publication of the known Scrolls and fragments has been drawn to an official close with the appearance of Emanuel Tov's final volume of the Discoveries in the Judaean Desert series (*The Texts from the Judaean Desert*). Volume 32 of that series that has yet to appear in print (Isaiah scrolls, edited by Eugene Ulrich and Peter Flint).

[23] Christopher Rowland, *The Open Heaven: A Study of Apocalyptic in Judaism and Early Christianity* (New York: Crossroad, 1982).

[24] This term, while still in use in some scholarship coming out of the U.K. and continental Europe, and in much New Testament scholarship, has fallen out of favor in North American research on Second Temple Judaism, which has tended to follow the distinctions (outlined in John J. Collins et al, *Semeia 14* [1979]) between "apocalypse" (a literary genre), "apocalyptic view of reality" (a worldview), and "apocalyptic movement" (a group of people with an apocalyptic worldview, who may or may not write apocalypses). See for example Klaus Koch, *The Rediscovery of Apocalyptic* (trans. M. Kohl; SBTh 22; London: SCM, 1972); Paul Hanson, *The Dawn of Apocalyptic: The Historical and Sociological Roots of Jewish Apocalyptic Eschatology* (Philadelphia: Fortress, 1975); Eibert J. C. Tigchelaar, *Prophets of Old and the Day of the End: Zechariah, the Book of Watchers and Apocalyptic* (OtSt 35; Leiden: Brill, 1996), 1–15; Lester L. Grabbe, "Prophetic and Apocalyptic: Time for New Definitions—and New Thinking," in *Knowing the*

attention away from the eschatological (or "horizontal") dimensions of apocalypticism and toward its revelatory or visionary (or "vertical") dimensions. The visionary texts he examines are

> distinguished from other Jewish and Christian literature by the underlying conviction that they contain visions, or disclosure by heavenly envoys, which unfold various aspects of God's will and other mysteries of the world and man's life in it. ... Truths which are beyond man's capacity to deduce from his circumstances are revealed directly by means of the manifestation of the divine counsels.[25]

Rowland underestimates the variety of modes in which mysteries come to be articulated in early Jewish traditions—especially in Qumran texts—and does not address the ways in which these various modes function within a specific community setting. This is perhaps a result of his focus on literature that may properly be called "apocalyptic"—that is literature that narrates an "unveiling"—and not, for example, on texts that describe interpretive acts (*Pesher Habakkuk*), liturgical experiences (*Songs of the Sabbath Sacrifice*), or wisdom instruction (4QInstruction). One aim of the present book is to deal not only with apocalyptic literature so narrowly defined but also with those other texts in which mystery language plays a significant role.[26] If Qumran was the site of an

---

End from the Beginning: The Prophetic, the Apocalyptic, and Their Relationships (ed. Lester L. Grabbe and Robert D. Haak; London: T&T Clark, 2003), 107–33. See also John J. Collins, "Prophecy, Apocalypse, and Eschatology: Reflections on the Proposals of Lester Grabbe," in *Knowing the End from the Beginning*, 44–52.

[25] Rowland, *Open Heaven*, 17.

[26] *The Open Heaven* succeeds to the degree that it reorients the question of "apocalyptic experience" toward the vertical dimension (cf. J. Carmignac, "Qu'est-ce que l'Apocalpytique? Son emploi à Qumrân," *RevQ* 10 [1979]: 3–33; Hartmut Stegemann, "Die Bedeutung der Qumranfunde für die Erforschung der Apokalyptik," in *Apocalypticism in the Mediterranean World and the Near East: Proceedings of the International Colloquium on Apocalypticism, Uppsala, August 12–17, 1979* [ed. David Hellholm; Tübingen: Mohr-Siebeck, 1983], 495–530), but it suffers from a lack of conceptual and lexical clarity as well as a from a somewhat arbitrary selection of source material. Additionally, Rowland's distinction between "direct" and "indirect" revelation of the heavenly mysteries is neither helpful nor accurate. As Adela Collins stated in a review of *The Open Heaven*, "Rowland's intention is to distinguish those ancient writers who explicitly claimed a divine origin for their texts from those who did not. The terms 'direct' and 'indirect' do not serve him well in making this distinction as the following statement shows: 'What we are faced with in apocalyptic, therefore, is a type of religion whose distinguishing feature is a belief in *direct* revelation of the things

apocalyptic community, and if many of the Scrolls reflect an apocalyptic worldview, then we are justified in looking beyond those texts that might be classified within the literary genre of "apocalypse."[27]

Whatever the shortcomings of Rowland's terminology and overarching categories, his book offers the first sustained, general study of the theme of mystery-revelation in Second Temple Jewish texts, and informs my own work to some degree, especially his notions of "vertical" and "horizontal" dimensions of mystery language. Rowland organized his work around the four topics whose consideration is proscribed in the Mishnah ("what is above, what is beneath, what was before, and what will be," *m. Ḥag.* 2.1), focusing in particular on "what is above" (the mysteries of the heavenly world) and "what will be" (the mysteries of what is to come). Whereas Rowland focused almost exclusively on elucidating the *content* of mystery-revelation, the present study considers more fully the *processes* and *uses* of mystery knowledge, i.e. the reception and transmission of "mysteries" in the context of Qumran esotericism.

In 1990 Markus Bockmuehl published an important monograph with the title, *Revelation and Mystery in Ancient Judaism and Pauline Christianity*. The similarity in theme (and title) between this work and Rowland's is evident, yet Bockmuehl offers a more cohesive account of the relationships between mystery language and the different modes of revelation in Second Temple Jewish religious expressions. He details the ways in which the themes of "mystery" and "revelation" are characterized in various collections of Jewish literature of the period (apocalyptic texts; Qumran compositions; wisdom literature; Targums and Greek translations of scriptural texts; Philo and Josephus; early

---

of God which was *mediated* through dream, vision, or divine intermediary' (p. 21; emphasis added). It does not make sense to speak of direct revelation being mediated. The term 'direct' better fits the oracle genre, through which divine secrets are simply announced, whereas 'indirect' is appropriate for the mediated revelation of the apocalypses" (Adela Yarbro Collins, review of *The Open Heaven*, *JBL* 103 (1984): 465–67, here 466).

[27] On Qumran as an apocalyptic community, see especially John J. Collins, *Apocalypticism in the Dead Sea Scrolls* (London: Routledge, 1997); Jörg Frey and Michael Becker, eds., *Apokalyptik und Qumran* (Einblicke 10; Paderborn: Bonifatius, 2007); Florentíno García Martínez, *Qumran and Apocalyptic: Studies on the Aramaic Texts from Qumran* (STDJ 9; Leiden: Brill, 1992); idem, "Apocalypticism in the Dead Sea Scrolls," in *Qumranica minora I: Qumran Origins and Apocalypticism* (ed. Eibert J. C. Tigchelaar; STDJ 63; Leiden: Brill, 2007), 195–226.

rabbinic literature), and concludes that "all ... affirm at least a measure
of continued divine revelation ... revealed to inspired, skilled, and
ethically qualified exegetes, [often] described in terms of divine
'mysteries.'"[28] This insight—that mysteries are somehow connected to
continued revelation—is an important one for understanding the dynamics
of mystery language in the Qumran Scrolls.

Indeed, as Bockmuehl briefly discusses, this notion of continued
revelation allows for the full range of Qumranic attitudes regarding the
relationship between scripture[29] and interpretation: legal exegesis of
torah, interpretation (*pesher*) of the prophets and writings, the role played
by the Teacher of Righteousness in many of the Qumran compositions,
and the status of texts such as the book of *Jubilees* and the *Temple Scroll*.
However, Bockmuehl's focus on mysteries as they relate to the technical
categories of revelation—which, to be fair, is the proper subject of his
book—precludes other, non-revelatory contexts in which mystery
language is used in Qumran texts. As the present work will demonstrate,
there are other important dimensions of mystery language in the Scrolls.
While these are related to notions of concealment and revelation, a
momentary bracketing of the customary ways of thinking about
"revelation" within the usual categories of traditional Judaism and
Christianity can help to crystallize several unique features of Qumran
esotericism.

Since the early 1990s—in the wake of the final push to publish all the
Qumran Scrolls[30]—a great deal of scholarly attention has been paid to

---

[28] Markus Bockmuehl, *Revelation and Mystery in Ancient Judaism and Pauline
Christianity* (WUNT 36; Tübingen: Mohr Siebeck, 1990; repr., Grand Rapids,
Mich.: Eerdmans, 1997), 124–25.

[29] Given the rather evident fact that there was no "Bible" during the period
under consideration, and that there were authoritative (scriptural) texts at
Qumran that are not later "canonized," I use this term in a loose sense
throughout this book. See for example Eugene Ulrich, *The Dead Sea Scrolls and the
Origins of the Bible* (SDSSRL; Grand Rapids, Mich.: Eerdmans, 1999); James C.
VanderKam, "Authoritative Literature in the Dead Sea Scrolls," *DSD* 5 (1998):
382–402; idem, "Revealed Literature in the Second Temple Period," in *From
Revelation to Canon: Studies in the Hebrew Bible and Second Temple Literature*
(Leiden: Brill, 2002), 1–30; Peter Flint, ed., *The Bible at Qumran: Text, Shape, and
Interpretation* (SDSSRL; Grand Rapids, Mich.: Eerdmans, 2001).

[30] For a cogent account of the publication history of the Scrolls see
VanderKam and Flint, *The Meaning of the Dead Sea Scrolls: Their Significance for
Understanding the Bible, Judaism, and Christianity* (San Francisco: Harper
SanFrancisco, 2002), 381–403.

4QInstruction and related compositions.[31] 4QInstruction has generated considerable excitement among scholars of early Judaism and

---

[31] Armin Lange, *Weisheit und Prädestination: Weisheitliche Urordnung und Prädestination in den Textfunden von Qumran* (STDJ 18; Leiden: Brill, 1995); idem, "Wisdom and Predestination in the Dead Sea Scrolls," *DSD* 2 (1995): 340–54; idem, "In Diskussion mit dem Tempel: zur Auseinandersetzung zwischen Kohelet und weisheitlichen Kreisen am Jerusalemer Tempel," in *Qohelet in the Context of Wisdom* (ed. Anton Schoors; BETL 136; Leuven: Leuven University Press, 1998), 113–59; John Strugnell, "The Sapiential Work 4Q415ff. and the Pre-Qumranic Works from Qumran," in *The Provo International Conference on the Dead Sea Scrolls* (ed. Donald W. Parry and Eugene Ulrich; STDJ 30; Leiden: Brill, 1999), 595–608; Torleif Elgvin, "An Analysis of 4QInstruction" (Ph.D. diss., Hebrew University of Jerusalem, 1997); idem, "Admonition Texts from Cave 4," in *Methods of Investigation of the Dead Sea Scrolls and the Khirbet Qumran Site: Present Realities and Future Prospects* (ed. Michael O. Wise et al; Annals of the New York Academy of Sciences 722; New York: New York Academy of Sciences, 1994), 179–96; idem, "Early Essene Eschatology: Judgment and Salvation According to Sapiential Work A," in *Current Research and Technological Development on the Dead Sea Scrolls: Conference on the Texts from the Judean Desert, Jerusalem, 30 April 1995* (ed. Donald W. Parry and S. D. Ricks; STDJ 20; Leiden: Brill, 1996), 126–65; idem, "'The Mystery to Come': Early Essene Theology of Revelation," in *Qumran between the Old and New Testaments* (ed. F. H. Cryer and T. L. Thompson; JSOTSup 290; Sheffield: Sheffield Academic Press, 1998), 113–50; idem, "Priestly Sages? The Milieus of Origin of 4QMysteries and 4QInstruction," in *Sapiential Perspectives: Wisdom Literature in Light of the Dead Sea Scrolls. Proceedings of the Sixth International Symposium of the Orion Center, 20-22 May 2001* (ed. Gregory Sterling and John J. Collins; STDJ 51; Leiden: Brill, 2004), 67–88; Daniel Harrington, "The *Rāz Nihyeh* in a Qumran Wisdom Text (1Q26, 4Q415–18, 423)," *RevQ* 17 (1996): 549–53; idem, "Recent Study of 4QInstruction," in *From 4QMMT to Resurrection: Mélanges qumraniens en hommage à Émile Puech* (ed. Florentino García Martínez, Annette Steudel and Eibert J. C. Tigchelaar; STDJ 61; Leiden: Brill, 2006), 105–23; idem, "Wisdom and Apocalyptic in 4QInstruction and 4 Ezra," in *Wisdom and Apocalypticism in the Dead Sea Scrolls and in the Biblical Tradition* (ed. Florentino García Martínez; BETL 168; Leuven: Leuven University Press, 2003), 343–55; Eibert J. C. Tigchelaar, *To Increase Learning for the Understanding Ones: Reading and Reconstructing the Fragmentary Early Jewish Sapiential Text 4QInstruction* (STDJ 44; Leiden: Brill, 2001); idem, "The Addressees of 4QInstruction," in *Sapiential, Liturgical and Poetical Texts from Qumran: Proceedings of the Third Meeting of the International Organization for Qumran Studies, Oslo 1998* (ed. Daniel Falk et al; STDJ 35; Leiden: Brill, 2000), 62–75; Darryl Jefferies, *Wisdom at Qumran: A Form-Critical Analysis of the Admonitions in 4QInstruction* (Gorgias Dissertations, Near Eastern Studies 3; Piscataway, N.J.: Gorgias Press, 2002); Loren T. Stuckenbruck, "4QInstruction and the Possible

Christianity in part because it contains elements of both wisdom and apocalypticism and throws important light on these two trends and their corresponding literary genres—helping to clarify what has been a point of controversy since Gerhard von Rad first began to argue that apocalyptic circles were successors not to the prophetic tradition but to sapiential streams of thought.[32] 4QInstruction has a clear wisdom orientation, and yet it is different from earlier Israelite wisdom texts such as Proverbs and from roughly contemporaneous works such as Sirach. Most important for our purposes, 4QInstruction "often appeals to supernatural revelation in the form of the *rāz nihyeh* (רז נהיה), which can be translated as 'the mystery that is to be.' The *rāz nihyeh* is the main tool by which the addressee acquires wisdom"[33] and it "constitutes an appeal to heavenly revelation that is at the core of 4QInstruction."[34] While the

---

Influence of Early Enochic Traditions: An Evaluation," in *The Wisdom Texts from Qumran and the Development of Sapiential Thought* (ed. Charlotte Hempel, Armin Lange and Herman Lichtenberger; BETL 159; Leuven: Leuven University Press, 2002), 245–61; John J. Collins, "The Mysteries of God: Creation and Eschatology in 4QInstruction and the Wisdom of Solomon," in *Wisdom and Apocalypticism in the Dead Sea Scrolls and in the Biblical Tradition* (ed. Florentino García Martínez; BETL 168; Leuven: Leuven University Press, 2003), 287–305; Matthew Goff, *The Worldly and Heavenly Wisdom of 4QInstruction* (STDJ 50; Leiden: Brill, 2003); idem, "The Mystery of Creation in 4QInstruction," *DSD* 10 (2003): 163–86; idem, "Reading Wisdom at Qumran: 4QInstruction and the Hodayot," *DSD* 11 (2004): 263–88; idem, *Discerning Wisdom: The Sapiential Literature of the Dead Sea Scrolls* (VTSup 116; Leiden: Brill, 2007); Joshua Ezra Burns, "Practical Wisdom in 4QInstruction," *DSD* 11 (2004): 12–42; Bilhah Nitzan, "The Ideological and Literary Unity of 4QInstruction and Its Authorship," *DSD* 12 (2005): 257–79; Benjamin G. Wold, *Women, Men and Angels: The Qumran Wisdom Document 'Musar leMevin' and Its Allusions to Genesis Creation Traditions* (WUNT 2/201; Tübingen: Mohr Siebeck, 2005); Émile Puech, "Les Fragments eschatologiques de 4QInstruction (4Q416 I et 4Q418 69 ii, 81–81a, 127)," *RevQ* 22 (2005): 89–119 Florentino García Martínez, "Marginalia on 4QInstruction," *DSD* 13 (2006): 24–37.

[32] Von Rad first began to make this argument in his *Theologie des Alten Testaments* (vol. 2; Munich: C. Kaiser, 1960), 315–37, an argument he refined in later editions and in *Weisheit in Israel* (Neukirchen–Vluyn: Neukirchener Verlag, 1970), translated into English as *Wisdom in Israel* (Nashville: Abingdon Press, 1972), 337–63. See also Magne Sæbø, *On the Way to Canon: Creative Tradition History in the Old Testament* (JSOTSup 191; Sheffield: Sheffield Academic Press, 1998), 232–47, which is the chapter, "Old Testament Apocalyptic in its Relation to Prophecy and Wisdom: The View of Gerhard von Rad Reconsidered."

[33] Goff, *Discerning Wisdom*, 10.

[34] Ibid., 13.

precise meaning of this phrase will itself likely remain something of a mystery, I return to a more extensive discussion of the significance of רז נהיה in chapter 4.

It will suffice for now simply to note that in all probability 4QInstruction, along with *Mysteries*, is a text that was of great importance to the Yaḥad,[35] and its use of "mystery" is thus an important piece of the overall puzzle. While discussion of the meaning of רז נהיה constitutes only a part of what follows, it is a salient reference point for any discussion of Qumran ideas about "mystery."

As might be expected, analysis of mystery language is often part and parcel of discussions about mysticism, mystagogy, mystical theology, theosophy, and similar topics. In recent years there have been several attempts to link Qumran mystery language—especially in texts like the *Songs of the Sabbath Sacrifice*—to mystical ideas and practices, which are then placed in continuity with later Jewish mysticism as refracted through texts like the Heikhalot literature (3 *Enoch*/*Heikhalot Rabbati, Heikhalot Zutarti*, etc.) and the *Zohar*. For example, in a recent essay Elliot Wolfson suggested a new category for thinking about Qumran "mystery," namely, that רז has a trajectory of meaning that he calls the "onto-theosophic."[36] For Wolfson, the cosmological and eschatological dimensions of "mystery" are grounded in this third, ontological, dimension, wherein the participant in a heavenly liturgy—as in the *Songs of the Sabbath Sacrifice*—experiences a transformation resulting in special access to the imaginal[37] realm of the eternal Temple. As such, the

---

[35] At least six manuscripts were discovered in the Qumran caves. See below for an explanation of how I understand and use the term "Yaḥad."

[36] Wolfson, "The Seven Mysteries of Knowledge."

[37] The term "imaginal" was originally coined by Henri Corbin in order to sidestep the connotation that something that takes place in the imagination, something that is "imaginary," is also "unreal"; see for example his *Spiritual Body and Celestial Earth: From Mazdean Iran to Shi'ite Iran* (Princeton, N.J.: Princeton University Press, 1977): "The imaginal is everything that surpasses the order of common empirical perception and is individualized in a personal vision, undemonstrable by simple recourse to the criteria of sensory knowledge or rational understanding. … It is often completely misconstrued through the habits of the rational mind, which identifies it simply with the unreal" (87). See Eibert J. C. Tigchelaar's recent article in the Florentino García Martínez *Festschrift*, "The Imaginal Context and the Visionary of the Aramaic *New Jerusalem*," in *Flores Florentino: Dead Sea Scrolls and Other Early Jewish Studies in Honor of Florentino García Martínez* (ed. Anthony Hilhorst, Émile Puech, and Eibert J. C. Tigchelaar; JSJSup 122; Leiden: Brill, 2007), 257–70.

participant gains knowledge (דעת, a key term for Wolfson)—which itself is a designation for the divine pleroma, "the imaginal world of the chariot-throne"—and is united in worship with the angels, or the "sons of heaven."[38] Thus the unification of the members of the Yaḥad with the angels is the result of an ontic transformation, so that "heavenly ascent [of the community] and incarnational presence [of the angels] may be viewed as two ways of considering the selfsame phenomenon."[39]

While Wolfson's observations were limited to only a small handful of texts, they suggest some potentially fruitful avenues of research. Nevertheless, one cannot escape the feeling that his assessment is overburdened by his desire to see in the *Sabbath Songs* a kind of precursor to later Jewish mystical traditions, and by his willingness to read neo-Platonic categories into Qumran texts without qualification.[40] Additionally, it still is not clear whether the evidence for inner transformation that he sees in a few liturgical texts from Qumran is descriptive of an individual experience or prescriptive for the Yaḥad as a whole. Despite these reservations, the connections with the temple and with worship—both heavenly and earthly—are important insights that will be developed at greater length in the following chapters.

Philip Alexander has subsequently broadened the approach to Qumran mysticism, arguing that there was indeed a form of mysticism and/or mystagogy practiced by the Yaḥad. Drawing on a history of religions model for assessing the character of Qumran religious experience, Alexander finds that "if we apply both our indicative [i.e. cross-cultural parallels] and abstract criteria for the definition of mysticism, we can readily identify a corpus of Qumran texts that *prima facie* qualify to be called mystical."[41] While the present book is not primarily about Qumran mysticism, some of what I present below will corroborate Alexander's overall formulation. In the process I also engage the work of other scholars who have commented on the question of Qumran mysticism.

---

[38] Wolfson, "The Seven Mysteries of Knowledge," 206.

[39] Ibid., 213.

[40] See esp. the philosophical terms "ontological" or "onto-theosophic."

[41] Philip S. Alexander, *The Mystical Texts* (LSTS 61; London: T&T Clark, 2006), 10. Alexander examines especially the *Songs of Sabbath Sacrifice*, 4QBlessings, 4QWords of the Luminaries, 4QPseudo Ezekiel, 11QMelchizedek, 4QSongs of the Sage[a], 4QDaily Prayers, and the *Hodayot*. See also Samuel Thomas, review of Philip S. Alexander, *The Mystical Texts: Songs of the Sabbath Sacrifice and Related Manuscripts*, Review of Biblical Literature [http://bookreviews.org] (2008).

"Mystery" and Translation

I have opted to place the word "mystery" in quotation marks for the following reasons. First, the usual translation of the Hebrew/Aramaic word רז by the English word "mystery" is somewhat problematic. It is difficult enough to uncover the meanings of the word in its ancient usage without the extra baggage that the word "mystery" implies. It is true that the usual Greek translation of רז is μυστήριον in texts like Daniel and *1 Enoch*, and this may help to explain the reflexive scholarly tendency to render the Aramaic term as such in English. Nevertheless, even if there is an affirmative semantic association between רז, μυστήριον, and "mystery," it will be important in the following study not to begin by assuming a one-to-one correspondence among these different terms.

The second reason for the quotation marks is that the Aramaic רז is itself often understood to be a direct borrowing from the Persian *raz*. But as I have discussed in the Appendix at the end of this book, the textual and linguistic evidence invites us to use some caution—or at least to be clear about the assumptions that support this association. While the English word "mystery" is a convenient and customary translation of רז, one that is rooted in the Greek translation into μυστήριον, it does not automatically indicate the meaning of *raz* in either its Persian or Aramaic/Hebrew uses.

Finally, "mystery" in quotation marks indicates the specific reference to רז, while I will typically use other English words to translate the related סוד (secret or council) and סתר/נסתרות (hidden things). The semantic values of these different terms receive more treatment in chapter 4, in part to confirm one thesis of the project as a whole, namely that within the broader language of secrecy and esoteric knowledge in the Qumran Scrolls, the term רז has a specific function and appears to be an important technical term in the many texts in which it is used. Without quotation marks, the term mystery (or mysteries) can apply in general to the full range of mystery language.

Throughout this book I operate with the notion that "mystery" is above all a "concept," an idea that serves as a shorthand reference to a body of knowledge, to the inner transformative power of that knowledge, and to the epistemological and social dynamics of access to and exclusion from matters of "ultimate concern."[42] Yet there is an

---

[42] The term "ultimate concern" is from Paul Tillich, *Systematic Theology* (vol. 1; Chicago: University of Chicago Press, 1951). While Tillich used the term with reference to Christian theology, his definition applies in a limited way to

important methodological point that deserves to be clarified.[43] In what follows I do not suppose by elucidating the various uses of רז in the Qumran Scrolls that I am saying anything final about the *inherent* value or meaning of the relevant terms. In fact, I do not even take it as a self-evident presupposition that *raz* means "mystery," but instead I am interested in testing the degree of equivalence of these two terms,[44] perhaps especially in order to sidestep the potential etymological fallacy that looms in the relationship between English "mystery" and Greek μυστήριον, and so on.[45] I wish to avoid falling prey to the tendency Jonathan Z. Smith calls to our attention: "Words are notoriously difficult and slippery affairs, yet, in recent years, we have seen them impeached,

---

"Qumran theology": "The religious concern is ultimate; it excludes all other concerns from ultimate significance; it makes them preliminary. The ultimate concern is unconditional, independent of any conditions of character, desire, or circumstance. The unconditional concern is total: no part of ourselves or of our world is excluded from it; there is no 'place' to flee from it."

[43] I would like to thank the anonymous reviewer of an early draft of this manuscript. This reviewer called my attention to a shortcoming that, I hope, has been overcome in the final version of the book. This reviewer aptly noted that my former use of terms like "*raz*-concept" was problematic, not least because "there is no inherent concept, however dynamic, imbedded in any word." The problem is reminiscent of James Barr's forceful critique of the Biblical Theology movement in the 1960s, a movement whose proponents perpetuated the methodological flaw of identifying linguistic phenomena with theological thought, often for the purpose of contrasting "the Hebrew and Greek minds." "As soon as evidence from linguistic phenomena is used in the contrast of Hebrew and Greek ways of thinking, a relation is being established between mental pattern and linguistic structure" (Barr, *The Semantics of Biblical Language* [Oxford: Oxford University Press, 1961], 21–45, here 25). Such was not my goal, of course, and I appreciate the redirection.

[44] "The test of explanations of words is by their contexts" (Barr, *Semantics*, 113). See for example Jonathan Z. Smith, *Drudgery Divine: On the Comparison of Early Christianities and the Religions of Late Antiquity* (Chicago: University of Chicago Press, 1990), 74: "If one places [Daniel 2] within the wider context of such royal wisdom contests, the most adequate substitution for the 'secret' represented by *rāz* or *mystērion* in Daniel would be something like 'puzzle.'"

[45] As Barr states, "The main point is that the etymology of a word is not a statement about its meaning but about its history" (*Semantics*, 109). See also Arthur Gibson, *Biblical Semantic Logic: A Preliminary Analysis* (New York: St. Martin's Press, 1981); J. P. Louw, *Semantics of Biblical Greek* (Philadelphia: Fortress, 1982).

by individuals within the field of religious studies, for their clarity and fixity."[46]

I am interested here in delineating the semantic diversity of mystery language in the Scrolls while also elucidating the conceptual frameworks in which this language is deployed. Words and concepts are not the same thing, but attending to the uses of רז in a given corpus will allow the contours of a dynamic concept to appear. After all, "words can only be intelligibly interpreted by what they meant at the time of their use, within the language system used by the speaker or writer."[47] My central aim is to animate the social history, the self-understanding, and the religious activities of the Yaḥad by paying sustained attention to the discursive unit of "mystery." After all, there is always a specific, historical dimension to language use, as well as social-contextual shifts that must be taken into account in any given analysis. We should not expect a word like "mystery" in Yaḥad-composed texts to have the same meaning(s) in, for example, the Pauline corpus—and the act of comparison can blur important distinctions even while it may draw out useful parallels.

"MYSTERIES," GREEK LANGUAGE, AND HELLENISM

The present study devotes limited attention to the use of mystery language in Greco-Roman literature and texts of early Judaism and Christianity written in (or translated into) Greek. Many studies have already attempted to tackle that vexed (and vexatious) problem.[48]

---

[46] Smith, *Drudgery Divine*, 54.

[47] Barr, *Semantics*, 140.

[48] The literature on ancient mystery religions in general is vast and will not be cataloged here. On Christian "mystery-terminology" in its Greco-Roman context, and for additional bibliography, see most recently Hans-Josef Klauck, *The Religious Context of Early Christianity: A Guide to Graeco-Roman Religions* (tr. Brian McNeil; Minneapolis: Fortress, 2003), esp. 81–89; A. E. Harvey, "The Use of Mystery Language in the Bible," *JThS* NS 31 (1980): 320–36; G. Bornkamm, "μυστήριον, μυέω," *TDNT* 4.802–28; C. Riedweg, *Mysterienterminologie bei Platon, Philon, und Klemens von Alexandrien* (Berlin: de Gruyter, 1987); Smith, *Drudgery Divine*, 54–84. For studies on Jewish Greek mysteries see discussion and notes below. As Smith explains in detail, Isaac Casaubon was apparently the first to endeavor a scholarly comparative investigation (in 1614) of mystery-terminology in early Christian texts in his *De rebus sacris et ecclesiasticis exercitationes XVI* (Smith, *Drudgery Divine*, 55–56). Smith goes on brilliantly to uncover the methodological fallacies that often attended earlier philological/etymological

Additionally, there is in general little evidence of direct dependence between the content of the Qumran Scrolls and the religious values and practices of Hellenistic culture.[49] In fact, it is possible that the Scrolls show signs of deliberate resistance to Greco-Roman cultural and linguistic incursions.[50] Of course, all this is not to underestimate the

---

work in religious studies, connecting the scholarly assessments of antiquity to contemporary Roman Catholic and Protestant theological preoccupations (see the entire third chapter, "On Comparing Words"), or to the desire to limit the sphere of influence on earliest Christianity to "Judaism" and its available theological concepts. See now recently Benjamin L. Gladd, *Revealing the Mysterion: The Use of Mystery in Daniel and Second Temple Judaism and Its Bearing on First Corinthians* (BZNW 160; Berlin: de Gruyter, 2008), esp. 8–15. Unfortunately, this work came to my attention too late in the process of revising this book for publication, and I have not been able to incorporate much of its salient commentary into this book.

[49] Some scholars have argued in favor of certain important parallels. For example, with respect to community structure, see Moshe Weinfeld, *The Organizational Pattern and the Penal Code of the Qumran Sect: A Comparison with Guilds and Religious Associations of the Hellenistic-Roman Period* (Göttingen: Vandenhoeck & Ruprecht, 1986); M. Klinghardt, "The Manual of Discipline in the Light of Statutes of Hellenistic Associations," in *Methods of Investigation of the Dead Sea Scrolls and the Khirbet Qumran Site: Present Realities and Future Prospects* (ed. Michael O. Wise et al; Annals of the New York Academy of Sciences 722; New York: The New York Academy of Sciences, 1994), 251–70; S. Walker-Ramisch, "Graeco-Roman Voluntary Associations and the Damascus Document: A Sociological Analysis," in *Voluntary Associations in the Graeco-Roman World* (ed. John S. Kloppenborg and S. G. Wilson; London: Routledge, 1996), 128–45; Albert I. Baumgarten, "Greco-Roman Voluntary Associations and Jewish Sects," in *Jews in a Greco-Roman World* (ed. Martin Goodman; Oxford: Clarendon Press, 1998), 93–111; John J. Collins, "Forms of Community in the Dead Sea Scrolls," in *Emanuel: Studies in Hebrew Bible, Septuagint, and Dead Sea Scrolls in Honor of Emanuel Tov* (ed. Shalom M. Paul et al; VTSup 94; Leiden: Brill, 2003), 97–111.

[50] See, for example, Hannah Cotton, "Greek," *EDSS*, 1.324–26. She states that "Qumran texts evince a deliberate and conscious avoidance of Greek loanwords. This runs counter to the prevailing trend in spoken and written Aramaic and Hebrew at the time" (324). Additionally, among the 930 manuscripts recovered from the eleven Qumran caves, only twenty-seven of them were written in Greek (3%). Of these, only one is a documentary text—in marked contrast to the remains of other find-sites around the Judean desert—and the rest are literary (probably scriptural) texts. While there are other possible explanations, Emanuel Tov's seems the most plausible: "The picture emerging from an analysis of the Greek texts from the Judean Desert is that the situation at Qumran differs totally from that of the other sites. At most sites, all the Greek texts (and in Wadi Murabba'at and Masada, the great majority) are

importance of the Greek sources for understanding Second Temple Judaism more broadly, or the claims that the Septuagint or Philo or the New Testament legitimately make for our attention, but for the most part consideration of the Greek texts has led to a tendency to read μυστήριον into Qumran (often by way of the New Testament). This, I contend, is not an entirely helpful tendency, and it potentially obscures the distinction between "mystery-terminology" and "mystery religion."[51]

In 1935 Erwin R. Goodenough published his monumental tome, *By Light, Light: The Mystic Gospel of Hellenistic Judaism*, a study which for all

---

documentary, showing that Greek was actively used among the persons who deposited the texts. ... On the other hand, there is no proof that the Greek language was in active use among the inhabitants of Qumran. It is possible that at least some of them knew Greek, since fragments of Greek Scripture were found in caves 4 and 7. However, cave 4 probably served as a depository of some kind (not a library) in which the Qumranites placed all their written texts (mainly Hebrew and Aramaic literary works, but also a number of *tefillin* and *mezuzot* as well as brief notes and scribal exercises). This depository in cave 4 contained eight Greek texts, which may signify that the person(s) who brought them to Qumran had used them prior to their arrival, thus implying a knowledge of Greek. ... Furthermore the small number of Greek texts found at Qumran is also in striking contrast to the large number from the other sites in the Judean Desert. The difference is partly chronological (most of the sites in the Judean Desert are from a later period than Qumran), but more so a matter of content since the Qumran Greek corpus is mainly religious" (Emanuel Tov, *Scribal Practices and Approaches Reflected in the Texts Found in the Judean Desert* [STDJ 54; Leiden: Brill, 2004], 301). Of course, avoidance of Greek was not total, and we must remain cautious about drawing definitive conclusions about its use at Qumran. See James C. VanderKam, "Greek at Qumran," in *Hellenism in the Land of Israel* (ed. John J. Collins and Gregory E. Sterling; CJAS 13; Notre Dame, Ind.: University of Notre Dame Press, 2001), 175–81; cf. A. R. C. Leaney, "Greek Manuscripts from the Judaean Desert," in *Studies in New Testament Language and Text: Essay in Honour of George D. Kilpatrick on the Occasion of His Sixty-fifth Birthday* (ed. J. K. Elliott; Leiden: Brill, 1976), 283–300; Leonard Greenspoon, "The Dead Sea Scrolls and the Greek Bible," in *The Dead Sea Scrolls after Fifty Years: A Comprehensive Assessment* (ed. Peter Flint and James C. VanderKam; 2 vols.; Leiden: Brill, 1999), 1.101–27. One should also take note of the use of Greek signs in the cryptic scripts from Qumran (see S. J. Pfann, "298. 4QCryptA Words of the Maskil to All Sons of Dawn," in DJD 20:1–31), as well as the in the Copper Scroll (3Q15) (see Judah Lefkovitz, *The Copper Scroll: 3Q15: A Reevaluation. A New Reading, Translation, and Commentary* [STDJ 25; Leiden: Brill, 2000], 498–504).

[51] For discussion of this issue see especially Gary Lease, "Jewish Mystery Cults Since Goodenough," *ANRW* 20.2:858–80.

its erudition and sheer intellectual force did not carry the day among scholars of Judaism of the Greco-Roman period.[52] Goodenough's central thesis—that the widespread presence of a Jewish mystical theology (and corresponding liturgical activity) could be detected in the writings of Philo of Alexandria and in monumental art of the period, and that this "mysticism" was appropriated from Hellenistic and Egyptian mystery religions—could not be supported by the evidence, however thoroughly marshaled.[53] Though Goodenough's effort was focused on the question of Jewish mystical theology in its Hellenistic (especially Greek Egyptian) setting, his underlying aim was to redefine the nature of early Judaism in its entirety.[54] Diasporic Judaism especially, he argued, was by the second century B.C.E. a thoroughly syncretistic religion, incorporating—and adapting into Jewish categories—elements from both the Greek and Egyptian mystical systems.[55] He claimed that

> after Judaism had, at least in its own eyes, been recognized as a religion
> offering a way to mystic objectives in conscious comparison with the

---

[52] Erwin R. Goodenough, *By Light, Light: The Mystic Gospel of Hellenistic Judaism* (New Haven: Yale University Press, 1935). For criticism of Goodenough's views in general see Morton Smith, "Goodenough's Jewish Symbols in Retrospect," *JBL* 86 (1967): 53–68; Jonathan A. Goldstein, "Review of Goodenough," in *Semites, Iranians, Greeks, and Romans* (BJS 217; Atlanta: Scholars Press, 1990), 57–66; Lease, "Jewish Mystery Cults Since Goodenough." See also Ernest S. Frerichs and Jacob Neusner, eds., *Goodenough on the History of Religion and on Judaism* (BJS 121; Atlanta: Scholars Press, 1986). Goodenough's conclusions were formulated in conversation with another important work of the period, Richard Reitzenstein's monumental *Die hellenistischen Mysterien-religionen, ihre Grundgedanken un Wirkungen* (Leipzig: Tübner, 1910).

[53] Goodenough also compiled some of the more impressive and erudite volumes in the history of all scholarship on ancient Judaism in his *Jewish Symbols in the Greco-Roman Period* (13 vols.; New York: Pantheon, 1953–68). In this work he continued to formulate and document the thesis he laid out in *By Light, Light*. See Samuel Thomas, "Goodenough, E. R.," and "Judaism: Mystery Religion as," in *Dictionary of Early Judaism* (ed. John J. Collins and Daniel Harlow; Grand Rapids, Mich.: Eerdmans, forthcoming).

[54] There is a passage in the preface to the final volume of *Jewish Symbols* that captures a kind of self-deprecating frustration: "Scholars have repeatedly said to me, 'At least you will always be remembered and used for your collection of material.' ... I have not spent thirty years as a mere collector: I was trying to make a point."

[55] A comprehensive review of Goodenough's thesis cannot be provided here; for a more detailed synopsis see his *By Light, Light*, 11–47 and Lease, "Jewish Mystery Cults."

other mysteries, it could go on to represent itself as the only true Mystery, and deal with its own mythology and the mystic philosophy with further reference to its competitors.[56]

But as I contend in this book, one need not appeal to Greco-Roman or Egyptian conceptions of mystery to explain the use of such language in the Qumran Scrolls. In fact, if there is a body of material that can help to evaluate the Qumran texts, we might look to the East, i.e. Babylon and Persia, to find it.

Of course, it cannot be denied that there is considerable overlap and hybridity among the religious systems of the Babylonian, Persian, and Greco-Roman periods. Such overlap has generated an enormous amount of speculation regarding the nature and direction of influences, similarities, and correspondences among the different traditions. In the last half-century, however, scholars of antiquity have generally become more cautious in the application of the older *religionsgeschichtliche* model for understanding the organization of religious concepts, words, motifs, and social realities. This is especially true in the case of parallels with broad reach, such as the presence of mystery language in religious texts. As James Davila has noted, "[i]n general, if a parallel or pattern of parallels between two texts or corpora or social groups turns out to be a shared element or pattern with much the same function in many texts, corpora, or social groups, one should be cautious of making much of the original comparison between just the two."[57]

This kind of caution restrains my own analysis: tempting as it may be to draw parallels between the use of mystery language in Philo and in Greco-Roman religious texts (or Palestinian texts in Aramaic and Hebrew), the fact remains that most religious systems employ this kind of language to express aspects of the relationship between humans and the divine and the difference between exoteric and esoteric religious knowledge and experience. As Jakob Petuchowski puts it, "[e]very religion professing belief in a super-human deity shows itself aware of the gulf separating the human from the divine, and of the truth that God

---

[56] Goodenough, *By Light, Light*, 7; cf. Max Radin, *The Jews Among the Greeks and Romans* (Philadelphia: The Jewish Publication Society, 1915), 153–72.

[57] James Davila, "The Peril of Parallels," n.p. [cited 25 May 2008]. Online: http://www.st-andrews.ac.uk/~www_sd/parallels.html; see also S. Sandmel, "Parallelomania," *JBL* 81 (1962): 1–13.

knows something which human beings do not."[58] Even if some influence of Greco-Roman or Egyptian mysteries upon Hellenistic Judaism might be found, Goodenough's thoroughgoing identification between them would hardly seem warranted. Similarly, the presence of some Persian motifs and words (say, dualism, or *raz*) in certain Second Temple Jewish texts cannot wholly affirm the "influence" of Persian culture and ideas in post-Exilic Judaism, even if extended contact between religious Jews and Persians is demonstrable.

Another tendency in the history of scholarship on Jewish mystery language is to appropriate the Qumran Scrolls (and other Jewish texts) as "background" for interpreting key New Testament passages. This can be a problematic procedure on linguistic and historical grounds, and while it may simply reflect a desire to construct Christian theological genealogies that can contextualize or illuminate Paul's understanding of this or that *theologoumenon*—a laudable goal in certain cases (done correctly, such comparisons might throw light on Paul's usage[59])—the results of such an approach often do not *eo ipso* leave us with a better understanding of the Qumran Scrolls in and of themselves. Of course, there is the added danger that this approach might harbor a kind of Christian supersessionism that renders early Judaism relevant only insofar as it creates part of the context for the life of Jesus and the early Christian movement.

SOME ADDITIONAL METHODOLOGICAL REMARKS

Several additional qualifications need to be addressed before proceeding to the substantive parts of this book. The first involves the dating of texts and manuscript remains found at Qumran (both the dates of composition and of copying); the second concerns the relationships among texts, especially the distinctions between sectarian and non-

---

[58] Jakob J. Petuchowski, "Judaism as 'Mystery'—The Hidden Agenda?" *HUCA* 52 (1981): 148.

[59] For particularly good examples of this, see Jörg Frey, "The Notion of 'Flesh' in 4QInstruction and the Background of Pauline Usage," in *Sapiential, Liturgical, and Poetical Texts from Qumran: Proceedings of the Third Meeting of the International Organization for Qumran Studies, Oslo 1998* (ed. Daniel K. Falk, Florentino García Martínez, and Eileen M. Schuller; STDJ 34; Leiden: Brill, 2000), 197–226; and the essays in George J. Brooke, *The Dead Sea Scrolls and the New Testament* (Minneapolis: Fortress, 2005). See now also Gladd (*Revealing the Mysterion*, 2–16), who attempts to be methodologically scrupulous about this issue even as he uses early Jewish material to illuminate the use of mystery terminology in 1 Corinthians.

sectarian compositions; and the third has to do with the connections between the site of Khirbet Qumran and the contents of the nearby caves. All three of these points are subjects of continuing scholarly controversies, none of which I have attempted to resolve here. Nevertheless, as these items impinge either directly or indirectly upon the results of this investigation, some words about my methodological assumptions are in order.

As James VanderKam and Peter Flint correctly note, "placing the Dead Sea Scrolls in their proper historical context is a crucial step in interpreting them."[60] Indeed, from the very beginnings of Qumran scholarship there has been an intense interest in establishing the dates of the various manuscripts (or fragments) and compositions, and, to be sure, relative datings often become the cornerstone for broader theories about the origins of the Scrolls and the history(-ies) of their author(s) and community(-ies).

The issue of dating is not central to many of my proposals, though in some instances it is germane to how I treat a particular text. For example, 4QInstruction is often thought to be "pre-sectarian," a judgment which would have implications for understanding how this composition is related to the Yaḥad: Why was it brought to Qumran? How was it used? How does "mystery" language in this composition figure in presumably later sectarian writings of the Yaḥad itself? Is it possible and fruitful to posit a textual and social progression from the limited information available to us?[61]

For the most part, my broad assumption is that any text preserved, copied, or composed at Qumran—regardless of its date or provenience— was of some value to members (or a member) of the Yaḥad, and that its contents are therefore relevant to this investigation. While I give some attention to the diachronic dimension of "mystery" language in the Scrolls—to the question of whether the concept developed over the course of time—there is much uncertainty in this area and my conclusions can be only suggestive and tentative. I offer an interpretation

---

[60] *The Meaning of the Dead Sea Scrolls*, 20.

[61] For example see Lange, *Weisheit und Prädestination*; idem, "Wisdom and Predestination in the Dead Sea Scrolls." Lange finds no "*yahad*-terminology" in 4QInstruction (which he refers to by its previous title, 4QSap A), and concludes on that basis that it is a "non-Essene" text. 4QInstruction is an important part of Lange's construction of a kind of intellectual genealogy from Qohelet to the *Treatise on the Two Spirits*, with 4QInstruction and *Mysteries* between them.

of the evidence that is generally synchronic while being sensitive to chronological relationships among the texts treated here.

The question whether a given text is sectarian is a related and important issue, especially if one wishes to say something about the function of the texts within, or as an expression of, the life of a particular community. It is a very difficult and problematic task to determine whether a text is sectarian. Correlating textual data with a reconstructed background group or community is notoriously problematic and thus should be undertaken with some caution.[62] Of course, chief among the dangers of using texts to determine or animate the contours of a social group is that of circular reasoning based on an arbitrary selection of representative compositions. Which texts are actually representative, and how would we know with any certainty? The criteria are difficult to establish, and in any case a general definition of "sectarianism" is far from universally agreed upon. Nevertheless, some important methodological guidelines have been offered, and there has been some recent progress in clarifying the issues involved.[63]

For the sake of clarity and convenience, I organize the non-biblical texts from Qumran into four main categories. In the first place are the sect-composed works like the *Community Rule*, the *Damascus Document*, the *Hodayot*, the *War Rule*, and the *pesharim*, among others. There is little dispute that there is an organic relationship among these texts and that they have in common a particular group responsible for their composition and preservation—even if this group itself evolved over time or comprised several related social formations. In any case, it is widely agreed that there is a core of texts that were authored by members of the Yaḥad during one stage of its existence or another.

The second category includes those compositions whose authorship by the Yaḥad is a matter of some dispute, e.g. the *Mysteries* texts from caves 1 and 4 (1Q27, 4Q299–300[301]) and the *Songs of the Sabbath Sacrifice* (4Q400–407; 11Q17; Mas1k). This category includes those texts which allegedly do not employ explicitly sectarian terminology yet display certain ideological affinities with the Qumran group, as well as texts whose distribution went beyond the site of Khirbet Qumran (for example, a copy of the *Songs of the Sabbath Sacrifice* was unearthed at Masada[64]). These texts may still have held some pride of place among the

---

[62] See, for example, the discussion in Wido van Peursen, "Qumran Origins: Some Remarks on the Enochic/Essene Hypothesis," *RevQ* 20 (2001): 250–53.

[63] See chapter 2 for a more extensive discussion of Qumran sectarianism as it relates to this study.

[64] See Carol Newsom, *Songs of the Sabbath Sacrifice: A Critical Edition* (HSM

Yaḥad, though it is more difficult to form conclusions about their precise function within the community. Although some of these texts play an important part in the following discussion, it will serve to keep in mind that they were possibly not composed by members of the group that inhabited the Qumran site. In the case of several of these texts, I will treat them in the same way as the explicitly sectarian texts, in part because I do not find the lack of sectarian terminology to make them decisively non- or pre-sectarian. The presence or lack of sectarian terminology may have as much to do with the particular *kind* or *genre* of text as it does with the social context in which the text was produced.[65] While I accept the argument that 4QInstruction differs from the sect-composed texts in terms of social location and date of composition, I am less convinced that the same is true for *Mysteries* and the *Songs of the Sabbath Sacrifice*. In fact, I treat these latter two texts in a way that is not appreciably different from the clearly sectarian compositions.

The third basic classification consists of those texts that were definitively not authored by the Qumran group and yet were esteemed by the community and thus preserved as part of its collection of writings. This category includes primarily Aramaic works such as portions of *1 Enoch*, the *Genesis Apocryphon*, *Visions of Amram*, the *Aramaic Levi Document*, and others.[66] Many of these texts were composed originally in

---

27; Atlanta: Scholars Press, 1985), 1–4, for a discussion of the Masada copy of this text; see also Y. Yadin, "The Excavations at Masada: 1963–64. Preliminary Report," *IEJ* 15 (1965): 105–108; C. Newsom and Y. Yadin, "The Masada Fragment of the Qumran Songs of the Sabbath Sacrifice," *IEJ* 34 (1984): 77–88.

[65] On the other hand, I am aware of the fact that in some cases there appears to be a direct correlation between groups and their chosen genres and ideologies. See, for example, John J. Collins, "Genre, Ideology and Social Movements in Jewish Apocalypticism," *Mysteries and Revelations: Apocalyptic Studies since the Uppsala Colloquium* (ed. J. J. Collins and J. H. Charlesworth; JSPSup 9; Sheffield: Sheffield Academic Press, 1991); Frances Flannery-Dailey, *Dreamers, Scribes, and Priests: Jewish Dreams in the Hellenistic and Roman Eras* (JSJSup 90; Leiden: Brill, 2004), 111–19.

[66] Robert Kugler makes the interesting argument that some non-sectarian texts like the *Aramaic Levi Document* may have *become* sectarian in the process of reception and transmission; see his "Whose Scripture? Whose Community? Reflections on the Dead Sea Scrolls Then and Now, By Way of Aramaic Levi," *DSD* 15 (2008): 5–23. Kugler argues that some works may have been "imported into the community and *adapted* for use among the covenanters, or ones composed *de novo* within the community from existing texts, traditions, and motifs. In either case, such texts, though made from material of non-Qumranic

Aramaic and as such their sectarian authorship is perhaps to be doubly doubted. However, the ways in which this congeries of Aramaic texts (and *Jubilees* and other related texts) employ mystery language may be suggestive about their inter-relationships, as they all seem concerned to present certain biblical heroes as ones who grasp "mysteries" (Enoch, Lamech, Methuselah, Noah, Amram, and so on), and who collectively form a chain of transmission of secret, esoteric knowledge.

Finally, there are works from Qumran that appear to have been brought to the community and translated from Aramaic into Hebrew or transcribed from Aramaic or Hebrew into one of several cryptic scripts. In other words, these works were incorporated into the Yaḥad by way of adaptive translation or transcription. These are especially interesting for the present study because they attest to a conscious effort either to update or to conceal (or both) a given text. In this category scientific and divinatory texts predominate, as Jonathan Ben Dov has amply documented.[67]

As will become apparent throughout the course of this study, it does not seem prudent to draw sharp lines between texts that may have preceded the formation of the Qumran group—such as the bulk of the Aramaic compositions—and those that were composed by members of the Yaḥad. Texts need not have been composed "at Qumran" to represent the views of, or to have been of some use to, its sectarian inhabitants. The word רז, for example, is a reliable feature of texts with other sectarian characteristics (*Community Rule*, *Damascus Document*, *Pesher Habakkuk*, *War Rule*, *Hodayot*), and indeed seems to be a central expression of the worldview found in those texts. Yet the word is neither limited to sectarian texts (*1 Enoch*, *Genesis Apocryphon*, 4QInstruction) nor does it occur in all such texts (e.g. 4QWords of the Maskil to All the Sons of Dawn [4Q298], *Rule of the Congregation* [1QSa], the *Temple Scroll* [11Q19ᵃ], etc.). Furthermore, so-called "Yaḥad-terminology" may not be directly linked to the sectarian authorship of a text, but rather to its genre or function.

---

origin, were perhaps nonetheless unique to Qumran. As such they are hitherto unrecognized 'sectarian' compositions" (10–11).

[67] Jonathan Ben Dov, *Head of All Years: Astronomy and Calendars at Qumran in Their Ancient Context* (STDJ 77; Leiden: Brill, 2008); and especially his "Scientific Writings in Aramaic and Hebrew at Qumran: Translation and Concealment," in *Aramaica Qumranica: The Aix-en-Provence Colloquium on the Aramaic Dead Sea Scrolls* (ed. Katell Berthelot and Daniel Stökl ben Ezra; STDJ; Leiden: Brill, forthcoming).

My use of terms like "Yaḥad" and "Qumran group" call for some explanation, even though I do not intend to resolve any of the larger questions about the history of the group(s) or about the relationship between the settlement of Khirbet Qumran and the manuscript remains of the Qumran caves. As VanderKam and Flint point out, "there are different theories about how the manuscripts in the eleven caves around Khirbet Qumran came to be there, and the theory one follows affects to some extent how one reads their contents."[68] This is one of the most disputed areas of Qumran research, generally pitting those who defend some form of the classic "Essene Hypothesis" against those who have sought to dismantle or revise this historical model on archeological, textual, or other grounds.[69] Naturally, in terms of the Qumran site itself, the question of what group inhabited the site is secondary to whether a relationship can be established in the first place between Khirbet Qumran and the contents of the nearby caves.

---

[68] *The Meaning of the Dead Sea Scrolls*, 255.

[69] One of the first scholars to argue against the Essene Hypothesis was Karl Rengstorf (*Hirbet Qumran und die Bibliothek vom Toten Meer* [Stuttgart: Kohlhammer, 1960]), who asserted that the scrolls came from the Jerusalem Temple library. Norman Golb (*Who Wrote the Dead Sea Scrolls? The Search for the Secret of Qumran* [New York: Scribner, 1995], esp. 143–49) adapted Rengstorf's idea to argue that the scrolls came not from one library but from several different ones. Recent refutations of the standard hypothesis are often based on alternative interpretations of the archeological site of Qumran. See esp. Yitzhak Magen and Yuval Peleg, "The Qumran Excavations 1993–2004: Prelimary Report," (JSP 6; Jerusalem: Israel Antiquities Authority, 2007); various articles in K. Galor, J. -B. Humbert, and J. Zangenberg, eds., *Qumran: The Site of the Dead Sea Scrolls: Archaeological Interpretation and Debates. Proceedings of a Conference Held at Brown University, November 17–19, 2002* (STDJ 57; Leiden: Brill, 2006); Yizhar Hirschfeld, *Qumran in Context: Reassessing the Archaeological Evidence* (Peabody, Mass.: Hendrickson, 2004); Robert Donceel, *Synthèse des observations faites en fouillant les tombes des necropolis de Khirbet Qumrân et des environs*, Qumran Chronicle 10 (Kraków: Enigma Press, 2002); Jürgen Zangenberg, "Wildnis unter Palmen? Khirbet Qumran im regionalen Kontext des Toten Meeres," in *Jericho und Qumran* (ed. B. Mayer; Regensburg: Friedrich Pustet, 2000), 129–64; Lena Cansdale, *Qumran and the Essenes: A Re-Evaluation of the Evidence* (Tübingen: Mohr Siebeck, 1997). For an assessment of what Josephus says about the Essenes, and how this relates to the inhabitants of Qumran, see Steve Mason, "What Josephus Says about the Essenes in His *Judean War*," in *Text and Artifact in the Religions of Mediterranean Antiquity: Essays in Honour of Peter Richardson* (ed. Stephen G. Wilson and Michel Desjardins; Waterloo: Wilfrid Laurier University Press, 2000) 423–52.

In short, I accept that there is a direct connection between the caves and the settlement, and that the community related to both was most likely Essene in character (or was related to an Essene "parent-group"). This group was responsible for the composing, copying, and preserving the manuscripts of the Qumran caves, and was most likely some version of the "Yaḥad," whose Qumran contigent was an exclusive and esoteric community of priestly-scribal adherents.[70] Nevertheless, I have opted not to dwell on the Essene identification—indeed it is not a crucial element of the overall project of this book, even if I do take the statements by Philo, Pliny, and Josephus into consideration—but rather I use the contents of the Scrolls themselves to describe aspects of the self-understanding of the Qumran group.

In this way I accept the broad outlines—if not each and every historical detail—of the "Groningen Hypothesis" formulated two decades ago and subsequently refined by Florentino García Martínez and Adam S. van der Woude.[71] The advantage of this hypothesis, in

---

[70] There are several possible theories about the relationships among the various groups evident from key sectarian texts such as the *Damascus Document*, the *Community Rule*, and the *Rule of the Congregation* (1QSa). See the following recent studies: Alison Schofield, *From Qumran to the Yahad: A New Paradigm of Textual Development for the Community Rule* (STDJ 77; Leiden: Brill, 2008); Sarianna Metso, "Whom Does the Term Yaḥad Identify?" in *Defining Identities: We, You, and the Other in the Dead Sea Scrolls, Proceedings of the Fifth Meeting of the IOQS in Groningen* (ed. Florentino García Martínez and Mladen Popović; STDJ 70; Leiden: Brill, 2008), 63–84; idem, "Qumran Community Structure and Terminology as Theological Statement," *RevQ* 20 (2002): 429–44; John J. Collins, "Forms of Community in the Dead Sea Scrolls"; idem, "The *Yaḥad* and the 'Qumran Community,'" in *Biblical Traditions in Transmission: Essays in Honour of Michael A. Knibb* (ed. Charlotte Hempel and Judith M. Lieu; JSJSup 111; Leiden: Brill, 2006), 81–96; Eyal Regev, "The *Yaḥad* and the *Damascus Covenant*: Structure, Organization and Relationship," *RevQ* 21 (2003): 233–62; Stephen Hultgren, *From the Damascus Covenant to the Covenant of the Community: Literary, Historical, and Theological Studies in the Dead Sea Scrolls* (STDJ 66; Leiden: Brill, 2007); cf. James C. VanderKam, "Identity and History of the Community," in *The Dead Sea Scrolls after Fifty Years: A Comprehensive Assessment* (ed. Peter W. Flint and James C. VanderKam; 2 vols.; Leiden: Brill 1999), 2.487–533.

[71] Florentino García Martínez, "Qumran Origins and Early History: A Groningen Hypothesis," *FO* 25 (1988): 113–36; Florentino García Martínez and Adam S. van der Woude, "A 'Groningen' Hypothesis of Qumran Origins and Early History," *RevQ* 14 (1990): 521–41; Florentino García Martínez and Julio Trebolle Barrera, *The People of the Dead Sea Scrolls* (trans. Wilfrid G. E. Watson; Leiden: Brill, 1995), esp. 92–96. See also the discussion of the Groningen Hypothesis in the proceedings from the second Enoch Seminar in Venice, Italy,

terms of how I understand and characterize the issue of "mysteries" and esoteric knowledge in the Qumran Scrolls, is that it reconstructs a historical scenario that allows for the relative ideological diversity of the texts, and that it approaches the textual remains as the deposit of a particular community (the Yaḥad) that variously preserved, copied, and composed the manuscripts—and, apparently, valued them for a variety of reasons. Thus it attempts to explain how it is that such a "library" (or, as in cave 4, a "depository") included non-sectarian, pre-sectarian, and sectarian texts, and attempts to retain the basic fact that these texts were found together and that even in their diversity they cohere in some important and interesting ways, even if they are not entirely internally consistent.[72]

While it may remain an important task to investigate the "original" *Sitze im Leben* of the many individual compositions preserved among the Qumran remains (such as *1 Enoch*, *Aramaic Levi*, 4QInstruction), insofar as we may understand the social history behind these texts without more concrete information, my approach here is compatible with what García Martínez has stated more recently about the Aramaic texts from Qumran: "the context we have ... is the context provided by the collection in which they have been found."[73] With regard to the collection as a whole, I concur with García Martínez that the classifications "biblical/non-biblical" and "sectarian/non-sectarian" are

---

July 1–4, 2003: Gabriele Boccaccini, ed., *Enoch and Qumran Origins: New Light on a Forgotten Connection* (Grand Rapids, Mich.: Eerdmans, 2005), especially "Part Four: The Groningen Hypothesis Revisited," which includes contributions from Charlotte Hempel, Albert I. Baumgarten, Mark A. Elliott, Torleif Elgvin, Lester L. Grabbe, Benjamin G. Wright III, Timothy H. Lim, Shemaryahu Talmon, Émile Puech, Gabriele Boccaccini, and a response from Florentino García Martínez (pages 249–326). The work of Gabriele Boccaccini and his attempt to reconstruct "Enochic Judaism" is also relevant in this regard; see especially his *Beyond the Essene Hypothesis: The Parting of the Ways between Qumran and Enochic Judaism* (Grand Rapids, Mich.: Eerdmans, 1998); and *Roots of Rabbinic Judaism: An Intellectual History, from Ezekiel to Daniel* (Grand Rapids, Mich.: Eerdmans, 2002); see the discussion of his theories in *Enoch and Qumran Origins*, pages 329–425.

[72] See also Perluigi Piovanelli, "Some Archaeological, Sociological, and Cross-Cultural Afterthoughts on the 'Groningen' and the 'Enochic/Essene' Hypotheses," in *Enoch and Qumran Origins: New Light on a Forgotten Connection* (Grand Rapids, Mich.: Eerdmans, 2005), 366–72.

[73] "*Aramaica qumranica apocalyptica?*" in *Aramaica Qumranica: The Aix-en-Provence Colloquium on the Aramaic Dead Sea Scrolls* (ed. Katell Berthelot and Daniel Stökl ben Ezra; STDJ; Leiden: Brill, forthcoming).

not always helpful, and they tend to obscure the fact that most if not all the texts found at Qumran were appropriated in one way or another by the "apocalyptic community" of the Yaḥad.[74]

Finally, there are several other topics that are closely related to this study. Given the focus of this book, however, and somewhat to my own regret, I have been able to treat them only occasionally and tangentially. While the results of my investigation are relevant to the study of the overlapping trends of ancient Jewish mysticism,[75] astronomy and astrology,[76] magic,[77] physiognomy,[78] and Gnosticism,[79]—and to later

[74] Florentino García Martínez, "¿Sectario, no-sectario, o qué? Problemas de una taxonomía correcta de los textos qumránicos," RevQ 23 (2008): 383–394.

[75] For recent studies see especially Moshe Halbertal, Concealment and Revelation: Esotericism in Jewish Thought and Its Philosophical Implications (trans. Jackie Feldman; Princeton, N.J.: Princeton University Press, 2007); April D. DeConick, ed., Paradise Now: Essays on Early Jewish and Christian Mysticism (SBLSS 11; Atlanta: Society of Biblical Literature, 2006); Alexander, The Mystical Texts; Andrei Orlov, The Enoch-Metatron Tradition (TSAJ 107; Tübingen: Mohr Siebeck, 2005); Ra'anan Boustan, From Martyr to Mystic: Rabbinic Martyrology and the Making of Merkavah Mysticism (Tübingen: Mohr Siebeck, 2005); Rachel Elior, The Three Temples: On the Emergence of Jewish Mysticism (trans. David Louvish; Oxford: The Littman Library of Jewish Civilization, 2004); Vita Daphna Arbel, Beholders of Divine Secrets: Mysticism and Myth in the Hekhalot and Merkavah Literature (Albany: State University of New York Press, 2003); Naomi Janowitz, Icons of Power: Ritual Practices in Late Antiquity (University Park: Pennsylvania State University Press, 2002); James R. Davila, Descenders to the Chariot: The People behind the Hekhalot Literature (JSJSup 70; Leiden: Brill, 2001); Rebecca Lesses, Ritual Practices to Gain Power: Angels, Incantations, and Revelation in Early Jewish Mysticism (Harrisburg, Penn.: Trinity Press International, 1998); Ithamar Gruenwald, Apocalyptic and Merkavah Mysticism (Leiden: Brill, 1980).

[76] See especially Ben Dov, Head of All Years; James H. Charlesworth, "Jewish Interest in Astrology during the Hellenistic and Roman Period," ANRW II 20.2: 926–51.

[77] See recently Gideon Bohak, Ancient Jewish Magic: A History (Cambridge: Cambridge University Press, 2008); Todd E. Klutz, ed., Magic in the Biblical World: From the Rod of Aaron to the Ring of Solomon (London: T&T Clark, 2003); Attilio Mastrocinque, From Jewish Magic to Gnosticism (STAC 24; Tübingen: Mohr Siebeck, 2005); Esther Eshel, "Genres of Magical Texts in the Dead Sea Scrolls," in Demons: The Demonology of Israelite-Jewish and Early Christian Literature in Context of their Environment (ed. A. Lange, H. Lichtenberger, and K. F. D. Römheld; Tübingen: Mohr Siebeck, 2003), 395–415; Florentino García Martínez, "Magic in the Dead Sea Scrolls," in The Metamorphosis of Magic from Late Antiquity to the Early Modern Period (ed. Jan N. Bremmer and J. R. Veenstra; Leuven: Peeters, 2002), 13–33; Michael Swartz, "The Dead Sea Scrolls and Later Jewish Magic and Mysticism," DSD 8 (2001): 182–93; Armin Lange, "The Essene Position on Magic

Jewish textual traditions such as the Heikhalot corpora, the Slavonic pseudepigrapha,[80] and other related works[81]—I do not attempt to offer a comprehensive synthesis of how the Qumran texts indicate the presence of related forms of knowledge and praxis among the Yaḥad. Each of these is an important and, for the most part, not well understood, phenomenon, and a full assessment of their interrelations remains a desideratum.

THE STRUCTURE OF THIS BOOK

Chapter 2 presents the theoretical and methodological foundations of this study. It comprises three main topics that are all interrelated, and each includes both general discussion as well as its specific relevance to

---

and Divination," in *Legal Texts and Legal Issues: Proceedings of the Second Meeting of the International Organization for Qumran Studies, Cambridge 1995* (ed. Moshe Bernstein, Florentino García Martínez, and John Kampen; STDJ 23; Leiden: Brill, 1997), 377–435; Philip S. Alexander, "Wrestling against Wickedness in High Places: Magic in the Worldview of the Qumran Community," in *The Scrolls and the Scriptures: Qumran Fifty Years After* (ed. Stanley E. Porter and Craig A. Evans; JSPSup 26; Sheffield: Sheffield Academic Press, 1997), 318–37; W. J. Lyons and A. M. Reimer, "The Demonic Virus and Qumran Studies: Some Preventative Measures," *DSD* 5 (1998): 16–32.

[78] See most recently Mladen Popović, *Reading the Human Body: Physiognomics and Astrology in the Dead Sea Scrolls and Hellenistic-Early Roman Period Judaism* (STDJ 67; Leiden: Brill, 2007); Philip S. Alexander, "Physiognomy, Initiation, and Rank in the Qumran Community," in *Geschichte—Tradition—Reflexion: Festschrift für Martin Hengel zum 70. Geburtstag* (ed. H. Cancik, Herman Lichtenberger, and Peter Schäfer; Tübingen: Mohr Siebeck, 1996), 385–94.

[79] There have been few attempts in recent years to link Qumran with Gnostic texts and movements, though in earlier years there was more enthusiasm for such an endeavor. See for example Bo Reicke, "Traces of Gnosticism in the Dead Sea Scrolls?" *NTS* 1 (1954): 137–41; Menahem Mansoor, "The Nature of Gnosticism in Qumran," in *Le origini dello gnosticismo: Colloquio di Messina 13–18 Aprile 1966* (ed. U. Bianchi; SHR 12; Leiden: Brill, 1970), 389–400; H. Ringgren, "Qumran and Gnosticism," in the same volume, 379–84; Ithamar Gruenwald, *From Apocalypticism to Gnosticism: Studies in Apocalypticism, Merkavah Mysticism and Gnosticism* (BEATAJ 14; Frankfurt: Peter Lang, 1988); Birger Pearson, "Gnosticism," *EDSS* 1.313–17.

[80] For a recent treatment and comprehensive bibliography of the Slavonic pseudepigrapha see A. Orlov, *From Apocalypticism to Merkabah Mysticism: Studies in the Slavonic Pseudepigrapha* (JSJSup 114; Leiden: Brill, 2007).

[81] Such as the *Sefer ha-Razim, Sefer Yeṣira,* and the *Asatir.*

Qumran: (1) Esotericism as a useful heuristic framework for interpreting the contents and context of the Scrolls, especially with its emphasis on esoteric knowledge, secrecy, and transmission; (2) Sectarianism in early Judaism and in the Qumran Scrolls; (3) Discourse theory and the "discourses of Qumran," with special attention to Carol Newsom's recent book, *The Self as Symbolic Space: Constructing Identity and Community at Qumran.*[82]

The third chapter provides an account of pre-Qumran conceptions of "mysteries" and secrets, in part to set the stage for the task of mapping out the relevant Qumran materials. I should state at this point that I have tried to avoid the genealogical fallacy that has often plagued studies of this sort, viz. that earlier concepts have a direct connection to later ones, and that we can simply "connect the dots" from one text to another. Moreover, I wish to contextualize the primary biblical and pseudepigraphical texts that bear on the investigation by calling attention also to important parallels in ancient Near Eastern and (some) Hellenistic works—especially when these pertain to ideas about "mystery," secrecy, and esotericism. I have attempted to limit such comparative material to those examples that will help to illuminate the Qumran texts.[83]

Turning in full to the Qumran manuscripts themselves in chapter 4, I deal with the lexicographical and philological issues attending the use of "mystery" in the Scrolls. For example, I ask questions such as, How are words combined to form new terms or ideas? Are phrases like רז נהיה technical terms? What verbs accompany the use of mystery terminology? The purpose of this section is to establish the conceptual values and semantic ranges of the various terms, and to present a catalog of word pairings, accompanying verbs, and syntactical patterns that can provide a sort of key to "mystery" language in the Qumran Scrolls. In short, this chapter forms the linguistic basis for the more constructive analysis that follows in chapter 5.

In chapter 5 I apply the heuristic model of the three religious discourses—prophetic, sapiential, and priestly—toward an evaluation of

---

[82] Carol Newsom, *The Self as Symbolic Space: Constructing Identity and Community at Qumran* (STDJ 52; Leiden: Brill, 2004).

[83] I am aware that my use of cross-cultural material as "background" to Qumran carries the danger mentioned above in relation to using Jewish material to construct the "background" of earliest Christianity. Perhaps I wish to have it both ways, but I hope I have been clear and selective enough in the way I use these materials to avoid this methodological error. It is primarily the social contexts of late Babylonian and early Jewish priestly-scribalism that gives rise to the phenomenological comparison—and not merely the linguistic/conceptual parallels that can be found there.

the function of mystery language in the Qumran Scrolls, focusing especially on the undisputed sectarian texts like the *Damascus Document*, the *Community Rule*, the *Hodayot*, and the *pesharim*, as well as *Mysteries*, the *Songs of the Sabbath Sacrifice*, and others. While these different discourses provide helpful categories by which to characterize the various ways in which mystery language is deployed in the texts most closely related to the Yaḥad, the distinctions among them are, in the end, somewhat artificial given the generic and thematic boundary-crossing to be observed in late Second Temple Jewish texts and traditions.

The final chapter provides a summary of my investigation and an attempt to integrate my findings into an overall idea of the "Vision, Knowledge, and Worship" of the Yaḥad This conclusion takes into account the functions of each of these themes in relation to Qumran ideas about "mystery," attitudes toward secrecy, practices of religious ritual, and communal self-understanding as constituted by esoteric knowledge.

CHAPTER TWO

ESOTERICISM, SECTARIANISM, AND RELIGIOUS DISCOURSES

> The book written in nature evokes the Tradition
> transmitted since the beginning and confided to the
> safekeeping of initiates: hidden and venerable book
> that shines in fragments scattered here and there.
>
> Maurice Blanchot

ESOTERIC KNOWLEDGE AND SECRECY

In recent years there has been increasing scholarly interest in secrecy and the social, political, and religious dimensions of secrecy and secret knowledge. In the words of Ann Williams Duncan, who published a bibliographic essay devoted to the topic in a special focus issue of the *Journal for the American Academy of Religion,*

> The events of the early twenty-first century have led to a resurgence of
> interest in the public and private expression of religion and the role of
> secrecy in religious traditions. In modern incarnations and throughout
> history, claims to secret knowledge, the limitations of knowledge of the
> divine, and private or secrete [sic] religious activities have existed in all
> types of religious traditions. From long-standing mystical traditions in
> Abrahamic faiths to smaller groups such as Theosophists, secrecy
> touches on many aspects of religious experience. Sociologists,
> anthropologists, political theorists, historians, and theologians have

---

Epigraph is from Maurice Blanchot, "The Book to Come," in *The Book to Come* (trans. Charlotte Mandel; Stanford, Calif.: Stanford University Press, 2003), 228.

undertaken studies of religion and secrecy in general and in reference to particular traditions and localities.[1]

Several recent studies have examined various aspects of secret knowledge in the broader context of ancient Near Eastern religious and cultural traditions, and some attempts have been made to trace out lines of continuity with biblical texts, the Qumran Scrolls and other Jewish and Christian corpora of antiquity.[2] The category of "secret knowledge"

---

[1] Ann Williams Duncan, "Religion and Secrecy: A Bibliographic Essay," *JAAR* 74 (2006): 469–82, here 469. Other recent contributions that are especially relevant to the present study include Hans G. Kippenberg and Guy Stroumsa, eds., *Secrecy and Concealment: Studies in the History of Mediterranean and Near Eastern Religions* (SHR 65; Leiden: Brill, 1995); Kees W. Bolle, ed., *Secrecy in Religions* (SHR 49; Leiden: Brill, 1987).

[2] Regarding the varieties and uses of secret knowledge in ancient Near Eastern literature, see Alan Lenzi, *Secrecy and the Gods: Secret Knowledge in Ancient Mesopotamia and Biblical Israel* (SAAS 19; Winona Lake, Ind.: Eisenbrauns, 2008) and the extensive bibliography cited there. See especially his first chapter for a lengthy review of the history of scholarship in this area, which includes discussion of the more recent controversies about secrecy and esotericism in ancient Mesopotamian texts and social contexts. See also Scott Noegel, *Nocturnal Ciphers: The Allusive Language of Dreams in the Ancient Near East* (AOS 89; New Haven, Conn.: American Oriental Society, 2007), esp. 11–88 and 113–82; Paul-Alain Beaulieu, "New Light on Secret Knowledge in Late Babylonian Culture," *ZAVA* 82 (1992): 98–99; Simo Parpola, "The Assyrian Tree of Life: Tracing the Origins of Jewish Monotheism and Greek Philosophy," *JNES* 52 (1993): 169; idem, "Mesopotamian Astrology and Astronomy as Domains of the Mesopotamian 'Wisdom,'" in *Die Rolle der Astronomie in den Kulturen Mesopotamiens: Beiträge zum 3. Grazer Morgenländischen Symposium (23–27 September 1991)* (ed. H. D. Galter; GMS 3; Graz, 1993), 47–59; idem "Monotheism in Ancient Assyria," in *One God or Many? Concepts of Divinity in the Ancient World* (ed. Bezalel N. Porter; TCBAI 1; Chebeague, Maine: Casco Bay Assyriological Institute, 2000), 165–209; H. Limet, "Le Secret et Les Écrits: Aspects du L'Ésotericisme en Mésopotamie Ancienne," in *Les Rites d'Initiation: Actes du Colloque de Liege et de Louvain-la-Neuve, 20–21 Novembre 1984* (ed. H. Limet and J. Ries; Louvain-la-Neuve: Centre d'Histoire des Religions, 1986), 243–54; J. G. Westenholz, "Thoughts on Esoteric Knowledge and Secret Lore," in *Intellectual Life of the Ancient Near East: Papers Presented at the 43rd Rencontre assyriologique internationale; Prague, July 1–5, 1996* (ed. J. Prosecky; Prague: Academy of Sciences of the Czech Republic Oriental Institute, 1998), 451–62; B. Pongratz-Leisten, *Herrschaftwissen in Mesopotamien: Formen der Kommunikation zwischen Gott und König im 2. und 1. Jahrtausend v. Chr.* (SAAS 10; Helsinki: The Neo-Assyrian Text Corpus Project, 1999); Alisdair Livingstone, *Mystical and Mythological Explanatory Works of Assyrian and Babylonian Scholars* (Oxford: Clarendon Press, 1986).

is empirically ubiquitous in human social life, and it should not come as a surprise that we might find it also in biblical and biblically-related literature.[3] Indeed, this may reflect a fundamental human reality that resides at the nexus between personal and social life, as "the repeated emphasis on the category of the mystery in the religious domain is an extension of the more general emphasis on concealment that is so essential to our disclosure in the realm of intersubjectivity."[4]

Given the fact that a secret, or secrecy itself, presumes some claim to special knowledge, there is always a corollary set of epistemological issues that need sorting out. Scholars of Second Temple Judaism have tended to counterpose the epistemologies found in various wisdom discourses, especially the more traditional empirical wisdom of observation, study, and contemplation (such as Proverbs, *Ahiqar*, Sirach)[5] and the revealed wisdom at home in priestly and apocalyptic milieux (Daniel, *1 Enoch*, 4QInstruction, etc.).[6] While such dichotomies are

---

[3]   See for example Chaim Cohen, "Was the P Document Secret?" *JANESCU* 1/2 (1968/69): 39–44, in which Cohen argues that the Priestly source shows clear similarities to a priestly ritual text from Babylon, which itself contains an explicit reference to the necessity of keeping the contents of the priestly knowledge secret.

[4]   Elliot Wolfson, "Introduction," in *Rending the Veil: Concealment and Secrecy in the History of Religions* (ed. Elliot R. Wolfson; New York: Seven Bridges Press, 1999), 2.

[5]   Even these categorizations have come under increasing scrutiny, and we may see, for example, that texts like Sirach are perhaps more closely aligned with portions of *1 Enoch* and other texts than has usually been assumed. See Randall Argall, *1 Enoch and Sirach: A Comparative Literary and Conceptual Analysis of the Themes of Revelation, Creation and Judgment* (EJL 8; Atlanta: Scholars Press, 1995); Annette Yoshiko Reed, *Fallen Angels and the History of Judaism and Christianity: The Reception of Enochic Literature* (Cambridge: Cambridge University Press, 2005). As Reed states, "in terms of socio-historical context, the Wisdom of ben Sira ironically exhibits more continuity with the *Book of the Watchers* than the *Book of Dreams* and *Epistle of Enoch* ..." and that "ben Sira's attitude towards apocalyptic epistemology is best seen as part of an internal debate within a single discourse of priestly scribalism" (60). See also Benjamin G. Wright III, "Putting the Puzzle Together: Some Suggestions Concerning the Social Location of the Wisdom of Ben Sira," in *Conflicted Boundaries in Wisdom and Apocalypticism* (ed. Benjamin G. Wright III and Lawrence M. Wills; SBLSS 35; Atlanta: Society of Biblical Literature, 2005), 89–112, and the bibliography he cites in this article.

[6]   See recently Matthew Goff, *Discerning Wisdom*; Reed, *Fallen Angels and the History of Judaism and Christianity*, chapter 1, "Angelic Descent and Apocalyptic

increasingly called into question—or at least further problematized—and
need to be approached cautiously, it is the case that many of the texts
from Qumran display elements of the latter category, insofar as special
knowledge is often characterized as originating in a moment of
revelation, whether in the form of a vision, a heavenly tour, a ritual
experience, or the reception of books that convey heavenly knowledge.
Such knowledge is often described by scholars as "esoteric," as in the
following:

> We know much about esoteric traditions in Palestinian Judaism, both
> among the Pharisees and the Essenes. ... Jewish esotericism has its own
> roots in apocalyptic literature, in texts which often claim to reveal the
> divine secrets. It is further reflected in the Dead Sea Scrolls, in particular
> in their insistence on "secrets" (*sod, raz*).[7]

Indeed, in apocalyptic discourses "lists of revealed things"[8] play a
central role, and constitute, at least in part, "esoteric knowledge
concerning man, nature, and the cosmos [that] did not remain hidden for
all of mankind but was revealed to some special individuals through
heavenly mediation."[9] According to this broad distinction (however we
may end up distributing the representative texts), empirical or
observation-based modes of wisdom are by nature not secret or
esoteric—they are in principle available to human beings generally—
whereas revealed wisdom holds the capacity for secrecy and esotericism
in its very modes of apprehension and transmission.[10] If we add to this

---

Epistemology: The Teachings of Enoch and the Fallen Angels in the *Book of the
Watchers"*; Collins, "The Mysteries of God."

[7] Stroumsa, *Hidden Wisdom*, 4–5. Elsewhere Stroumsa makes a similar
statement: "Such vocables as *sod* or *raz*, for instance, which appear time and
again in the Qumran texts, seem to refer to a *mysterium* of sorts, difficult to define
precisely, but in any case esoteric by nature" ("From Esotericism to Mysticism in
Early Christianity," in *Secrecy and Concealment: Studies in the History of
Mediterranean and Near Eastern Religions* [ed. Hans G. Kippenberg and Guy G.
Stroumsa; SHR 65; Leiden: Brill, 1995], 294).

[8] See the oft-cited article by Michael Stone, "Lists of Revealed Things in
Apocalyptic Literature," in *Magnalia Dei: The Mighty Acts of God: Essays on the
Bible and Archaeology in Memory of G. Ernest Wright* (ed. Frank Moore Cross,
Werner E. Lemke, and Patrick D. Miller, Jr.; Garden City, N.Y.: Doubleday, 1976),
414–54

[9] Popović, *Reading the Human Body*, 221–22.

[10] Ithamar Gruenwald, "The Jewish Esoteric Literature in the Time of the
Mishnah and Talmud," *Immanuel* 4 (1974): 37–46, which includes a discussion
about the esotericism of Jewish apocalyptic literature. Some apocalyptic texts,

the more specific role of "mantic wisdom" in apocalyptic strains of Judaism, including those represented in the Qumran Scrolls, the specialized divinatory skills of the mantic sage further suggest an esoteric framework.[11]

The social or ethical dimensions of secrecy are another crucial part of any attempt to explain the use of mystery language in the Scrolls. In this sense, a secret is information that is "intentionally hidden" to prevent those outside the in-group from "possessing it, making use of it, or revealing it."[12] But a secret in the religious sense is not merely some piece of information, but is, as Georg Simmel asserted in his seminal study of secrecy, "the hiding of realities by negative or positive means" in order to constitute a new and different reality, "a second world alongside the manifest world" where "the latter is decisively influenced by the former."[13] But surely even with this definition of a "secret" we may make a further distinction between religious secrets—what a given religious group may consider part of its *private* domain of knowledge, practice, and experience—and religious "mysteries," which usually entail the conjunction of esoteric knowledge and ritual practice within a specific group of insiders.

---

like chapter 2 of the book of Daniel, portray revealed wisdom in a way that is ostensibly not esoteric or secretive; see Alan Lenzi, "Secrecy, Textual Legitimation, and Inter-Cultural Polemics in the Book of Daniel," *CBQ* 71 (2009): 330–48. I would like to thank Dr. Lenzi for making this article available to me before its publication.

[11] On "mantic wisdom" in Second Temple Judaism see especially H. -P. Müller, "Mantische Weisheit und Apokalyptik," in *Congress Volume: Uppsala 1971* (VTSup 22; Leiden: Brill, 1972), 268–93; idem, "Magisch-mantische Weisheit und die Gestalt Daniels," *UF* 1 (1969): 79–94; James C. VanderKam, "Mantic Wisdom in the Dead Sea Scrolls," *DSD* 4 (1997): 336–53; Andreas Bedenbender ("Jewish Apocalypticism: A Child of Mantic Wisdom?" *Henoch* 24 [2002]: 189–96) argues that there is very little solid evidence relating Jewish apocalypticism to the mantic practices of ancient Babylonian diviners; Bedenbender prefers the term "revealed wisdom" to "mantic wisdom." See also the chapter on "Mantological Exegesis" in Michael Fishbane, *Biblical Interpretation in Ancient Israel* (Oxford: Oxford University Press, 1985), 445–505.

[12] Sissela Bok, *Secrets: On the Ethics of Concealment and Revelation* (New York: Vintage, 1989), 5, 6.

[13] *The Sociology of Georg Simmel* (tr. and ed. K. H. Wolff; Glencoe, Ill.: Free Press, 1950), 330. See also Michael Barkun, "Religion and Secrecy After September 11," *JAAR* 74 (2006): 277, where he discusses this same topic.

Kees W. Bolle has rightly noted that there is nothing remarkable about secrecy insofar as "there are communities or persons who know something that another one does not know," and that this in itself would hardly be worth investigating. "Communicating facts of information or the refusal to do so becomes interesting only to the extent that it reflects a mystery central to human existence" or a tradition that "as a whole preserves the recollection of the central mysteries of creation, of life and death, of initiatory rites, or purpose and meaning, of 'ultimate assumptions.'"[14] Even after its *secrets* are revealed, "a religion's mysteries remain. ... By contrast, a mystery remains a mystery in plain sight, impervious to logic, common sense, and ordinary powers of observation."[15]

A mystery is not simply some piece of hidden information, and thus something to be merely *disclosed* (by a deity or another human being) or registered cognitively. Rather it is something that presumes some inward knowledge that comes from a combination of tradition, contemplation, and experience—in other words, it is knowledge of a "reality" that is not immediately manifest and is therefore not easily perceptible to those who are outside the fold. Such knowledge itself is constructed and cultivated in apocalyptic literature by appeal to symbolic, mythological language, insider exegesis, and, perhaps in some cases, mystical experience and theurgic praxis.

All this is not to say that mysteries are not also potential secrets. It seems that no matter which cultural/religious tradition one considers, appeals to mystery language are inherently bound up in the complex dynamic of secrecy and disclosure, whether in the theological or in the interpersonal sense. There can be no such thing as a secret without the potential for its disclosure—or at the very least, a secret loses its potency and rationale if disclosure is not always possible or imminent. The very appeal to a divine or human "mystery" itself presumes an unveiling, and such an appeal is usually also a claim to knowledge that is restricted to a particular group. If "the best way to keep a secret is not to talk or write about it,"[16] i.e., if a secret loses its potential for disclosure, it also loses much of its theological and social force.

The present book is devoted to exploring and mapping the territory of Qumran ideas about secrecy, mystery, and esoteric knowledge, and seeing whether such characterizations as given above are appropriate or

---

[14] Kees W. Bolle, "Secrecy in Religion," in *Secrecy in Religions* (ed. Kees W. Bolle; SHR 49; Leiden: Brill, 1987), 2–3.

[15] Barkun, "Religion and Secrecy," 278.

[16] Werner Kelber, "Narrative and Disclosure: Mechanisms of Concealing, Revealing, and Reveiling," *Semeia* 43 (1988): 3

adequate to describe the relevant Qumran material.[17] My assertion is that the secrets most guarded by the Qumran group are the ones that pertain to "mysteries," and that there are other kinds of secrets that are distinct from the epistemological domain of "mystery." This latter category might include, for example, sectarian halakhah, which is often characterized under the rubric of "hidden things" (נסתרות), though even this distinction is perhaps somewhat artificial given the relatively seamless and dynamic relationship between scriptural interpretation, religious experience, and other expressions of knowledge claims in Qumran texts.

There were apparently different levels at which secrecy was operative within the Yaḥad, starting with the basic distinction between "Israel" and the "community of the renewed covenant." The *Community Rule* states that

1QS 8:11–14

11 ... וכול דבר הׄנסתר מישראל ונמצאו לאיש

12 הדורש אל יסתרהו מאלה מיראת רוח נסוגה *vacat* ובהיות אלה ליׄחׄד

בישראל

13 יבדלו בתכונים האלה מתוך מושב הנשי העול ללכת למדבר לפנות שם

את דרך הואהא[18]

14 כאשר כתוב במדבר פנו דרך '''' ישרו בערבה מסלה לאלוהינו[19]

11 ... And every matter hidden from Israel but which has been found out by the

12 Interpreter, he should not keep hidden [from those holy ones in the midst of the council of the men of the community] for fear of a spirit of desertion. *vacat* When such men as these come to the Yaḥad in

---

[17] Jonathan Z. Smith has rightly cautioned scholars (perhaps especially of religion) not to equate the "maps" we make—our cartographies by which we navigate worlds we do not inhabit—with the "territories" they reflect, and to retain a healthy sense of the distance between ourselves and the thing we are attempting to describe. Only this can help us to avoid the tendency toward reification of our subject matter, subjects we know only as objects manipulated by our imaginations. See especially Smith's "Map is Not Territory," in *Map is Not Territory: Studies in the History of Religions* (Chicago: University of Chicago Press, 1993), 289–309.

[18] 4Q259 (4QS^e) has the variant דרך האמת in this position.

[19] Text from Alison Schofield, *From Qumran to the Yaḥad*. A critical text that incorporates all the manuscripts can be found in an appendix at the end of her book.

Israel,

13 they will separate, upholding these things, from among the dwelling of the men of iniquity, in order to go to the wilderness, there to prepare the way of truth,

14 as it is written, "In the wilderness prepare the way of the LORD, make straight in the desert a highway for our God" (Isaiah 40:3).

At the most elemental level there was knowledge shared by the entire community that was "hidden from Israel" at large.[20] One puzzling aspect of this injunction is that it suggests a scenario in which knowledge was shared equally among the members of the group—i.e. that the epistemological domain of the sect was not internally exclusive or hierarchical but communitarian in nature, even if the organizational structure was hierarchical and internally exclusive.[21]

Another passage from the *Community Rule* seems to convey the same idea, namely that knowledge was corporately derived and communally shared:

1QS 6:8–10

8 ... וזה הסרך למושב הרבים איש בתכונו הכוהנים ישבו לרשונה והזקנים
בשנית ושאר
9 כול העם ישבו איש בתכונו וכן ישאלו למשפט ולכול עצה ודבר אשר
יהיה לרבים להשיב איש את מדעו
10 לעצת היחד ...

8 ... This is the rule for the session of the Many. Each one by his measure (or rank): the priests will sit down first, the elders next, and the remainder

9 of all the people will sit down in order of measure. And following the same system they will be questioned with regard to judgment, all counsel and any matter referred to the Many, so that each can impart his knowledge

10 to the council of the community ...

---

[20] Josephus says of the Essenes (*J.W.* 2.141) that they swear oaths "to conceal nothing from the members of the sect and to report none of their secrets to others, even though tortured to death" (καὶ μήτε κρύψειν τι τοὺς αἱρετιστὰς μήθ᾽ ἑτέροις αὐτῶν τι μηνύσειν, κἂν μέχρι θανάτου τις βιάζηται).

[21] As Mladen Popović notes, "It is good group maintenance to erect boundaries against the outside world, but it seems improbable that nothing was kept hidden from other sectarians, although this ideal may have been held in high regard" ("Physiognomic Knowledge in Qumran and Babylonia," *DSD* 13 [2006]: 174).

On the other hand, there appear to have been levels of secrecy—or gradations of authority that corresponded to the degrees of esoteric knowledge attained by different members—within the community itself. Elsewhere the *Community Rule* states:

1QS 5:23–24

23 וכתבם בסרך איש לפני רעהו לפי שכלו ומעשיו[22] להשמע הכול איש
לרעהו הקטן לגדול ולהיות
24 פוקדם את רוחם ומעשיהם[23] שנה בשנה להעלות איש לפי שכלו ותום
דרכו ולאחרו כנעוויתו

23 [Those who freely volunteer to join the community] will be enrolled by rank, one before the other, each according to his insight and his deeds, in such a way that each one obeys another, the junior and the senior.

24 And their spirit and their deeds must be tested, year after year, in order to upgrade each one to the extent of his insight and the perfection of his path, or to demote him according to his failings.

Furthermore, the Maskil is to have "acquired all insight (כול השכל) that has been gained according to the periods … and he should separate and weigh the sons of Zadok according to their spirits … and promote [each one] according to his intellect" (1QS 9:13–16). This passage culminates in what appears to be a kind of credo or epitome of the Maskil's (and the community's) purpose, a statement I discuss in additional detail in chapter 5: "He should lead them with knowledge and in this way teach them the mysteries of wonder and truth (רזי פלא ואמת) in the midst of the men of the community, so that they walk perfectly, one with another, in all that has been revealed to them" (1QS 9:18–19).[24]

It appears then that while there may in fact have been hierarchies of knowledge within the Yaḥad—and opportunities to change positions based on the acquisition of new or superior levels of knowledge or insight—it was also the case that individual members were expected to contribute their own advances in understanding to the collectivity as a whole (but perhaps only under schematized and controlled

---

[22] 4Q258 (4QS[d]) includes בתורה to read "his works in/of *torah*"

[23] See previous note. The copyist of 4Q258 seems to want to clarify just what kind of works are being described.

[24] See chapter 4 for extended discussion of the Maskil and his/their role among the Yaḥad.

circumstances[25]). The resulting deposit of secret knowledge, all of which was to have been apprehended at least by the Maskil (if not by other community leaders), was the totality of those things known by the community and unknown to the world at large. Thus, this strictly hierarchical and secretive group could simultaneously have reinforced the internal structure of the community, given to its members each his own role in contributing to the collective task of learning and understanding, and solidified its position vis-à-vis the outside world.[26]

The nature of the esoteric knowledge of the Yaḥad was manifold.[27] On the one hand, true knowledge was considered to be "revealed" in some fashion or another. Members of the community were actively involved in the derivation of new forms of understanding and insight— they were interpreters of revelation, and, for them, it appears that to interpret correctly was itself a way of generating newly revealed knowledge. In other words, revelation, for them, could come in many forms, and they understood themselves to be in the business of "receiving" new revelations through study and interpretation.

But the literary-prophetic task was not the only form of revelation embraced by the Yaḥad. Some representations of religious *experience*, whether related to liturgical praxis or not, reflect the tone of the prophetic tradition in which a solitary figure (an "I") recounts his own experience of revelation—an experience of "seeing" or "hearing" (or having his "ears opened") something otherwise unknown to the human world. In this regard some of the poetic-liturgical texts—like the *Hodayot* and *Barkhi Nafshi*—come to mind. In these texts it is perhaps the "experience" of revelation—or the revelation that comes with the experience—that leads to new knowledge.

---

[25] It is difficult to reconcile statements like this—statements that reflect the possibility of "upward mobility"—with the rather extreme brand of determinism also present in the sectarian scrolls, namely the "lot" (גורל) of each individual member and the use of physiognomy to establish the distribution of parts of light and darkness. In any case, one's position in the Yaḥad was likely not based on some predetermined system of hierarchy or ranking, but was based on one's knowledge relative to other (non-Maskil) members (it was not as if one could move from being a "green belt" to a "black belt"—thanks to Molly Zahn for this perceptive analogy).

[26] "In the first place, esoteric secrecy serves to defend and strengthen the identity of a small, distinctive group. The more restricted and distinguishable a group, the more likely is the occurrence of esoteric secrecy. ... Esoteric secrecy thrives in and on isolation" (Kelber, "Narrative and Disclosure," 5).

[27] What follows here is just a brief description; these statements are elaborated more fully below, and in chapters 5 and 6.

Additionally there is the strong theme of esoteric wisdom in the Qumran Scrolls, of knowledge rooted in the reception of, reflection upon, and integration of specially revealed information about human nature, creation, cosmic structures, and so on. Such a theme takes up in various ways the traditions found in the Enochic works and the book of Daniel, as well as other Aramaic texts preserved in the Qumran caves including the physiognomic, astrological, and magico-medical texts (such as 4Q561, 4Q318, 4Q186, and 4Q510–11).

ESOTERICISM

Scholars of early Judaism often refer to certain aspects of Qumran and other apocalyptic literature as "esoteric," but they typically do not give a clear definition of what they take "esoteric" to mean.[28] The general usage implies a restricted or elite context in which recondite information is generated and preserved, but there are other associations with the term that require a more sustained attempt at a definition. Furthermore, we must inquire whether there is a distinction to be made between the category of "esoteric knowledge" and the social phenomenon of "esotericism."[29]

---

[28] An example is Paul Owen, "The Relationship of Eschatology to Esoteric Wisdom in the Jewish Pseudepigraphal Apocalypses," in *Of Scribes and Sages: Early Jewish Interpretation and Transmission of Scripture. Vol. 1: Ancient Versions and Traditions* (ed. Craig A. Evans; LSTS 50; London: T&T Clark, 2004), 122–33.

[29] The word "esotericism" was first used in French in 1828: "l'ésotérisme" was coined by Jacques Matter in his *Histoire du gnosticisme*; see Pierre Riffard, *L'ésotérisme* (Paris: Payot, 1990), 63–137. To be sure, matters of *esoterica* have long been pursued in the context of learning and scholarship, but it is only since the nineteenth century that an academic discourse regarding *esotericism* has existed. Esotericism as a social phenomenon has recently become an object of heightened scholarly inquiry, catalyzed in part by Edward Tiryakian's essay "Toward the Sociology of Esoteric Culture," *American Journal of Sociology* 78 (1972): 491–512. The term "esotericism," however useful, is a scholarly construct to be used for heuristic purposes. "'Esotericism' does not exist as an object. 'Esotericism' exists only in the heads of scholars, who classify objects in [a] meaningful way to themselves, in order to analyse processes of European [or another] cultural history. Put differently: definitions are tools of *interpretation*; they should not be used essentially." For this reason von Stuckrad prefers to speak of "the esoteric" rather than of "esotericism," i.e. to avoid giving the impression that it represents a "coherent doctrine or clearly defined body of tradition," yet he continues to use the category "esotericism" (Kocku von Stuckrad, *Western Esotericism: A Brief History of Secret Knowledge* [trans. N. Goodrick-Clarke; London: Equinox, 2005],

In his important essay, "Toward the Sociology of Esoteric Culture" Edward Tiryakian defined esoteric matters in the following way:

> By "esoteric" I refer to those religiophilosophic belief systems which underlie techniques and practices; that is, it refers to the more comprehensive cognitive mappings of nature and the cosmos, the epistemological and ontological reflections of ultimate reality, which mappings constitute a stock of knowledge that provides the ground for occult procedures. . . . But a crucial aspect of esoteric knowledge is that it is a secret knowledge of the reality of things, of hidden truths, handed down, frequently orally and not all at once, to a relatively small number of persons who are typically ritually initiated by those already holding this knowledge.[30]

Nearly every aspect of this definition of esotericism applies to the textual material from Qumran, and to the supposed group/s responsible for the production and use of many of those texts. There is concern not only for

---

10). Dr. von Stuckrad was kind enough to send to me several of his unpublished works, for which I am grateful. I am indebted to von Stuckrad for his abundant scholarship, which has guided me into the broader field of esoteric studies. In his wide-ranging body of work, von Stuckrad has begun to elaborate what amounts to a new program for the study of esotericism using (and reformulating) a history of religions approach. The objects of von Stuckrad's study have included the history of Jewish and Christian astrology (including some discussion of Qumran texts), Renaissance paganism, and modern Western Neoshamanism, among other esotericisms, and with its broad comparativist perspective his work can help to frame some of the issues encountered in the present study. To be sure, von Stuckrad himself is interacting with a field of scholarship that is wide-ranging and broader that I am able to engage in the present study; I draw upon his work with the knowledge that his voice is one among many in the study of esotericism, but one that I trust to speak with a confidently articulated synthesis of this field. See for example his "Jewish and Christian Astrology in Late Antiquity—A New Approach," *Numen* 47 (2000): 1–40, here 10–15; *Frömmigkeit und Wissenschaft. Astrologie in Tanach, Qumran und frührabbinischer Literatur* (Frankfurt: Peter Lang, 1996); *Das Ringen um die Astrologie. Jüdische und christliche Beiträge zum antiken Zeitverständnis* (RVV 49; Berlin: de Gruyter, 2000; "Reenchanting Nature: Modern Western Shamanism and Nineteenth-Century Thought," *JAAR* 70 (2002): 771–99; *Schamanismus und Esoterik. Kultur- und wissenschaftsgeschichtliche Betrachtungen* (GTI 4; Leuven: Peeters, 2003); *Geschichte der Astrologie. Von den Anfängen bis zur Gegenwart* (rev. ed.; Munich: Beck, 2007), which has been translated into Spanish, Portugese, Italian, and English; *Was ist Esoterik? Kleine Geschichte des geheimen Wissens* (Munich: Beck, 2004), translated into English as *Western Esotericism*.

[30] Tiryakian, "Toward the Sociology of Esoteric Culture," 265.

cosmology and the structural components of the universe, but also for their connection with human moral and ontological meaning; there is great preoccupation with proper "occult"[31]—and also cultic—procedures and the divine rationales that underlie them; and many of the Qumran texts most certainly display an attitude of secrecy, i.e. that there are hidden truths known only to the members of the elect group, those initiated into the sectarian conventicle(s). This is a "relatively small number of persons" who receive the secret knowledge by a process of transmission that goes—or is imagined by the sectarians to go—all the way back to the primeval past and to the ancestral heroes of Israel's covenant with its God.[32]

Some may object to the use of "esotericism" as a way to describe Qumran texts and social realities. Admittedly, the term does carry some baggage that makes its use problematic in this context. The category itself is artificially constructed from areas of overlap and similarity among comparative materials, i.e. it is a construct that is built up by observing texts and social trends that come from (sometimes vastly) different cultural, historical, and social locations. This means that the act of comparison itself must be accepted as a legitimate procedure that reveals something new and true about each of the *comparanda*, something that may become helpful in the interpretation of one or another of them.[33]

The present investigation is rooted in an approach that gives pride of place to philology and historical criticism. But these are simply the tools I use to say something about the functions of secrecy and esoteric knowledge within the "discourses" of the Yaḥad, discourses that appropriate sapiential, prophetic, and priestly language and attempt to form a new synthesis of self-understanding. The broader conclusions of

---

[31] Usually practices associated with the "occult" include magic, theurgy, exorcism, astrology, and physiognomy, nearly all of which are attested in the Qumran Scrolls. We shall inquire below, however, whether we should imagine the same social setting for such texts and those that evidence a cultic or priestly background.

[32] See discussion below and in chapter 3, especially the sections on the Aramaic literature from Qumran.

[33] Or, as Jonathan Z. Smith states the matter, "A comparison is a disciplined exaggeration in the service of knowledge. It lifts out and strongly marks certain features within difference as being of possible intellectual significance, expressed in the rhetoric of their being 'like' in some stipulated fashion. Comparison provides the means by which *we* 're-vision' phenomena as *our* data in order to solve *our* theoretical problems" (*Drudgery Divine*, 52).

the study, therefore, also bring the Qumran material into conversation with other areas of inquiry. While the "esotericism" label does come with some potential pitfalls, overall it serves well to illuminate important aspects—both particular and general—of the Qumran Scrolls, and the thought and practice of the Yaḥad.

It would be difficult to argue, for example, that the following description of "esoteric discourse" would not apply to much of the Jewish apocalyptic literature of the Second Temple period, and especially the sectarian material from Qumran:

> What makes a discourse esoteric is the rhetoric of a hidden truth, which can be unveiled in a specific way and established contrary to other interpretations of the universe and history—often that of the institutionalized majority. Mediation may be conceived as such a means: the link between hidden and revealed knowledge, between transcendence and immanence, is frequently attributed to specific authorities—for example Hermes or Zoroaster—who act as mediators and place a "perfect" knowledge at the disposal of human beings. That eternal knowledge, the *philosophia perennis*, can be achieved by some distinguished persons even without mediation, but the notion of a chain of "initiates" and sages, who determine the course of revelation, is a recurrent motif in the history of esotericism from ancient times up until the present. This claim to knowledge is often combined with an emphasis on individual *experience*, wherein a seeker attains higher knowledge through extraordinary states of consciousness.[34]

Another reason why some might wish to resist the esotericism framework is that it carries perhaps too strong a suggestion that there may have been magic, mysticism, and other "occult" beliefs and practices among the Yaḥad. Scholars of the Dead Sea Scrolls might be rightly nervous about a direct comparison between the Qumran materials and those of neo-Platonism, Pythagoreanism, Hermeticism, Gnosticism, Renaissance paganism, and New Age theosophism—all of which might fall into the category of esotericism[35]—especially when lines of influence are drawn from one to another. And yet, the problem is not one of *kind* but of *definition* and of *degree*: the fact remains that certain tendencies manifest themselves among sectarian and/or esoteric groups, and approaches based in comparative work can help to illumine the

---

[34] von Stuckrad, *Western Esotericism*, 10; his emphasis.

[35] The proliferation of "-isms" is itself telling, and underscores the fact that all of these categorizations are provisional and limited constructs for modeling and understanding an objectified reality that is rather removed from the scholar in time, place, and culture.

contours and contents of any given body of evidence. Even so, it is important to keep in mind that undeniable parallels between the various exempla of different brands of esotericism do not carry any necessary implications for across-the-board comparison. In other words, and to give a specific example, the ostensible rejection of most forms of "magic" at Qumran[36] does not render the Scrolls unfit for comparison with other esoteric traditions in which magic is highlighted—it merely means that esotericism is (and must be) a relatively fluid category of description, and we must resist any temptation to carry the comparison too far.[37]

There is still the question whether esoteric knowledge necessarily implies secrecy, whether something that originates in an esoteric milieu is by nature secret (Latin *secretus* = "to separate, divide"). These are indeed two different ways of characterizing a given item of knowledge, overlapping and yet with apparently distinct social contexts and purposes. Esoteric knowledge is knowledge supposedly derived from an esoteric setting—a setting that includes "an innermost circle of advanced or privileged students."[38] In its moment of origination it may be considered previously "hidden" (from human view in general), but it may or may not be considered "secret," i.e. restricted, apart from the bare fact that it happens to be limited to those capable of grasping and

---

[36] See Lange, "The Essene Position on Magic and Divination." Lange judiciously concludes that "since neither magic nor divination were completely rejected, even by Essenes, it can be concluded that the various phenomena described today as magic or divination were not understood by them as belonging to the same group of practices which they judged to be part of the dominion of Belial" (435). See also Lyons and Reimer, "The Demonic Virus": "For the Qumran sectarians who created, preserved, and cherished these texts, nothing in them resembled magic or sorcery. These were simply texts that allowed them to deal with threats to their community, much as community discipline and purification rites dealt with various threats" (32).

[37] The construction of a taxonomy that is not overly rigid yet still heuristically useful can be seen in the work of scholars who have labored to elucidate the contours of ancient Jewish and Christian "apocalypses," "apocalypticism," and "apocalyptic worldviews." See especially the voluminous work of John Collins (and others) in this area, whose symbolic beginning has become "Apocalypse: Toward the Morphology of a Genre," and the entire issue of *Semeia* 14 (1979).

[38] J. G. Westenholz, "Thoughts on Esoteric Knowledge and Secret Lore," 451–62, here 452. Westenholz notes that the word "esoteric" comes from the Greek ἐσωτερικ–, the comparative of ἔσω "within."

dealing with the knowledge. Whatever the original purpose or scope of esoteric knowledge, it is always potentially secret, but this is a question that is determined by the status and use of esoteric knowledge in a given social setting. For esoteric knowledge to become secret it must be self-consciously and formally restricted to a highly defined social group such as the Yaḥad.

To give a specific example, apocalyptic texts are often deemed by scholars to convey "esoteric" matters, even though these may *not* be intended to be kept secret—on the contrary they are often meant to be publicized and shared beyond the "conventicles" in which they arise. The book of Daniel is a good example of this type of esotericism. Possibly assembled by an esoteric conclave of pious elites (the *maśkîlîm*?[39]), "there is no evidence that anyone ever guarded the book from outsiders. In fact, given the general message of the book, keeping it secret would have worked against its purpose."[40] The book may indeed betray a polemical stance toward the secret-keeping practices of the various Babylonian diviners, making the point that not only their gods but also their methods are incapable of revealing anything worth guarding in the first place. But already here we have made a distinction between the product of a particular group—a "book"—and the group

---

[39] It has long been a scholarly theory that the group behind the redaction of Daniel is related to the several mentions of the "wise ones" (המשכלים), such as in Dan 11:33–35; 12:3, 10. See Philip R. Davies, "Reading Daniel Sociologically," in *The Book of Daniel in the Light of New Findings* (ed. A. S. van der Woude; BETL 106; Leuven: Leuven University, 1993), 345–61; John J. Collins, *Daniel with an Introduction to Apocalyptic Literature* (FOTL 20; Grand Rapids: Eerdmans, 1984), 53; idem, *Daniel* (Hermeneia; Minneapolis: Fortress, 1993), 66–70.

[40] Lenzi, "Secrecy, Textual Legitimation, and Inter-Cultural Polemics." Lenzi goes on to explain this remark: "From a critical perspective, therefore, these injunctions [to seal the book and keep it secret; Dan 8:26, 12:4, 9] must be considered a literary-rhetorical ploy to gain authority for the book and to deal with the problem of transmission created by the book's choice of pseudonym. Concerning the latter: a putative neo-Babylonian/early Persian period mediator of divine secrets somehow had to pass his knowledge down to a late Hellenistic audience without that knowledge having ever become public in the intervening years. An injunction to seal and hide the words of his book is the final redactor's literary attempt to rectify this chronological problem. As for gaining authority, secrecy in the Book of Daniel seems to be a rhetorical means to display the revelatory abilities of the Jewish deity and his mediator and thereby create legitimation and gain authority for the revelatory corpus as a whole. Thus, even if the Hellenistic Jewish readers considered themselves privileged readers of a secret revelatory corpus, there is no evidence from a critical perspective to consider the Book of Daniel historically as such."

itself, and along with it the implicit assumption that if the book was public then the group must not have been secretive. But what do we really know about this group? And why should we assume that the book of Daniel represents the extent of its teachings? Could it not simply be the publicly disseminated teaching that derives from a larger store of secret, guarded, esoteric knowledge?

I should clarify at this point what I consider to have been within the "esoteric domain" of Qumran, i.e. the overall stock of esoteric knowledge of the Qumran group. This is a complicated question, and any brief answer runs the risk of over-simplification, but the following can serve as the basic outline whose details will be filled out during the course of the study as a whole. The variety of non-biblical material from the Qumran caves is difficult to synthesize into a coherent explanatory model, and yet upon careful inspection there are some unifying features by which one might characterize the Qumran material as "esoteric" in nature, a characterization that is of course related to the oft-issued statement that the inhabitants of Qumran constituted an "apocalyptic community."[41] In the case of the Qumran group(s), at least some of the esoteric knowledge was also apparently secret, given the explicit statements to that effect as well as the presence of material encoded into several different cryptic scripts.[42]

I stress again that I am approaching the Qumran Scrolls not as if they represent a single group at a single moment in time, but as a *collection* of texts taken to be valuable (if not all immediately useful) by a particular group of people whom I consider to be the Yaḥad. I am not interested as much in the groups behind, say, *1 Enoch*, *Aramaic Levi*, and other texts, but in *why the Yaḥad* would be interested in texts like these. The brand of apocalyptic thought at Qumran was a kind of priestly scribalism that integrated aspects of previously existing wisdom and apocalypticism with a *torah*-centered covenantal theology. The corresponding body of knowledge represented by the Qumran Scrolls was part of an effort to acquire and employ total knowledge of the cosmos and history.

If we take a composite definition derived from Tiryakian's and von Stuckrad's descriptions of esotericism as a guide, the following features of the Qumran material are worthy of note—regardless of whether specific to Qumran or not. Indeed, there are other aspects of esotericism that will play into the discussion as it unfolds here, but this provides a good starting point.

---

[41] See pages 8–9, n. 28.
[42] See Stephen Pfann, DJD 36.

1. **The rhetoric of a previously hidden truth delivered by mediation by a specific authority.** Examples: *1 Enoch, Visions of Amram, Genesis Apocryphon, Aramaic Levi, Jubilees, Pesher Habakkuk.*

2. **The notion of a chain of "initiates" and sages who determine the course of revelation.** Examples: *Visions of Amram, Genesis Apocryphon, Aramaic Levi, Jubilees,* 4QInstruction, *Community Rule*

3. **The claim that knowledge is combined with individual religious experience.** Examples: *1 Enoch* (*Book of the Watchers, Epistle of Enoch, Birth of Noah* pericope), Daniel, *Hodayot, Community Rule* (esp. column 11), *Songs of the Sabbath Sacrifice, Self-Glorification Hymn* , 4QInstruction, *Mysteries.*

4. **Comprehensive cognitive mappings of nature and the cosmos, and of the ontological reflections of ultimate reality.** Examples: *1 Enoch* (*Book of the Watchers, Astronomical Book*), *Hodayot*, physiognomies and astrologies (4Q186, 4Q318, 4Q561), *Jubilees, Ages of Creation* (4Q180–81), *Treatise on the Two Spirits* (1QS 3–4; 4QpapS^a; 4QS^b; 4QpapS^c).

5. **Ritual initiation of new members by those already holding esoteric knowledge.** Examples: *Aramaic Levi, Community Rule, Damascus Document, Hodayot.*

This basic framework can be compared with the summary of Qumran esotericism provided by Jey Kanagaraj in his study of the Jewish mysticism of the Gospel of John. While he is not entirely clear about how he defines "esotericism," his statement is apt nevertheless in the way it anticipates much of the present study:

> In sum, the רז passages in Qumran literature bring out the following elements as esoteric, which, at the same time, reflect a "mystical" character: (1) the knowledge of the divine order of creation, hidden for an ordinary human being but revealed to the initiates; (2) the splendour of God's glory as perceived in the heavenly council and the name and glory of God in creation; (3) the right interpretation of Scripture that is made known only to whom God wills; (4) and the whole system of evil that works against God now, but which will be dealt with ... when God will reveal his eschatological plan to him.[43]

---

[43] Jey Kanagaraj, *Mysticism in the Gospel of John: An Inquiry into Its Background* (JSNTSup 158; Sheffield: Sheffield Academic Press, 1998), 101.

To consider one part of the collection, the presence in much of the Aramaic literature of material—stories, teachings, traditions—that describe the processes of revelation and transmission of esoteric knowledge is one good reason why *these particular* Aramaic writings were of value to the Qumran group despite its ostensible predilection for Hebrew as the language of the elect.[44] Additionally, scientific texts such as the astronomical and physiognomic writings may actually *constitute* some of the content of esoteric knowledge that is passed along from one generation to the next. But again it is important to stress the distinction between the origins (and "original intent" or even "original audience") of the various Aramaic texts and their *reception* and *use* among the Qumran sectarians. It is also important to stress that not all of the knowledge would have been current, useful, or even accepted as legitimate or representative.[45] While the early Enochic works, for example, may derive initially from a priestly-scribal group at home in the Jerusalem Temple, such a possibility does not finally determine the social setting of these works as they are transmitted and interpreted by successive apocalyptically-oriented groups.[46]

---

[44] See chapter 3 for additional discussion of this issue.

[45] See the fascinating discussion by Michael Barkun in his *A Culture of Conspiracy: Apocalyptic Visions in Contemporary America* (Berkeley: University of California Press, 2003), 26–29. Describing the intersections between modern apocalyptic and conspiratorial modes of thinking, Barkun asserts that there is such a thing as "stigmatized knowledge" that is embraced by apocalypticists—knowledge that includes forgotten knowledge, superseded knowledge, ignored knowledge, rejected knowledge, suppressed knowledge. I have John Collins to thank for this reference. Regarding the *Astronomical Book*, for instance, several scholars have argued that it reflects an "outdated" understanding of astronomy with respect to the surrounding Hellenistic environment. See Michael Stone, "Enoch, Aramaic Levi, and Sectarian Origins," *JSJ* 19 (1988): 159–70; Ben Dov, *Head of All Years*, 245-50.

[46] Gabriele Boccaccini, *Beyond the Essene Hypothesis*, 77–78; Reed, *Fallen Angels*, 69: "The most salient features of [the *Book of the Watchers* and the *Astronomical Book*] are their self-conscious scribalism and their development of a unique type of wisdom that combined 'scientific,' exegetical, mythic, and ethical components. One cannot underestimate the economic and social preconditions for the cultivation of such learning, nor for the continued transmission of Mesopotamian lore alongside Israelite traditions. Together with the priestly interests of both apocalypses, these factors suggest that the production of the earliest Enochic writings fits most plausibly with scribes in the orbit of the Jerusalem Temple."

Even if a given text may not have been esoteric when composed or compiled,[47] it can be "esotericized" in its later reception and interpretation. In this way it seems that even the non-sectarian/pre-sectarian texts helped the people of the Damascus Covenant and the Yaḥad to interpret not only their sacred traditions, but also *themselves*, in light of the great cultural, political and religious vicissitudes of the third to the first centuries B.C.E. If, as is often claimed, these people comprised a priestly community of scribal-intellectual elites, their store of esoteric knowledge went well beyond the material they themselves were composing—and yet it was to some extent crystallized into their own (apparently secret) complex religious and intellectual system.[48]

Before proceeding it is worth considering an important observation by Moshe Halbertal on the nature of Jewish esotericism in general. He

---

[47] Reed, *Fallen Angels*, 67: "'Scientific' interests of the circles responsible for the *Astronomical Book* and the *Book of the Watchers* were probably only 'esoteric' insofar as they were scribal."

[48] Take for example Philip Alexander's statement: "The standard explanation of Qumranian interest in Enoch is that the Qumranians, in opposition to the Jerusalem priesthood, had adopted the Enochic solar calendar, and needed both the Enochic science and the authority of the Enochic literature to sustain its position," a view that is itself "not without its problems." Nevertheless, "the calendar may have been retained as an ideal model of time—a kind of model not unknown to modern science. It may have come to represent how time ideally should run, and perhaps would run in the future, when the natural order was no longer disturbed by evil. It is, of course, possible that as a community of scholars, the Qumranians valued the Enochic texts for their own sake as learned, and, indeed, edifying literature, without being too deeply influenced by them. But the simplest explanation is surely that Enoch features at Qumran because the circles who founded Qumran were linked in some way to the circles that studied the Enochic tradition. Enoch was part of their intellectual baggage. The Jerusalem Temple in the Second Temple period was probably a locus not just of ritual, but of a vigorous intellectual life, and may have housed a school or schools. This should, in principle, cause no surprise: great temples had from hoary antiquity been centres of learning in the Near East. Qumran was founded by renegade Jerusalem priests. The founders of Qumran were associated with the school, or the circle, in the Jerusalem Temple which had preserved and studied the Enochic literature, and they brought copies of the texts with them from there to Qumran" ("Enoch and the Beginnings of Jewish Interest in Natural Science," in *The Wisdom Texts from Qumran and the Development of Sapiential Thought* [ed. Charlotte Hempel, Armin Lange, and Hermann Lichtenberger; BETL 159; Leuven: Leuven University Press, 2002], 223–43, here 239–40).

points out a paradox that lies at the heart of esotericism, one that can be found in its ancient, medieval, and modern manifestations:

> The justification for esotericism reflects an attempt to preserve part-icular knowledge in a state of purity, without fault or distortion, as a protected, well-guarded realm. Because, however, the esoteric realm is a closed one, it cannot be effectively controlled. An esotericist may claim that a new body of knowledge is actually the transmission of an ur-ancient esoteric Jewish tradition. In response to those who dispute him, claiming that they had never heard of such a teaching in Jewish tradition, he will claim: "This knowledge was kept secret; consequently, it left no trace in the traditions known to you." Thus the most guarded realm is also the least restricted.[49]

Perhaps the most salient example of this kind of Jewish esotericism in antiquity is the collection of Enochic writings, and the way in which the book of *Jubilees* writes the (secretly-transmitted) Enochic lore into the sacred (public) narrative of Moses and the reception of *torah* on Mount Sinai. But there are many examples of this kind of claim—especially in Aramaic texts of the mid-late Second Temple period—and these will be discussed in more detail in the next chapter.

What Halbertal's observation brings to the fore is the potential implicit deceit that lurks in claims to esoteric knowledge. Ironically, the very appeal to authority, which rests finally in the claim to antiquity and hiddenness, can also undermine the legitimacy of the text when it finds itself in a context outside of its authorizing or legitimating community. In this way it is perhaps not surprising that the majority of apocalyptic (and Gnostic and other) texts were not deemed authoritative by the mainstream religious bodies later responsible for biblical canonization, who on the whole apparently viewed such texts and their adherents to be hostile to the emerging Jewish and Christian orthodoxies.

EXCURSUS: ESOTERIC KNOWLEDGE AND THE SCRIBAL CRAFT

In general, ancient Near Eastern societies appear to show an interest at some level in mystery, secrecy, and esoteric knowledge. The revelation or acquisition of special knowledge from the divine realm is a ubiquitous aspect of ancient Near Eastern religious culture, and though its expressions and underlying practices vary from one context to another,

---

[49] Halbertal, *Concealment and Revelation*, 12.

usually the *Sitz im Leben* of language about mystery and secrecy is predictably the temple or the royal court.[50]

In various discussions about the *Aramaic Levi Document* (1Q21; 4Q213, 213a, 213b, 214, 214a, 214b) and related Aramaic compositions such as the *Visions of Amram* and the Aramaic "testaments," Henryk Drawnel has described some of these texts as "priestly didactic literature" that is concerned with the practice and transmission of the "scribal craft."[51] This craft involves much more than simply learning how to read and write, but also includes the acquisition of knowledge regarding metrological,[52] astrological, and astronomical matters, as well as sacrificial and marital purity concerns. In these texts, the special, esoteric knowledge of a highly defined group of priestly (levitical) tradents informs the presentation of how the patriarchs receive and transmit sacred knowledge. Indeed, their acquisition of special knowledge represents a set of ideals that has been retrojected upon the earlier figures in ways that are echoed in many of the Qumran sectarian texts.

---

[50] For example, for discussion of the royal and cultic significance of the *Epic of Gilgamesh* (and the *Atrahasis Epic*), or at least Tablet XI of its later redaction (by Sîn-lēqi-unninī, a *kalû* priest), see Paul-Alain Beaulieu, "The Descendants of Sîn-lēqi-unnini," in *Assyriologica et Semitica: Festschrift für Joachim Oelsner* (ed. J. Marzahn and H. Neumann; AOAT 252; Münster: Ugarit-Verlag, 2000), 1–16; James R. Davila, "The Flood Hero as King and Priest," *JNES* 54 (1995): 199–214; Scott Noegel, *Nocturnal Ciphers*, 69–76; Lenzi, *Secrecy and the Gods*, passim.

[51] See especially his *An Aramaic Wisdom Text from Qumran: A New Interpretation of the Levi Document* (JSJSup 86; Leiden: Brill, 2004); "Priestly Education in the *Aramaic Levi Document* (*Visions of Levi*) and *Aramaic Astronomical Book* (4Q208–211)," *RevQ* 22 (2006): 547–74; "Moon Computation in the *Aramaic Astronomical Book* (1)," *RevQ* 23 (2007): 3–41; "Some Notes on Scribal Craft and the Origins of the Enochic Literature," paper presented at the Fourth Enoch Seminar, Camaldoli, Italy, July 8–12, 2007. Drawnel also refers to this document as the "Visions of Levi."

[52] Robert Kugler critiques Drawnel's reconstruction of the metrological section of the Qumran copies of *Aramaic Levi*. As Kugler notes, "no fragments of the metrological details reported in the G [Greek] and C [Cairo Geniza] (§§31–47) survive" ("Whose Scripture? Whose Community?" 10 n. 13). Drawnel, however, claims that such details can be found in 4Q214b 5–6 ii 6, which attests a ת, the first letter of what Drawnel reconstructs to be תותב, which is part of the first verse of the metrological section in Bodl. d 18; here Puech agrees. See Drawnel, *An Aramaic Wisdom Text from Qumran*, 189; Émile Puech, "Le *Testament de Lévi* en araméen de la Geniza du Caire," *RevQ* 20 (2002): 532.

This notion of a "scribal craft" is found also in ancient Assyrian and Babylonian scribal circles.[53] As Alan Lenzi persuasively demonstrates, this scribal craft in Mesopotamian traditions developed an association with secrecy, whereby "the attachment of secrecy to the scribal craft was an ideologically motivated move—it was part of their divine secret knowledge mythmaking strategy—intended to buttress the social position of a very select group of individuals and the authority of their knowledge."[54] One may cite texts such as "In Praise of the Scribal Art,"[55] which states,

> The scribal art is a "house of richness," the secret of Amanki (Enki/Ea),
> Work ceaselessly with the scribal art and it will reveal its secret to you.

The word for "secret" here is *niṣirtu*, which can also be found in other texts such as VAB VII 254:13, in which Ashurbanipal claims that "I have learned the hidden secret (*niṣirtu*), the entire scribal craft (*tupšarrūtu*);

---

[53] One might also note the similarities between Mesopotamian and Egyptian scribal cultures; see Karel Van der Toorn, *Scribal Culture and the Making of the Hebrew Bible* (Cambridge, Mass.: Harvard University Press, 2007), 51–73.

[54] *Secrecy and the Gods*, esp. 1–220.

[55] See A. W. Sjöberg, "In Praise of the Scribal Art," *JCS* 24 (1972): 126–27, lines 7-8. Scott Noegel has also treated this text in his *Nocturnal Ciphers* (36–37). Noegel's overall thesis is that punning is a ubiquitous and important feature of ancient Near Eastern scribal/divinatory culture, and the use of puns as a device witnesses to "the existence of a scribal perception in which the written word or 'sign' has the potential to be a great deal more than what it signifies. Like the diviner who embodies his profession, it is a container of divine secrets. The exegetes who deciphered omens and texts via punning extrapolations clearly viewed their interpretive strategies as more than mere academic embellishment, for as many of the colophons to the commentaries explicitly state, the interpretive system in which we find this punning constituted *amāt niṣirti* 'hidden word' and *piristu ša ilī* 'secret(s) of the gods.' Since the punning hermeneutic aims to reveal divine secrets hidden in texts, to some degree we must consider wordplays as containers of divine secrets and/or tools for revealing them" (37–38). Noegel proposes the possibility that the Sumerian signs KI.URÌ, translated into Akkadian as *niṣirtu*, can also make a reverse ligature (without the DINGIR sign) of NANNA(R), god of the new moon. As he asks, "Is this the secret to which the scribe draws attention?" (36). It strikes me that an investigation of the use of such punning in Qumran texts—especially the ones that display aspects of oneiromancy such as the *Genesis Apocryphon, Aramaic Levi Document*, and others—might be a fruitful path of study.

with my own eyes I have seen the tablets of heaven and earth," or in Nabonidus' Verse Account 8'-10' in which the king proclaims,

> I stood in the assembly; I praised myself, (saying):
> "I am wise. I am learned. I have seen ('read'?) secret things.
> (Though) I am illiterate, I have seen ('read'?) secret knowledge."[56]

Many of these passages constitute "*Geheimwissen* colophons" that "designate a text as *niṣirtu* 'restricted,' or as *pirištu* 'secret,'" and that pertain to the realm of priests, sages, diviners, scholars, and even kings,[57] or as Simo Parpola has described it, to the five scholarly crafts of the Neo-Assyrian court: exorcism, divination, lamentation-appeasement, astrology, and medical practices.[58] In first millennium texts such colophons often take the following form: "The initiate may show the initiate. The uninitiated may not see."[59] In a Late Babylonian colophon we find the statement, "reading what has to do with the great gods is the secret lore concerning heaven and earth, reading commentary is the

---

[56] See Lenzi, *Secrets of the Gods*, 144. Nabonidus text is from H. Schaudig, *Die Inschriften Nabonids von Babylon und Kyros' des Großen samt den in ihrem Umfeld entstandenen Tendenzschriften: Textausgabe und Grammatik* (AOAT 256; Münster: Ugarit, 2001), 569. From the mouth of Nabonidus this would seem a patently absurd claim to the minds of the priestly-scribal elite of the Neo-Babylonian empire (see Paul-Alain Beaulieu, *The Reign of Nabonidus King of Babylon, 556–539 B.C.* [YNER 10; New Haven: Yale University Press, 1989]), and one can imagine that the reception of traditions about Nabonidus in early Judaism would have been accompanied by a similar evaluation. In the surviving Jewish references to Nabonidus the Babylonian king is confused with Nebuchadnezzar (Dan 4–5) and is subordinated to the God of Israel and his representative sage, for whom no "mystery" is too difficult (see also 4QPrayer of Nabonidus [4Q242]). Nabonidus certainly is not given to know mysteries or secrets, which in mid-late Second Temple Jewish literature is the prerogative of religious-intellectual elites.

[57] Beaulieu, "New Light on Secret Knowledge," 98–99.

[58] Parpola, "The Assyrian Tree of Life," 169; idem, "Mesopotamian Astrology and Astronomy as Domains of the Mesopotamian 'Wisdom,'" 47–9; and "Monotheism in Ancient Assyria," 165–209. Parpola's views have been challenged within the Assyriological community, though Lenzi concurs with modifications; see discussion in Lenzi, *Secrecy and the Gods*, 19–21. See also H. Limet, "Le Secret et Les Écrits," 243–54; Westenholz, "Thoughts on Esoteric Knowledge and Secret Lore"; and Pongratz-Leisten, *Herrschaftwissen in Mesopotamien*; Livingstone, *Mystical and Mythological Explanatory Works*.

[59] Beaulieu, "New Light on Secret Knowledge," 98.

secret of the scholar."[60] These colophons underscore at least two salient facts about the functions of secrecy and esotericism in Mesopotamian scribal circles: 1) special knowledge was controlled and limited to defined groups; 2) such knowledge was transmitted from one member (and generation) to another.[61]

There are some important connections to be made between Mesopotamian and early Jewish scribal practices. To take but one important example, scholars have increasingly focused on the ways in which Babylonian materials can help to illuminate the scientific and mantic writings from Qumran, and to explain their presence among the other works represented in the caves.[62] For example, as Mladen Popović has demonstrated in his recent book, several Qumran Aramaic and Hebrew texts display an interest in physiognomic knowledge, or reflect more generally the "physiognomic consciousness" of mid-late Second Temple Judaism.[63] While he is not the first to discuss the phenomenon,[64]

---

[60] H. Hunger, *Babylonische und assyrische Kolophone* (Neukirchen-Vluyn: Neukirchener Verlag, 1968), No. 519 r. 26; Noegel, *Nocturnal Ciphers*, 37 n. 128.

[61] Pongratz-Leisten argues in *Herrschaftwissen in Mesopotamien* that these areas of knowledge were kept secret largely to vouchsafe the power of the king (304–309). Compare 4QProto-Esther ar (4Q550) in which a "sealed scroll" of Darius is addressed to kings who will come after him. It contains some kind of warning against "oppressors" and "liars."

[62] It is not possible to discuss in detail all of the Aramaic scientific texts. It must suffice to say that there is a diverse set of texts and areas of knowledge represented here. In his contribution to a recent conference, Jonathan Ben Dov put the Aramaic scientific texts into six categories: Astronomy; Geography; Metrology; Physiognomy; Astrology; Exorcism ("Scientific Writings in Aramaic and Hebrew at Qumran"). The scientific material is packaged in free-standing presentations (as in 4Q318, 4Q561) and is also embedded in narrative texts (as in *Astronomical Book* of *1 Enoch*, the *Genesis Apocryphon*, *Aramaic Levi Document*, and others).

[63] Popović, *Reading the Human Body*. The texts he discusses include 4QZodiacal Physiognomy (4Q186), 4QPhysiognomy ar (4Q561), 4QBirth of Noah ar (4Q534–35), the description of the newborn Noah in *1 En* 106, and the description of Sarai in the *Genesis Apocryphon* (1QapGen ar 20).

[64] See for example Menachem Brayer, "Psychosomatics, Hermetic Medicine, and Dream Interpretation in the Qumran Literature (Psychological and Exegetical Considerations)," *JQR* 60 (1969): 112–127; Florentino García Martínez, "4QMes. Aram. y el libro de Noé," *Salmanticensis* 28 (1981): 195–232; Jonas C. Greenfield and Michael Sokoloff, "Astrological and Related Omen Texts in Jewish Palestinian Aramaic," *JNES* 48 (1989): 201–214; Mark J. Geller, "New Documents from the Dead Sea: Babylonian Science in Aramaic," in *Boundaries in*

Popović situates the physiognomic and astrological (zodiacal) texts from Qumran within the broader Babylonian and Greco-Roman cultural trends, and more particularly, demonstrates the ways in which Babylonian and Hellenistic scientific knowledge has been appropriated and modified in the relevant Qumran texts. As he states, the physiognomic and astrological texts "perhaps objectified the speculative, scientific interests of some of elite members of Hellenistic-Early Roman period Jewish society or of the Qumran community. The pursuit and possession of that knowledge may have confirmed that elite status."[65] Such a scenario would likely mirror the social reality of physiognomic and astrological learning in ancient Mesopotamian scholarly/scribal circles, in which

> the interdiction against persons outside the circle of "knowers" reflects the efforts of a particular scribal body to maintain control over its tradition and to protect a particular body of knowledge. The special status of the tradition in the view of the scribes, however, is expressed in the claim that the knowledge contained in the tablets was transmitted from a divine source.[66]

The interest in the Qumran texts in matters pertaining to physiognomy, astrology, astronomy, medicine, and other esoteric arts—all presumed to be given by divine revelation—points to a context in which these forms of learning and practice were cultivated in a way analogous to late Babylonian scribal circles.

Another parallel exists at the level of writing practices. "A sub-category of writing which embodies the principles of secrecy is that of cryptic writing systems" which are found in both Babylonian and Qumran scribal settings.[67] The purpose of employing cryptic scripts is rather self-evident, even if the coded meanings are often difficult to reconstruct with real clarity. Information that was highly valued by—or was especially germane to bolstering the esoteric identity of—the group

---

the Ancient Near Eastern World: A Tribute to Cyrus H. Gordon (ed. Meir Lubetski, Claire Gottlieb and Sharon Keller; JSOTSup 273; Sheffield: Sheffield Academic Press, 1998), 224–29; Barbara Böck, "An Esoteric Babylonian Commentary" Revisited, *JAOS* 120 (2000): 615–20; Alexander, "Physiognomy, Rank and Initiation," 385–94. See now also Ben Dov, *Head of All Years*.

[65] *Reading the Human Body*, 231.

[66] Francesca Rochberg, *The Heavenly Writing: Divination, Horoscopy, and Astronomy in Mesopotamian Culture* (Cambridge: Cambridge University Press, 2004), 217.

[67] Westenholz, "Thoughts on Esoteric Knowledge and Secret Lore," 457.

was concealed by means of encryption. While this is an aspect of the Qumran Scrolls that needs considerably more research, Jonathan Ben Dov has suggested that

> as legitimate descendants of the Mesopotamian scientific discipline, both the Hebrew and the Aramaic sages adopted the doctrine of secrecy into their teaching. However, while Aramaic-writing scribes only warned against the illicit distribution without taking any practical measure to prevent it, the circle of Hebrew-writing authors centered around the yahad devised some forms of encryption in order to reinforce the limitations on illicit distribution of knowledge. In the Hebrew-writing sectarian sphere, the doctrine of secrecy and concealment seems to have joined forces with the hierarchy of knowledge, which may have been the norm in the sectarian setting.[68]

SECTARIAN THEORY AND QUMRAN SECTARIANISM

Recently scholars have given renewed attention to the issue of Qumran sectarianism in an attempt to give further definition and nuance to the social history of the Qumran group(s) and its relationship to other Jewish groups of the period. Many have noted the "tendency toward sectarianism" in Second Temple Judaism, beginning with the Restoration and the allegedly schismatic movements behind Ezra-Nehemiah, Second-Third Isaiah, Enochic works (especially the earliest among them, the *Book of the Watchers* and the *Astronomical Book*), *Jubilees*, and other texts, and culminating in the varieties of Judaism manifested in the first centuries B.C.E. and C.E.[69] At stake, it seems, has been an effort to tease

---

[68] Ben Dov, "Scientific Writings in Aramaic and Hebrew at Qumran."

[69] Most recently see David Chalcraft, ed., *Sectarianism in Early Judaism: Sociological Advances* (London: Equinox, 2007), which includes illuminating essays by Chalcraft, Lester L. Grabbe, Philip R. Davies, Perluigi Piovanelli, Eyal Regev, Cecilia Wassen and Jutta Jokiranta, and Albert I. Baumgarten. The term "tendency toward sectarianism" is from Joseph Blenkinsopp, who was among the first of the contemporary scholars to deal with this issue in his "Interpretation and the Tendency Toward Sectarianism: An Aspect of Second Temple History," in *Jewish and Christian Self-Definition, Vol. 2: Aspects of Judaism in the Graeco-Roman Period* (ed. E. P. Sanders, Albert I. Baumgarten and Alan Mendelson; Philadelphia: Fortress, 1981), 1–26. See also Blenkinsopp, "A Jewish Sect of the Persian Period," *CBQ* 52 (1990): 5–20; Shemaryahu Talmon, "The Internal Diversification of Judaism in the Early Second Temple Period," in *Jewish Civilization in the Hellenistic-Roman Period* (ed. Shemaryahu Talmon; Philadelphia: Trinity Press International, 1991), 16–43; idem, "The Emergence of Jewish

out of a limited number of sources (of the "dark" period of Achaemenid and early Hellenistic hegemony) the contours of the fractious mid-late Second Temple Jewish *ethnos*,[70] and to account for the rise of apocalyptic

---

Sectarianism in the Early Second Temple Period," in *Ancient Israelite Religion: Essays in Honor of Frank Moore Cross* (ed. Patrick D. Miller, Paul Hanson, and S. Dean McBride; Philadelphia: Fortress, 1987), 587–616; Michael Stone, *Scriptures, Sects and Visions: A Profile of Judaism from Ezra to the Jewish Revolts* (Philadelphia: Fortress, 1980); Albert I. Baumgarten, *The Flourishing of Jewish Sects in the Maccabean Era: An Interpretation* (JSJSup 55; Leiden: Brill, 1997). See also the recent compilation of articles (both previously published and unpublished) by Moshe Weinfeld, *Normative and Sectarian Judaism in the Second Temple Period* (LSTS 54; London: T&T Clark, 2005). It is not clear why this particular title has been given to the collection; there is no preface or epilogue that explains it, and the articles deal with such a vast array of topics that it is difficult to discern which of them represent Weinfeld's understanding of "normative" Judaism during the Second Temple period, and thus which of them deal with "sectarian" matters. He does seem to presuppose that certain later normative practices such as the *Amidah* were normative also during the Second Temple period. (I am not suggesting that such practices were not in existence, but rather that it remains to be seen whether they were normative.) Of particular interest are, "Prayer and Liturgical Practice in the Qumran Sect," 53–67; and "The Crystallization of the 'Congregation of the Exile' (קהל הגולה) and the Sectarian Nature of Post-Exilic Judaism," 232–38. Unfortunately it was too late for this study when I came across what appears to be a helpful recent contribution to the topic of Jewish sectarianism: H. Newman and R. Ludlam, *Proximity to Power and Jewish Sectarian Groups of the Ancient Period: A Review of Lifestyle, Values, and Halacha in the Pharisees, Sadducees, Essenes, and Qumran* (Leiden: Brill, 2006), especially chapters 2 ("Jewish Groups in the Hasmonean Period and Their Proximity to the Regime") and 5 ("Seceding Groups and Dissenting Groups: Theology and Ideology").

[70] Articulating the nature of Second Temple "Judaism" is dogged even taxonomically: What is Judaism during this period? When does it begin? And does it include non-Judean elements of the people formerly constituted as "Israel" prior to the Babylonian conquest? If "Jewish" and "Judaism" are taxons derived from the ethno-geographic category "Judean," what terminology might include "Jews" from Benjamin, Yeb/Elephantine, Samaria, and later, diasporic communities? For discussion of this problem see Philip R. Davies, "Sect Formation in Early Judaism," in *Sectarianism in Early Judaism: Sociological Advances* (ed. David Chalcraft; London: Equinox, 2007), 133–55; Perluigi Piovanelli, "Was There Sectarian Behaviour before the Flourishing of Jewish Sects? A Long-Term Approach to the History and Sociology of Second Temple Judaism," in *Sectarianism in Early Judaism*, 156–79. See also Shaye D. Cohen, *The Beginnings of Jewishness: Boundaries, Varieties, Uncertainties* (Berkeley: University of California Press, 1999); M. Hamilton, "Who Was a Jew? Jewish Ethnicity during the Achaemenid Period," *Restoration Quarterly* 37 (2001): 102–17.

groups, the transformation of the wisdom schools, the nature and functions of the priesthood, and the internecine strife over the question of how properly to constitute the people Israel.

One important problem, of course, is the way we may speak of "sects" or of self-consciously segregating groups in the context of a Judaism for which there may not have been a mainstream or normative manifestation.[71] What then was the center from which such sects/ sectarians deviated?[72] And how do our primary sources, if they reflect different strains of these segregating groups (or different historio-graphical accounts of them, as in the case of the descriptions by Josephus, Philo, Hippolytus, and Pliny, among others[73]), help us to construct an accurate picture of the social and religious world of Palestinian Judaism during the Persian, Hellenistic, and early Roman periods?[74] And finally, how does the phenomenon of early Jewish

---

[71] While there is by no means universal agreement on the question of whether there was such a thing as mainstream or normative Judaism during this time, scholars have tended in recent years to assume that there was not. See the summary of contemporary scholarly views in Boccaccini, *Roots of Rabbinic Judaism*, 8–14.

[72] Or, as Davies states, "The existence of a sect implies the existence of a 'parent,' from which the sect obtains some of its identity but against which it matches its identity also. ... What *was* that 'parent' Judaism?" ("Sect Formation," 133). Davies goes on in the article to provide a rich and nuanced discussion of scholarly approaches that have posited a "centrifugal" model for the varieties of early Judaism (groups that break away from a center), and those that have seen a "centripetal" process at work (various disparate groups overlapping to create a kind of consensus about what constitutes Judaism). The former category includes scholars like Paul Hanson (esp. his *The Dawn of Apocalyptic*) and Otto Plöger (esp. his *Theocracy and Eschatology* [trans. S. Rudman; Richmond: John Knox Press, 1968]); the latter category includes most notably the work of E. P. Sanders, esp. *Paul and Palestinian Judaism: A Comparison of Patterns of Religion* (Philadelphia: Fortress, 1977) and *Judaism: Practice and Belief 63 BCE to 66 CE* (London: SCM/Philadelphia: Trinity Press International, 1992). In a different but related category would be the work of Jacob Neusner, "for whom 'Judaism' in any kind of normative sense, or expressing a coherent religious system, is hard to discern before the efforts of the rabbis to create it" (Davies, "Sect Formation," 142).

[73] Josephus *Ant.* 18, *J.W.* 2; Philo *Hypoth.* 11, *Good Person* 75-91, *Contemp. Life*; Hippolytus *Ref.* 9.13-25; Pliny *Nat. Hist.* 5.17, 4.

[74] See the two cautionary treatments in *The Early Enoch Literature* (ed. Gabriele Boccaccini and John J. Collins; JSJSup 121; Leiden: Brill, 2007): James C. VanderKam, "Mapping Second Temple Judaism," 1–20; Florentino García Martínez, "Conclusion: Mapping the Threads," 329–36.

sectarianism reflect corollary claims to authentic and true knowledge, and in what ways is such knowledge held to be secret or esoteric?

Since the beginning of Qumran scholarship there has been a concern to explain the nature of the sect(s) associated with the preservation and composition of the Qumran Scrolls.[75] In recent years the overall picture has become more complicated, yet scholars have continued to use the language of "sect" and "sectarian" to describe the Qumran group(s). In general I agree with the mediating position of Albert Baumgarten:

> Ancient Jewish sectarianism as I understand it did not require the existence of a normative orthodoxy, from which a sect had split off, as a prerequisite. All it needed was the choice made by sectarians to declare war against significant aspects of the religious world in which they lived.[76]

---

[75] See most recently Eyal Regev, *Sectarianism in Qumran: A Cross-Cultural Perspective* (Religion and Society 45; Berlin: de Gruyter, 2007); John J. Collins, "Sectarian Consciousness in the Dead Sea Scrolls," in *Heavenly Tablets: Interpretation, Identity and Tradition in Ancient Judaism* (ed. L. LiDonnici and A. Lieber; JSJSup 119; Leiden: Brill, 2007), 177–92; idem, "'Enochic Judaism' and the Sect of the Dead Sea Scrolls," in *The Early Enoch Literature* (ed. Gabriele Boccaccini and John J. Collins; JSJSup 121; Leiden: Brill, 2007), 283–300; Gabriele Boccaccini, "Enochians, Urban Essenes, Qumranites: Three Social Groups, One Intellectual Movement," in *The Early Enoch Literature* (ed. Gabriele Boccaccini and John J. Collins; JSJSup 121; Leiden: Brill, 2007), 301–28; Jutta M. Jokiranta, "'Sectarianism' of the Qumran 'Sect': Sociological Notes," *RevQ* 20 (2001): 223–40; Schofield, *From Qumran to the Yaḥad*, 21–33. See also the important article by Carol Newsom, "'Sectually Explicit' Literature from Qumran," in *The Hebrew Bible and Its Interpreters* (ed. William H. Propp, Baruch Halpern and David Noel Freedman; Winona Lake, Ind.: Eisenbrauns, 1990), 167–87; Devorah Dimant, "Qumran Sectarian Literature," in *Jewish Writings of the Second Temple Period: Apocrypha, Pseudepigrapha, Qumran Sectarian Writings, Philo, Josephus* (ed. Michael Stone; CRINT 2.2; Philadelphia: Fortress, 1984), 483–550; Armin Lange, "Kriterien essenischer Texte," in *Qumran kontrovers: Beiträge zu den Textfunden vom Toten Meer* (ed. Jörg Frey and Hartmut Stegemann, with the collaboration of Michael Becker and Alexander Maurer; Einblicke 6; Paderborn: Bonifatius, 2003), 59–69; idem, "Kriterien zur Bestimmung 'essenischer Ver-fasserschaft' von Qumrantexten," in *Qumran kontrovers*, 71–85; idem, "Dream Visions and Apocalyptic Milieus," in *Enoch and Qumran Origins: New Light on a Forgotten Connection* (ed. Gabriele Boccaccini; Grand Rapids, Mich.: Eerdmans, 2005), 27–34.

[76] "Ancient Jewish Sectarianism," *Judaism* 47 (1998): 388; compare Baumgarten's "He Knew that He Knew that He Knew that He Was an Essene," *JJS* 48 (1997): 53–61.

Perhaps the most comprehensive recent attempt to explain the phenomenon of Qumran sectarianism has been Eyal Regev's *Sectarianism in Qumran: A Cross-Cultural Perspective*.[77] In this work, which is an extension and elaboration of some of his earlier studies,[78] Regev takes a broad comparative and sociological approach to elucidating the contours of Qumran sectarianism, and concludes that such an approach can help us identify the appropriate language—or nomenclature—with which to characterize the kind of sectarianism we find "in Qumran."[79] Drawing on the sociological models of both Bryan Wilson[80] and Rodney Stark and William S. Bainbridge,[81] Regev finds that the four main elements of "Qumranic ideology" are "introversion (separation), revolution (messianism and eschatology), atonement, and divine revelation."[82] And

---

[77] Regev, *Sectarianism in Qumran*. While the broad comparative dimension in Regev's work is potentially somewhat problematic, he attempts to anticipate and answer possible objections (he has sections on "The Social Sciences," "Postmodern History" [by which he may mean Historiography], and "The Comparative Method"), though the critical issue of comparability and the wide application of social-scientific methodology may remain a problem for some readers.

[78] These include his "Abominated Temple and a Holy Community: The Formation of the Concepts of Purity and Impurity at Qumran," *DSD* 10 (2003): 243–78; "The *Yaḥad* and the Damascus Covenant: Structure, Organization, and Relationship," *RevQ* 21 (2003): 233–62; "Comparing Sectarian Practice and Organization: The Qumran Sect in Light of the Regulations of the Shakers, Hutterites, Mennonites and Amish," *Numen* 51 (2004): 146–81.

[79] Regev is sensitive to the fact that "Qumran" is not a monolithic representation of the group(s) associated with the Qumran Scrolls; though not everyone will agree with the historical scenario he posits, he remains constantly attentive to the diachronic dimension of the Scrolls and to the fact that they represent different moments in the life of the Qumran group. Regev understands this group to have had two major phases and corollary textual corpora (in this chronological order): (1) the Yaḥad, represented by the *Community Rule*, the *pesharim* and other texts, and (2) the Damascus Covenant, represented by the *Damascus Document*. He also discusses at length his assessment of pre-sectarian and related texts and groups (1 *Enoch*, *Jubilees*, *Temple Scroll*, 4QMMT) as well as the classical descriptions of the Essenes, which group he takes to be an outgrowth of the Qumran movement.

[80] Especially *The Social Dimensions of Sectarianism*; *Religion in Sociological Perspective*.

[81] Especially *The Future of Religion: Secularization, Revival, and Cult Formation* (Berkeley: University of California Press, 1985).

[82] Regev, *Sectarianism in Qumran*, 33.

as he states, "Like most ideologies, [these aspects] reflect an aspiration for an ideal realization of cognitive and moral values, contained in the sacred, through the 'total transformation' of society."[83]

Following Stark and Bainbridge, Regev discusses Qumran sectarianism as being essentially "in tension" with the surrounding social environment. This tension has three markers: *antagonism* with respect to society as a whole (or certain segments of it); *separation* from society and the creation of a closed social world; and an insistence upon *difference* from others, a difference that is reinforced with considerable effort. While I cannot engage his complex study in detail here (and while I do not embrace all aspects of his use of the sociological models or his resulting historical reconstruction), his work is helpful for the way it illuminates both the ideological and social contexts of Qumran sectarianism. Especially important is the impact his study has upon the way we might characterize the functions of secrecy, esotericism, and appeals to special knowledge (of "mysteries") in Qumran texts and within the sectarian milieu.

With respect to the first of the three markers of sectarianism and social tension, antagonism is a constituent feature of Qumran sectarianism and of apocalyptic movements in general. If a signature element of an apocalyptic worldview is the motif of judgment after death,[84] apocalyptic views of reality assume an essential antagonism between the righteous and the wicked, the saved and the damned. The constituents of these groups are defined in different ways depending upon the text in question (e.g. *Jubilees* compared to the *Community Rule*), but the basic pattern remains the same in "apocalyptic constructions of reality."[85]

Indeed this is what we find in key Qumran sectarian texts such as the *Damascus Document* and the *Community Rule*. For example, in the *Damascus Document* those who are not part of the in-group are characterized as a "congregation of traitors" who "depart from the way" (CD 1:12–13). This description is part of the opening section of the

---

[83] Ibid., 33.

[84] See John J. Collins, "Apocalyptic Eschatology as the Transcendence of Death," *CBQ* 36 (1974): 21–42; idem, "Response: The Apocalyptic Worldview of Daniel," in *Enoch and Qumran Origins: New Light on a Forgotten Connection* (ed. Gabriele Boccaccini; Grand Rapids, Mich.: Eerdmans, 2005), 60; idem, "Genre, Ideology, and Social Movements in Jewish Apocalypticism," 15–17.

[85] The phrase is George W. E. Nickelsburg's: "The Apocalyptic Construction of Reality in 1 Enoch," in *Mysteries and Revelations: Apocalyptic Studies since the Uppsala Colloquium* (ed. John J. Collins and James H. Charlesworth; JSPSup 9; Sheffield: Sheffield Academic Press, 1991), 51–64.

Damascus Document, the "historical prologue," in which the rise of the Teacher of Righteousness is contrasted with the "Man of Mockery" (איש הלצון) who "turned aside from paths of righteousness" (CD 1:15–16). Throughout this text there is a preoccupation with those who have deviated and their impending judgment and destruction, all of which is linked in various ways to claims to "true" and "false" knowledge.[86]

At a few points the *Damascus Document* is explicit about the relationship between knowledge of "hidden things" (נסתרות) and redemption, and about the atoning power of God's "mysteries of wonder" (רזי פלא).[87] Those who are "outside the wall" (CD 4:19) are finally people without any insight at all (אין בהם בינה).[88] Correct knowledge—limited, special, esoteric knowledge—is presumed a necessary precursor to election and, by extension, to salvation.

In the *Community Rule* we find a similar pattern of sectarian boundary-formation and identity-marking, one that accentuates the themes of social tension even more dramatically than the *Damascus Document* and also highlights the motif of cosmic tension between the heavenly forces of good and evil. The *Community Rule* repeatedly portrays the Yaḥad as arrayed against the Sons of Darkness (בני חושך), and those who volunteer to join the elect group are to bring "all their knowledge, strength, and wealth into the Yaḥad of God." They will have their knowledge "purified" in the "truth of God's statutes," and they will live in a "covenant of mercy," as a "society of God" that is to be separate from the works of Belial and from all evil (1QS 1:1–19).

In this text, which itself has undergone several stages of transmission and redaction reflecting different moments in the life of the community that stands behind it, the Yaḥad is the locus of special, esoteric, indeed salvific, knowledge. As in the *Damascus Document* (and other texts), the appeal to such knowledge forms the basis for the sectarian self-understanding, and informs the depiction of communal history, rationale, and practice. Even the central rites of passage described in the *Community Rule*—initiation and covenant renewal—presuppose

---

[86] Maxine Grossman has also discussed the way perceptions of "insider-status" are reinforced by textual/scriptural "virtuosity" in her "Cultivating Identity: Textual Virtuosity and 'Insider' Status," in *Defining Identities: We, You, and the Other in the Dead Sea Scrolls: Proceedings of the Fifth Meeting of the IOQS in Groningen* (ed. Florentino García Martínez; STDJ 70; Leiden: Brill, 2008), 1–11.

[87] CD 3:12–18.

[88] CD 5:16–17. Regev translates בינה as "intelligence," which is also an apt way to understand this passage (Regev, *Sectarianism in Qumran*, 35).

sectarian knowledge as a fundamental orienting and organizing principle. According to 1QS 5–6 new members are required to undergo periods of examination and incubation before being considered full members of the Yaḥad. The judgment rendered by the various community authorities was based on an assessment of the initiate's knowledge and whether the "lot" fell in his favor:

1QS 6:13–19

If anyone of Israel volunteers to join with the Council of the Yaḥad, the man appointed as leader of the Many will examine him with respect to his understanding (שכלו) and his works (מעשיו). If he has the potential for instruction, he is to bring him into the covenant, returning to the truth and turning away from all iniquity. ... When he has passed a full year in the midst of the Yaḥad, the Many will inquire regarding the matters pertaining to his understanding and his works of torah (מעשיו בתורה). If the lot falls to him (אם יצא לו הגורל) according to the opinion of the priests and the Many, he will be brought into the (secret?) council (סוד) of the Yaḥad.

If after the second year of provisional association the initiate was granted full membership in the Yaḥad, he would then be allowed to share his "counsel and judgment" with the rest of the group (1QS 6:21–23). His separation from the broader society would then be made complete.

The rituals of initiation and covenant renewal were also boundary-forming expressions of the Yaḥad's attempt to separate from wickedness and from its enemies—which, to be sure, were understood to be manifestations of one and the same reality, i.e. the men who were under the dominion of Belial. The dualistic framework of good vs. evil (and its various permutations) is characteristic of sectarian religiosity. Furthermore, "as a voluntary sectarian community, Qumran had to develop ways to reconstruct a person's identity, to separate them from their old identity within the mainstream of society, and create for them an identity that situated them within the Qumran community."[89] Claims to special knowledge of hidden matters and "mysteries" were also a crucial part of the group self-fashioning for which such rituals were effective vehicles.[90] And in the worldview of the Yaḥad these beneficent "mysteries" were placed in stark contrast and opposition to the "mysteries" of evil, thereby

---

[89] Russell C. D. Arnold, *The Social Role of Liturgy in the Religion of the Qumran Community* (STDJ 60; Leiden: Brill, 2006), 53 n. 7.

[90] See below, chapters 4 and 5, for a more detailed treatment of these texts and issues.

expressing also the perceived cosmic tension which was mirrored in the
earthly social tension of the community.

1QH^a 12:28–29

28 ... ובי האירותה פני רבים ותגבר עד לאין מספר כי הודעתני ברזי
29 פלאכה ובסוד פלאכה הגברתה עמדי

28 ... but by me you have illumined the face of many (i.e. the general
membership of the Yaḥad) and have strengthened them countless
times. For you have given me understanding in/of the mysteries
29 of your wonder, and in the council of your wonder you have
confirmed my standing.

1QM 13:10–12

10 ... ואתה
11 עשיתה בליעל לשחת מלאך משטמה ובחוש[ך ממשל]תו ובעצתו
להרשיע ולהאשים וכול רוחי
12 גורלו מלאכי חבל בחוקי חושך יתהלכו ואליו [תשו]קתמה יחד

10 ... You
11 have made Belial to corrupt, a hostile angel—his dominion is in
darkness and his counsel is for wickedness and guilt. All the spirits
12 of his lot are angels of destruction. They walk in the laws of darkness
and toward it; [darkness] is their only desire.

1QM 14:8–10

8 ... [ברוך] שמכה אל החסדים השומר ברית לאבותינו ועם
9 כול דורותינו הפלתה חסדיכה לשאר[ית נחלתכה] בממשלת בליעל
ובכול רזי שטמתו לוא הדיחונ[ו]
10 מבריתכה ...

8 ... [Blessed] be your name, God of mercies, the one who guards the
covenant of our fathers, and with
9 all our generations you have wondrously [bestowed] your mercies to
the remn[ant of your inheritance] during the dominion of Belial. But
with all the mysteries of his enmity, they [the mysteries?] have not
separated (us)
10 from your covenant ...

An important aspect of the present study is the way it draws upon
more general trends in the study of religion to help to illuminate the
contours of Qumran esotericism, and to define further the nature of the

Qumran group in terms of its boundary-making social, religious, and intellectual stances. One particularly striking feature of the Qumran Scrolls that has received but scant attention in scholarship is the resemblance of the Yaḥad and its intellectual and religious interests to other, later trends in (Western) esotericism. Regev's work, for example, though often helpful in its comparative approach to Qumran sectarianism, does not sufficiently (or explicitly) relate the sectarian outlook to its epistemological grounding in esoteric knowledge.[91] While his cross-cultural perspective elicits a more vivid picture of Qumran social practices and attitudes, it does not engage the closely related issue of esotericism despite the centrality of this way of thinking to the self-understanding of the Qumran group *as sectarians*.

DISCOURSE THEORY AND QUMRAN DISCOURSES

In an excellent recent treatment of Qumran self-identity, which also delves into the issues of language, knowledge, "discourses," and sectarianism, Carol Newsom has offered a theoretically—and even poetically—sophisticated account of the symbolic world of Qumran and the ideals it engendered within the community of the Yaḥad.[92] Newsom does not, however, present her findings in the broader terms of esotericism (which, to be fair, is not the aim of her study), and does not dwell upon the important role of secrecy or the claim to knowledge of "mysteries" in Qumran identity- and community-formation.

One extremely illuminating and helpful aspect of Newsom's study is the way she orients her approach to the texts in terms of the "discourses" of the Qumran community.[93] The word "discourse" itself has become a notorious—and often abused—*terme technique* of post-modernist literary, social, political, and philosophical work, and its definitions and/or functions can vary considerably from one school (or discourse) to the

---

[91] Regev does discuss these matters briefly; see especially pages 81–93 and 351–76.

[92] Carol Newsom, *The Self as Symbolic Space*.

[93] I have become somewhat self-conscious about my own use of terms like "discourse," "esotericism," and "sectarianism" by reading Russell McCutcheon's *Manufacturing Religion: The Discourse on Sui Generis Religion and the Politics of Nostalgia* (Oxford: Oxford University Press, 1997). It is indeed the case that in scholarship on religion, the study of discourses—whether ancient or modern—is tied intimately to the discourse of academic culture, which itself has lately insisted on the importance of articulating the shape, nature and function of various discourses (without, I might add, consciously and deliberately attempting to reify its own discourses).

next.[94] Despite potential pitfalls, several recent studies on early Jewish literature have appropriated this framework to good effect, using it to build heuristic models for interpreting the Qumran Scrolls and the works of Philo as well as the more general literary and cultural trends of Second Temple Judaism.[95] Regarding the Scrolls, as Newsom puts it, "because the Qumran community reflected self-consciously on the nature of its life together and embodied those reflections in texts, we know a significant amount about that life and the way in which it formed a community of discourse."[96]

As the present analysis attempts to show, one may see in the Qumran references to "mystery" that this term was embedded in three distinguishable discourses—namely the prophetic, the priestly, and the sapiential—which were incorporated into (or which formed the discursive bases for) the social, intellectual and religious life of the Yaḥad. Once again, to quote Newsom:

> In Second Temple Judaism, of course, one can note the spread of several discourses that offer a perspective from which others might be dialogically engaged. The language of the Deuteronomic movement becomes broadly influential, as does sapiential discourse. In a somewhat different way the highly technical language of the priesthood also becomes a moral language of extended scope. An apocalyptic way of talking is encountered in a wide variety of texts. *These do not remain radically separate discourses, of course, although their distinctiveness is often sufficient to allow one to identify them.* But such questions as whether Qumran was an apocalyptic community or a priestly community or a sapiential community might be more fruitfully addressed by examining how the various discourses are dialogically related in Qumran literature. These would not be questions about whether the members

---

[94] See Newsom, *Self as Symbolic Space*, 1–21 for further discussion and bibliography.

[95] For example Newsom, *The Self as Symbolic Space*; Hindy Najman, *Seconding Sinai: The Development of Mosaic Discourse in Second Temple Judaism* (JSJSup 77; Leiden: Brill, 2003); see also the approach of Maxine Grossman, *Reading for History in the Damascus Document: A Methodological Study* (STDJ 45; Leiden: Brill, 2002); eadem, "Priesthood as Authority: Interpretative Competition in First-Century Judaism and Christianity," in *The Dead Sea Scrolls as Background to Postbiblical Judaism and Early Christianity: Papers from an International Conference at St. Andrews in 2001* (ed. James R. Davila; STDJ 46; Leiden: Brill, 2003), 117–31; eadem, "Reading for Gender in the Damascus Document," *DSD* 11 (2004): 212–39.

[96] Newsom, *Self as Symbolic Space*, 1.

were themselves priests or sages or seers but questions about the relationship of various discursive traditions within the speech community of Qumran.[97]

Here I focus on a "discursive unit"—or a related set of them—that has to do with many of the same issues Newsom deals with such as knowledge, *torah*, identity, community, and worship. This discursive unit is the concept(s) of "mystery" and the related topics of secrets, secrecy, revelation, esoteric knowledge, and mysticism.

   In conversation with cultural and linguistic theorists such as those in the Bakhtin circle, Newsom also uses the term "ideological sign," which is another apt way of describing the use of "mystery" terminology in the Scrolls. Other examples of such signs include words like "Israel," "*torah*," "covenant," "righteousness," words that can take on different accents when used by different communities of discourse (Newsom gives the example of the use of *torah* in Maccabean literature vs. the Qumranic "those who do *torah*" [מעשי התורה] in texts like 1QpHab 7:11; 8:1). According to such a view of the discursive power of ideological signs, people usually use words that have already been charged with meaning in some context or another, and

> the characteristic of [such] used words is that they bear the traces of their previous use within them. ... To use a word, but especially a word that is particularly weighted with past usage, is implicitly to respond to other utterances of the word. ... As a community formed in significant measure by adult converts, the Qumran sect was not a closed community of discourse, but one that had to take account of a variety of conceptual horizons in establishing its own language. These are present in [for example, the *Community Rule*] in the way in which received language is incorporated, engaged, and reaccented.[98]

There are essentially three overlapping modalities by which—or contexts in which—one gains access to or apprehends "mysteries" according to the Qumran literature, and these may be designated the prophetic, the sapiential, and the priestly.[99] Each of these modalities is rooted in a more or less distinct social sphere in Israel's history, and thus each carries its own discourse or set of discourses as an inheritance of the

---

[97] Newsom, *Self as Symbolic Space*, 9; my emphasis.

[98] Ibid., 11–12; Mikhail Bakhtin, *The Dialogic Imagination* (trans. C. Emerson and M. Holquist; vol. 1; Austin: University of Texas Press, 1981), 275–85

[99] I shall have much more to say about these modalities and their discourses in chapter 5; what follows here is a preliminary outline.

tradition to which it is tied. The first of these, the prophetic, has to do with claims of revelatory knowledge of the divine will—claims historically tied to specific figures endowed with a kind of charismatic authority. To be sure, the institutions and forms of prophetic communication would evolve during the Second Temple period, yet despite later claims that "prophecy ceased" with, say, Malachi, the discourse of prophecy itself did not recede into history. As mediating activity it became as much interpretive as proclamatory, but in any case prophetic discourse was extended into new religious, political, and social situations in Second Temple Jewish life.

With respect to sapiential discourse, one may also chart an evolution during the Second Temple period, when the earlier ("traditional"?) wisdom of the Israelite sages underwent a social and epistemological transformation that included a reassessment of the relationship between reward and punishment, the limits and sources of human knowledge, and "the viability of earlier Wisdom, especially the gap between the promise of reliability and actual human experience."[100] Such a reassessment led to increased "eschatologizing" of wisdom, and the blending of wisdom constructs with notions of prophetic revelation participated in the rise of apocalyptic modes of thought and literary expression. Such a move relocated the focus of wisdom discourse from the earthly realm of human action and the laws of nature toward concern with and speculation about the cosmic structures and the mythic principles of reality. Fusing with ideas imported from Babylonian, Persian, and Greek traditions, these new sapiential pursuits were also concerned with the identification of correspondences between heavenly and earthly realities, between the timeless empyrean and the unfolding human historical drama. A corollary of this development was a fundamental shift in the epistemological basis for knowledge, a reorientation toward divine revelation as a—perhaps as the—cornerstone of legitimate wisdom. It is nonetheless possible to identify features of the sapiential discourse reflected in the use of mystery language in the Qumran Scrolls.[101]

---

[100] See recently the excellent study of Samuel Adams, *Wisdom in Transition: Act and Consequence in Second Temple Instructions* (JSJSup 125; Leiden: Brill, 2008), especially the summary in pages 273–77; also John J. Collins, "Wisdom Reconsidered, in Light of the Scrolls," *DSD* 4 (1997): 265–81.

[101] Collins ("Wisdom Reconsidered," 269–70) points out, however, that the more traditional wisdom was also alive and well at Qumran, citing 4Q413, 4Q420–21, and 4Q424 as examples.

Finally, the discourse surrounding the priestly tradition, or regarding the priesthood itself, is an important aspect of mystery language. To be sure, defining the nature and the limits of priestly concerns is a complex task, and in any case if the Yaḥad was a community of priests then in that sense everything in the sectarian texts must be considered "priestly." Moreover, it would not be prudent to assume that texts/contexts that are liturgical therefore pertain necessarily to a priestly discourse. Thus, in my discussion in chapter 5 I limit my treatment of priestly "mysteries" to (1) passages that display concern with issues of calendar and cosmology, cultic festivals, ritual impurity, or atonement for iniquity, and (2) the use of mystery language in compositions that otherwise show a keen interest in priests or the priesthood.

By the time of the mid- to late-Second Temple period we witness a high degree of boundary-crossing among these centers of intellectual and religious authority and the literary genres with which they were often associated.[102] At issue, at least in part, was an attempt to work out the proper basis of religious and political authority in the post-exilic communities of Judea and the Diaspora, a process that was itself bound up with profound aporias about the nature of the continuation of God's covenant, the definition of what (or who) constituted "Israel," the status and delimitation of *torah*, and the possibility for continued revelation in the post-exilic era.

All this, of course, is not to mention the difficulties brought on by the extreme vicissitudes of the Jewish polity within the larger framework of

---

[102] In 1960 R. B. Y. Scott observed in his SBL Presidential address: "In any case there is evidence for a certain mingling of the functions of prophet, priest, and sage, and of a common element in their teachings. This is so in spite of the fact that the classical prophets appear fundamentally critical of both priests and wise men, that the priests were unhappy about the intrusion of prophets like Amos and Jeremiah, and that the wise—at least as they are represented in the books of Proverbs, Job, and Qohelet—stand aloof from both. Prophets as well as priests gave *torah*, and they delivered many of their public oracles in the cult. Samuel and Elijah offered sacrifice. Jeremiah (possibly) and Ezekiel (certainly) were priests. Haggai and Malachi concerned themselves with the proper operation of the temple cult. ... Isaiah and Jeremiah scorn the wise men of their time, yet they themselves adopt some of the language, forms, and ideas of the wisdom teachers. ... Scribes were undoubtedly attached to the temple. ... Yet for all their interaction, the *ways to the knowledge of God* represented by prophet, priest, and sage remain distinct. Each appears to claim priority, and they are held together in creative tension" ("Priesthood, Prophecy, Wisdom, and the Knowledge of God," *JBL* 80 [1961]: 3–4).

power struggles among the Persians, Seleucids, Ptolemies, and Romans—in other words, the *realpolitik* of Jewish life in the Persian, Hellenistic, and early Roman periods. Not surprisingly, a concomitant struggle for religious authority—and all its corollary political, social, and fiduciary entanglements—became part of the reality of Second Temple Jewish life, as various groups sought to align themselves according to their own identities and goals. If the truism that "knowledge is power" holds any water, one way to trace out the lines of this picture is to investigate the use of key appeals to authority—or, in other words, the discursive claims to authoritative knowledge that are codified in literary and documentary texts.

To return to Newsom's notion of dialogically-related discourses in the Qumran literature, this is an extremely helpful way of explaining the presence of different religious ideas, traditions, languages, and genres among the recovered manuscripts. With such a model for understanding the contents of the Scrolls, it becomes unnecessary to be bound by the rigid frameworks that have customarily come into play when one labels the Qumran group to be an "apocalyptic community" or a "priestly community," or other designations like these. It also can help to explain the Qumran library as a reflection of various overlapping discourses, ones that were encoded in texts that represent various religious sensibilities yet also have unifying features. In order to understand the dynamic use of mystery language in the Qumran Scrolls we must investigate the ways in which it is carried along in the discourses that make up the "community of discourse" of the Qumran group.

As Newsom elucidates in her own way, these discourses all cast issues of knowledge in a central role; knowledge was, after all, the stock-in-trade in the competitive intellectual and religious marketplace of Second Temple Jewish leadership. What one could claim to know, and how one could claim to know it, would say something important about that person's place in the society.[103] In the case of the Yaḥad, the acquisition and safeguarding of knowledge was perhaps the most salient rationale and guiding principle for the life of the community. Even central concerns like proper observance of *torah* or priestly ritual were understood in terms of the true and unique knowledge of the group.

---

[103] As Newsom rightly points out, however, there were indeed groups whose authority was not predicated upon the knowledge that comes with "scribal expertise." Here she cites 1 Maccabees, in which the theme of knowledge is nearly absent altogether, and in which "zeal for *torah*" does not involve scribal intervention (*Self as Symbolic Space*, 59–60).

Of course, the prophetic, sapiential, and priestly discourses are themselves bound up—each in their own way—with that other emerging authoritative entity: scripture. Textually scripture was not yet a fixed quantity, but rather it was reflexively shaping and being shaped by these various traditions of religious authority during the course of the Second Temple period. Additionally the related issue of "scribalism," that is, the roles, social locations, practices, and self-understanding of scribes, is also an important aspect of each of these modes of religious authority. Some scribes were more than copyists or workaday tradents of scriptural traditions: there was in all likelihood a kind of "priestly-scribal" tradition—along a continuum that would include the Yaḥad—that involved knowing (or at least claiming to know) the details of astronomical lore, medicine, eschatology, and other fields of knowledge.

> The characteristics of torah (its immutability, its numerological symmetries, its foundations in cosmic realia and primordial events, its uniting of heaven and earth) can only be adequately comprehended by those who understand the mysteries of cosmic structures and of history. Thus the speech of those who talk about torah without such comprehensive intellectual contexts is likely to be defective.[104]

As Newsom argues, knowing how to understand scripture involved knowing lots of other things, too. In a section with the title "Qumran: How Knowledge of Torah Requires Knowledge of Other Things," Newsom calls attention to both the diversity of materials and types of scribal activity at Qumran, as well as the curious fact that there is almost no "scribal self-consciousness" reflected in the Qumran sectarian compositions.[105] While she does not really elucidate the contours of what this other knowledge might comprise (apart from knowledge of human nature and of history), she discusses the several statements about "revealed" and "hidden" matters of *torah*, and rightly notes that at Qumran "no longer is torah both a common possession and a special possession. True torah can be known *only* in the sect."[106]

---

[104] Ibid., 54–55. Here Newsom is discussing *Jubilees*, but, as she states, "the priestly scribalism of Jubilees with its apocalyptic overtones is very close to that of the Qumran community."

[105] Newsom, *Self as Symbolic Space*, 68–73; Christine Schams, *Jewish Scribes in the Second Temple Period* (JSOTSup 291; Sheffield: Sheffield Academic Press, 1998), 251, 257–60. Of course, this may suggest that such self-conscious identifications were not felt to be necessary, but rather the scribal self-awareness was taken for granted in the sectarian writings.

[106] Newsom, *Self as Symbolic Space*, 71.

One of the principle features of sectarianism of any stripe is the claim to possess (or at least to have access to) special knowledge available solely to a highly defined and restrictive group, often in the form of a religious conventicle (see discussion of sectarianism and esotericism above). Such a feature often arises among groups that have become isolated or marginalized from centers of real political and social power; their special knowledge is inherently "over-against" competing or prevailing constructions of reality. In this sense, on the one hand knowledge is *not* power, but often signals the lack of real power and the corollary desire for its possession.

On the other hand, the restricted knowledge can lend to the sectarian group a different sort of power, the ideological and moral upper hand of those who exhibit (often by their own standards) the most stringent and pure form of religious practice and language—what Newsom and others have called "symbolic power."[107] Furthermore, in the case of the group responsible for the authorship and preservation of the Qumran Scrolls, it is possible (if not highly likely) that their removal from the center in Jerusalem was self-imposed—it was a retreat to the wilderness as a response to the perceived impurity in the temple and the expected "end of days."[108]

---

[107] Ibid., 23. Here symbolic power is defined as "the social power that comes from the ability to define the meaning of common cultural symbols," i.e. *torah* or covenant or priesthood. Newsom also quotes the work of Pierre Bourdieu, *Language and Symbolic Power* (trans. Gino Raymond and M. Adamson; Cambridge, Mass.: Harvard University Press, 1995): symbolic power is "a power of constituting the given through utterances, of making people see and believe, of confirming and transforming the vision of the world and, thereby, action on the world and thus the world itself, an almost magical power which enables one to obtain the equivalent of what is obtained through force (whether physical or economic), by virtue of the specific effect of mobilization" (170).

[108] For a clear review of the problems involved in this question see VanderKam and Flint, *Meaning of the Dead Sea Scrolls*, 275–92. For a discussion of a particular aspect of Qumran "priestly" sectarianism—that of the purity of the *ḥullin*—see Meir Bar-Ilan, "Reasons for Sectarianism According to the Tannaim and Josephus' Allegation of the Impurity of the Oil for the Essenes," in *The Dead Sea Scrolls Fifty Years After Their Discovery, 1947–97* (ed. Lawrence Schiffman, Emanuel Tov, and James C. VanderKam; Jerusalem: Israel Exploration Society in Cooperation with The Shrine of the Book, Israel Museum, 2000), 587–99. On the retreat to the wilderness, see especially Shemaryahu Talmon, "The 'Desert Motif' in the Bible and in Qumran Literature," in *Biblical Motifs, Origins, and Transformations* (ed. A. Altmann; Cambridge, Mass.: Harvard University Press,

Whatever the exact reasons for separation in the case of the Yaḥad, Newsom is also correct to point out that as an "outsider" discourse, the apocalypticism of Qumran is a "language of those who elect a stance of marginality and seek to use that marginal status to find a place in the cultural conversation."[109] One text that demonstrates this rather well is the so-called *Halakhic Letter* (4QMMT or *Miqṣat Maʿaśe ha-Torah*), in which the author, possibly an early leader of the Yaḥad (or of a parent group), issues a series of suggested "corrections" to the practices then engaged in the Jerusalem temple and apparently condoned by the "letter's" recipient(s).[110] In that text, it is from the place of marginality

---

1966), 31–63; James C. VanderKam, "The Judean Desert and the Community of the Dead Sea Scrolls," in *Antikes Judentum und Frühes Christentum: Festschrift für Hartmut Stegemann zum 65. Geburtstag* (ed. B. Kollmann, W. Reinbold, and A. Steudel; Berlin: Walter de Gruyter, 1999), 159–71; Alison Schofield, "The Wilderness Motif in the Dead Sea Scrolls," in *Themes in Biblical Narrative: Israel in the Wilderness* (ed. K. Pomykala; Leiden: Brill, 2008), 37–53. Among Qumran texts see 1QS 8:12–14, 9:18–21; 1QM 1:2–3.

[109] Newsom, *Self as Symbolic Space*, 48; see also Robert R. Wilson, "From Prophecy to Apocalyptic: Reflections on the Shape of Israelite Religion," *Semeia* 21 (1981): 79–95 (esp. 84–85).

[110] See most recently Hanne von Weissenberg, *4QMMT: Reevaluating the Text, the Function, and the Meaning of the Epilogue* (STDJ 82; Leiden: Brill, 2008), especially the discussion in the Introduction; also Elisha Qimron and John Strugnell, "An Unpublished Halakhic Letter from Qumran," in *Biblical Archaeology Today* (Jerusalem: Israel Exploration Society, 1985), 400–407; Lawrence Schiffman, "The New Halakhic Letter (4QMMT) and the Origins of the Qumran Sect," *BA* 53 (1990): 64–73. Von Weissenberg aptly writes that in the epilogue of 4QMMT, "the reader is addressed in the 2nd person singular and plural. It has been proposed that the 2nd person singular references and the kings mentioned in the epilogue suggest that the text was a letter and the addressee was a political and religious leader, possibly even one of the Hasmonean kings or high priests. However, the comparison with Semitic epistolary texts showed that 4QMMT lacks the formal features typical of a personal letter, such as a *praescriptio* and an epistolary conclusion. The text itself gives no explicit identification of either the author or the addressee, and it is important to remember that the title 'Halakhic Letter' was given to 4QMMT by its modern readers. ... Even though the use of direct speech discourse is suggestive of the epistolary genre, it is not exclusive to this genre and cannot therefore be used as a sole criterion for genre identification. Rather than being a private letter, 4QMMT was a text that was meant to be circulated and studied by a wider, more general audience. Both the members of the community responsible for the copying of 4QMMT, and persons outside this community, for instance the priests of Jerusalem, could have been addressed by this text." I would like to

that the author(s) exhorts his (their) audience to "reflect on all these [things] and seek from him that he might support your counsel and keep far from you the evil plans and counsel of Belial, so that at the end of time (באחרית העת) you might rejoice in finding that some of our words were true" (4Q398 14–17 ii 4–6). From the periphery, or perhaps because of its peripheral status, the letter presumes the authority to instruct its recipient, an authority that must not derive from immediate association with the goings-on in the temple.

SUMMARY AND CONCLUSION

In this chapter I have provided the conceptual framework for the chapters that follow. "Esotericism" is a useful heuristic category not only for broad phenomenological comparison of socially analogous movements, but also because it can help to crystallize many of the salient features of the Yahad's interests, practices, and boundary-marking rhetorical expressions. Related to this, I have briefly discussed the issue of "sectarianism" as it pertains to Second Temple Judaism and to Qumran in particular. Finally, I offered an account of Carol Newsom's work on Qumran discourse and argued that her characterization of the Yahad's "group self-fashioning" is a helpful way to frame the present investigation of "mystery" in the Scrolls.

This overall conceptual framework—unwieldy as it may be at times—draws on three interlacing ways of speaking about the ideological language of the Yahad. To be sure, the formation of this group was preceded by other social, intellectual, and religious trends in Second Temple Jewish society, and the Yahad and its related groups inherited a broad array of texts and traditions that it (they) shaped in its (their) own important ways. It is to some of this preceding material that we turn in the next chapter.

thank Dr. von Weissenberg for making parts of the manuscript of her book available to me before publication.

CHAPTER THREE

SECRETS, MYSTERIES, AND THE DEVELOPMENT OF APOCALYPTIC THOUGHT

> To map an apocalyptic world is to map a cognitive world.
>
> Leonard L. Thompson

In this chapter I discuss a diverse, though by no means comprehensive, sample of ancient Israelite, ancient Near Eastern, and early Jewish (Second Temple) texts and traditions that bear importance for understanding the broad cultural and religious context of mystery language in the Qumran Scrolls.[1] I should be clear that I am not suggesting a particular line of genealogical development, but rather that there are important analogs in earlier texts and social contexts, and these can help us to understand what we encounter in the Qumran Scrolls.[2]

The epigraph is drawn from Leonard L. Thompson, "Mapping an Apocalyptic World," in *Sacred Places and Profane Spaces: Essays in the Geographics of Judaism, Christianity, and Islam* (ed. Jamie Scott and Paul Simpson-Housley; CSR 30; New York: Greenwood Press, 1991), 125.

[1] I have limited my treatment below to texts I think are helpful for illuminating the Qumran material in particular. I have not endeavored to provide an exhaustive analysis of texts from the Hebrew Bible, the ancient Near East, or early Jewish apocalyptic literature, but rather to provide a sketch of the broader discursive contexts regarding "mysteries" and secrets in early Judaism. For a broad treatment of secrecy in the ancient Near East and in the Hebrew Bible see Lenzi, *Secrecy and the Gods*.

[2] Maureen Bloom (*Jewish Mysticism and Magic: An Anthropological Perspective* [London: Routledge, 2007], 17) writes about ancient Mesopotamia as a "watershed" culture that can serve as the broad backdrop for understanding developments in ancient Israelite and early Jewish religion. This is especially true

THE "DIVINE COUNCIL" AND THE BIBLICAL *SOD*

Scholars have long discussed the presence and meaning of ancient Near Eastern traditions about the divine council (or divine assembly), especially as they relate to biblical traditions regarding the סוד *sod*, the heavenly assembly to which the Hebrew prophet gains special access for the purpose of delivering a divine message to a human community.[3] The modern study of the divine assembly motif in ancient Near Eastern literature (especially as it relates to the Hebrew Bible) was initiated in the middle of the twentieth century by H. Wheeler Robinson in his essay "The Council of Yahweh." Since Robinson's publication scholars have continued to debate the nature of the correspondences in Hebrew, Sumerian, Akkadian, and Ugaritic texts that deal with this motif.[4] Although an exhaustive presentation of these traditions cannot be

---

in the areas of wisdom and divination, or in other words, in the realm of religious knowledge and the forms and social contexts in which it operated.

[3] Theodore E. Mullen, *Assembly of the Gods: The Divine Council in Canaanite and Early Hebrew Literature* (HSM 24; Chico, Calif.: Scholars Press, 1980); H. Wheeler Robinson, "The Council of Yahweh," *JTS* 45 (1944): 151–57; Frank Moore Cross, Jr., "The Council of Yahweh in Second Isaiah," *JNES* 12 (1953): 274–77; G. Cooke, "The Sons of (the) God(s)," *ZAW* 76 (1964): 22–47; E. C. Kingsbury, "Prophets and the Council of Yahweh," *JBL* 83 (1964): 279–86; R. N. Whybray, *The Heavenly Counsellor in Isaiah xl 13–14: A Study of the Sources of the Theology of Deutero-Isaiah* (Cambridge: Cambridge University Press, 1971); Richard J. Clifford, *The Cosmic Mountain in Canaan and the Old Testament* (Cambridge, Mass.: Harvard University Press, 1972); Patrick D. Miller, "Cosmology and World Order in the Old Testament: The Divine Council As Cosmic-Political Symbol," *HBT* 9 (1987): 53–78; Robert Gordon, "From Mari to Moses: Prophecy at Mari and in Ancient Israel," in *Of Prophets' Visions and the Wisdom of Sages: Essays in Honour of R. Norman Whybray on His Seventieth Birthday* (ed. Heather McKay and David Clines; JSOTSup 162; Sheffield: JSOT Press, 1993), 63–79; Heinz-Dieter Neef, *Gottes himmlischer Thronat: Hintergrund und Bedeutung von sôd JHWH im Alten Testament* (Stuttgart: Calwer, 1994); Martti Nissinen, "Prophets and the Divine Council," in *Kein Land für sich allein: Studien zum Kulturkontakt in Kanaan, Israel/Palästina und Ebirnâri für Manfred Weippert zum 65. Geburtstag* (ed. Ulrich Hübner and Ernst Axel Knauf; OBO 186; Freiburg: Universitätsverlag/ Göttingen: Vandenhoeck & Ruprecht, 2002), 4–19; Lenzi, *Secrecy and the Gods*, 221–71. There are other words that are used to refer to the heavenly gathering: קהל (Ps 89:6), עדה (82:1), מועד (Isa 14:13), though these do not usually carry the additional connotation of "secret."

[4] See the discussion in Lenzi, *Secrecy and the Gods*, 221–71; cf. Neef, *Gottes himmlischer Thronat*, for comprehensive discussion of the word סוד and its ancient Near Eastern cognates, as well as in later texts and translations.

offered here, several examples from the Hebrew Bible will suffice to demonstrate the antiquity of this theme and its relevance to later Jewish notions of secrecy, access to the heavenly reality, and divinely-revealed knowledge. As Alan Lenzi demonstrates in considerable detail, "the divine סוד reflects several characteristics of a human סוד, especially limited access, unity in loyalty or purpose, and secrecy with regard its plans."[5]

The word סוד, though etymologically obscure,[6] is an important term in the Hebrew Bible, having a fairly wide semantic range with both concrete and abstract connotations as well as both religious and secular applications. It can refer to various kinds of earthly assemblies (or "councils"), such as a gathering of tribes or clans (Gen 49:6), a "circle of youth" (Jer 6:11), a "circle of friends" (Job 19:19), or a council of the faithful (Ps 111:1). It can also refer in some of the earlier biblical texts to the council of Yahweh (Ps 89:8[7]; 1 Kgs 22:19–22; Jer 23:18–22; Amos 3:7; Job 15:8, etc.) in which heavenly decrees are decided and issued.

It is often observed that there are fundamentally two separate, but related, meanings of סוד in the Hebrew Bible.

> The word סוד, as is known, is mentioned in the Bible in two different but closely inter-related meanings. In the opinion of most scholars, the concept of סוד in the sense of something hidden and concealed, is not, contrary to first impression, the basic meaning of the word. Its basic meaning is derived from the other sense: a "secret council," an inner, closed circle.[7]

Perhaps as a natural outgrowth of the exclusive setting of the סוד, the word developed also the connotation of something hidden or concealed, a "secret" whose origin and meaning derive from the council itself. The deliberations of a council (whether understood as an earthly or heavenly conclave) comprise knowledge that is inherently secret on the basis of its remove from the general public, even if some of the results are subsequently disseminated to a wider audience.

---

[5] Lenzi, *Secrecy and the Gods*, 236.

[6] Heinz-Joseph Fabry, "סוד," *TDOT* 12.171–78; idem, "סוד. Der himmlische Thronrat als ekklesiologisches Modell," *Bausteine biblischer Theologie. FS G. J. Botterweck. BBB* 50 (1977): 99–126.

[7] A. Malamat, "The Secret Council and Prophetic Involvement in Mari and Israel," in *Prophetie und geschichtliche Wirklichkeit im alten Israel: Festschrift für Seigfried Herrmann zum 65. Geburtstag* (ed. Rüdiger Liwak and Siegfried Wagner; Stuttgart: Verlag W. Kohlhammer, 1991), 231–36.

This notion is likely rooted in the realm of royal politics and warfare, and its theological dimensions reflect an image of human social reality into the heavenly world.[8] But to whatever extent political and social realities form the backdrop to the heavenly council idea in the ancient Near East, the connotation of a divine sodality finds purchase in ancient Israelite and early Jewish religious imagination. The rhetoric of both prophecy and later wisdom is linked in a fundamental way with ancient Near Eastern traditions about the divine assembly and the role of the human (and sometimes angelic or divine) messenger to communicate the verdicts of the heavenly council. Even insofar as the Israelite prophets may have participated in restricted human colloquies, their claims to genuine authority, and true knowledge, were based in part on the premise of their having access to the divine realm where the decisions regarding human affairs were deliberated.

A few salient examples can demonstrate the use of this motif in ancient Israel's prophetic tradition. As both the Hebrew and Ugaritic (Canaanite) material attest,[9] an integral part of the divine council were the messengers who delivered the decrees of the assembly. These messengers often took the form of divine beings who were "sent" by the gods or by the LORD: for example, the רוח of 1 Kgs 22:19–23 is sent out to be a "lying spirit" in the mouths of the false prophets. Another example is the "angel of the LORD" (מלאך יהוה) who features in many biblical texts.[10] As Mullen points out, there is a parallel here between the ways in

---

[8]　But see Lenzi, *Secrecy and the Gods*: "there is no proof that prophecy, an intuitive form of divination, functioned as a state secret in the Israelite or Judean royal councils. That is not to say that the royal courts in the two ancient kingdoms did not actually utilize secret prophecies in their proceedings (for a hint of secrecy in general, see Isa 29:15 and 30:1–2); but, *according to the biblical presentation* prophecy is simply not represented in this manner. How then shall we understand the significance of the secret origin of prophetic messages in the Hebrew Bible, i.e. the occasional claim that these messages derive from the divine assembly? I would suggest that the secret origin of a prophetic message was part of a common mythmaking strategy to *authorize* prophetic statements and activities, both historically by individual prophets, to the extent that we may know about this, and literarily by various editors of prophetic material at our disposal" (266).

[9]　For Ugaritic (and Phoenician) examples see E. Theodore Mullen, Jr., "Divine Assembly," *ABD* 2.214.

[10]　It is not always explicitly stated that the messenger goes out from the divine assembly, though this is usually the implied context. See Exod 3:2, 14:19, 23:20; Num 20:16, 22:31; Josh 5:13–15; Judg 13:8; 2 Sam 24:16–17; Isa 44:26; Zech 3:1; Pss 103:20, 104:4, 148:2; Job 4:18, 33:23, etc. The point is especially well made

which a divine messenger is "sent" (שלח) and the commissioning of a prophet who is dispatched with a message from the LORD.[11] Indeed, it has long been observed that the Israelite prophet is called to proclaim the will of God from the assembly, and yet the prophet in the biblical tradition is somewhat sui generis in the ancient Near East. No exact parallel exists for the role of the Israelite prophet, who according to the tradition is not merely sent with a message or endowed with interpretive skill, but who actually stands among the council and participates in the assembly in a unique way.

Let us examine a few key passages. There are three particularly good examples of this conception of prophecy in the Hebrew Bible, each with its own emphasis on the role and position of the prophet in the divine council. The first of these offers a clear formulation of this theme as it attempts to articulate the difference between false prophets and the genuine vehicle of God's word:

Jeremiah 23:16–18

16 כה־אמר יהו הצבאות אל־תשמעו על־דברי הנבאים הנבאים לכם מהבלים המ
אתכם חזון לבם ידברו לא מפי יהוה:
17 אמרים אמור למנאצי דבר יהוה שלום יהיה לכם וכל הלך בשררות לבו אמרו
לא־תבואעליכם רעה:
18 כי מי עמד בסוד יהוה וירא וישמע את־דברו מי־הקשיב דברי וישמע:

16 Thus says the LORD of hosts: Do not listen to the words of the
prophets who prophesy to you; they speak in vain to you. They
speak visions to you that are not from the mouth of the LORD.

---

in Ps 103:20: ברכו יהוה מלאכיו גברי כח עשי דברו לשמע בקול דברו. G. E. Wright asserted that whenever a prophetic indictment is given, e.g. Isa 1:2 or Mic 6:2, the background must be that of the divine assembly (*The Old Testament Against Its Environment* [SBT 2; Naperville, Ill.: Allenson, 1957]). Additionally, Frank Moore Cross (*Canaanite Myth and Hebrew Epic* [Cambridge, Mass.: Harvard University Press, 1973], 187) and Mullen (*Assembly of the Gods*, 216) have demonstrated that the addresses of the divine assembly are constituted by plural imperatives and first person plural indicatives.

[11] Exod 3:10, 15, 7:16; Deut 34:11; Josh 24:5; 1 Sam 15:1; 2 Sam 12:1, 25; Isa 6:8–9; Jer 1:7, 7:25, 19:14, Ezek 2:3–4; Mic 6:4; Hag 1:12; Zech 2:12, 13, 15; Mal 3:23; Ps 105:26. The same word—שלח—is often used for the commissioning of the prophet, e.g. Ezek 2:3: ויאמר אלי בן־אדם שולח אני אותך אל־בני ישראל. See also James Ross, "The Prophet as Yahweh's Messenger," in *Israel's Prophetic Heritage: Essays in Honor of James Muilenburg* (ed. Bernhard W. Anderson and Walter Harrelson; New York: Harper & Row, 1962), 98–107.

17 They declare to those who despise me: "The LORD has said: 'All will
   be well with you.'" And to all who stubbornly follow their willful
   hearts they say, "No evil will befall you."
18 For who [among them?] has stood in the council of the LORD so as to
   see and hear his word? Who has heeded my word and listened?

Here a clear distinction is made between those who speak words from
their own minds and those who (like Jeremiah) actually stand in the
council of the LORD—whose authority thus comes from a direct
encounter with God among the deliberative assembly. This claim is
further refined a few verses later when the author exclaims on behalf of
God,

21 לא־שלחתי את־הנבאים והם רצו לא־דברתי אליהם והם נבאו:
22 ואם־עמדו בסודי וישמעו דברי את־עמי וישבום מדרכם הרע ומרע מעלליהם:

21 I did not send the prophets, and yet they ran. I did not speak to them,
   and yet they prophesied.
22 But if they had stood in my council, they would have proclaimed my
   words to my people; and they would have turned them away from
   their evil way, and from the evil of their deeds.

In these passages, access to the divine assembly thus constitutes one
important rhetorical feature of prophetic legitimation. False prophets do
not have access to the council,[12] whereas, presumably, Jeremiah speaks
from the experience of one who has stood in the council and been sent to
proclaim God's word.

Perhaps the most well known example of this scenario (though the
word סוד is not specifically used) is the famous call vision of Isaiah, in
which the prophet receives his commission through a kind of angelic
purification:

Isaiah 6:1–8

In the year that King Uzziah died, I the LORD sitting on a throne, high
and lofty; and the hem of his robe filled the temple. Seraphs were in
attendance above him; each had six wings: with two they covered their
faces, and with two they covered their feet, and with two they flew.
And one called to another and said: "Holy, holy, holy is the LORD of
hosts; the whole earth is full of his glory." The pivots on the thresholds
shook at the voices of those who called, and the house filled with

---

[12] Unless they speaking words given by false (or "lying") spirits who have
been sent out of the assembly—see 1 Kgs 22:8–23.

smoke. And I said, "Woe is me! I am lost, for I am a man of unclean lips, and I live among a people of unclean lips; yet my eyes have seen the King, the LORD of hosts!" Then one of the seraphs flew to me, holding a live coal that had been taken from the altar with a pair of tongs. The seraph touched my mouth with it and said, "Now that this has touched your lips, you guilt has departed and your sin is blotted out." Then I heard the voice of the LORD saying, "Whom shall I send, and who will go for us?" And I said, "Here I am; send me!"[13]

In this text the prophet does not simply receive a commission; he actively answers the question posed by the LORD, and his *participation* becomes a central feature of the scene—indeed, he becomes indispensable for the dissemination of the divine message. God seems at a loss for a suitable herald, and having been purified Isaiah steps into the breach, ready to bear the news of the LORD's wrath. As Mullen correctly notes, "the participant who brings the scene to its climax is the prophet himself."[14] Of course, the scene described in this text becomes a foundational reference point for later elaborations of how one participates in, or gains access to, the "mysteries" of God, and along with Ezekiel's *Merkavah* vision it becomes the basis for later Jewish mystical speculation in the circles responsible for the production of the Heikhalot and Zoharic texts. While the scene is not precisely analogous to other images of the divine council in the ancient Near East, it constitutes a reworking of this motif into a throne-room scenario, where specific ranks of angels attend to the deity and are perpetually poised to do his bidding.[15]

The most apposite example of the use of סוד in the Hebrew Bible is that found in Amos 3:7–8, which states even more boldly than the Isaiah passage that the role of the prophet is a *sine qua non* for divine communication. It is here, too, that we may see the most explicit use of סוד as something to be revealed—as something that otherwise remains hidden or known only to God, i.e. as a "secret."

---

[13] Translation from the NRSV.

[14] Mullen, *Assembly of the Gods*, 218.

[15] Max E. Polley, "Hebrew Prophecy Within the Council of Yahweh, Examined in Its Ancient Near Eastern Setting," in *Scripture in Context: Essays on the Comparative Method* (ed. W. W. Hallo, J. B. White, and C. D. Evans; Pittsburgh, Penn.: The Pickwick Press, 1980), 155, n. 31; Cooke, "The Sons of (the) God(s)," 37-38.

Amos 3:7–8

7 כי לא יעשה אדני יהוה דבר כי אם־גלה סודו[17] אל־עבדיו הנביאים:[16]
8 אריה שאג מי לא יירא אדני יהוה דבר מי לא ינבא:

7 Indeed, my lord YHWH does nothing without having revealed his
(secret) purpose to his servants the prophets.
8 A lion has roared, who can but fear? My lord YHWH has spoken, who
can but prophesy?[18]

Here the word סוד takes on its secondary meaning (though often
translated as "plans" or "purpose"), with the implication that God has
made known to the prophet the secret deliberations of the divine
assembly.[19] Amos appears to claim not only that the prophets are *allowed*
access to the divine reality, but, indeed, that God *does nothing* without
revealing his purposes to his servants the prophets. Although this

---

[16] The phrase עבדיו הנביאים is characteristic of Deuteronom(ist)ic language
(2 Kgs 9:7, 17:13, 23, 21:10, 24:2; Jer 7:25, 25:4, 26:5, 29:29, 35:15, 44:4), though it is
found elsewhere as well (e.g. Ezek 38:17; Zech 1:6; Dan 9:6; Ezra 9:11). This
phrase also surfaces in some important sectarian texts from Qumran (the
Community Rule, *Pesher Habakkuk*, *Pesher Hosea*).

[17] This phrase often reflects the context of proverbial wisdom, i.e. where סוד
refers to a human gathering and the importance of *not* revealing secrets (see Prov
11:13, 20:19, 25:9).

[18] Verse 7 is usually taken to be an editorial insertion on the part of a later
(Deuteronomistic) redactor. It seems to break with the surrounding structure (it
is a declarative sentence as opposed to the preceding series of interrogative
couplets) and is a "dogmatic assertion (not a rhetorical question)" (Shalom Paul,
Amos: A Commentary on the Book of Amos [Hermeneia; Minneapolis: Fortress,
1991], 112). In any case, whether the statement is a literary addition or a natural
extension of the logic set up in verses 3–6 (or both), it attests to an important
tradition regarding the role and place of the prophet in conceptions of divine
revelation in ancient Israel: the prophet is the spokesman for God *par excellence*,
and his authority derives from his being made privy to the activity of the divine
council.

[19] F. I. Anderson and D. N. Freedman (*Amos: A New Translation with
Introduction and Commentary* [AB 24A; New York: Doubleday, 1989]) assert that
Amos's auditions with the LORD were likely private (398); elsewhere, however,
they state that "Amos became a prophet with a message from God as a result of
his vision of God in the divine assembly of which he, the shepherd and farmer,
was an invited member" (399–400). Compare Lenzi, however: "The divine
assembly as a body … is not in view in Amos 3:7 at all; rather, the verse treats the
deliberations that take place there" (*Secrecy and the Gods*, 251).

potentially bold aspect of Amos's claim is often simply overlooked in studies of this passage,[20] F. I. Anderson and D. N. Freedman propose a compelling alternative to reading it in this way. They point out that the word דבר could mean "decree," suggesting that the LORD will not issue a decree without first calling a prophet.

> In neither Jonathan's [1 Sam 20:2] nor Amos' case can *dābār* mean "anything." Obviously God does most things without first telling a prophet. ... In the context the *dābār* is a specific course of action in response to an unusual situation, one requiring forethought and planning—not a situation for a routine, predictable response, but a departure from the norm that needs to be identified and explained as an act of God.[21]

In any case, "the communication of Yahweh's secret to prophets is a legitimate, and theologically even necessary, activity," a communication that stresses the moment and point of origination of a secret and not its transmission or dissemination.[22] (As in other prophetic texts, the point is that this information will indeed be shared, that it will not be kept secret in the human realm.) Furthermore,

> even though the counsel-aspect of סוד (Yahweh's "secret plan") in Amos 3:7 is in the forefront semantically so as to underline the secret and exclusive nature of prophetic knowledge, conceptually there can be little doubt that the Deuteronomistic commentator would have connected the secret plan (סוד) to the divine assembly (the סוד of Jer 23:18, 22).[23]

Therefore, as seems clear by now, סוד in this instance carries both aspects of its definition: it is both the heavenly conclave and, by metonymy, the secret plan or purpose that the LORD decrees in the council. There is thus some justification for seeing, as Raymond Brown and others have seen, an important connection between the biblical סוד and the later use of רז in Jewish apocalyptic literature of the Second Temple period.[24] Though Brown tends to present the סוד-related material as if it is somehow

---

[20] See for example Shalom Paul, *Amos.*

[21] Anderson and Freedman, *Amos*, 398–99.

[22] Lenzi, *Secrecy and the Gods*, 253.

[23] Ibid., 254.

[24] Brown, "The Semitic Background," 2–6; Bockmuehl, *Revelation and Mystery*, 12–16.

genetically linked with later uses of רז, I prefer to think of the relationship as a thematic or motific one. סוד is not simply the Hebrew counterpart of the Aramaic רז, but it represents an idea that will later come to be expressed in partially analogous terms in the latter word (see below for additional discussion).

Here I must return briefly to a qualification made above. As noted long ago by Yehezkel Kaufmann and reiterated by Lenzi, "a 'word of God' can be a 'secret word,' but according to its essence it is intended to be spoken openly and also to an audience of people."[25] Lenzi cites Isa 45:18c–19 as good evidence of this:

18c אני יהוה ואין עוד:
19 לא בסתר דברתי במקום ארץ חשך לא אמרתי לזרע יעקב תהו בקשוני
אני יהוה דבר צדק מגיד מישרים:

18c I am the LORD, there is no other.
19 I did not speak in secret, in a place of land of darkness. I did not say
    to the seed of Jacob, "Seek me in a void!" I, the LORD, speak the truth,
    proclaim what is right.

Indeed, like some later apocalyptic literature whose authority is predicated upon the access its protagonists have to a restricted kind of knowledge (e.g. Daniel, *1 Enoch*), there is no indication that prophetic knowledge was to remain secret. Nevertheless, the way authoritative ("biblical" or "pseudepigraphical") texts render the moment of revelation as a delivery of otherwise restricted divine information does suggest that a notion of secrecy is often at work.

The prophetic function in the Hebrew biblical tradition was postulated, at least in part, on the notion of having access to the divine realm through visions (or some other mode of perception) of the heavenly assembly, which itself generated knowledge that was understood to be a heavenly secret to be grasped by means of the prophetic mode. The word רז, then, whatever the precise mechanism by which it entered into Aramaic and Hebrew usage, was a suitable term to capture the secondary meaning of סוד, yet without the potential association with a (often polytheistic) scenario of divine deliberation. In this way, too, perhaps it served to shift the notion of prophetic authority toward its epistemological side: prophecy was not solely the domain of those men of old who drew down fire from heaven or wandered in the hillsides in ecstatic conventicles; it was the domain of those who acquired the true knowledge of God's realm and his purposes for human

---

[25] Lenzi, *Secrecy and the Gods*, 264.

history. The prophetic valence of סוד would be taken up in later Jewish texts of the Second Temple period (and, it seems, downplayed in some wisdom contexts), and would find new expression along with what seems to have been a burgeoning interest in the goings-on of the world beyond the visible, manifest dimensions of human life.

SOD, WISDOM, AND REVEALED KNOWLEDGE

The word סוד is also used in a wisdom context, especially in texts that display skepticism about the possibility of real human knowledge of the divine realm. The wisdom tradition—if we may reduce it to such a designation[26]—appears to have undergone a profound transformation during the Second Temple period, when earlier attitudes about human knowledge of the divine came increasingly into question under the strain of Israel's various historical exigencies. Especially important was the question of theodicy—how the omnipotence of Israel's God could be squared with the fact of Israel's oppression by foreign rulers—but also at stake were the related issues of election, covenant, and salvation. Given the perhaps widespread perception of a *Deus absconditus* (Job 13:24: למה פניך תסתיר "Why do you hide your face?"; Isa 45:15: אכן אתה אל מסתתר "Indeed you are a God who hides himself") the literary products of sapiential pursuits—especially as in we find Job and Qohelet—display an increasingly skeptical disposition with respect to how and whether it is possible to know the nature of God and God's workings in the world.

> Over the six centuries in which [wisdom] literature was produced the answer [to the question, "How did those who wrote wisdom literature think they gained access to God and his ways?"] changed from an emphasis on individual freedom and the use of the human natural resources of reason and experience to an emphasis on God's special revelation obtainable only through the divine gift of wisdom that ultimately was seen to be embodied in the Torah (Ben Sira) or the Spirit of God (Wisdom of Solomon).[27]

---

[26] For a summary of the difficulty of defining and delimiting "the wisdom tradition," see James L. Crenshaw, *Old Testament Wisdom: An Introduction* (Atlanta: John Knox, 1981), 1–19; John J. Collins, *Jewish Wisdom in the Hellenistic Age* (Louisville, Ky.: Westminster John Knox, 1997), 1–21.

[27] Leo Perdue, "Revelation and the Problem of the Hidden God in Second Temple Wisdom Literature," in *Shall Not the Judge of the Earth Do What Is Right? Studies on the Nature of God in Tribute to James L. Crenshaw* (ed. David Penchansky

This rough schema, though it fails to account fully for the complexity of wisdom traditions in the Second Temple period, contains an important observation about at least one issue that seems to have been at stake: the role of revelation in the acquisition of true knowledge about the universe, human nature, and the goal and meaning of history.

Against the tradition of the prophet being granted special access to the heavenly council (סוד) stands the book of Job. Job is in a sense the anti-prophet: not only is he not an emissary of God, but his predicament functions throughout the text as an indictment and, finally, exaltation of God, whose justice, mercy, and supreme knowledge are affirmed at the end of the book. In any case, the book of Job is rather clear about the limitations of the human capacity to enter into God's council and to comprehend the matters deliberated therein. As Eliphaz the Temanite rebukes Job for his presumption to question God and his motives for "punishing" Job, his rhetorical questions cut through to the heart of Job's accusations:

Job 15:6–9

6 יַרְשִׁיעֲךָ פִיךָ וְלֹא־אָנִי וּשְׂפָתֶיךָ יַעֲנוּ־בָךְ:
7 הֲרִאישׁוֹן אָדָם תִּוָּלֵד וְלִפְנֵי גְבָעוֹת חוֹלָלְתָּ:
8 הַבְסוֹד אֱלוֹהַ תִּשְׁמָע וְתִגְרַע אֵלֶיךָ חָכְמָה:
9 מַה־יָּדַעְתָּ וְלֹא נֵדָע תָּבִין וְלֹא־עִמָּנוּ הוּא:

6 Your own mouth condemns you—not I; your lips testify against you.
7 Were you the first man born? Were you created before the hills?
8 Have you listened in on the council of God? Have you sole possession of wisdom?
9 What do you know that we do not know, or understand that we do not understand?

The author of Job suggests that only the "first man born" ("Adam") might be able to say anything more meaningful about hidden realities than the average person; though he seems to concede the possibility of a higher knowledge based on contact with heaven, the righteousness of Job is apparently not enough to merit an invitation to the heavenly council.[28] The irony here is jarring: "Have you listened in on the council

---

and Paul L. Redditt; Winona Lake, Ind.: Eisenbrauns, 2000), 201–222; J. C. Rylaarsdam, *Revelation in Jewish Wisdom Literature* (Chicago: University of Chicago Press, 1946); Collins, *Jewish Wisdom in the Hellenistic Age*, 80–131.

[28] Lenzi connects the reference to the "first man" to the widespread myth of the Primal Human, which "posits that the first human was present at creation and thus privy to the secret knowledge of the creation of the cosmos" (*Secrecy*

of God?" Of course not! is the implied answer. Lenzi again summarizes the matter quite nicely:

> The irony of this discussion [between Job and Eliphaz] of the divine סוד in Job 15 lies, of course, in the fact that it would not be taking place at all had Eliphaz and Job known about the activities and discussions of the divine assembly recounted in Job 1–2. The disputants may know about the existence of the divine assembly, but they certainly do not know of its proceedings.[29]

Indeed, the depiction of the heavenly council in the opening chapters of Job consists only of heavenly figures engaged in debate about human nature and behavior. There is no prophet who comes bearing the results of the divine deliberations; there is only silence until God himself decides to speak directly to Job in answer to his challenges. And when God finally answers (esp. Job 38–42), he echoes the rhetorical charges issued by Eliphaz, saying,

Job 38:2–4

מי זה מחשיך עצה במלין בלי־דעת: 2
אזר־נא כגבר חלציך ואשאלך והודיעני: 3
איפה היית ביסדי־ארץ הגד אם־ידעת בינה: 4

2 Who is this that darkens counsel by words without knowledge?
3 Gird up your loins like a man, I will question you, and you will declare to me.
4 Where were you when I laid the foundation of the earth? Tell me, if you have understanding.[30]

In the text cited above (Job 15:6–9) the author makes an association between standing in the council of God (בסוד אלוה) and the possession of wisdom (חכמה), an association not made by any prophetic texts, or, for that matter, any other wisdom text from the Hebrew Bible.[31] For the

---

and the Gods, 245). See also Dexter E. Callendar, Jr., *Adam in Myth and History: Ancient Israelite Perspective on the Primal Human* (HSS 48; Winona Lake, Ind.: Eisenbrauns, 2000), 137–76. See below for further discussion of this issue.

[29] Lenzi, *Secrecy and the Gods*, 246.

[30] NRSV translation.

[31] The closest analogy is Amos 3:3–8, where the style of a wisdom teacher is adopted to demonstrate the authority and inherent causality of the prophetic commission. See Paul, *Amos*, 104–105; Hans Walter Wolff, *Joel and Amos: A*

author of Job, the source of all true wisdom is indeed God himself, and yet this is a God whose knowledge remains obscure, hidden from the sight of human beings. "[T]he real obstacle to obtaining divine knowledge in these texts is not necessarily, or at least obviously, the exclusive nature of the divine סוד; rather, it is the great chasm that exists between humans and the location of that knowledge."[32]

Elsewhere, the statement of Zophar the Naamathite makes explicit that the relationship between wisdom and the divine is one of concealment and human incomprehension:

Job 11:5–6

5 ואולם מי־יתן אלוה דבר ויפתח שפתיו עמך:
6 ויגד־לך תעלמות[34] חכמה כי־פלאים[33] לתושיה ... :

5 If only God would speak, and open his lips to you!
6 Then he would tell you the secrets of wisdom—indeed, of the wonders that accompany understanding. ...

This passage also reveals something interesting about the underlying assumptions of its author(s). God's ways are imponderable, yet humans desire knowledge that surpasses understanding—knowledge that can only come by bridging the cosmographical divide between humans and the all-knowing deity.

It is this same impulse that animates the later apocalyptic twist on the wisdom tradition, namely that essential knowledge—knowledge of

---

Commentary on the Books of the Prophets Joel and Amos (trans. Waldemar Janzen et al; Hermeneia; Philadelphia: Fortress, 1977), 91–100; for a refutation of the idea that this section of Amos is associated with the wisdom tradition, see Lenzi, *Secrecy and the Gods*, 252.

[32] Lenzi, *Secrecy and the Gods*, 246. Lenzi calls this "cosmographical distance," an apt term for this idea.

[33] The Masoretic Text reads here כי־כפלים, which has bred no shortage of confusion for interpretation (NRSV translates "For wisdom is many-sided"). Here I follow the judicious argument made by Lenzi: "The *kaf* may have arisen via dittography of the *pe* which was then made intelligible when 'corrected' to a *kaf*. The *alef* was simply omitted" (*Secrecy and the Gods*, 233). As it turns out, this emendation meshes nicely with the statement Job makes at the end of the book: "I have uttered things I did not understand, things too wonderful for me (נפלאות ממני), which I did not know" (Job 42:3); cf. David Clines, *Job 1–20* (WBC; Dallas: Word, 1989), 254, n.6.a.

[34] For analogous uses of the term תעלמה as "secrets," see Ps 44:21 and Job 28:11.

the cosmos and of the historical world, which includes the future—is revealed by means of mediating figures who are worthy vehicles for otherwise hidden information. In some ways the book of Job hints at this notion of "revealed wisdom," but does not embrace it the way the author(s) of, say, the *Book of the Watchers* will do in a subsequent century.[35]

FROM *SOD* TO *RAZ*: REVEALED WISDOM AND APOCALYPTICISM

There are several trajectories of Jewish wisdom tradition in Second Temple period, and there is a long-standing scholarly awareness of the tensions in early Jewish wisdom literature regarding the sources of knowledge about the imperceptible God and God's activity in the perceptible world. If writings such as Job and Qohelet convey a certain reticence regarding human knowledge of God's ways, there are also wisdom texts that affirm the human capacity to know God and the divine will for humanity through more the more "traditional" epistemological modes of observation and inquiry. Ben Sira, for example, famously embraces the study and contemplation of prior revelation as it is enshrined in scriptural texts (Sir 1, 24) while shunning the pursuit of matters hidden or otherwise unseen (Sir 3:21–24):

21 Things too marvelous for you, do not investigate,[36]
    And things too evil for you, do not research.
22 On what is authorized, give attention,
    But you have no business with secret things (נסתרות)[37].
23 And into what is beyond you, do not meddle,
    For that which is too great has been shown to you.
24 For many are the thoughts of the sons of men,
    Evil and erring imaginations.[38]

---

[35] For example, while overall the content of the book of Job expresses skepticism about what humans can know about "ultimate realities," the whole story builds up to the climactic confrontation between Job and God—a confrontation in which God reveals himself to Job (if only long enough to upbraid him for his unknowing)!

[36] Compare Job 42:3; see below chapter 4 for discussion of the use of נפלאות/פלא in combination with mystery language in the Qumran Scrolls.

[37] See chapter 4 for a brief discussion of the term נסתרות in the Qumran Scrolls.

[38] Translation is from Argall, *1 Enoch and Sirach*, 74.

As Benjamin Wright recommends, it is best to see this passage not as a polemic against Greek philosophical inquiry,[39] but to read it "against the backdrop of the mysteries revealed to Enoch [in *1 Enoch*] and Levi [in *Aramaic Levi*], especially cosmological speculation and eschatological realities, and together with others that seem to address similar kinds of inner-Jewish concerns."[40] Elsewhere in Ben Sira there are statements that incorporate secrecy or mystery language explicitly, though not in the way usually implied in apocalyptic contexts.[41] In these passages, secrecy functions in an ethical capacity to encourage the withholding of guarded personal information—an ancient Jewish equivalent of the old Spanish proverb, "Cautious silence is where prudence takes refuge."[42] It reflects a kind of folk wisdom that is concerned with what is customarily proper and not with the cultivation and restriction of sacred, arcane knowledge.

One way of understanding wisdom traditions and their development is in terms of interest in causality—in finding and expressing suitable ways to speak about cause-and-effect and to integrate such knowledge into a monotheistic system that posits an omnipotent deity who differentiates between the good and the wicked. A related way to understand wisdom is in terms of what Dexter Callendar has called "effective knowledge," which is

> knowledge of the laws and constituents of the cosmos. ... Discovery and knowledge of natural laws (order and causation) leads to the practical articulation or application in technology. The ancient mind had no reason to separate natural and spiritual causes; all phenomena operated in accordance with the cosmos—the order of which was not always possible to trace. ... The practical outcome of wisdom is potentiality. ... To have *ḥokmâ* is to have power over something.[43]

Here we may cite an important passage from the Wisdom of Solomon, a first century B.C.E. (C.E.?) text that shows some alignment with both "traditional wisdom" and with developments in later "revealed wisdom." The passage is Wis 7:15–22:

---

[39] As proposed by Patrick Skehan and Alexander Di Lella, *The Wisdom of Ben Sira* (AB 38; New York: Doubleday, 1987), 160–61.

[40] Wright, "Putting the Puzzle Together," 97. Wright refers to these mysteries as "esoteric matters."

[41] For example Sir 8:18; 27:16–17.

[42] Baltasar Gracián, *The Art of Worldly Wisdom* (trans. Christopher Maurer; New York: Doubleday, 1991).

[43] Callendar, *Primal Human*, 149–50.

15 May God grant me to speak with judgment,
   and to have thoughts worthy of what I have received;
   for he is the guide even of wisdom and the corrector of the wise.
16 For both we and our words are in his hand,
   as are all understanding and skill in crafts.
17 For it is he who gave me unerring knowledge of what exists,
   to know the structure of the world and the activity of the elements;
18 the beginning and the end and middle of times,
   the alternations of the solstices and the changes of the seasons,
19 the cycles of the year and the constellations of the stars,
20 the natures of animals and the tempers of wild animals,
   the powers of spirits and thoughts of human beings,
   the varieties of plants and the virtues of roots;
21 I learned both what is secret and what is manifest,
22 for wisdom, the fashioner of all things, taught me.[44]

Callendar also adduces this passage in his discussion of the way the ancient Near Eastern motif of the "primal human" is appropriated and deployed in different ways in biblical and apocryphal/pseudepigraphical texts. This is an important point that is relevant not only to the texts he discusses but also for the development of Enochic traditions and for the rise of apocalypticism in general. Such a primal human, as reflected variously in Gen 1:26–28, Gen 2–3, Ezek 28:11–19 (the King of Tyre pericope), Job 15:7–16, and Prov 8:22–31, has its counterpart in Mesopotamian figures such as Adapa, Enmeduranki, Utnapishtim, and others.

The first of these, Adapa, was a priest of Eridu and a devotee of Ea, and in the Mesopotamian traditions was "a sage who brings higher knowledge to humanity" after cursing the wind (and thereby "breaking its wing") and being summoned by the high Anu to explain his behavior. He is depicted as a culture-bringer by Berossus, the third-century Babylonian historiographer writing in Greek, who stated that Adapa (or U'an/Oannes) "gave to men the knowledge of letters and sciences and crafts of all types ... [and] taught them how to found cities, establish temples, introduce laws and measure land."[45] In the *Myth of Adapa*, the protagonist is said to be "perfect in wisdom," knowing the "designs of the land," i.e. the plan or order of the cosmos. He is the first of the *apkallū* sages, one who sets the standard for others who follow, and whose

---

[44] NRSV translation.

[45] Stanley Burstein, *Berossus the Chaldean* (SANE 1,3; Malibu, Calif.: Undena, 1977), 13–14; Callendar, *Adam in Myth and History*, 82.

knowledge is associated with magic, astrology, and priestly purificatory ritual.[46] He is, in other words, a paradigmatic mediator figure who is understood also to be an important bearer of culture and religious knowledge. As Callendar notes,

> An interesting part of the Adapa myth comes in the fragment from Amarna. Upon discovering Adapa's ability to break the wing of the south wind, Anu asks, "Why did Ea disclose what pertains to heaven and earth to an uncouth mortal?" This concern over the revelation of divine information to a human recalls Ea's disclosure of divine knowledge to Utnapishtim, called Atrahasis, in the flood tablet of the Gilgamesh Epic, and the subsequent decision with which the gods were faced—what to do with a human who had attained divine knowledge (cf. Gen 3:11, 22–24).

Early traditions about Utnapishtim present the protagonist as a worthy prophet- and sage-like figure who is granted total knowledge and has access even to the secret and hidden aspects of the world. In his eponymous tale, Gilgamesh seeks information about the time before the flood—knowledge of the antediluvian (primordial?) nature of creation— from Utnapishtim, who himself has been invited into the assembly of the gods and has been granted eternal life at the "source of the rivers," or in other words, in Paradise. As one who has gained insight into the secret things of the divine habitation, Utnapishtim is transformed into an eternal being and purports to transmit his knowledge to Gilgamesh, who, despite his desire to gain access, is not admitted into the council of the gods.

Tablet I of the *Epic of Gilgamesh* opens with this dramatic statement:

> 1 [He who saw the Deep, the] foundation of the country,
> 2   [who knew … ,] was wise in everything!
> 3 [Gilgameš, who] saw the Deep, the foundation of the country,
> 4   [who] knew […,] was wise in everything!
> 5 […] … equally [… ,]
> 6   he [*learnt*] the totality of wisdom about everything.
> 7 He saw the secret (*ni-ṣir-tu*) and uncovered the hidden,
> 8   he brought back a message from the antediluvian age.[47]

---

[46] Ibid., 82–83; see also text sources and bibliography cited there. See also P. Michalowski, "Adapa and the Ritual Process," *RO* 41 (1980): 77–82.

[47] Text and translation from A. R. George, *The Babylonian Gilgamesh: Introduction, Critical Edition, and Cuneiform Texts* (2 vols.; Oxford: Oxford University Press, 2003), 1.539.

In Tablet XI there are two passages in particular that hint at both the concept of divine disclosure of secrets and at the ambivalence that often goes along with the problem of human attainment of sacred knowledge. In the first part of the tablet, Utnapishtim says that he will convey to Gilgamesh information that is both secret and mysterious:

> 8 Ūta-napišti spoke to him, to Gilgameš:
> 9 "I will disclose to you, Gilgameš, a secret matter . ...."
> 10 and I will tell you a mystery of the gods.[48]

Later in the same tablet, Ea declares that

> 196 I did not myself disclose the great gods' secret;
> 197 I let Atra-ḫasīs see a dream and so he heard the gods' secret.

And according to the Epic, Atrahasis [Utnapishtim] "obtained entrance to Paradise only by the decree of the divine assembly. Gilgamesh, lacking such a decree, would be unable to remain."[49] Several of these themes are echoed in later Jewish formulations about Enoch the sage, as well as in other Aramaic texts that depict various antediluvian biblical figures and their acquisition of special (heavenly) knowledge.[50]

---

[48] Ibid., 1.703.

[49] Mullen, *Assembly of the Gods*, 153.

[50] It deserves mention here that the figures Gilgamesh and Hobabish (Humbaba)—and possibly Atambish = Utnapishtim—were known to the author(s) of the *Book of Giants* preserved among the Qumran Scrolls. This does not mean that the author(s) were conversant with the entire body of Sumerian and Akkadian traditions about these figures, but that they were at least aware of some of them. See Loren Stuckenbruck, *The Book of Giants from Qumran* (TSAJ 63; Tübingen: Mohr Siebeck, 1997), 24–40; idem, "The 'Angels' and 'Giants' of Genesis 6:1–4 in Second and Third Century BCE Jewish Interpretation: Reflections on the Posture of Early Apocalyptic Traditions," *DSD* 7 (2000): 354–77; idem, "Giant Mythology and Demonology: From the Ancient Near East to the Dead Sea Scrolls," in *Demons: The Demonology of Israelite-Jewish and Early Christian Literature in Context of their Environment* (ed. Armin Lange, Hermann Lichtenberger, and K. F. Diethard Römheld; Tübingen: Mohr Siebeck, 2003), 318–38; John Reeves, *Jewish Lore and Manichaean Cosmogony: Studies in the* Book of Giants *Traditions* (MHUC 14; Cincinnati, Ohio: Hebrew Union College Press, 1992), 51–164; idem, "Utnapishtim in the Book of Giants?" *JBL* 112 (1993): 110–15; R. V. Huggins, "Noah and the Giants: A Response to John C. Reeves," *JBL* 114 (1995): 103–10; É. Puech, DJD 31:28–30; 74–78.

James VanderKam and Helge Kvanvig have demonstrated that the depictions of Enoch in the earliest Jewish apocalyptic traditions (the *Book of the Watchers* and the *Astronomical Book*) show clear affinities with Mesopotamian traditions about both Utnapishtim and Enmeduranki.[51] Especially important here is the fact that these heroes have mediatorial roles, that they learn "the secrets of the gods" and transmit those to humanity after spectacular journeys to otherwise inaccessible regions of the cosmos. As for the choice in the Enochic lore to endow Enoch with the role of the one who brings knowledge of the divine secrets (and not, say, Noah, the actual flood hero in Genesis, who, unlike Utnapishtim, is not made immortal), VanderKam writes that for the author of *1 Enoch* 106–107,

> The concept of a man who lives among divine beings, who has access to their choicest secrets, but who nevertheless remains somewhat accessible ... [was] attached to Enoch who also associated with celestial beings according to the tradition but about whose paternity there could be no question. The writer managed to have it both ways: he retained the idea of an accessible human being in divine company but avoided any danger that his readers would infer a divine status for the Jewish survivor of the flood. ... With his unparalleled knowledge of the cosmos, history, and the *eschaton*, Enoch was the ideal preacher of hope, comfort, and warning to the last generations. While his words echo the language of ancient prophecy, Enoch appears preeminently as the supreme Jewish sage whose wisdom knows no bounds and whose message rests on unfailing divine revelation.[52]

Writing now fifty years ago P. Grelot made the association between the Mesopotamian hero Enmeduranki and the Jewish sage Enoch.[53] Drawing heavily on Berossus' account in the *Babyloniaka*, Grelot demonstrated that Enoch inherited from the ancient king the attributes of both divinely-inspired culture-bearer and transmitter of antediluvian

---

[51] James C. VanderKam, *Enoch and the Growth of an Apocalyptic Tradition* (CBQMS 16; Washington, D.C.: The Catholic Biblical Association of America, 1984); Helge Kvanvig, *The Roots of Apocalyptic: The Mesopotamian Background of the Enoch Figure and of the Son of Man* (WMANT 61; Neukirchen-Vluyn: Neukirchener Verlag, 1988); H. Ludin Jansen, *Die Henochgestalt: Eine vergleichende religionsgeschichtliche Untersuchung* (Oslo: Dybwad, 1939); P. Grelot, "La légende d'Hénoch dans les apocryphes et dans la Bible: Origine et significance," *RSR* 46 (1958): 5–26, 181–210; idem, "La géographie mythique d'Hénoch et ses sources orientales," *RB* 65 (1958): 33–69.

[52] VanderKam, *Enoch and the Growth of an Apocalyptic Tradition*, 176–77.

[53] Grelot, "La légende d'Hénoch"; "La géographie mythique d'Hénoch."

wisdom, wisdom that encompasses "the beginnings and the middles and the ends of all writings," which itself may be another way of saying "everything." For his part, Enoch was indeed depicted in the Enochic collection as knowing and teaching about creation, the course of history, and eschatology, topics that would each receive varying emphasis as the traditions about this figure evolved over the centuries.[54]

There are many examples from the ancient world of similar kinds of culture-bringer figures. In fact, it appears that such a motif was even a kind of international trend during a several-hundred year period, during which various human characters took on mythological significance in Babylonian, Hellenistic, and Egyptian cultures. One may cite U'an/ Oannes of the Berossus account, Prometheus of classical lore,[55] and Taautos, who, according to Philo of Byblos' *Phoenician History*, is to be identified with Thoth, the Egyptian (Alexandrian) god who invented arts, sciences, writings, and other aspects of human culture.[56] This latter figure is also equated by the Phoenician Philo with Hermes who, in Greek (and Latin) traditions, is endowed with similar characteristics. Later this Thoth/Hermes syncretism would form the basis for the esoteric founder *par excellence* of the Hermetic tradition, Hermes Trismegistus, who himself was understood to be the master of astronomy, astrology, magic, alchemy, medicine, and other esoteric arts.[57]

The presentation of Enoch as culture-bringer connects also with the ancient myth of the primal human, as one who gains "knowledge of everything" by virtue of his special status as *Urmensch*, as one who bridges the gap between the human and the divine.[58] The primal human

---

[54] Grelot, "La légende d'Hénoch," 6–25; VanderKam, *Enoch and the Growth of an Apocalyptic Tradition*, 17–18.

[55] See especially Aeschylus' *Prometheus Bound* in H. W. Smyth, *Aeschylus I* (LCL; Cambridge, Mass.: Harvard University Press, 1922).

[56] See VanderKam, *Enoch and the Growth of an Apocalyptic Tradition*, 181–84.

[57] See for example Florian Ebeling, *The Secret History of Hermes Trismegistus: Hermeticism from Ancient to Modern Times* (trans. David Lorton; Ithaca, N.Y.: Cornell University Press, 2007); Garth Fowden, *The Egyptian Hermes: A Historical Approach to the Late Pagan Mind* (Cambridge: Cambridge University Press, 1986); A. -J. Festugière, *La revelation dHermès Trismégiste* (3 vols.; Paris: Les Belles Lettres, 1981); Antoine Faivre, *The Eternal Hermes: From Greek God to Alchemical Magus* (York Beach, Maine: Phanes Press, 1995).

[58] For the idea of Enoch as a culture-bringer see VanderKam, *Enoch and the Growth of an Apocalyptic Tradition*, 182; Alexander, "Enoch and the Beginnings of Jewish Interest in Natural Science," 223–42; Paul Hanson, "Rebellion in Heaven,

functioned as a tool for exploring a host of ideas. Among these are the question of the relation between "humanity" and "deity," and the place of individuals in "elevated" ritual positions of intermediation (e.g. the king, priests, prophets). Authors invoked the symbol of the primal human to engage these questions in various ways. The questions comprise not only the task of discerning the essential boundaries between humanity and the divine, but ultimately the very task of *defining* humanity and the divine.[59]

In the Second Temple period in particular, the quest for knowledge of the universe and of history was part of a theological revaluation brought on in part by the experience of national rupture and cultural incursions, but also by the intellectual renaissance resulting from contact with neighboring Babylonian, Persian, Greek, and Roman cultural traditions. In this period "the yearning to breach the gap to the transcendent God is also the desire to live in consonance with the constitution of the universe and to make the life of man and the course of the cosmos whole."[60]

The Jewish interest in the primal human is also doubtless related in the fourth and third centuries B.C.E. to oncoming Hellenism and its cultural traditions about the *prōtos heurētes*.[61] The third century (?) Jewish Samaritan author of the Pseudo-Eupolemos fragments, writing in Greek, connected this idea to Enoch through the figure of Abraham:

> Abraham excelled all in nobility and wisdom; he sought and obtained the knowledge of astrology and the Chaldean craft, and pleased God because he eagerly sought to be reverent. ... Abraham lived in Heliopolis with the Egyptian priests and taught them much: He explained astrology and the other sciences to them, saying that the Babylonians and he himself had obtained this knowledge. However, he attributed the discovery of them to Enoch. ... The Greeks say that Atlas discovered astrology. However, Atlas is the same as Enoch. The son of

---

Azazel, and Euhemeristic Heroes in 1Enoch 6–11," *JBL* 96 (1977): 195–233; Davila, "Flood Hero as King and Priest."

[59] *Adam in Myth and History*, 17.

[60] Michael E. Stone, "Three Transformations in Judaism: Scripture, History, and Redemption," *Numen* 32 (1985): 229.

[61] See A. Kleingünther, *ΠΡΩΤΟΣ ΕΥΡΗΤΕΣ: Untersuchungen zur Geschichte einer Fragestellung* (Leipzig: Dietrich, 1933; repr. New York: Arno, 1976); R. Netz, "The First Jewish Scientist?" *SCI* 17 (1998): 27–33.

Enoch was Methuselah. He learned everything through the angels of God, and so knowledge came to us.[62]

Early Jewish apocalyptic writings such as 1 Enoch thus participated in a more widespread cultural trend in which Jewish writers were engaged in the appropriation and use of mythic/mythological motifs in the reproduction and elaboration of scriptural traditions. As mentioned above, some scholars have tried to see in this development an attempt to reconcile an understanding of God's historical relationship with Israel with the post-exilic experience of a Deus absconditus whose self-communication and continued presence have been called into question. One way of accomplishing such a theological renovation was to find new ways of expressing the relationship between myth and history, new formulations that attributed to biblical figures superhuman wisdom and knowledge that transcended the mere observation of "the way things are," or, at least, the way things seem.

Though it would be a mistake to assume that all apocalyptic texts reflect this synthesis equally and in the same way, there is much to be gained in the insight that apocalyptic texts—and apocalyptic groups—display a concern to know about both the cosmic and the earthly realms, and that claims to knowledge are expressed in terms of both "vision" and "reality," which, in spite of Paul Hanson's assessment, turn out to be two sides of the same coin.[63] As Hanson states,

---

[62] Text and translation from Robert Doran, "Pseudo-Eupolemus," OTP 2.880–81. Doran asks the pertinent question: To whom does this "us" refer? Given the widespread interest in the transmission of knowledge as itself an authorizing principle, I would have to answer (if tentatively) that the "us" in question is the author and his audience.

[63] Hanson draws on work in the sociology of religion for his categories of "visionary" and "realistic" elements in Second Temple Judaism; see Max Weber, The Sociology of Religion (trans. E. Fischoff; Boston: Beacon Press, 1963); Karl Mannheim, Ideology and Utopia: An Introduction to the Sociology of Knowledge (trans. L. Wirth and E. Shils; New York: Harcourt Brace, 1936). I do not agree with Hanson's conclusion that the transformation that took place in the institution of prophecy in the early Second Temple period was due to a conflict between "visionary" (prophetic) and "realistic" (hierocratic) groups. Such a model, though elegant in certain respects, has not been able to stand and does not account for much of what we now can say about the social location(s) of apocalyptic groups. Furthermore, it is becoming increasingly clear that developments within the apocalyptic tradition also took place within the priestly (hierocratic) and sapiential milieux.

The realm of the cosmic vision is the world of myth, whereas the realm of mundane reality is the sphere of human history. The tension between vision and reality, between myth and history, was not universal in the Ancient Near East, for such a tension could result only when the historical realm assumed a position distinct from the realm of the gods.[64]

According to Hanson, this is precisely the case with respect to ancient Israel, whose own historiographical traditions (esp. the Deuteronomic and Priestly traditions) presented cosmogony in terms of the unfolding relationship between two distinct entities: YHWH who inhabits the uncreated ("mythic") realm, and the people Israel, who come into being and inhabit the created, historically-contingent world. Thus, for Hanson, in such patterns of thought, "for the first time in the Near East, the cosmic realm and the realm of the real world are recognized as two truly distinct realms," and it is this situation that creates the conditions for the apocalyptic synthesis in which the two "realms" would be reunited under the right historical and cultural conditions.[65] Though Frank Moore Cross is probably more correct about the way "myth" and "history" are interwoven into "epic" even in ancient Israel's sacred historiographical traditions (and as such they were not viewed as strictly distinct), Hanson's characterization of the early stages of apocalypticism retains some of its value.[66]

Whatever the problems with Hanson's overall assessment of the origins of apocalypticism, he is correct to link the development of apocalyptic ways of speaking to a Jewish domestication of ancient mythological language in order to express ideas about the cosmic, "mythic" dimensions of divine reality. Of course this way of speaking was in fact a way of speaking also about time and history, as the interest in cosmic *mythoi* was tied to an intense desire to read the future, to place the (then) present in terms of both the past and the future, and to know how God's cosmic mastery would be translated into his mastery in the world. From the perspective of apocalyptic writers, this translation would naturally be expressed most fully in his redemption of Israel, which, with some variation based on the particular view of any given apocalyptist, would itself have final and complete world-historical ramifications. The beginning of such an *Urzeit und Endzeit* preoccupation

---

[64] Paul Hanson, "Jewish Apocalyptic Against Its Near Eastern Environment," *RB* 78 (1971): 31–58.

[65] Ibid., 41. Whether indeed this is the "first time" such a distinction is made is probably impossible to say, but this does not mitigate his overall point.

[66] Cross, *Canaanite Myth and Hebrew Epic*.

appears to be rooted in Jewish cultural and political conditions during the fourth–third centuries B.C.E., and becomes a well-known feature of Jewish (and Christian) apocalypticism down through the ages. With his characteristic clarity, Michael Stone has aptly summarized the situation obtaining in post-exilic Judaism in general: "It is the balance between the mythical and the historical elements that changes in the Second Temple period. ... There was a remythologization of cosmology as well as of history."[67]

One result of this shift was the emergence of a new kind of figure in the landscape of apocalyptic Judaism: the figure who knows everything. Seen most clearly in the representations of Enoch, such a figure served as the human counterpart to another emergent locus of the "knowledge of everything" during the Second Temple period, viz. the heavenly tablets (*Jubilees*; 1 *En* 93:2, 103:2). In the case of Enoch (especially the *Book of the Watchers*) we may see evidence of an attempt to synthesize (even systematize) knowledge of the cosmos—to the point that it becomes difficult to distinguish between natural science and religion, astronomy and divination, geography and eschatology.[68] VanderKam demonstrates that

> as a sage, Enoch reveals information about the *Urzeit* during which he lived, periodizes history, learns and teaches astronomical lore, and divulges the cosmological details that he has discovered on his remarkable journeys . ... When Enoch is pictured as a divine figure, he appears as the one who in effect saves Noah from the flood by disclosing salvific information to him, as Ea did to Utnapishtim, the Babylonian flood hero.[69]

There are other ways in which the depictions of Enoch's knowledge reflect a Babylonian background, and we may venture to guess at a loosely analogous "priestly-scribal" tradition in which early Enochic literature took shape in antiquity.[70] The sources of the "knowledge of everything" in 1 *Enoch* include angelic mediation, cosmic journeys, consultation of the heavenly tablets, and, finally, in later traditions, taking up residence in the divine abode itself, from which Enoch mediates and vouchsafes the transmission of perfect knowledge to needful mortals (e.g. 1 *En* 106).

---

[67] "Three Transformations in Judaism," 24, 27.

[68] Tigchelaar, *Prophets of Old and the Day of the End,* 253–54.

[69] VanderKam, *Enoch and the Growth of an Apocalyptic Tradition,* 13.

[70] See Reed, *Fallen Angels.*

RAZ IN PRE-QUMRAN TEXTS

Because of its late entry into the biblical lexicon, the word רז is not widespread in the Hebrew Bible. In fact, it occurs definitively only in the Aramaic portions of the book of Daniel, though there is also a likely attestation in the book of Isaiah. Outside the Hebrew Bible, the word is attested in the *Book of the Watchers* and in a handful of other non-sectarian Aramaic texts from Qumran. Because many of these Aramaic compositions likely pre-dated the establishment of the Yaḥad (and were preserved and copied by its members), I will discuss several of them briefly in this section. Because it continues to be difficult to ascertain precise dates for many of these texts, have have had to be somewhat selective in my approach to them.

ISAIAH 24:16B

One disputed but potentially important early reference to רז is in the late addition to Isaiah known as the "Isaiah Apocalypse" (chapters 24–27).[71] In Isa 24:16b we encounter the phrase, רזי־לי רזי־לי, which is embedded in its broader context as follows:

Isaiah 24:14–16

14 המה ישאו קולם ירנו בגאון יהוה צהלו מים:
15 על־כן בארים כבדו יהוה באיי הים שם יהוה אלהי ישראל:
16 מכנף הארץ זמרת שמענו צבי לצדיק ואמר רזי־לי רזי־לי
אוי לי בגדים בגדו ובגד בוגדים בגדו:

14 They will lift up their voices, they will sing for joy; they shout from the west about the majesty of the LORD

15 So in the east give glory to the LORD; in the coastlands of the west glorify the name of the LORD the God of Israel.

16 From the end of the earth we hear singing: Glory to the Righteous One! But I say, "I have my mystery,' I have my 'mystery!' Woe is me, for the faithless have acted faithlessly, the faithless have broken faith!"

---

[71] The designation of these chapters as an "apocalypse" was first made by Bernhard Duhm in his famous commentary, *Das Buch Jesaja* (Göttingen: Vandenhoeck & Ruprecht, 1922). While this label has been rightly criticized in subsequent generations of scholarship, his late dating of the material in chapters 24–27 has been generally embraced.

The phrase רזי־לי רזי־לי has been parsed and translated in various ways. For example, in the Jewish Publication Society version of the Tanakh, the editors take רזי to derive from the root רזה (to become lean) and translate accordingly: "I waste away, I waste away!" This is not an uncommon position to take, and indeed some lexicons offer רזי as a masculine noun meaning "leanness" or "wasting," thus rendering רזי־לי literally as "to me, wasting."[72] In this case the word would be a *hapax legomenon* (it occurs twice here, but nowhere else), it would be something of a grammatical oddity, and it would fit somewhat awkwardly in its context. Additionally, there is little support for this reading from the other ancient versions.

As Joseph Blenkinsopp notes, this phrase is a "notorious crux, simply omitted by the [Old Greek] LXX," and he goes on to point out that most of the early versions support reading רזי as "my mystery" or "my secret" (Blenkinsopp prefers the latter).[73] On the one hand, the fact that the Old Greek of Isaiah simply fails to acknowledge the presence of the רזי־לי couplet might suggest that it is a late interpolation (or gloss?) in the Hebrew.[74] On the other hand, it is also possible that the Greek translator simply did not know what to make of this passage, a position that Ron Troxel appears to endorse: "The translator's path in the first half of v. 16 is traceable from the MT, but he seems to have been at a loss

---

[72] See BDB, 931. See also A. S. Herbert, *The Book of the Prophet: Isaiah 1–39* (CBC; Cambridge: Cambridge University Press, 1973), 147: "But I thought, Villainy! Villainy!" (he provides no additional comments on this translation); Christopher Seitz, *Isaiah 1–39* (Louisville, Ky.: John Knox, 1993), 184: "I pine away. I pine away"; George Buchanan Gray, *A Critical and Exegetical Commentary on the Book of Isaiah Volume 1* (ICC; Edinburg: T&T Clark, 1912), 418: "I have leanness, I have leanness." Gray also notes that "רז is in Aramaic a loan word from Persian … and may well have been used by some glossator here" (419).

[73] Blenkinsopp, *Isaiah 1–39: A New Translation with Introduction and Commentary* (AB 19; New York: Doubleday, 2000), 353–54.

[74] This is the view that Blenkinsopp takes. Such a possibility would limit the interpolation of this phrase to some time between the production of the Old Greek of Isaiah (250 B.C.E.?) and the copying of the Great Isaiah Scroll (1QIsaᵃ), the oldest extant manuscript witness, which includes the phrase רזי־לי. If Eugene Ulrich is correct that 1QIsaᵃ "preserves the original text most often" compared to LXX and MT ("The Developmental Composition of the Book of Isaiah: Light from 1QIsaᵃ on Additions in the MT," *DSD* 8 [2001]: 18), this would logically entail that the phrase first makes its way into the textual tradition behind 1QIsaᵃ and thereby into MT, and that the Vorlage for LXX either did not contain the phrase or the translator(s) did not know what to make of it.

for what to do with the second half, particularly רזי לי רזי לי, which he omits, perhaps reckoning it 'implied by the interjection' [אוי־לי], as Ottley inferred."[75]

Other early translations usually dealt with this difficult phrase by (apparently) assuming a connection with the word רז. Other Greek versions such as Symmachus and Theodotion employ μυστήριον in their translations, possibly taking their cue from the use of רז in the book of Daniel. (Would the original translators of Old Greek Isaiah not have had the benefit of knowing the text of Daniel? This might explain their confusion about the phrase, and their reticence on this passage.)

Picking up on the apocalyptic and eschatological themes of Isaiah 24–27, Targum Jonathan later understands Isa 24:16b to mean, "The prophet said, 'The mystery of the reward for the righteous is visible to me, the mystery of the retribution for the wicked is revealed to me!'" (רז אגר לצדיקיא איתחזי לי רז פורענו לרשיעיא אתגלי לי). Thus in this version the eschatological theme of reward and retribution is given to the prophet as a visible revelation, which is perhaps a way of reading Isa 24 in light of the call narrative and the famous vision of Isa 6. After all, the Targum connects the sparse utterance רזי־לי רזי־לי with the mode of its revelation: it is visible, or in other words, it is a vision (using חזא). The obscure double utterance of רז also seems to have triggered for the Targumist the notion that there are "good mysteries" and "bad mysteries," that רזי־לי רזי־לי conceals a reference to the two different kinds of "mysteries" that unfold as part of God's final reckoning.

When we turn to the larger context of the Isaiah passage, we see that in contrast to the ones lifting up their voices joyfully to sing of God's majesty, Isaiah has his own vision, his "mystery," and he knows that the euphoric refrain comes from a false understanding of God's plan of judgment. Despite the rejoicing of the people from East to West, Isaiah is unable to join the liturgy; his "mystery" tells him that destruction is yet to come, that there is yet a final punishment of the wicked and a vindication of the Lord's "elders" (whoever they may be).

---

[75] Ron Troxel, *LXX-Isaiah as Translation and Interpretation: The Strategies of the Translator of the Septuagint of Isaiah* (JSJSup 124; Leiden: Brill, 2008), 235. The reference to Richard Ottley is to his *The Book of Isaiah According to the Septuagint* (2 vols.; Cambridge: Cambridge University Press, 1904–06), 2:223. Troxel continues in a footnote: "The translator was probably perplexed by רזי, judging from his rendering of ישלח האדון יהוה צבאות במשמניו רזון by ἀποστελεῖ κύριοσ σαβαωθ εἰσ τὴν σὴν τιμὴν ἀτιμίαν in 10:16 and of ומשמן בשרו ירזה by καὶ τὰ πίονα τῆς δόξης αὐτοῦ σεισθήσεται in 17:4" (235, n. 145).

This "mystery" is clearly a special kind of revelation to which only Isaiah has access (at least according to the redactor[s] of this passage). Isaiah mediates the significance of this revelation for understanding God's plan for history and for the cosmos, and yet the content of the revelation remains concealed. Contrary to, say, Dan 2, there is no explanation, in the context of the passage, of how and by what authority Isaiah "sees" this "mystery." As I suggested above, though there is scarcely a way to prove the point, I am tempted therefore to read this passage in light of Isaiah's call narrative and throne vision in chapter 6, and to see it also in connection with the proclamation that God is "creating a new heaven and a new earth" in Third Isaiah (Isa 65:17–66:24)—a new reality that is both cosmic and eschatological. The vision of chapter 6 is perhaps itself interpreted in Isa 24 as Isaiah's "mystery," the vision that allows him to see not only the divine imperium but also the horizontal dimension of earthly history.

It is interesting that the content of the "mystery" of Isa 24 seems to involve both the consummation of history as such, i.e. the history of false worship (whether Israelite or pagan) and the reigns of earthly kings, and also the judgment of the cosmos—the "hosts of the high heavens" and the moon and the sun. To be sure, other apocalyptic writings include both heavenly agents and earthly rulers among those who will be punished, and in some cases the actions of both are causally linked.[76] First Enoch 18–19 is rather explicit about this:

1 Enoch 19:1–2

And Uriel said to me, "There stand the angels who mingled with the women. And their spirits—having assumed many forms—bring destruction on men and lead them astray to sacrifice to demons as to gods until the day of great judgment, in which they will be judged with finality."[77]

---

[76] Alexander Toepel makes a compelling case that the Qumran fragments 4Q552–53 and the *Testament of Reuben* 2:1–3:7 demonstrate an association between earthly rulers or kingdoms and planetary demons in his "Planetary Demons in Early Jewish Literature," *JSP* 14 (2005): 231–38; as he points out, there is a strong correlation between these Qumran fragments and Danielic traditions regarding the scheme of four succeeding nations (e.g. Dan 2, 7). For other examples see *1 En* 89:59–70; Dan 10:13; 1QM 12–13.

[77] Translation is from George W. E. Nickelsburg and James C. VanderKam, *1 Enoch: A New Translation* (Minneapolis: Fortress, 2004), 39.

Another theme this part of *1 Enoch* shares with Isa 24 is the motif of imprisonment: when Enoch inquires of Uriel about the "desolate and fearful" place beyond the angels, he replies, "This place is the end of heaven and earth; this has become a prison for the stars and the hosts of heaven" (*1 En* 18:14). Though this theme of celestial rebellion is a typical part of ancient cosmogonies and theogonies (cf. *Enuma Elish*, Hesiod's *Works and Days*), it is at least conceivable that there is a more directly shared tradition between *1 En* 18–19 and Isa 24.

Whatever the "original" sense of the construction רזי־לי in Isaiah, understanding it to be a reference to Isaiah's "mystery" makes considerable good sense of the context in which it occurs, and offers an intriguing possibility for outlining the development of the apocalyptic tradition in Jewish texts of the latter half of the Second Temple period. This section of Isaiah as a whole (Isa 24–27) displays characteristics typical of an apocalyptic worldview, and thus is usually dated to some time in the third (or as late as the second) century B.C.E.[78] Though it should not be taken as conclusive evidence of a late date for this section, the word רז is otherwise attested only during and after the third century B.C.E., and almost exclusively in apocalyptically-oriented texts such as *1 Enoch*, Daniel, and many of the Aramaic and sectarian texts from Qumran. As Blenkinsopp suggests, this section of Isaiah indicates "the uneven progress of the Isaian tradition in the direction of the apocalyptic world view familiar from the book of Daniel and therefore raise[s] the question in an acute form regarding the bearers of that tradition and the social situation in which it came to final expression."[79] While this statement necessarily over-simplifies the problem as a whole, Blenkinsopp is not the only one to see an important connection between Isa 24 and the book of Daniel.[80]

Whether the phrase רזי־לי רזי־לי in Isaiah reflects deliberate use of the word for "mystery" is, finally, impossible to know with certainty, even if the available evidence does point in that direction. What is clear is that

---

[78] See Blenkinsopp *Isaiah 1–39*, 346–49.

[79] Ibid., 355. In his more recent book Blenkinsopp elaborates on the possibility of an Isaiah-Daniel trajectory, and offers some speculation on the place the Yaḥad might occupy along the extended continuum of such a trajectory (*Opening the Sealed Book: Interpretations of the Book of Isaiah in Late Antiquity* (Grand Rapids, Mich.: Eerdmans, 2006), esp. 1–27.

[80] See also J. F. A. Sawyer, "'My Secret Is With Me' (Isaiah 24:16): Some Semantic Links between Isaiah 24–27 and Daniel," in *Understanding Poets and Prophets: Essays in Honor of George Wishart Anderson* (ed. A. Graeme Auld; JSOTSup 152; Sheffield: JSOT Press, 1993), 307–17; Jeffrey Niehaus, "*RĀZ-PᴱŠAR* in Isaiah XXIV," *VT* 31 (1981): 376–78.

later interpreters understood it to have this meaning, and it is perhaps simply an unfortunate accident of (un)preservation that we do not know how Isa 24:16b was interpreted among the Yaḥad. The closest we may come is in the *Damascus Document*'s exposition of the next verse in Isaiah, פחד ופחת ופח עליך יושב הארץ "Terror, and the pit, and the snare are upon you, O inhabitant of the earth," which is itself a famously enigmatic passage:

CD 4:14–19

14 ... פשרו
15 שלושת מצודות בליעל אשר אמר עליהם לוי בן יעקב
16 אשר הוא תפש בהם בישראל ויתנם פניהם לשלושת מיני
17 הצדק הראשונה היא הזנות השנית ההון השלישית
18 טמא המקדש העולה מזה יתפש בזה והניצל מזה יתפש
19 בזה ...

14 ... Its interpretation:
15 the three traps of Belial which Levi son of Jacob told them
16 that he [Belial] would catch Israel in, and so he directed them to three kinds of
17 righteousness. The first is illegal marriage; the second is wealth; the third is
18 defiling the sanctuary. Whoever gets out of one is caught in another; and whoever gets out from that one is caught
19 in yet another. ...

Even here there is possibly an implicit association between the "mystery" of Isa 24 and the "mysteries" known by those of the members of the Damascus Covenant. According to the logic of the *Damascus Document*, this knowledge provides for the proper preemption of the "three nets of Belial," the avoidance of which is a defining feature of those who belong to the continued (or new) covenant.

THE *BOOK OF THE WATCHERS*

Because I am concerned here to describe the use of "mystery" in Second Temple Jewish texts before the advent of the Yaḥad, I have for the sake of convenience restricted the investigation of *1 Enoch* to those sections whose pre-Maccabean composition are beyond dispute, namely the *Book of the Watchers* (רז is not used in the *Astronomical Book*). Though much of what we find in the other books of the collection (especially the *Parables of Enoch*, the *Birth of Noah* and, less so, the *Epistle*) is indeed relevant to the broad study of "mystery" language, these will not figure in the present discussion. The relationship between the groups responsible for the production of the Qumran sectarian texts and the later compositions of the Enochic corpus remains an open yet elusive question.

In the *Book of the Watchers*, we can identify a tradition of "mystery" revelation that bears some similarity to Isa 24. In this case, the good "mysteries" granted to the scribe Enoch are set against the illicit, or evil, "mysteries" of the Watchers. It is difficult to speak with certainty about exactly where the word רז occurs in the *Book of the Watchers*. One may cite the Aramaic fragments found in Qumran cave 4, in which only one attestation of רז remains, namely that of *1 En* 8:3. But the Greek and Ethiopic recensions indicate the likely presence of at least three other appearances in the *Book of the Watchers*: 9:6, 10:7 and 16:3 (twice). Despite general reservations about retro-translating from Greek and Ethiopic to a presumed Aramaic *Vorlage* (which is probably not represented in a pristine way even by the Qumran manuscripts), I will proceed with the assumption that רז is a term known to several parts of the *Book of the Watchers*, and that it functions in a special way in the text.

The famous section of mythic materials in *1 En* 6–11 offers an account (or several intertwined accounts) of evil in the world, focusing on the activity of the Watchers and their dealings with humankind. In this narrative, the "sons of heaven" conspire to takes wives from among the "daughters of men," and the result of their unions is the birth of obscure "giants," Nephilim, and Elioud (successively), as well as the proliferation of evil upon the earth. In short, the Watchers and their offspring violate the boundary between heaven and earth, and proceed to devastate the creation. The four archangels take note of the disaster unfolding on earth, and despite Enoch's intercessory commission, they proceed to imprison and punish the Watchers for their transgressions.

The traditional core of the narrative—centered around the Watcher Shemihazah—is complemented, scholars generally agree, by a secondary, "instruction motif" associated with the Watcher Asael.[81] Included in the instruction motif are various kinds of teachings: the fabrication of war implements and bodily ornaments; magic arts such as sorcery and charms and the cutting of roots and plants; and the interpretation of different kinds of omens (lightning flashes, shooting stars, and the movements of celestial bodies). It is with respect to these teachings that "mystery" is invoked as an important reference point in the *Book of the Watchers*.

---

[81] Nickelsburg, *1 Enoch*, 171–72; 190–93.

Nickelsburg reconstructs the schematic history of this motif in the following way: the parallel notices at *1 En* 7:1 and 9:8 are the initial interpolations into the Shemihazah story, reflecting interest only in the magical arts; the list in 8:3, with Shemihazah at its head, reflects the hierarchy of 6:7—which means that it predates the Asael material—and is an elaboration and extension of 7:1 and 9:8, including new material on the interpretation of omens; the material about Asael constitutes the final interpolation, including 8:1–2, 9:6 and 10:4–8, and is concerned primarily with instruction in the arts of killing and self-ornamentation. These stages perhaps reflect the changing interests of the authors as the tradition developed over the period from ca. 300 B.C.E. to ca. 165 B.C.E.

If Nickelsburg's reconstruction is correct, we can detect something of a dichotomy between the "occult arts" (cutting of roots and plants, reading the heavenly signs) and the "artifactual arts" (fashioning of war implements, jewelry, cosmetics, etc.). In terms of the contents of the various "mysteries," then, the occult arts involve some form of divination, while the artifactual arts are concerned with the application of knowledge to the production of material goods. Indeed, both kinds of knowledge are presumed to be illicit and evil, but the dichotomy seems to be present throughout these chapters of *1 Enoch*.

The first reference to the instruction motif comes in *1 En* 7:1: "And they [the Watchers] began to go in to [their wives], and to defile themselves through them, and to teach them sorcery and charms, and to reveal to them the cutting of roots and plants." "Mystery" is not specifically used here, but is tied into this theme at the end of 8:1–3:

1 Enoch 8:1–3

Shemihazah taught spells and the cutting of roots.
Hermani taught sorcery for the loosing of spells and magic and skill.
Baraqel taught the signs of the lightning flashes.
Kokabel taught the signs of the stars.
Ziqel taught the signs of the shooting stars.
Arteqoph taught the signs of the earth.
Shamsiel taught the signs of the sun.
Sahriel taught the signs of the moon.
And they all began to reveal mysteries to their wives and to their children.[82]

---

[82] 4Q201 1 iv 5–6: ‏ובלהן רזין לנשיהן‎ [‏וכלהן שריו לגלי‎]‏ה‎; "and to their children" is attested in the Greek version of Syncellus, perhaps as a later gloss to explain why

The last line of 8:3 could be read either as a summary of all that the Watchers taught or as something extra, viz. "in addition to all these things, they taught them mysteries," though the former sense seems more likely. So what begins as a reference only to magical arts in 7:1— sorcery, cutting of roots, and so on—later encompasses the occult arts in general, including the interpretation of celestial omens. Yet, presumably, the community behind the production of these Enochic motifs was not entirely hostile to omen-interpretation; throughout the entire collection there is intense interest in the movements of the sun and moon, and in the laws of the stars (the *Astronomical Book*, among others); and the *Book of Parables* declares that Enoch knows the secrets of lightning, thunder, and the luminaries (*1 En* 59). As Nickelsburg and others have suggested, perhaps "the references to prognostication from signs in the heavenly bodies ... may be a foil to Enoch's 'true' astronomical revelation."[83] In other words, it is only because it comes from an unauthorized source that it is in any way proscribed.

In any case, in *1 En* 6–11 the problem seems to be primarily the transmission from heaven to earth of information not authorized by God.[84] In *1 En* 8:3, the Watchers begin to teach "mysteries" to their wives and children under the auspices of Shemihazah; in 9:4, it is Asael who reveals the "eternal mysteries that are in heaven" (note also in 9:16, "which men were striving to learn" is a possible reference to the futility of humans *striving* to learn God's secrets—cf. Dan 2). And in 10:7 the angel Raphael is sent to heal the earthly destruction caused by the "mystery that the Watchers told and taught their sons." Finally, in chapter 16, Enoch is told to say to the Watchers in response to their petition: "You were in heaven, and no mystery was revealed to you; but a *stolen* mystery you learned; and this you made known to the women in your hardness of heart; and through this mystery the women and men are multiplying evils upon the earth" (*1 En* 16:3). But again, surely not all revelations of "mystery" were thought to be illicit: throughout the narrative—and this is perhaps one of the primary points of the entire *1 Enoch* collection—the evil "mysteries" that the Watchers reveal is set against the good and authorized "mysteries" revealed to Enoch. The mystery "stolen" by the Watchers is set up as a foil to the mystery

the Giants also possessed knowledge of evil things by which they led human beings astray.

[83] Nickelsburg, *1 Enoch*, 191.

[84] H. Bietenhard, *Die himmlische Welt im Urchristentum und Spätjudentum* (WUNT 2; Tübingen: Mohr Siebeck, 1951), 268.

revealed intentionally to Enoch by God and the angels. The explanation for rampant destruction and idolatry is tied to the revelation of the Watchers' mysteries, while the mysteries made known to Enoch provide the basis for understanding what will happen at the end regarding the judgment of the wicked and the vindication of the righteous.

Though Enoch himself is not explicitly tied directly to knowledge of רזין in the *Book of the Watchers*, we are to understand from later developments of the tradition that the information derived from Enoch's contact with heaven constituted just such "mysteries." For example, in the *Birth of Noah* narrative in chapters 106–107, Enoch assures his son Methuselah that despite the iniquity of the Watchers and the subsequent destruction of the earth, Methuselah's grandson Noah will be saved from all corruption. But Enoch also knows that the cleansing of the flood will only give way to ever greater iniquity, generation after generation of evil, until the final reckoning. "For," Enoch says, "I know the mysteries that the holy ones have revealed and shown to me, and that I have read in the tablets of heaven" (106:19).

One additional consideration here is the status of the recipients of רזין. On the one hand are Enoch and his progeny, to whom he reveals an esoteric teaching about the contents of the tablets of heaven. On the other hand are the recipients of the dangerous knowledge imparted by the Watchers, namely, all the other inhabitants of the earth. Enoch's family line is portrayed not only as the carrier of divine knowledge, but also, in the figure of Noah, as the vehicle for righteousness and salvation. Indeed, Noah's status is a salient feature of several Second Temple Jewish compositions which involve the revelation of "mysteries" (*1 Enoch*, *Jubilees*, *Genesis Apocryphon*); he does not participate in the multiplication of evils upon the earth, and he is something of a savior whose righteousness comforts the earth after all its corruption. Furthermore, Noah seems to be depicted as a foil to the Watchers themselves: the narratives about Noah's birth[85] in *1 Enoch* and the *Genesis Apocryphon* describe that event in almost miraculous terms, in which the child has supernatural characteristics. He had a body "whiter than snow

---

[85] See James C. VanderKam, "The Birth of Noah," in *Intertestamental Essays in Honor of Jósef Tadeusz Milik* (ed. Z. J. Kapera; Kraków: The Enigma Press, 1992), 213–31; idem, "The Righteousness of Noah," in *Ideal Figures in Ancient Judaism: Profiles and Paradigms* (ed. John J. Collins and George W. E. Nickelsburg; SBLSCS 12; Chico, Calif.: Scholars Press, 1980), 13–32; D. Dimant, "Noah in Early Jewish Literature," in *Biblical Figures Outside the Bible* (ed. Michael E. Stone and T. A. Bergren; Harrisburg, Penn.: Trinity Press International, 1998), 123–50.

and redder than a rose"; hair "like white wool"; "when he opened his
eyes the house shone like the sun"; he spoke words of praise almost
immediately after being born. Indeed, Lamech was afraid, because his
son was not like other human beings, but was "like the sons of the angels
of heaven." When Methushelah went to the ends of the earth to inquire
of Enoch regarding the strange child, Enoch recounted to him the story
of the Watchers and assured him that Noah's role was in fact to outlive
the iniquity of the fallen angels and their "stolen mysteries."[86]

THE BOOK OF DANIEL

Turning now to the book of Daniel, we find another perspective on how
one gains access to the "mysteries," and what the contents of the
mysteries entail. The word רז occurs in chapters 2 and 4, in both places in
the context of Daniel's interpretation of Nebuchadnezzar's dreams.
These chapters fall into the genre of the ancient Near Eastern "court-
tale," and they likely reflect fourth- or third-century B.C.E. traditions
about Daniel the sage.[87] These tales are literary records of the practice of
what has often been called "mantic wisdom," by which a diviner or sage
is given to know divine truths by the practice of dream-interpretation or
other mantic arts.[88] In any case, the underlying motive of the stories is to

---

[86] Several centuries later, the connection between Noah and special
revelation of "mysteries" is made complete: the *Sefer ha-Razim* claims to be one of
the books of "mysteries" given to Noah (זה ספר מספרי הרזים שנתן לנוח בן למך).
Like in *1 Enoch*, in *Sefer ha-Razim* a connection is made between possession of
"mysteries" and knowledge of astrological signs; here, as in *1 Enoch*, the
knowledge of such matters that comes down to Noah is cast in a positive light (as
opposed to the knowledge of the Watchers). But unlike Enoch, Noah does not
gain access to the "mysteries" by direct experience, as in a vision or journey;
instead, he receives them in a book, or perhaps by instruction. See Michael
Morgan, trans., *Sefer ha-Razim: The Book of Mysteries* (SBLTT 25; Chico, Calif.:
Scholars Press).

[87] See especially Collins, *Daniel*, 38–52; idem, "The Court-Tales in Daniel
and the Development of Apocalyptic," *JBL* 94 (1975): 218–34; Susan Niditch and
Robert Doran, "The Success Story of the Wise Courtier," *JBL* 96 (1977): 179–93;
Lawrence M. Wills, *The Jew in the Court of the Foreign King* (HDR 26; Minneapolis:
Fortress, 1990).

[88] James C. VanderKam, "The Prophetic-Sapiential Origins of Apocalyptic
Thought" in *A Word in Season: Essays in Honour of William McKane* (ed. James D.
Martin and Philip R. Davies; JSOTSup 42; Sheffield: JSOT Press, 1986), 163–79;
idem, "Mantic Wisdom in the Dead Sea Scrolls"; Müller, "Magisch-mantische
Weisheit und die Gestalt Daniels."

demonstrate the effectiveness of God's revelation and inspiration over against the futile divinatory methods of Babylonian occult artists, reflecting a similar dichotomy as in the *Book of the Watchers* between authorized and unauthorized revelation, between the genuine article of God-given knowledge and the bankrupt wisdom of illicit "mysteries."

In Dan 2:17–19, Daniel urges his companions to seek God's compassion—in other words to pray—that the "mystery" of Nebuchadnezzar's dream might be revealed. Accordingly, the "mystery" was given to Daniel in a "vision of the night," that is, in a dream:

> 17 Then Daniel went to his house and informed his companions, Hananiah, Mishael, and Azariah, of the matter, 18 that they might implore the God of Heaven for help regarding this mystery (רזה דנה), so that Daniel and his colleagues would not be put to death together with the other wise men of Babylon. 19 The mystery (רזה) was revealed to Daniel in a night vision (בחזוה די־ליליא) then Daniel blessed the God of Heaven.

It is significant that at this point in the narrative, the singular רז is used in reference to the "mystery" of Nebuchadnezzar's dream. The "mystery" of its interpretation is one of a different kind, one that Daniel himself will reveal by the wisdom granted to him through his prayer in 2:20–23:

> 20 Daniel spoke up and said: "Let the name of God be blessed forever and ever, for wisdom and power are His. 21 He changes times and seasons, removes kings and installs kings; He gives the wise their wisdom and knowledge to those who know. 22 He reveals deep and hidden things (עמיקתא ומסתרתא), knows what is in the darkness, and light dwells with Him. 23 I acknowledge and praise You, O God of my fathers, You who have given me wisdom and power, for now You have let me know what we asked of You; You have let us know what concerns the king."

As a preface to Daniel's description of the dream he says to the king, "it is not because of wisdom that is in me beyond all living things that this mystery was revealed to me but so that the interpretation should be made known to the king ..." (2:30). And in the coda to the episode, just after Daniel has expounded the dream, the king says to Daniel, "Truly your God is God of gods and Lord of kings and revealer of mysteries, since *you* have been able to *reveal* this mystery," which mystery is the interpretation of the dream (2:47). The plural רזין is used only in reference to God's *general* ability to maintain and reveal "mysteries" (2:28, 29, 47), whereas the singular can be used either for the content of a direct revelation or for the interpretation of that revelation. This possibility is reinforced in Dan 4:6: Nebuchadnezzar does not bother to ask Daniel for the content of the dream, only for its interpretation; he knows that a "divine spirit" is in Daniel, and that "no mystery is too difficult" for him. "Mystery" here can only refer to the interpretation of the dream; no direct revelation to Daniel is recounted, but only his inspired exegesis of the dream.

In chapter 2, Daniel's prayer immediately after receiving the dream-revelation includes several characteristic features of apocalyptic writings: reference to God's control over "seasons and times" as well as the enthronement and deposition of kings; and dualistic language of darkness and light. Furthermore God is said to reveal "deep and hidden things." Here the word for "hidden" is מסתרתא, perhaps in order to distinguish the generic category of "hidden things" from the specific technical meaning of רז which the author seems to employ. In any case, all of these things are related to the work of Daniel the sage, to whom practical wisdom is given to understand visionary revelation. In other words, the episode involves both the (passive) reception of a vision, and the (active) work of an interpreter endowed with divinely enhanced skill—and the content of each of these aspects is to be considered a "mystery."

Surely there is more one could say about Daniel's use of "mystery," but most of it has already been said and it would not help to rehearse what several recent studies have documented.[89] My aim here has not been to provide an exhaustive treatise on revelatory functions in Daniel, but to highlight certain features of the text that will be relevant to the latter portions of this study.

OTHER ARAMAIC LITERATURE FROM QUMRAN

There are quite a number of Aramaic texts that accentuate the transmission of a special stream of knowledge in prediluvian and patriarchal times. Indeed, this seems to be one of the salient and uniting features of the Aramaic narrative compositions, a feature also found in the book of *Jubilees*. Often such special knowledge takes the form of "books" that ostensibly contain "hidden" or "sealed" knowledge that is available to the elect. In 4Q534, which is one of the fragmentary Aramaic

---

[89] For example, Gladd, *Revealing the* Mysterion, 17–50.

texts dealing with the birth of Noah,[90] there is a clear association between eternality or immortality and the books or scrolls that are at issue in that passage. The text begins with a description of Noah, stating, "In his youth he will be adept and like a man who does not know anything until he knows the three books (ספריא תלתת). Then he will be wise ... prudence will be with him, and he will know the mysteries of men (רזי אנשא), and his wisdom shall come to all peoples, and he will know the mysteries of all living things (רזי כול חייא) ... his purposes will last forever."[91] And later, "Would that someone would write these words of mine in a book that will not wear out and keep my utterance in a scroll that will not pass away." Though the text places Noah's acquisition of "mysteries" in the future—after he has read the books—it also presumes that he has already done so and has duly learned such "mysteries." He not only learns them, but according to this text "he will reveal mysteries like the Most High ones" (4Q536 2i+3 8), and will pass them along in a line of transmission among the remnant elect (4Q536 2i+3 13).

Throughout the Noah materials there is an association between special knowledge and election, which is interesting especially in light of one of the known etymologies of Noah's name: that of "being left," i.e. as a righteous "remnant" (נוח). As both Devorah Dimant and James VanderKam have argued, this may well underlie the fact that many of the Aramaic texts show an interest in Noah as a kind of precursor to all such remnant elect.[92] Like Levi, who retroactively becomes a symbolic representative of the levitical priestly-scribal craft, Noah (like Enoch) becomes a primeval synecdoche for those who receive and adhere to a special kind of revelation—revelation that is salvific perhaps by simple virtue of its possession.

In the *Visions of Amram* "the transmission of teaching to Amram from Abraham, via Isaac, Jacob and Levi is stressed,"[93] and the group of

---

[90] For the history of scholarship on this text see Dorothy Peters, *Noah Traditions in the Dead Sea Scrolls: Conversations and Controversies in Antiquity* (SBLEJL 26; Atlanta: Society of Biblical Literature, 2008), 101–106.

[91] *1 En* 106:19.

[92] Dimant, "Noah in Early Jewish Literature," 125–26; VanderKam, "The Birth of Noah," 220–21.

[93] Michael Stone, "The Axis of History at Qumran," in *Pseudepigraphic Perspectives: The Apocrypha and Pseudepigrapha in Light of the Dead Sea Scrolls* (ed. M. E. Stone and E. Chazon; STDJ 31; Leiden: Brill, 1999), 140.

texts with which the work is associated[94] are concerned with the "generations of Levi down to Aaron, the direct father of the priestly line of Israel."[95] This is especially important to the present topic because at one point this text declares that "concerning A[aron and the (high) priesthood] [I] will tell you the mystery of his work (רז עובדה): he is a holy priest [to God Most High, for] his descendents will be holy to him for all the generations of e[ternity ...]" (4Q545 4 15–17).

It would appear that Amram and Aaron are associated with "mysteries" because they are descendants of Levi, who is understood to be the first priest and the father of all priests. The *incipit* to the *Visions of Amram* states that what follows in the text is a "copy of the book of 'The Words of the Vision of Amram son of Kohath son of Levi.'[96] It contains everything that he told his sons and everything that he commanded them on the day he died. ..." In this text Aaron is elevated even above Moses, who is barely mentioned. This cluster of Aramaic texts wishes to say something important about priests and the kind of knowledge they possess and the authority in which such knowledge is grounded. Levi takes a special place as the recipient of special teaching that goes back to Enoch, and presumably goes forward all the way to the readers and interpreters of the priestly-scribal tradition.[97]

To return to the figure of Noah, it may be a peripheral connection, but in a fragmentary portion of 4QInstruction there is a passage that may refer to "the mystery that is to be and he made it known to Noah."[98] Is

---

[94] *Aramaic Levi Document, Testament of Qahat,* and *Visions of Amram* were possibly understood to be a collection; see Michael Stone, "Levi, Aramaic," *EDSS* 1.486–88.

[95] Drawnel, *Aramaic Wisdom Text,* 31.

[96] פרשגן כתב מלי חזות עמרם

[97] See also 4QTestament of Jacob ar (4Q537); 4QTestament of Qahat ar (4Q542); 4QBiblical Chronology ar (4Q559).

[98] רז נהיה ויודיע אל נח—4Q418 201 1 (reconstructed by T. Elgvin along with 4Q416 1 3); cf. 4Q253 1 4. See Torleif Elgvin, "Wisdom, Revelation and Eschatology in an Early Essene Writing," in *SBL Seminar Papers 1995* (ed. E. H. Lovering; Atlanta: Scholars Press, 1995), 459; Moshe Bernstein, "Noah and the Flood at Qumran," in *The Provo International Conference on the Dead Sea Scrolls: Technological Innovations, New Texts, and Reformulated Issues* (ed. Donald W. Parry and Eugene Ulrich; STDJ 30; Leiden: Brill, 1999), 217–18. The DJD editors of 4QInstruction did not accept Elgvin's reconstruction here, based in part upon the fact that elsewhere in the Dead Sea Scrolls the name Noah invariably has the plene spelling, נוח, making Elgvin's suggestion "orthographically very unlikely in this manuscript" (DJD 34:422–23). See also Peters, *Noah Traditions in the Dead Sea Scrolls,* 64–65; Peters notes here that Elgvin has since changed his position on

the author of 4QInstruction familiar with these traditions about Noah's esoteric knowledge? While I do not wish to dwell here on the meaning and shape of the referent in its various extant uses,[99] it is significant that an important Hebrew text displays the association between Noah and the "mystery that is to be." Even if 4QInstruction is not a strictly sectarian composition, it is written in Hebrew and was clearly an important text for the Yaḥad. I take the references to the רז נהיה in 4QInstruction (and elsewhere) to indicate a special body of teaching, a compendium that itself was perhaps (but need not have been) written.

It is well known that several of the Aramaic compositions from Qumran participate in a tradition about primordial "Watchers" and "giants" who transmit illicit knowledge.[100] Their primary transgression appears to be a crossing of boundaries, an unauthorized mixing of heavenly and earthly forms of being and knowing. While one of the functions of the Watchers story is to provide an etiology for the presence of sin and evil in the world, another is to provide a suitable antithesis to the true nature of Enoch's knowledge and the knowledge of the group associating itself with him.[101] While there are several possibilities for the social setting in which such traditions took shape, what is of interest here is the representation of competing claims to knowledge and the presentation of the antagonists as bankrupt, corrupt, and damned.

In addition to the oft-cited passages in the *Book of the Watchers* (e.g. *1 En* 6–11; esp. 8:1–3, 9:5–8), there are other passages that attest to an interest in both illicit and esoteric knowledge. In 1Q23—a fragment of the *Book of Giants*—there is perhaps a reference to רז / רזין, though this is a best-guess reconstruction based on the presence of [--]ר וידעו [--] in the context of a passage that is apparently about the proliferation of sin on the earth and the begetting of Giants. In the first column of the *Genesis Apocryphon* the story of the Watchers is loosely recounted along with reference to the "instruction motif," in order, it seems, to introduce the

---

this reconstruction, and yet Peters argues that there are other indications in the text that might suggest a Noachic context.

[99]   Goff, *Worldly and Heavenly Wisdom*, 54-61.

[100]   As Annette Reed has recently shown, the "instruction motif" in the *Book of the Watchers* itself has a complex history that includes both the embrace and the rejection of the idea of illicit angelic conveyance of heavenly knowledge. See her *Fallen Angels and the History of Judaism and Christianity*, esp. chapters 1–3.

[101]   See Samuel I. Thomas, "'Riddled with Guilt': The Mysteries of Transgression, the Sealed Vision, and the Art of Interpretation in 4Q300 and Related Texts," *DSD* 15 (2008): 155–71.

birth of Noah trope. In this text it is Noah who serves as the foil to the Watchers, and in col. 6 Noah himself learns ("in a vision" בחזיון) of the descent and transgression of the "Sons of Heaven," knowledge that he in turn keeps hidden in his heart (ולכול אנוש לא אחויתה וטמרת רזא דן בלבבי). This particular locution, "to hide X in my heart," is interesting and it is attested also in one of the *Aramaic Levi* manuscripts from Qumran (4Q213b 3; CTL Bodl. a). The phrase "I [hid] this (vision) too in my heart and [I revealed it] to nobody" (בלבבי ולכל אנש לא [גליתה וטמר[ת אף דן) occurs in the context of a dream vision, just prior to Jacob's tithing and Levi's elevation to the "head of the priesthood" of the "God of eternity."[102] (If indeed *Aramaic Levi* is cited in the *Damascus Document* ["words of Levi, son of Jacob," CD 4:15 / ALD 6:3], as Jonas Greenfield has argued, it is interesting that the citation occurs as part of a reference to the "three nets of Belial" and in the broader context of the Admonition which underscores the special revelation of "hidden matters" (נסתרות) that are limited to those who inhabit the "safe home in Israel" [CD 3:13–19]).[103]

These texts do not state why it is important to hide such knowledge in the heart, but this same impulse is present in the *Hodayot*. In one of the hymns the speaker refers to the "mysteries of [God's] wonder" (רזי פלאך) by which he has come to understand the "depth of [God's] insight" and the "paths [of truth] (and) the works of evil" (דרכי [אמת] מעשי רע).[104] Such knowledge is apparently proper to the "men of truth" (אשני אמת) or the "men of Your vision" (אנשי חזונכה),[105] men who are part of the Yaḥad and thus the "council" of the speaker (וכן הוגשתי ביחד כול אנשי סודי).[106] Yet the special knowledge, the "mystery," was apparently also a vehicle of betrayal by some members of the community:

1QHᵃ 13:26–29

Even those who share my bread have lifted up their heel against me, and all those who have committed themselves to my counsel speak perversely against me with unjust lips. The men of my council rebel and grumble about. And concerning the mystery *which You hid in me*, they go about as slanderers to the children of destruction. Because You have

---

[102] See Jonas C. Greenfield, Michael Stone, and Esther Eshel, *Aramaic Levi Document: Text, Translation and Commentary* (SVTP 19; Leiden: Brill, 2004), 66–69.

[103] Greenfield, "The Words of Levi Son of Jacob in Damascus Document IV.15-19," *RevQ* 13 (1988): 319–22.

[104] 1QHᵃ 5:19–20.

[105] 1QHᵃ 6:13; 6:18.

[106] 1QHᵃ 6:29.

exalted Yourself in me, and for the sake of their guilt, *You have hidden in me* the spring of understanding and the counsel of truth. But they devise the ruination of their heart and with the words of Belial they have exhibited a lying tongue; as the poison of serpents it bursts forth continuously.

A similar sentiment is encountered in an Aramaic fragment (PAM 41.590) that has been associated with 4QPhysiognomy (4Q561).[107] Indeed, there is considerable terminological overlap between this fragment and other key Qumran Aramaic texts such as the *Book of Giants*, *Genesis Apocryphon*, the testaments of Judah, Jacob, and Qahat, *Aramaic Levi*, the *Birth of Noah*, and the *Astronomical Book* (though, curiously, not with fragments 1–6 of 4Q561). The fragment represents an apparently apocalyptic (or more properly, eschatological) section of the text in which the phrase "and you shall walk ... you shall hide in [your] heart" (ותלך [ו]תטשא בלבך) occurs in proximity to "teaching" (אלף) and "writing" (רשם) and a reference to "eternal" or "eternity" (עלמא).

Finally, one could cite the presence of an exorcism, or "Incantation Formula" among the Aramaic texts from Qumran (4Q560). As Philip S. Alexander notes, the "magical" character of this text "has been demonstrated beyond reasonable doubt," and it reflects a complex demonology that "fits in well with the ethos of 4Q510–11 and 11Q11," which display other incantatory material.[108] While 11QApocryphal Psalms[a] (11Q11) is not definitively sectarian, 4QSongs of the Maskil[a-b] (4Q510–11) represent a Qumran sectarian application of the idea of efficacious, apotropaic incantation/adjuration in the form of prayer.

---

[107] Søren Holst and Jesper Høgenhaven "Physiognomy and Eschatology: Some More Fragments of 4Q561," *JJS* 57 (2006): 26–43. The authors conclude that the fragments in question (9–11) are probably not part of the *Aramaic Physiognomy*, even if they come from a text written by the same scribe on the same manuscript. "Whilst an ultimate verdict should, of course, await the final publication of 4Q561 by É. Puech, the evidence at the present state of research points to the original editors being right in considering 4Q561 frgs 9–11 as an independent text distinct from 'Aramaic Horoscope' or 'Aramaic Physiognomy'" (43). Popović does not treat this fragment in his *Reading the Human Body*, presumably because he does not take it to be part of 4Q561. Puech has confirmed in a private conversation that he does not take fragments 9–11 to be part of 4Q561; they were merely photographed together.

[108] Philip S. Alexander, "'Wrestling against Wickedness in High Places,'" 329–30; see also D. L. Penney and Michael O. Wise, "By the Power of Beelzebub: An Aramaic Incantation Formula from Qumran (4Q560)," *JBL* 113 (1994): 627–50.

(Curiously, the word רז is likely extant in both 4Q511 and 11Q11.) And one should not overlook the fact that several other Qumran Aramaic texts display concern with spiritual healing that involves the expulsion of demons and evil spirits, texts that include Tobit (Tob 6:16–17; 8:3; cf. 4Q196–197), *Genesis Apocryphon* (1QapGen 20:16–22), and the *Prayer of Nabonidus* (4Q242).[109]

If we may assume that the people behind the production and preservation of the Qumran texts wrote only in Hebrew—and presumably valued and reclaimed Hebrew as the primordial language of God[110]—we might ask why so many Aramaic works were also preserved and/or copied.[111] And why were some of them apparently authoritative in some way? And is it significant that the book of *Jubilees* is written in Hebrew when it has such close affinity with, say, the *Genesis Apocryphon*, the Enochic literature, and other Aramaic compositions, several of which could very well precede the composition of *Jubilees*? Might this suggest something about the relationship between *Jubilees* and the Hebrew sectarian literature? If we are to think of Aramaic-speaking adherents bringing their own Aramaic texts to Qumran (which is one possibility for explaining their presence there), how then should we think about the rather high level of correspondence in themes, styles, and motifs among the various Aramaic compositions? Is this mere coincidence? Is this

---

[109]   Alexander, "'Wrestling against Wickedness in High Places,'" 328–29. To these I might add *Jub* 10:12–14, which makes reference to Noah writing in a book "all kinds of medicine" that apparently preclude "evil spirits"; and *Aramaic Levi Document*'s "book of Noah concerning the blood" (10:10). For the latter see Greenfield, Stone, and Eshel, *Aramaic Levi Document*, 90–91, 180; this portion is extant only in the Greek: ἐν τῇ γραφῇ τῆς βίβλου τοῦ Νῶε περὶ τοῦ αἵματος.

[110]   For discussions about the use of Hebrew at Qumran, see esp. S. Segert, "Die Sprachenfragen in der Qumran Gemeinschaft," in *Qumran-Probleme: Vorträge des Leipziger Symposions über Qumran-Probleme vom 9. bis 14. Oktober 1961* (ed. Hans Bardtke; DAWBSSA 42; Berlin: Akademie-Verlag, 1963), 315–19; William Schniedewind, "Qumran Hebrew As an Antilanguage," *JBL* 118 (1999): 235–52; idem, "Linguistic Ideology in Qumran Hebrew," in *Diggers at the Well: Proceedings of a Third International Symposium on the Hebrew of the Dead Sea Scrolls and Ben Sira* (ed. T. Muraoka and J. F. Elwolde; STDJ 36; Leiden: Brill, 2000), 245–55; Steven Weitzman, "Why Did the Qumran Community Write in Hebrew?" *JAOS* 119 (1999): 35–45; S. Schwartz, "Language, Power and Identity," *Past and Present* 148 (1995): 21–31; M. Stone and E. Eshel, "The Holy Language at the End of Days in Light of a Qumran Fragment," *Tarbiz* 62 (1993): 169–77 (Hebrew). This "fragment" is 4Q464; cf. *Jub* 12:25–26.

[111]   There are approximately 129 Aramaic manuscripts from Qumran, and about 87 of them are well enough preserved for modern study.

merely a random sample of literary and documentary texts available in general to Aramaic-speaking (reading) Jewish scribes? Or do these manuscripts represent something more? And finally, why would the Qumran scribes (or those of related communities) continue to copy these Aramaic texts if they were not considered "sectarian" in some way?

In short, in addition to any other reasons these texts were valued, it appears that many of the Aramaic compositions contain a number of important features of what we might call the "esoteric knowledge" that was constitutive of the Yahad's own social and religious self-understanding. In many of the Aramaic compositions we find the kind of material that corresponds with what the Qumran group(s) apparently understood to be within its own special epistemological domain. This includes the transmission of special "books" and interpretations, scientific knowledge about astronomy, astrology, physiognomy, etc., as well as the possibility for personal, revelatory religious experience made possible for those whose righteousness merited it.

SUMMARY AND CONCLUSION

This chapter has covered a wide range of material in an attempt to set the stage for a detailed discussion of Qumran (especially) sectarian texts. I have treated material from the ancient Near East, the Hebrew Bible, and biblical and non-biblical Aramaic texts, with several objectives in mind. One goal was to demonstrate that the functions and conceptual values of mystery language in the Qumran Scrolls are both in continuity with previous manifestations and yet represent a new development in the traditions and practices of ancient Judaism. In particular, we have charted the use of סוד in the Hebrew Bible as it developed from ancient Near Eastern and prophetic to wisdom-oriented texts and contexts, noting along the way the changing cultural conditions in which such developments took place. By the time of the third century B.C.E., the word רז had been introduced into the Aramaic lexicon,[112] and while it expressed a number of meanings parallel to the uses of סוד, it also appears to have taken on specialized meanings within apocalyptic strains of thought.

Another aim of this chapter was to highlight the parallel social contexts for secrecy, "mystery," and esoteric knowledge in the ancient Near East and in early (Palestinian) Judaism. We observed in chapter 2 that in Mesopotamian cultures, the "house of wisdom"—the realm of

---

[112] For discussion see the Appendix at the end of the book.

scholars, priests, and kings—was a place where esoteric knowledge of divination, astronomy, astrology, and other "mantic arts" was cultivated and guarded. In the present chapter it became evident that appeals to revealed, restricted, recondite knowledge in the "biblical tradition" are to be found in early (pre-exilic) prophetic works—whose connections with Mesopotamian divination have been well-documented—and also in certain strains of the wisdom tradition of the early-mid Second Temple period. With respect to the use of רז in pre-Yaḥad literature, we noted the affiliation with prophetic, sapiential, and priestly kinds of texts and discourses, and that "mystery" terminology was embedded within social contexts compatible with secrecy and esotericism. In addition, רז is also used in texts that reflect esoteric practices such as astronomy and astrology, divination, and exorcism.

While some caution is in order, the following conclusion presents itself for further consideration. The Mesopotamian (esp. Babylonian, and later, Persian) heritage of certain aspects of early Jewish apocalypticism presupposes not mere literary or cultural "borrowing." There is likely a (shared?) social sphere in which traditions and practices were transmitted and shaped in analogous ways, and in which these Mesopotamian reflexes could have been worked into the fabric of emerging Jewish apocalyptic thought. This invites the possibility that apocalypticism was a relatively broad movement that was integrally tied to, or derived from, the intellectual center of Second Temple Judean society—namely the temple and its scribal apparatus, which itself was already a restricted, esoteric realm in which the mantic arts and cultic machinery were preserved, elaborated, inscribed, and guarded.

Thus, even while some of the conceptual potential for "mystery" was already framed in the earlier (Hebrew) prophetic and sapiential traditions, it was in the context of an Aramaic-speaking priestly-scribal guild that apocalyptic themes were developed and רז was introduced into the lexicon during the late Achaemenid or early Hellenistic period. From this point forward, "mystery" would come to take on a new range of uses and meanings as it made its way beyond Aramaic and into the Hebrew of the Yaḥad—a "temple community," a "house of wisdom," and, for its members, a place of ongoing prophecy.

CHAPTER FOUR

A LEXICOLOGY OF MYSTERY IN THE QUMRAN SCROLLS

> The "real world" is to a large extent unconsciously
> built up in the language habits of a group. ... The
> worlds in which different societies live are distinct
> worlds, not merely the same world with different
> labels attached. ... We see and hear and otherwise
> experience very largely as we do because the
> language habits of our community predispose certain
> choices of interpretation.
>
> Edward Sapir

Having considered the general context of mystery language and concepts of secrecy in the ancient Near East and in early Judaism, and with a basic outline of the uses of mystery language in apocalyptically-oriented literature of the Second Temple period, we may now focus our attention on the Qumran Scrolls themselves. After briefly describing the uses of סוד and נסתרות in the Scrolls, this chapter will turn to the various uses of רז in the Scrolls, including word combinations and accompanying verbs. The goal of this chapter is to provide an overall semantic map for רז, and to lay the foundation for what follows in chapter 5. While there is some conceptual overlap among these three terms in the Qumran corpus, the decision to center on רז stems from its centrality in the ideological self-communication of the Yaḥad and from its broader conceptual range.[1]

The epigraph for this chapter is taken from Edward Sapir, *Culture, Language and Personality* (Berkeley: University of California Press, 1970), 69.

[1] There are some attestations of רז that are too fragmentary to allow for any contextual evaluation. For obvious reasons these will not be dealt with in detail here: 1Q36 9 1; 1Q40 1 2; 4Q385a 3a–c 8; 4Q464a 3.

The impetus for this part of the study has come in part from a small note by Devorah Dimant in her widely cited article, "Qumran Sectarian Literature": "That the term 'the mysteries of God' refers to the divine plan is evident from passages like 1QS 3:23, 4:18; 1QM 3:9; 1QpHab 7:5, 8, 14. The term may have a wider application according to the various combinations of terms (cf. רזי פלא, רזי שכל, רזי פשע)."[2] To be sure, one of the first things to notice about the use of רז in the Scrolls is that it is most often used in construct,[3] that it is usually deployed in ways that indicate a broader range of application. This is in contrast to its use in *1 Enoch* and in Daniel (and in other Aramaic compositions such as the *Genesis Apocryphon*), where it occurs in the absolute form without any qualifying words. This may indicate a development in the use of the term in the Qumran sectarian texts, a topic we will take up again below. All this has important implications for how we should understand the function of mystery language (and in particular, רז) within the worldview of the Yaḥad.

Whether a general concept or a specific category, wherever "mystery" shows up in the Scrolls it must *do* something, or someone must do something with it. There are certain verbs that tend to provide for the action associated with mysteries, and these can also help to illuminate aspects of "mystery" and its corresponding religious and social functions. The verbal associations with "mystery" include verbs of revelation, of knowledge acquisition and understanding, and of concealing, among others. The subjects of these actions vary according to the contexts of the relevant passages.

Of course, immediate literary context is not the only way to determine the meaning or significance of a word. One must also take into account the genre of the text as a whole and its overarching formal purposes. It is possible, for example, that the word רז conveys subtle but important differences in meaning depending on the type of literature in which it is employed. As we might expect, a "mystery" in the context of a wisdom-oriented composition could carry connotations that are different from a "mystery" in the context of a rule book, a liturgical text, or a calendrical document. To take another example, the use of סוד may also shift from one kind of text to another: in texts that deal with community life and structure the valence of "human council" will outweigh the connotation of "heavenly council" that might be found in liturgical texts. For this reason, I will consider the matter of genre

---

[2] Dimant, "Qumran Sectarian Literature," 536 n. 256.
[3] Or, for example, in a phrase like רז נהיה, which is a noun + participle; see below.

wherever such distinctions can provide help in interpreting a given passage.

As we will see, a "mystery" can have either good or evil connotations. In addition to the many examples of "mysteries" that are cited in the positive sense, there are several interesting statements about "mysteries of transgression" (רזי פשע) or "mysteries of Belial" (רזי בליעל). Such language corresponds closely with the kind of dualistic thought prevalent in the Qumran Scrolls,[4] and it is perhaps significant that the sectarian texts in which dualism is especially highlighted also contain "mystery" language. This "cosmic dualism" finds its counterpart in the social (or ethical) dualism that underlines the strict delineation between the elect and the wicked.[5] Such social dualism is in turn related to the rhetoric and practices of concealment among the Yaḥad. In my view, while we may profit from the idea that Qumran dualism is indebted in part to Persian or Greek influences, the most immediate roots of its association with mystery language can be found in Isaiah, 1 Enoch, and the book of Daniel.

From a statistical point of view, "mystery" language is rather prominent in the Qumran Scrolls, comparable in frequency to other characteristically sectarian expressions (or to words and concepts that appear to have been especially important to the Yaḥad).[6] The word רז occurs at least 140 times in at least twenty-eight different non-biblical compositions, including all of the major sectarian texts and many of the otherwise well-attested compositions. While we cannot make too much

---

[4] As both Devorah Dimant ("Qumran Sectarian Literature," 533–34) and Shaul Shaked ("Qumran and Iran," 433–34) are careful to note, the word "dualism" can be misleading insofar as it may imply the opposition of good and evil forces that are equal in scope or power, as in the Zoroastrian system—which is manifestly not the sense of "dualism" found in the Qumran texts.

[5] Often these forms of dualism are called "cosmic dualism" and "ethical" or "psychological dualism," respectively, though Dimant is correct to point out that both may be "understood as aspects of the same basic cosmic dualism, which have a necessary counterpart on the moral and psychological level" ("Qumran Sectarian Literature," 535). See also John G. Gammie, "Spatial and Ethical Dualism"; Peter von der Osten-Sacken, Gott und Belial: Traditions-geschichtliche Unter-suchungen zum Dualismus in den Texten aus Qumran (SUNT 6; Göttingen: Vandenhoeck & Ruprecht, 1969), 239–40.

[6] For example: גורל (111 times); משיח (30 times); בליעל (105 times); יחד (141 times); הון (109 times). These numbers are derived by a simple count of entries in the Dead Sea Scrolls Concordance: Martin Abegg et al, The Dead Sea Scrolls Concordance: The Non-Biblical Texts from Qumran (2 vols.; Leiden: Brill, 2003).

of the frequency of a given word—the evidence is fragmentary and therefore potentially misleading, some words are simply more common and useful than others, etc.—at the very least we can say that the word רז is an important term that relates to "the theological and metaphysical outlook of [the Yaḥad]," which itself is clearly linked in some important ways to the writings of *1 Enoch*, the book of Daniel, and other relevant texts.[7] While we find the word in compositions not limited to Qumran, in my view it is employed as "sectually explicit" language in the sectarian texts of the Yaḥad.[8]

EVOLUTION IN THE USE OF *SOD*—THE QUMRAN SCROLLS

Heinz-Josef Fabry sees an overall evolution in the use of סוד from the pre-exilic to the post-exilic periods: the Canaanite and Mesopotamian mythological elements were adopted by Israelite tradents and conformed to a more purely monotheistic framework in which "Yahweh becomes the monopotentate within a polytheistic council of the gods"; the possibility that human beings might belong to the heavenly council was opened up by the definition of its members (mostly prophets) as *qᵉḏôšîm* (1 Kgs 22:19–22; Isa 6, 40:1–8; Jer 23:18–22; Amos 3:7, etc.); and finally in the post-exilic period "every limitation is suspended, and Yahweh's throne council is democratized to the point that every person 'who fears Yahweh' is able to participate in his *sôḏ*" (Ps 25:14). During this latter period, the word סוד refers almost exclusively to the religious-cultic community centered in the Jerusalem temple (Pss 111:1; 55:15[14]); the

---

[7] Devorah Dimant, "The Qumran Manuscripts: Contents and Significance," in *Time to Prepare a Way in the Wilderness*. (ed. Devorah Dimant and Lawrence Schiffman; STDJ 16; Leiden: Brill, 1995), 27–28. Dimant lists words that reflect "terminology connected to the Qumran community," which itself includes several categories: (1) words that pertain to community organization (סרך, יחד, etc.); (2) words that reflect the community's history and circumstances (חלקות, מורה הצדק, etc.); (3) words that convey the community's theological/ metaphysical outlook (references to the spirits of light and darkness, רז, תעודה, etc.); and (4) words that deal with the particular exegesis of the community (פשר, etc.). Dimant rightly cautions that the third category is potentially problematic given that certain characteristics of such an "outlook" are shared by other texts that are not specific to the Yaḥad, such as *Jubilees, 1 Enoch*, and others (27–28). But this concern reflects perhaps an inordinately strict application of the rule that we may only count as sectarian those usages that are not found elsewhere. I think it is fruitful also to see how sectarian texts remake pre-existing usages into sectarian contexts.

[8] The term is Newsom's: "'Sectually Explicit' Language."

"council of the holy ones" is now not simply composed of the members of God's heavenly entourage, but is the cultic community assembled in the fear of God and the most upright conduct.[9]

Fabry's point is suggestive of an important development in Second Temple Jewish ideas: that the members of the cultic community ritually enact in the temple service the earthly liturgy that mirrors or participates in some way the activity in heaven. The participants are, in this respect, recipients of a special kind of knowledge grounded in the cultic experience itself. Fabry goes on:

> Not only can one evaluate the notion of Yahweh's throne council as a hermeneutical model addressing the specific quality of the *sôd* congregation, one can also attribute at least a remnant perspective to its etymological connotation in the abstract meaning "secret." A confluence of the two semantic levels, however, is first visibly actualized only in the esotericism of the Qumran community.[10]

This is another way of saying that a liturgical function of the word סוד gains in importance as (presumably temple-based) worship appropriates the idea of a heavenly congregation arrayed in service to the God of Israel, yet the valence of secrecy that derived from the restrictive nature of the סוד remained a latent meaning that could be deployed in certain circumstances. Perhaps we may see a connection here with the claim by the Chronicler that the activity of the levitical singers in the sanctuary was itself "prophecy" (1 Chron 25:1–8), which may reflect a post-exilic priestly co-option of prophetic authority whereby the exclusive claim of the prophet to gain access to the heavenly assembly is transferred to the worshiping community.[11] Fabry is correct that the cultic, temple-oriented understanding of סוד (among a few other meanings) can be found in the Qumran texts:

1QS 8:4–6

4 ... ולהתהלך עם כול ב( )מדת האמת ובתכון העת בהיות אלה בישראל
5 נכונה (ה)עצת היחד באמת (ל) *vacat* למע°ת עולם בית קודש לישראל
וסוד קודש (6) קודשים לאהרון ...[12] ·

---

[9] Fabry, "סוד," *TDOT* 12.175.

[10] Ibid., 176.

[11] See W. Schniedewind, *The Word of God in Transition: From Prophet to Exegete in the Second Temple Period* (JSOTSup 197; Sheffield: Sheffield Academic Press, 1995), 174–88.

[12] Text from Schofield, *From Quman to the Yaḥad*, appendix.

4 They are to walk with all by the standard of truth and the measure of
   the age. When these men come to be in Israel,
5 the assembly of the Yaḥad will be established in truth *vacat* an eternal
   planting, a holy house [temple] for Israel, and a council of the holy of
6 holies to Aaron. ...

1QHᵃ 19:7–8

7 [הבינ]ותני בסוד אמתכה ותשכילני במעשי פלאכה ותתן מפי הודות ובלשוני
8 [תהל]ה ומזל שפתי במכון רנה ...

7 [You have enlighten]ed me in the council of your truth, and you have
   given me insight into your works of wonder. You put praises in my
   mouth, and on my tongue
8 [a psal]m; the utterance of my lips is at the foundation of exaltation. ...

It is worth noting that these texts also associate being in the סוד with the
acquisition of wisdom, true knowledge, and enlightenment. Here the
social connotation of a defined circle of people "in the know" is
combined with the religious imagery of temple worship, imagery that is
also well-known from later Jewish mystical texts (e.g. Heikhalot
literature). Several Qumran texts are even more explicit about this
imagery. For example, in a text widely thought to be part of the annual
covenant renewal ceremony among the Yaḥad,[13] there is what appears to
be a description of the heavenly sanctuary, which is itself a mirror of the
earthly temple:

4QBerakhotᵃ (4Q286) 1ii2–8

2 ... ומרכבות כבודכה כרוביהמה ואופניהמה וכול סודי[המה]
3 מוס[י]י אש ושביבי נוגה וזהרי הוד נה[ור]י אורים ומאורי פלא
4 [הו]ד והדר ורום כבוד סוד קודש ומק[ור ז]והר ורום תפארת פ[לא]
5 [הוד]ות ומקוה גבורות הדר תשבוחות וגדול נוראות ורפאו[ת -- [
6 ומעשי פלאים סוד חוכמא ותבנית דעה ומקור מבינה[14] מקור ערמה
7 ועצת קודש וסוד אמת אוצר שכל מבני צדק ומכוני יוש[ר רב]
8 חסדים וענות טוב וחסדי אמת ורחמי עולמים[15]

---

[13] See Bilhah Nitzan, "4QBerakhot (4Q286–90): A Preliminary Report," in
*New Qumran Texts and Studies: Proceedings of the First Meeting of the International
Organization for Qumran Studies*, (ed. George J. Brooke and Florentino García
Martínez; STDJ 15; Leiden: Brill, 1994), 53–71.

[14] There is a cancellation dot over the *mem*; according to Bilhah Nitzan, "the
scribe intended to write ומקור בינה" (DJD 11:12).

2 ... and chariots of your glory, with their cherubim and their wheels
  and all [their] councils:

3 their bases of fire, flames of brightness, illuminations of splendor,
  luminescent lights, luminaries of wonder,

4 splendor and majesty, glorious height, holy council and [sh]ining
  fou[nt], height of beauty and wonder,

5 [prais]es, a reservoir of powers, a majesty of glorifications, a greatness
  of fears and heali[ngs --]

6 works of wonder, a council[16] of wisdom, a pattern of knowledge, a
  fount of understanding, a fount of prudence,

7 a holy assembly, a council of truth, a storehouse of insight, structures
  of righteousness, foundations of uprightness, greatness

8 of mercies, genuine humility, mercies of truth, and acts of everlasting
  compassion.

This text shows some affinity with another important liturgical text from
Qumran, the *Songs of the Sabbath Sacrifice*, in which סוד is also used in a
way that captures the various levels of its meaning. In this text, the
conjunction of the heavenly and earthly temples is clear, and while it is
not explicit that the human worshipers are part of the heavenly סוד, one
may infer as much from the overall context of the text, from fragmentary
references such as [-- אל]ים בסוד כבודו "his glory in the council of the
heavenly beings," and from passages like the following:

4QShir^d (4Q403) 1 ii 18–20

18 למשכיל שיר עולת השבת השמינית בשלושה ועֹ[שרים לחודש השני הללו
   לאלוהי כול מ -- כול קדושיֹ]

19 עולמים שניים בכוהני קורב סוד שני במעוץ פלא בשבע[-- בכול ידועיֹ]

20 עולמים ורוממוהו ראשי נשיאים במנה פלאיו הללוֹ] לאל אלוהים שבע
   כהונת קורבו -- [

18 For the Instructor: song of the sacrifice for the eighth Sabbath, on the
   tw[enty-]third [of the second month. Praise the God of all ... all who
   are holy

19 forever, the second ones among the priests who draw near,[17] the

---

[15] The text continues here with reference to רזי פאלים "mysteries of
wonders/wondrous mysteries," a passage we will discuss in detail below .

[16] Here and in line 7 Nitzan translates סוד to "foundation," based on
analogy with 1QH^a 2:10 and 5:26, whereas she renders the plural in line 2 as
"councils" (DJD 11:13).

[17] Carol Newsom translates the phrase בכוהני קורב as "priests of the inner
sanctum" (DJD 11:282); also v. 20.

second council in the wondrous abode among the seven [… among all those who know]

20 eternal things. Exalt him, leaders of princes, among (or with) the portion of his wonders. Praise the [God of gods, the seven priesthoods who are near him …].

Whether סוד is used explicitly to connote secrecy or something like "mystery" in the Qumran Scrolls is another matter. סוד does not often carry the overt tone of secrecy in Qumran texts, but insofar as it tends to denote a restricted human colloquy we might assume that some measure of secrecy is implied. But apart from a couple instances in which סוד and רז are used in parallel with one another, the two terms often have distinct valences and semantic ranges in most of the Qumran texts.

נסתרות—"HIDDEN THINGS"

In a famous passage, the book of Deuteronomy proclaims that "the secret things (הנסתרת) belong to the LORD our God, but the revealed things (הנגלת) belong to us and to our children forever, to observe all the words of this law" (Deut 29:29). This passage relates itself explicitly to the *torah* which Moses himself is depicted as delivering (התורה הזאת), making the distinction, apparently, between aspects of *torah* that cannot be known (they belong to the LORD) and those that are to be promulgated and passed down from one generation to another. While the passage suggests implicitly that one ought not inquire about those hidden matters, the very distinction indicates a Deuteronomic awareness of the potential for "reading beyond the text"—which Deuteronomy as a whole apparently strives to discourage. Indeed, the passage occurs in the middle of a discourse on the curses that will visit wayward generations when they fail to uphold the covenant, and thus the implication is clear: the only thing one needs to know about *torah*—and thus about divine purposes—has been made public, and attending to hidden matters does not curry divine favor.

By the time the book of Daniel was compiled, however, its authors could state, perhaps in direct contradiction of the Deuteronomic theology, that God "*reveals* deep and hidden things (גלא עמיקתא ומסתרתא)" (Dan 2:22), and indeed one of the basic points of the court tales in Daniel is that God reveals "mysteries" (רזין) to worthy recipients such as Daniel himself. This theme is of course a central tenet of apocalyptic literature in general, and finds important analogs in the Qumran Scrolls.

The juxtaposition of concealment and revelation is a prevalent feature of Qumran sectarian texts, and for several decades scholars have written about the development of ideas regarding הנסתרת and הנגלת in Jewish literature of the late Second Temple period in general. In his important monograph on sectarian *halakhah* at Qumran, Lawrence Schiffman argued that these two rubrics were used to classify sectarian *halakhah* on the one hand (הנסתרות) and laws given to all Israel on the other (הנגלות). The hidden things were thus equivalent to those matters "found out" (מצא, דרש, etc.) by the sect and its leaders by a process of intensive study; they represent "the correct legal interpretations known only to the sect."[18]

Subsequent studies have tended to confirm or to nuance Schiffman's pioneering work, focusing as well on the relationship between text, interpretation (or "exegesis"), and the process of generating new standards of normativity in the face of changing circumstances (*halakhah*).[19] There is general agreement that while the נסתרות refer in part to things hidden "in" the law (and therefore they need to be discovered by a process of inspired inquiry), this rubric also suggests that the hidden matters were themselves guarded by the sect from the rest of Judean society.

Going beyond this basic distinction, Paul Heger also argues that the category נסתרות had two important dimensions or applications: on the one hand were the halakhic norms known by the sect as a whole, and on the other hand were those things known only by the Maskil—knowledge that was guarded even from other members of the community.[20] While this point may remain a matter of some speculation, what is clear from the use of נסתרות in the Scrolls is that it does pertain especially to legal matters, and that even while the rhetoric of concealment and disclosure attends both terms, there is a distinction to be made between נסתרות and רז. The latter term had a wider application, denoting not only legal rulings but also knowledge of history and of the cosmos as a whole.

---

[18] Lawrence Schiffman, *The Halakhah at Qumran* (SJLA 16; Leiden: Brill, 1975), 23.

[19] See especially Aharon Shemesh and Cana Werman, "Hidden Things and Their Revelation," *RevQ* 18 (1998): 409–27; Paul Heger, "The Development of Qumran Law: *Nistarot, Niglot*, and the Issue of 'Contemporization,'" *RevQ* 23 (2007): 167–206; cf. Israel Knohl, "נגלות ונסתרות—Revealed and Hidden Torah," *JQR* 85 (1994): 103–108.

[20] Heger, "The Development of Qumran Law."

"MYSTERIES OF WONDER"

Judging by the use of the root פלא in the Qumran texts, and the apparent willingness to contemplate the "mysteries of wonder," members of the Yaḥad seem not to have internalized the psalmist's confession: "I do not aspire to great things, or to wonders that are beyond me (לא־הלכתי בגדלות ובנפלאות ממני)" (Ps 131:1). One of the most prominent constructs with רז in Qumran texts is with some form of the word פלא, or "wonder." There are several different possibilities for understanding how this term functions. It is often translated as "wonderful mysteries," a translation that captures neither the variability in usage nor the fact that there are several grammatical possibilities for understanding the phrase.[21] "Wonderful mysteries" is analogous to the substantive + attributive adjective formation, but this translation—while perhaps warranted grammatically—does not always represent the best semantic possibility for the phrase. A more straightforward reading of the construct-genitive might be "mysteries of wonder," wherein פלא (in a few different grammatical forms) is taken to be not simply a modifier of רז but is a thing in and of itself—it is a "wonder."

The meaning of פלא in biblical texts can throw some light on its use in construct with רז. The former is most often found in narratives or poetic texts (especially psalms) that describe God's dealings with his people, and, more specifically, God's acts of judgment and redemption. Such acts of God were evidently understood to be the "wonders" themselves.[22] As Rainer Albertz states,

---

[21] See for example the edition of Florentino García Martínez, *The Dead Sea Scrolls Translated: The Qumran Texts in English* (trans. Wilfred G. E. Watson; 2nd ed.; Leiden: Brill, 1996).

[22] See Conrad, "פלא, plʾ," *TDOT* 11.533–46. Conrad asserts that "the word group *pālāʾ* does not describe the act or effect as such, but rather qualifies it as transcending human knowledge or power. In other words, we must distinguish between the basic meaning and its application to specific subjects. The former requires a stative definition such as 'be inscrutable, incredible.' … Primarily, then, an observation is made concerning a line that human beings cannot cross but that can be crossed from the other side." It strikes me that this distinction is rather unnecessary: in its nominal or participial forms, פלא nearly always refers to the acts of God and not the acts of human beings; it therefore seems redundant to insist that "the word group thus also marks the contrast between the finitude of what is possible on one side of the line and the infinite range of what is possible on the other side" (535). In any case, Conrad later seems to endorse the view that this word group does in fact refer to the very acts of God themselves:

The language of *pele'* is the language of joyous reaction (praise). The wonder, the astonishment, includes the recognition of the limits of one's own power to conceptualize and comprehend. Since the *pele'* event signifies a transcendence of customary, normal expectations, it is predominantly understood as God's activity.[23]

There are two forms in which the word occurs with this meaning: in the *niphal* feminine plural participial form (נפלאות) and in the nominal singular or plural (פלא or פלאים / פלאות). The semantic differences among these different forms appear to be somewhat negligible, though the former is more common in the biblical corpus.[24] It is possible that in the Qumran non-biblical texts there is a more clear distinction between the two basic forms. The following are a few specific examples of both forms; these are more or less representative of the Hebrew Bible as a whole, though a few exceptions will be noted.

Exodus 3:20:

ושלחתי את־ידי והכיתי את־מצרים בכל נפלאתי אשר אעשה בקרבו ואחרי־כן
ישלח אתכם

So I will stretch out My hand and smite Egypt with all my wonders which I will work in his midst; after that [Pharaoh] will let you go.

Joshua 3:5:

ויאמר יהושע אל־העם התקדשו כי מחר יעשה יהוה בקרבכם נפלאות

And Joshua said to the people, "Purify yourselves, for tomorrow the Lord will perform wonders in your midst."

---

on page 540 he writes that "the nominalized ptcp. *niplā'ot* refers to mighty acts of God that are humanly inexplicable and indescribable, but are experienced as extremely efficacious events that shape human lives." The participial form נפלאות is used solely with nominalized connotations, and always refers to the activity of God.

[23] "*pele'*," *TLOT* 2.932.

[24] The participial form occurs only in the plural. This form occurs in the following texts (orthography varies between *plene* and *defectiva*): Exod 3:20, 34:10; Judg 6:13; Josh 3:5; Jer 21:2; Mic 7:15; Pss 9:2, 26:7, 40:6, 71:17, 72:18, 75:2, 78:4, 78:11, 78:32, 86:10, 96:3, 98:1, 105:2, 105:5, 106:7, 107:8, 107:15, 107:21, 107:24, 107:31, 111:4, 119:18, 119:27, 119:129, 131:1, 136:4, 139:14

1 Chronicles 16:8–9, 12–13:

8 הודו ליהוה קראו בשמו הודיעו בעמים עלילתיו
9 שירו לו זמרו־לו שיחו בכל־נפלאתיו ...
12 זכרו נפלאתיו אשר עשה מפתיו ומשפטי־פיהו
13 זרע ישראל עבדו בני יעקב בחיריו

8 Praise the Lord; call on his name; make known His deeds among the peoples.

9 Sing to Him; make music to Him; muse upon all His wonders. ...

12 Remember His wonders that He has done—His portents and the judgments He has pronounced,

13 seed of Israel, His servant, descendents of Jacob, His chosen ones.

Psalm 77:12–16

12 אזכיר [אזכור] מעללי־יה כי־אזכרה מקדם פלאך
13 והגיתי בכל־פעלך ובעלילותיך אשיחה
14 אלהים בקדש דרכך מי־אל גדול כאלהים
15 אתה האל עשה פלא הודעת בעמים עזך
16 גאלת בזרוע עמך בני־יעקב ויוסף סלה

12 I recall the deeds of the Lord; I recall Your wonder(s) of old.

13 I recount all Your works, and I speak of Your acts.

14 God, Your ways are holiness—what god is as great as God?

15 You are the God who works by wonder(s). You have made Your strength known among the peoples.

16 By Your arm You redeemed Your people, the children of Jacob and Joseph. Selah.

It is clear from these few examples that a "wonder," as an act of judgment or deliverance, can also be an act of war in the Hebrew Bible. In fact, with few exceptions the word has martial connotations, most often with respect to the activity of God on behalf of Israel. It is interesting that several occurrences of the word פלא are in older texts that share with other ancient Near Eastern traditions the themes of cosmic warfare (Pss 77, 89), and yet there appears to be no direct semantic parallel to this usage in non-biblical texts.[25] Thus while it is possible that, in terms of its ancient associations, the "wonders" of God are tied to the idea of a primordial victory over celestial powers, the use of פלא in the Hebrew Bible is restricted to the results of God's work as

---

[25] The etymology of פלא is uncertain, and its only reliable cognates are in later languages like Syriac and Arabic.

they pertain to the fate of Israel within the framework of redemption history. In the theology and cosmology of ancient Near Eastern cultures in general, however, this theme of divine warfare was also inextricably linked to ideas about the creation of the heavens and the earth (for example, the *Enuma Elish* and the *Baal Cycle*). Though this tendency is subverted in the creation stories of Genesis in order to present a God who creates by simple divine prerogative rather than by some primordial struggle, the association of the root פלא with creation imagery is evident in both the Hebrew Bible and in the Qumran Scrolls.

This association is presented most vividly in the book of Job, where the reader is challenged to come to terms with the knowledge that God does marvelous things that humans cannot comprehend. According to the book as a whole, the work of God in the making and sustaining of creation is fathomless and the proper response to it is solely awe and wonder (esp. Job 37–41; cf. Jer 32:17). The wonderful things God does in creation are called נפלאות and are considered to be part of the inscrutable ways of God. The book of Job insists upon the limits of human knowledge as it pertains to the will of God, and underscores the radical discontinuity between the conditioned and compromised nature of the human realm and the majestic life of divine autonomy (esp. Job 37–38). After the lengthy series of rhetorical questions God poses to Job about the wonders of creation, Job capitulates and says meekly, "I have uttered what I did not understand, things too wonderful for me, (which) I did not know" ולא אבין נפלאות ממני ולא אדע (Job 42:3).[26]

The association between wisdom, creation, and cosmology is apparent here, and as Albertz writes,

> Theological wisdom links the astounded observation of nature with the hymnic praise of God's wondrous acts. Only here do God's wonders lose their association with the historical acts of deliverance and are seen in his mysterious activity in "natural processes" and in the amazing, wise arrangement of his creation.[27]

As we will see in the following pages, this understanding of "wonders" as they pertain to knowledge of creation is also present in the Qumran Scrolls. Indeed, in the *Hodayot*, for example, the hymnist often meditates on the "wonders" of creation and asks about himself, "But I, a creature of

---

[26] Compare Prov 30:18; Zech 8:6.
[27] Albertz, *"pele'*," 935; see also Gerhard von Rad, *Old Testament Theology*, 1.449.

clay, what am I? Mixed with water, like whom should I be considered? What is my strength?" (1QHª 11:23–24).

In the book of Daniel, on the other hand, the salvific "wonders" of God made an important transition from describing the works of the past, and taking on eschatological dimensions began also to point forward to God's future acts of deliverance.[28] In this historiologic reorientation, the hymnic recollection of God's historic acts in a cultic setting was perhaps translated to a mantic-wisdom setting by which knowledge of a future deliverance could be mediated:

Daniel 12:5–7

5 וראיתי אני דניאל והנה שנים אחרים עמדים אחד הנה לשפת היאר ואחד
הנה לשפת היאר 6 ויאמר לאיש לבוש הבדים אשר ממעל למימי היאר עד־
מתי קץ הפלאות[29] 7 ואשמע את־האיש לבוש הבדים אשר ממעל למימי
היאר וירם ימינו ושמאלו אל־השמים וישבע בחי העולם כי למועד מועדים
וחצי וככלות נפץ יד־עם־קדש תכלינה כל־אלה

> 5 Then I, Daniel, looked and saw two others standing, one on one bank of the river, the other on the other bank of the river. 6 One said to the man clothed in linen, who was above the water of the river, "How long until the end of (these) wonders?" 7 Then I heard the man dressed in linen, who was above the water of the river, swear by the Ever-Living One as he lifted his right hand and his left hand to heaven: "For a time, times, and half a time; and when the breaking of the power of the holy people comes to an end, then shall all these things be fulfilled."

If this use of פלאות is consistent with its occurrence in Dan 8:24 and 11:36—which seems likely—these "wonders" appear to be a reference not directly to the work of God, but to that of Antiochus Epiphanes IV. Given the context and the presumed outcome of the events in the background of the passage, it is certainly possible that פלאות here refers to the events that take place within the framework of the overall triumph of God over Israel's enemies. The most straight-forward conclusion, however, is that here פלאות should be read not as the "wonders" of God, but as the "awful things" to be done by Antiochus as part of the

---

[28] The root פלא is not attested in the Aramaic sections of Daniel (or in Biblical Aramaic in general); instead the word תמה is employed to denote a similar idea (Dan 3:33; 6:28).

[29] Symmachus omits "wonders." Theodotion: Ἕως πότε τὸ πέρας ὧν εἴρηκας τῶν θαυμασίων; Old Greek: Πότε οὖν συντέλεια ὧν εἴρηκας μοι τῶν θαυμαστῶν καὶ ὁ καθαρισμὸς τούτων.

unfolding eschatological drama.[30] Nevertheless, at least one ancient Greek translator understood this to be part of a larger process by which God redeems his people, adding to these "awful things" the phrase "and their purification" (καὶ ὁ καθαρισμὸς—Old Greek).

An eschatological dimension of "wonders" is reflected also in some Qumran texts such as the *War Rule* and some of the hymns from the *Hodayot*. As Conrad points out, it is only rarely that the Scrolls "mention God's mighty acts in the early history of Israel (1QM 11:9; cf. 11:1–10). What is critical is instead God's work in the community itself, since only within it does true salvation begin; for it is there that God mysteriously and unfathomably takes away sin and guilt."[31] While this latter statement may well be true, it may obscure the degree to which the Yaḥad's eschatological hope entailed real, historical and physical deliverance.

There is a variation on the use of פלא in the Hebrew Bible that is not reflected in the Qumran Scrolls. In Isa 29:14 the author employs the term to refer not to Israel's deliverance but to God's judgment of Israel itself. It is not clear in the passage, however, just what the threat might entail: because of Israel's unfaithfulness of heart, God will cause the people to marvel at his wondrous works against them.

Isaiah 29:11–14

11 ותהי לכם חזות הכל כדברי הספר החתום אשר־יתנו אתו אל־יודע הספר
לאמר קרא נא־זה ואמר לא אוכל כי חתום הוא
12 ונתן הספר על אשר לא־ידע ספר לאמר קרא נא־זה ואמר לא ידעתי ספר
13 ויאמר אדני יען כי נגש העם הזה בפיו ובשפתיו כבדוני ולבו רחק ממני
ותהי יראתם אתי מצות אנשים מלמדה
14 לכן הנני יוסף להפליא את־העם־הזה הפלא ופלא ואבדה חכמת חכמיו
ובינת נבניו תסתתר

11 The vision of all these things has become for you like the words of a sealed book. When they hand it to one who knows how to read saying, "Read this," he replies, "I can't, for it is sealed."

12 When they hand the book to one who cannot read saying, "Read this," he replies, "I don't know how to read."

13 The Lord says: Because this people approach me with their mouths and honor me with their lips, while their hearts are far from me, and their reverence for me is a human commandment, learnt by rote,

---

[30] See for example Collins, *Daniel*, 369.

[31] Conrad, "פלא, *plʾ*," 545.

14 I will perform yet more strange and wonderful things with this
people; the wisdom of their sages shall vanish, and the discernment
of their knowing ones shall disappear.[32]

It is interesting that this passage is part of a broader statement about the
bafflement of the people as a part of the plan of judgment and
redemption. God will make his ways hidden before revealing them at a
later time. Those who might have read the signs are foreclosed any
understanding—they can no longer read, for "the book" has been sealed
to them.[33] In this passage the object of the "wonder" that God will work
is transferred from Israel's enemies to Israel itself—not all Israel but only
those who are not given to proper understanding. The passage is yet
another reflection of the growing tendency toward sectarianism in post-
exilic Judaism, and highlights the motif of special knowledge given to
the elect found so prominently during this period.[34]

In the Qumran Scrolls, the vast majority of the occurrences of פלא (in
any form) are found in the Hodayot and in the Songs of the Sabbath
Sacrifice, as well as other important liturgical and hymnic texts—a fact
which reflects similar preponderance of the term in the Psalms and
related compositions from the Hebrew Bible.[35] The simplest explanation
for both of these observations is that the term has primarily poetic uses,
and that the language of "wonder" most aptly belongs in a hymnic or
laudatory setting. The rehearsal of God's activity on behalf of Israel, after
all, would have been proper to either a cultic or a prayer setting in which
such remembrances were collectively and ritually called to mind. In
addition, these kinds of poetic/hymnic texts often deal with matters
pertaining to creation and cosmology, and thus the "wonders" could
also refer to the particular works of God in creating and sustaining the

---

[32] Translation is from Blenkinsopp, Isaiah 1–39, 403.

[33] For additional treatment of this passage as it pertains to Mysteries
(especially 4Q300), see my "'Riddled' with Guilt"; see also below in chapter 5.

[34] This passage has been treated elsewhere by Blenkinsopp, often in
conjunction with other texts such as Isa 8, Dan 12, and key Qumran texts. See
especially his Opening the Sealed Book, 1–27.

[35] While the participial form is more common than the nominal form in the
Hebrew Bible, the opposite is the case in the Qumran Scrolls, where the nominal
form predominates by a rather large margin. It is not clear what this discrepancy
might suggest, and it probably unwise to overinterpret the observation. One
point worth noting, however, is that with the exception of the Hodayot there is
very little overlap in the texts that employ the word; the various scribes or
authors seem to prefer one or the other form.

world, motifs which often connect in varying degrees of directness with ideas about the heavenly and earthly temples in some Qumran texts.

Both aspects of God's works of "wonder"—salvation and creation— are proper to the textual and presumed social setting of many of the Qumran compositions, and it is perhaps these things that the psalmist of the *Hodayot* has in mind when he writes that "I give thanks, Lord, according to the greatness of your strength and the abundance of your wonders [נפלאותיך] from eternity and for eternity [מעולם ועד עולם]" (1QHᵃ 6:23). The hymnist continually underscores his earthly, lowly nature ("I am but dust"), but he also regularly claims to know about the "wonders" God has taught him despite his unimpressive station vis-à-vis the transcendent deity. "And I, what am I that you have taught me the basis of your truth, and have instructed me in your works of wonder?" (1QHᵃ 19:3; cf. 1QS 11:17–22).

For the author(s) of the *Hodayot*, the acts of creation and deliverance are made manifest simultaneously in his inner, psychological landscape (or are intended to be made so in the mind of the reader, depending upon the use to which a given psalm may have been put). The thanksgiving is a heartfelt and natural expression of the internal conviction that God "saves" both in fashioning the creation and bringing it to its ultimate destination. Such a sentiment is uttered also in the prayer known as *Barkhi Nafshi*: "Bless, my soul, the Lord for all his wonders [נפלאותיו], forever. And blessed be his name, because he has saved the soul of the poor" (4Q434 1 i 1). Thus, in terms of knowledge of the נפלאות, there is an apparent and continuous counterposition of both their utter remove from the realm of the knowable and their intelligibility in the mind of the speaker(s).

In other texts one finds similar connotations as in the *Hodayot*. For example, 4QTanhumim (4Q176)[36] exhorts God to follow through on his promise of deliverance and invokes the language of Isaiah 40: "Perform your wonder [פלאכה], do your people justice and … […] your temple … Argue with kingdoms over the blood of […] Jerusalem. See the corpses of your priests […] there is no one to bury them. And from the book of

---

[36] As John Strugnell pointed out in his famous book-length recension of DJD V ("Notes en marge du Volume V des <<Discoveries in the Judaean Desert of Jordan>>," *RevQ* 7 [1970]: 229), "J. M. Allegro nous présente quelques grands fragments d'un ouvrage qu'il appelle <<*Tanhûmîm*>>, un titre cependant qu'on pourrait hésiter à appliquer à *tout* l'ouvrage." In other words, though the text cites from Isaiah's "words of consolation," the other passages in the composition "sont plus difficiles à caractériser."

Isaiah [quotes Isa 40:1-5]" (4Q176 1–2 i 1–4).[37] In this prayer text, the eschatological dimensions of God's "wonders" are brought to bear in a work that imagines the restoration (or perhaps reconsecration) of the temple, Jerusalem, and the priesthood, through an extended exegetical meditation on select passages from Isaiah.[38] Though the text is fragmentary and its reconstruction controversial,[39] it is possible that toward the end of the extant portions of the composition the predestinarian cosmology found in other sectarian texts emerges:

> Because he created every [spirit] of the eternal [generation]s, and [according to] his judgment [he established] the paths of them all. The ear[th] he cre[ated with] his [rig]ht (hand) before they existed, and he con[tinually superv]ises everything th[ere is in it. And in] his mystery (וברזו) he causes the lot (גורל) to fall on man in order to give [...].

In this text, then, the "wonders" of God's creation and deliverance of humanity are both seen as part of God's "mystery," by which the leaders of the Yaḥad are able to assess the spirits of the candidates for entrance into the community.[40] The way in which this idea functions within the broad corpus of the Qumran Scrolls will be taken up again in chapter 5.

Given these preliminary considerations about the use of פלא in the Qumran Scrolls, we may now turn to the רז פלא construct. We have seen that the word פלא most often denotes a "wonder" that is an act of God on behalf of a subject, or an act of God in creation. It is usually used to recount some moment of deliverance (for Israel) or judgment (against the nations) in the past, the memory of which can be invoked toward the hope of similar acts in the future. In other words, it is a term of salvation—with respect to both past and future—and as such it plays an important role in the vocabulary of redemption in the Qumran Scrolls. But in some cases, as we have seen, the "wonder" is a phenomenon of creation whose ultimate explanation or understanding is beyond the ken of the human observer.

---

[37] The imagery in this passage also seems to reflect or draw upon Ps 79:2–3 (cf. 1 Macc 7:17). Elsewhere (1QS 8:14–15), the "preparing the way of the ****" is likened to studying the law "in order to act in compliance with all that has been revealed from age to age."

[38] C. D. Stanley, "The Importance of 4QTanḥumim (4Q176)," *RevQ* 15 (1992): 569–82.

[39] The reconstruction used here essentially follows the one offered by Strugnell ("Notes en marge," 234).

[40] Compare, for example, 1QS 3:13ff.

In some cases it may appear that רז and פלא are roughly synony-
mous, especially when it comes to categories of special knowledge
attained by members of the community of the elect. Again, as Conrad
demonstrates, the noun פלא

> emphasizes on the one hand that human beings cannot understand the
> mighty acts of God by their own power (1QHᵃ 7:32). On the other hand,
> it attests that God has nevertheless given understanding of them to
> those who belong to the community, thus incorporating them into the
> salvation bestowed on the community (1QHᵃ 11:4; niplāʾôṯ, 10:4).[41]

To be sure, in terms of the interplay between the hidden and manifest
dimensions of God's overall plan for creation, there is some degree of
parallel meaning. Nevertheless, in light of the frequent combination of
the two words in a construct chain, they must also be able to signify
different referents. While a רז and a פלא may display similar aspects,
their combination must signal a connotation of a different kind.

As Craig Evans has noted, the notion of God's "wonders" might also
reflect a revelatory context in some Qumran texts.[42] All the passages
which he includes in this category also make reference to "mystery"
(though there are certainly more examples than he lists in his article),
and it is perhaps this association he has in mind—though he is not
explicit about it. In other words, it is not the "wonder" itself that is
revelatory, but the "mystery of wonder," and it is revelatory only insofar
as there is a connotation of revelation that often accompanies notions of
"mystery" in Jewish texts of the period.[43] As noted above, the
epistemological nature of a "wonder" is that while its effects can be
known, its causes often are understood to remain hidden in the "mind"
of God unless they are revealed to the knower.

While the particular combination of רז and פלא in the Qumran
Scrolls attests to the notion that there are hidden things that God reveals,
the "mysteries of wonder" are also thought to be efficacious in some
way—as seen most clearly in the historical prologue of the *Damascus
Document*. This text presents a sweeping overview of the long series of
Israel's failures to live up to the demands of the covenant, culminating in
the argument that the successive stages of Israel's covenantal life reach

---

[41] Conrad, "פלא, plʾ," 545.

[42] Craig A. Evans, "A Note on the 'First-Born Son' of 4Q369," *DSD* 2 (1995):
196.

[43] See especially Bockmuehl, *Revelation and Mystery*.

their apogee in the community of the Damascus Covenant, those who inhabit the "safe home in Israel" (CD 3:19). The whole history of Israel is collapsed into a story of God's repeated preservation of the covenant relationship, which is concentrated into an ever smaller and more consecrated group of people who inherit the mantle of election. All of this is accomplished in the "mysteries of [God's] wonder":

CD 3:12–20:

12 ... ובמחזיקים במצות אל
13 אשר נותרו מהם הקים אל את בריתו לישראל עד עולם לגלות
14 להם נסתרות אשר תעו בם בם כל ישראל [--] שבתות קדשו ומועדי
15 כבודו עידות צדקו ודרכי אמתו וחפצי רצונו אשר יעשה
16 האדם והיה בהם [--] פתח לפניהם ויחפרו באר למים רבים
17 ומואסיהם לא יהיה והם התגוללו בפשע אנוש ובדרכי נדה
18 ויאמרו כי לנו היא ואל ברזי פלאו כפר בעד עונם וישא לפשעם
19 ויבן להם בית נאמן בישראל אשר לא עמד כמהו למלפנים ועד
20 הנה המחזיקים בו לחיי נצח וכל כבוד אדם להם הוא

12 ... And when they held firm to the commandments of God—

13 those who yet remained—God held firm his covenant with Israel forever, revealing

14 to them hidden things in which all Israel had erred [...] his holy Sabbaths, his glorious festivals,

15 his righteous laws, his true ways, the delights of his will which humanity should practice,

16 so to live by them [...] he disclosed [these things] to them and they dug a well of plentiful water;

17 and whoever spurns them will not live. But they had defiled themselves with human sin and unclean paths,

18 and they said, "This is ours." But God, in the mysteries of his wonder, atoned for their iniquity and pardoned their sin.

19 And he built for them a safe home in Israel, such as there has not been since ancient times, not even until

20 now. Those who remained steadfast in it will acquire eternal life, and all the glory of Adam is for them.

These "mysteries of wonder" were apparently known to the leadership of the sect, and were passed on to "those who who choose the path." This was, it seems, primarily the job of the Maskil (משכיל), who was "to lead them with knowledge and in this way teach them the mysteries of wonder and of truth (להשכילם ברזי פלא ואמת) in the midst of the men of the community, so that they walk perfectly, one with another, in all that has been revealed to them" (1QS 9:18–19). Similarly, the psalmist of the *Hodayot* proclaims that God has "set me like a banner for the elect of justice, like a banner for the elect of justice, like a mediator of knowledge of the mysteries of wonder (ומליץ דעת ברזי פלא)" (1QH[a] 10:13).[44]

It is quite possible in view of these passages that the "wonder" here envisioned is salvific in a way that is different in at least one respect from God's wondrous works of old. The "mysteries of wonder" might here refer not only to the enactment of some miraculous feat of physical deliverance, but to the provision of additional revelation which itself was salvific insofar as it allowed for the continuation of the covenant in the face of ongoing iniquity. In other words, it is the special, esoteric knowledge of the "true" meaning and scope of revelation that is the "wonder," and it provides for the deliverance of those who inhabit the "safe home in Israel." Although this seems to be the direction in which column 3 of the *Damascus Document* is moving, this possibility should not eclipse the equally likely expectation of a natural, physical deliverance of the community from those it understood to be its "earthly" foes.[45]

In a different but related vein, the term רזי פלא may have yet another valence: it may refer to the "wondrous" aspects of a kind of mystical temple setting whose architecture accords with the structures of the created order. This notion can be detected to varying degrees in several different texts, all of them sectarian or closely related texts. For example, in the eighth song of the *Songs of the Sabbath Sacrifice*, there is a reference to the "seven mysteries of knowledge in the mystery of the wonder of the seven regions of the holy of holies (שבע רזי דעת ברז הפלא לשבעת גבולי קודש קדשים)."[46] This passages points rather clearly to the

---

[44] Compare 1QH[a] 12:27: "Through me you have enlightened the face of the Many, you have increased them, so that they are uncountable, for you have shown me the mysteries of your wonder." This passage goes on to declare that God has "strengthened the position" of the hymnist, and "worked wonders in the present of the Many on account of your glory, and to show your powerful acts to all living things" (1QH[a] 12:28–29).

[45] I do not intend to give the impression that I am collapsing the *Damascus Document* and the *Community Rule* into a single social context. I recognize that they reflect different historical moments and social arrangements, but I take them to express a relatively consistent ideology.

[46] 4Q403 1 ii 27.

notion that the "wonder" here imagined is associated with a temple-like setting.[47]

In another passage of the *Songs of the Sabbath Sacrifice* that is perhaps part of the second Song, there is a fragmentary mention of רזי נפלאותיו "mysteries of his wonders" followed by the statement that "they [the angels?] make known hidden things (נסתרות)" (4Q401 14 ii 6–8). As I will discuss further below, it may be possible to gain from this fragment an important insight into one function of "mystery" language in the sectarian scrolls. In a recent article on the *Songs of the Sabbath Sacrifice*, Judith Newman stated about this passage that

> it seems significant that *raz* with its esoteric connotations seems here to be entirely a possession of God and it is the priestly angels who are acquiring instruction in holy mysteries as a kind of specialized catechesis.[48]

In a similar passage in the *War Rule*, a worship scenario is presented as part of the eschatological vision; the "remnant of [God's] people" (1QM 14:8) will enact the true and cosmically ordained order of temple worship according to the "eternal edicts":

1QM 14:12–15

12 ואנו עם קודשכה במעשי אמתכה נהללה שמכה

13 ובגבורותיכה נרוממה תפ[ארתכה בכול] עתים ומועדי תעודות עולמים
עם מ[בו]א יונם ולילה

14 ומוצאי ערב ובוקר כיא גדולה מ[חשבת כבו]דכה ורזי נפלאותיכה
במרומי[כה] ל[הרי]ם לכה מעפר

15 ולהשפיל מאלים

12 We, your holy people, will praise your name for your works of truth,
13 for your mighty deeds we will extol [your splendor at every] moment

---

[47] See below for additional discussion of this passage and of the "mysteries of knowledge."

[48] Judith Newman, "Priestly Prophets at Qumran: Summoning Sinai through the Songs of the Sabbath Sacrifice," in *The Significance of Sinai: Traditions about Sinai and Divine Revelation in Judaism and Christianity* (ed. G. J. Brooke, H. Najman, and L. T. Stuckenbruck; TBN 13; Leiden: Brill, 2008), 49. Newman further suggests that "it seems that the appearance here and in the eighth song of *raz* without the verbal qualification [of *nihyeh*] would support the idea that the Songs portray the mystery's realized eschatological revelation to the angelic priests and their imitators through the liturgical practice on the first thirteen Sabbaths of the year" (48).

and (during) the fixed times of the eternal *tᵉʿûdôt*: with the coming of
day and night,

14 at the fall of evening and morning. For great is the plan of your glory,
and the "mysteries" of your wonders in your heights, that you might
raise up to yourself (those) from the dust

15 and bring low (those) among the divine beings.

The "mysteries" of God's wonders in this case pertain to a different
realm in which the covenanters may participate in proper worship
according to the correct reckoning of time.[49] Even more interesting is the
possibility that the phrase "the plan of your glory" (מחשבת כבודכה)
refers to a kind of (imagined) temple setting in which the human
participants meet the angelic retinue in a mutually transformational
worship experience.[50] This explanation would also render the rest of the
passage more intelligible, though it would not be without its difficulties.

The פלא-רז couplet in the Qumran Scrolls is perhaps an emblem of a
particular way of understanding past events within their broader salvific
context, and of projecting similar significance onto an interpretation of
the present and future acts of God. But in many of the Qumran texts, the
notions of judgment and deliverance also take on a particular, re-
concretized meaning. The "mysteries of wonder" therefore pertain to the
contemporary predicaments of the Yaḥad and their historical resolution
by God who is expected to perform acts of wonder on behalf of the "true
Israel." The "mysteries of wonder" also point to another kind of God's
work in the world, namely that of creating and sustaining the structures
of the created order. This intersection of eschatological and cosmological

---

[49] Compare 1QS 3:9–10: "May [one who enters the community], then, steady
his steps in order to walk with perfection on all the paths of God, as he has
decreed concerning the appointed times of his assemblies (כאשר צוה למועדי
תעודתיו) and not turn aside, either right or left. ..."

[50] כבוד is an important term in the Hebrew Bible, and has a number of
different applications. See Moshe Weinfeld, "כָּבוֹד *kābôḏ*," *TDOT* 7.22–38. The
association of God's "glory" with the tabernacle and the temple (or in other
words God's dwelling place) is well-known, and has its roots in ancient Near
Eastern traditions. In the Hebrew Bible this can be seen especially in the P source
of the Pentateuch, in Ezekiel, and in Isaiah (esp. chapters 4 and 6), where in some
passages it takes on eschatological connotations. In the Qumran Scrolls, nearly
half of the (almost 400) occurrences of the word are in the *Hodayot*, though it is
also common in the *War Rule*, the *Community Rule*, and in the *Songs of the Sabbath
Sacrifice*. As noted by Weinfeld, the occurrences in the *Sabbath Songs* "extend the
notion of *kābôḏ* found in Ezekiel" (37).

concerns in the phrase רזי פלא is a good example of how these ideas often come together in the thought world of the Yaḥad.

One other compelling aspect of this phrase is that the "mysteries of wonder" may have something to do with a temple setting, or at least with an ideal temple whose cosmic proportions are understood and experienced by the members (or at least the leaders) of the Yaḥad. There is in this way a mystical element to the "mysteries of wonder" that could have served as a locus for integrating ideas about the relationship between the cosmic order of creation, the march of historical time, and the ritual re-creation of space and time in the context of heavenly worship. It is possible, as Newman has argued, that this ritual enactment may itself have had a revelatory effect insofar as the participating priests would be rendered capable of new oracular performance.

"THE MYSTERY THAT IS TO BE"[51]

As noted in the Introduction, the phrase רז נהיה has garnered a considerable amount of attention and no shortage of speculation about its meaning. The phrase is not a very frequent one, but it is used in several important texts and appears to have been a significant point of reference for the group(s) associated with the Qumran Scrolls. It is especially prominent in the text now known as 4QInstruction, which has been the object of much scholarly investigation in recent years, and is also attested in *Mysteries* (1Q27/4Q299–300 [301?[52]]), and in the *Community Rule*.[53]

In his work on 4QInstruction, Matthew Goff correctly noted that the phrase רז נהיה is "difficult to interpret."[54] This difficulty is evident in the array of translations that have been offered for the phrase: "mystery of

---

[51] I have adopted here Matthew Goff's translation of רז נהיה as "the mystery that is to be"; see especially his *Worldly and Heavenly Wisdom*, passim.

[52] For discussion about whether 4Q301 might be a *Mysteries* manuscript, see Matthew Goff, *Discerning Wisdom*, 71–73, and bibliography cited there.

[53] See pages 11–13 for bibliography and brief history of scholarship. The phrase occurs more than twenty times in 4QInstruction: 4Q415 6 4; 4Q416 2 i 5 (par 4Q417 2 i 10); 4Q416 2 iii 9, 14, 18, 21 (par 4Q418 9 8, 15; 4Q418 10 1, 3); 4Q417 1 i 3, 6, 8, 18, 21 (par 4Q418 43 2, 4, 6, 14, 16); 4Q417 1 ii 3; 4Q418 77 2, 4; 4Q418 123 ii 4; 4Q418 172 1; 4Q418 184 2; and 4Q423 4 1, 4 (par 1Q26 1 1, 4). According to Goff (*Discerning Wisdom*, 13), "the phrase is reasonably reconstructed in 4Q415 24 1; 4Q416 17 3; 4Q418 179 3; 4Q418 190 2–3; 4Q418 201 1; 4Q418c 8; 4Q423 3 2; 4Q423 5 2; and 4Q423 7 7." The phrase also occurs in the *Community Rule* (1QS 11:3–4) and in *Mysteries* (1Q27 1i3, 4 [par 4Q300 3 3, 4]).

[54] Goff, *Worldly and Heavenly Wisdom*, 30.

what has passed";[55] "mystery of existence" or "mystery of being";[56] "mystery of becoming";[57] "mystery to come";[58] "mystery of that which was coming into being";[59] "mystery of the future";[60] and "mystery that is to be."[61] This is to name just the most prominent translations. The different senses captured in these translations reflect the various opinions of the grammatical form and function of נהיה, which is usually taken to be a *nifal* participle, the precise meaning of which is open to debate.

---

[55] My translation of Roland de Vaux's "le mystère passé" in his "La Grotte des manuscrits hébreux," 605; here de Vaux was commenting on the fragments of 1Q26 and 1Q27, both of which contain the phrase רז נהיה.

[56] See Florentino García Martínez and Eibert J. C. Tigchelaar, *The Dead Sea Srolls Study Edition* (2 vols.; Leiden: Brill, 1997–98), passim; Robert Eisenman and Michael Wise, *The Dead Sea Scrolls Uncovered: The First Complete Translation and Interpretation of 50 Key Documents Withheld for Over 35 Years* (Shaftsbury: Element Books, 1992), passim; Giovanni Ibba, "Il 'Libro dei Misteri' (1Q27, f.1): testo escatologico," *Henoch* 21 (1999): 73–84. Ibba makes the point that *Mysteries* and 4QInstruction convey different senses for רז נהיה: while in the former it should be translated eschatologically as "mistero futuro," in 4QInstruction it has a more existential connotation as "mistero dell'estistenza." See also Goff, *Discerning Wisdom*, 77–80.

[57] Lange, *Weisheit und Prädestination*, 97; and "Wisdom and Predestination in the Dead Sea Scrolls," 341. In my view, Lange's "Geheimnis des Werdens" ("the mystery of becoming") reflects a slight misreading of the evidence. Lange's translation (and corresponding conception) is based in part on a comparison of נהיה with the נהיות of Sir 42:19, which is translated in the Greek (LXX) as τὰ ἐσόμενα. On the contrary, it seems that on both linguistic and contextual grounds τὰ ἐσόμενα should be understood to mean "the *things* that will be/happen." See for example H. W. Smyth, *Greek Grammar* (Cambridge, Mass.: Harvard University Press, 1920), 455–56, for an explanation of the Greek substantive participle.

[58] See especially Elgvin, "The Mystery to Come," 132.

[59] Lawrence Schiffman, 4QMysteries[a]: A Preliminary Edition and Translation," in *Solving Riddles and Untying Knots: Biblical, Epigraphic, and Semitic Studies in Honor of Jonas C. Greenfield* (ed. Ziony Zevit et al; Winona Lake, Ind.: Eisenbrauns, 1995), 210; idem, "4QMysteries," in DJD 20.

[60] "Le mystère future," which is J. T. Milik's translation of the phrase in 1Q26 and 1Q27 (DJD 1).

[61] Goff, *Worldly and Heavenly Wisdom*, passim; Collins, "Wisdom Reconsidered, in Light of the Scrolls," 272; idem, "The Mysteries of God"; Daniel Harrington, *Wisdom Texts from Qumran* (London: Routledge, 1996), e.g. 49.

Having comprehensively reviewed the evidence from the Hebrew Bible and the Qumran literature, Matthew Goff has argued that the *nifal* participle is used in this construction in order to overcome the temporal restrictions of other verb forms, so that that the choice of נהיה reflects an underlying theological and cosmological claim in the way 4QInstruction (and *Mysteries*) uses the phrase. It is worth quoting Goff in full on this issue:

> The temporal meaning of the word [נהיה] makes translating this phrase inherently problematic. I doubt whether any translation can fully convey its temporal sense. Any translation of נהיה must specify a single tense—past, present, or future. The word itself, however, is trying to convey the fact that רז נהיה extends throughout all of history. ... While no translation is fully adequate, this rendering of the phrase ["the mystery that is to be"] is better than other choices that have been suggested.[62]

Goff does not attempt to remove a strictly temporal sense from נהיה (as do those translators who prefer "existence" or "being"), but seeks to articulate the nature of its temporality and corollary conceptual value. According to Goff, then, this phrase implicitly denotes the claim

> that divine mastery extends throughout the entire chronological scope of the created order. 4Q417 1 i 3–4 and 4Q418 123 ii 3–4, for example, connect the mystery that is to be with the past, present and future. This mystery gives the addressee the ability to understand the full chronological extent of God's deterministic framework.[63]

Goff's own translation of רז נהיה to "the mystery that is to be," while giving due favor to the evidence for an eschatological connotation, reflects the difficulty of finding an English expression to correspond with the sense of the Hebrew he attempts to draw out. His (and any) English translation undermines to some degree his interpretation of the phrase in 4QInstruction as having a broader temporal meaning than the phrase "the mystery that is to be" might indicate.[64] Additionally, while the temporal dimension of the phrase is indeed prominent, the word רז itself

---

[62] Goff, *Worldly and Heavenly Wisdom*, 34.

[63] Ibid., 33; see also 54–61.

[64] In his review of Goff's book [*CBQ* 67 (2005): 118], James C. VanderKam states that the "meaning of the indefinite expression רז נהיה continues to be difficult. It does have something to do with the 'big picture,' and the verbs used with it leave open the possibility that it was written." See below for further discussion of this issue.

often points to the perception of an existential reality that transcends time—or in other words to the fullness of spatio-temporal reality.

In any case, Goff goes on to offer an extended and rather convincing exposition of the significance of the phrase in 4QInstruction, including a comprehensive review of the relevant recent scholarship. For this reason—and because I largely agree with Goff's presentation of the scholarship and his treatment of the relevant issues—it will not be necessary to duplicate his efforts in detail here.[65] While Goff's investigation of the phrase רז נהיה is directed toward his analysis of 4QInstruction, he also offers a brief general account of the significance of רז as an expression relating to esoteric (revealed) knowledge in late Second Temple Jewish literature.[66] In a subsequent work, Goff continued his treatment of 4QInstruction and expanded his investigation to include analysis of *Mysteries* and other related texts.[67]

Given his focus on 4QInstruction, *Mysteries*, and their relationship to wisdom and apocalypticism, however, he is concerned primarily to understand the use of רז in epistemological terms.[68] In other words, he discusses רז as it relates to knowledge, but does not address its function in different kinds of literature and the various modes by which one gains access to "mysteries." In this regard his discussion is limited to the acquisition of knowledge by contemplation of revealed content, i.e. "mysteries" or the רז נהיה as it appears in the relevant texts.

Goff isolates seven major themes that intersect with and are influenced by the notion of the רז נהיה in 4QInstruction. These are: (1) temporal dominion of God; (2) eschatology; (3) creation; (4) determinism; (5) *torah*; (6) instruction for daily life; and (7) ethical dualism.[69] The phrase רז נהיה has been of particular interest to scholars because of the way in which it serves as a focal point in texts that display the concerns of both wisdom and apocalyptic literature—concerns more or less represented by Goff's list above. Some scholars have asserted that 4QInstruction as a whole provides a heretofore unavailable bridge or missing link between these two worldviews and their corresponding literary genres. Often at issue is the question of how each tradition grounds its understanding of the sources of knowledge: in traditional wisdom, knowledge is gained by observation and perception; in

---

[65] Goff, *Worldly and Heavenly Wisdom*, 30–79.
[66] Ibid., 30–42; 47–51.
[67] Goff, *Discerning Wisdom*.
[68] Collins, "The Mysteries of God."
[69] Ibid., 42.

apocalypticism, appeals to special revelation form the basis for knowledge claims. Often the distinction between the two trends has been cast in terms of a tension that necessarily exists between these two ways of thinking about the acquisition of knowledge regarding matters both divine and mundane.

In recent years, however, scholars of ancient Judaism and Christianity have become increasingly aware of the ways in which the blending of sapiential, prophetic, and apocalyptic (and, I would argue, priestly) concerns led to new forms of Jewish thought and literature during the Second Temple period.[70] It is therefore somewhat surprising that some continue to advance the argument that any co-existence of wisdom and apocalypticism in a single composition must be due to successive historical and literary stages.[71] As I argue, however, it is just this kind of juxtaposition that characterizes the flexibility with which "mystery" language is employed in Qumran texts. In other words, notions of "mystery" find purchase in a variety of texts and literary types associated with different kinds of religious authority and expression which are often brought together in Qumran texts. In my view it is not at all surprising that we might find ideas typically associated with apocalypticism or apocalyptic eschatology alongside ideas typically associated with traditional wisdom, even despite Ben Sira's well-known dictum, "What is committed to you, attend to; for what is hidden is not your concern" (Sir 3:21).[72]

Goff summarizes in the following way his own assessment of 4QInstruction as it pertains to these issues:

> 4QInstruction should be considered a wisdom text because it draws on traditional wisdom in terms of form and content. Yet its appeals to

---

[70] See for example the recent volume *Conflicted Boundaries in Wisdom and Apocalypticism* (ed. Benjamin G. Wright III and Lawrence M. Wills; SBLSS 35; Atlanta: Society of Biblical Literature, 2005), a collection of essays reflecting some of the recent work of the Wisdom and Apocalypticism Group of the Society of Biblical Literature. See also the stimulating essay by Carol Newsom, "What Do We Mean by Genre? A Report from Genology" (paper presented at the annual meeting of the SBL, San Antonio, Tex., November, 2004), where she provides a helpful review of the ways in which scholars of early Judaism and Christianity have talked about genre and generic theory.

[71] Elgvin, "An Analysis of 4QInstruction," 80–81.

[72] It seems that scholars have cast the relationship between wisdom and apocalypticism in oppositional terms in part based on Sirach's attitude toward the possession of "special" revelation claimed in apocalyptic circles. See for example Argall, *1 Enoch and Sirach*.

revelation distinguish it from older wisdom. Biblical wisdom promotes the acquisition of knowledge through perception of the natural order. The address of 4QInstruction, however, learns about the world through the contemplation of revealed knowledge. In terms of pre-Christian Jewish literature, the epistemology of 4QInstruction has its closest parallels in the apocalypses. ... Israel's sapiential tradition was both conservative and flexible. Great value was placed on wisdom that was handed down from generation to generation. Yet the wisdom tradition was able to merge with other ideas and new developments. As Ben Sira's reception of traditional wisdom incorporates covenantal theology, 4QInstruction combines practical wisdom with an apocalyptic worldview. ... It is not required to attribute 4QInstruction's wisdom to a crisis in the sapiential tradition or to assume that its author considered traditional wisdom in need of revision. 4QInstruction's apocalyptic worldview is more simply understood as a consequence of the reception of older wisdom in the late Second Temple period in light of perspectives and traditions common to this era.

Though he does not state it explicitly, Goff correctly hints that we should not be too rigid in our categorizations of late Second Temple Jewish writings. Generic classification can be a helpful way to organize and interpret material from the ancient world, so long as it does not then determine what we might (or might not) expect a given text to contain. If there is anything we can say about late Second Temple Judaism, it is that religious traditions and social realities were in a state of considerable flux. The literary conventions of the time mirror this social and religious fluidity.

In any case, the רז נהיה couplet is one of the more intriguing combinations of רז + X in the extant texts from Qumran, and because it occurs in 4QInstruction and *Mysteries*, and in the final column of the *Community Rule* (1QS 11:3–4), it has been interpreted as an important bridge between those texts, representing as it does a measure of ideological continuity.[73] I will present and briefly discuss several important passages in what follows.[74]

In 4QInstruction, the phrase "constitutes an appeal to heavenly revelation that is at the core" of the work.[75] It is a multivalent reference to

---

[73] As, for example, in Lange, "Wisdom and Predestination in the Dead Sea Scrolls."

[74] Given that the focus here is on the use of mystery language, I will not provide extensive commentary on the full texts. For such commentary and exhaustive, relevant bibliography, see Goff, *Discerning Wisdom*.

[75] Goff, *Discerning Wisdom*, 13.

a particular locus of knowledge that encompasses the full range of what the authors of 4QInstruction thought it worthy to know about. By means of the רז נהיה God brings the cosmos into being and maintains and governs it (4Q417 1 i 8–9). By means of the רז נהיה the addressee may understand the nature of creation, the workings of (and the difference between) good and evil, and the course of history from beginning to end. The רז נהיה is not equivalent to the Torah, but, like much of the early Enoch literature, is ostensibly compatible with it.[76] It is esoteric insofar as it is available only to the members of the elect group envisioned in the text—a group that should not be identified with the Yaḥad but that shares important ideological and religious values with it.

In each of the texts in which the רז נהיה is mentioned, the phrase functions as an important boundary-marker between those who have access to it and those who do not. The verbs most often used in conjunction with the phrase have to do with knowledge or perception, the possession of which relates to issues of election, salvation, and eschatology—and, by implicit or explicit extension, to inclusion and/or exclusion from the community of the righteous. For example, in *Mysteries* there is an emphasis on the contrast between those who grasp the רז נהיה and those who adhere to the evil "mysteries" (or the "mysteries of transgression"), and a focus on the eschatological reckoning that will take place between them.

The following is a composite text of *Mysteries* reconstructed from 1Q27, 4Q299, and 4Q300:[77]

02 [... בעבור ידעו בין טוב ובין רע ובין שקר לא[מת] -- [
03 [ויבינו] רזי פשע כל חוכמתם ולא ידעו רז נהיה ובקדמוניות לוא
04 התבוננו ולא ידעו מה אשר יבוא עליהם ונפשם לא מלטו מרז נהיה
05 וזה לכם האות כי יהיה בהסגר מולדי עולה וגלה הרשע מפני הצדק

---

[76] In *Weisheit und Prädestination*, Lange argued that the רז נהיה and the Torah should be identified with one another (for example, page 58); cf. Goff, *Discerning Wisdom*, 28–29. In my opinion the identification is not warranted by the contents of 4QInstruction. Even if there are several interesting shared themes between the רז נהיה and the Torah, overall the similarities are too vague and difficult to interpret adequately. Furthermore, it is important to use caution when using terms like "the Torah" in the context of the Dead Sea Scrolls.

[77] The reconstruction and translation is from Schiffman, "4QMysteries[a]," DJD 20:35–36. While this is an edition of 4Q299, the numbering (02, 03, etc.) reflects the composite nature of the reconstruction, since the text reproduced here precedes the portions where 4Q299 is extant. This part of the text is preserved mostly in 1Q27 (with overlaps in 4Q300), the first edition of which can be found in DJD 1.

06 כגלות [ח]ושך מפני אור וכתום עשן וא[ינ]ו עוד כן יתם הרשע לעד

07 והצדק יגלה כשמש תכון תבל וכול תומכי רזי [פשע[78] אינמה עוד

02 [in order that they might know (the difference) between good and evil, and between falsehood and truth,]

03 [and that they might understand] the mysteries of transgression, (with) all their wisdom. But they did not know the mystery of that which was coming into being, and the former things they did not consider.

04 Nor did they know what shall befall them. And they did not save their lives from the mystery that was coming into being.

05 And this shall be the sign to you that it is taking place: When the begotten of unrighteousness are delivered up, and wickedness is removed from before unrighteousness,

06 as darkness is removed from before light. (Then,) just as smoke wholly ceases and is no more, so shall wickedness cease forever,

07 and righteousness shall be revealed as the sun (throughout) the full measure of the world. And all the adherents of the mysteries [of transgression] will be no more.

This passage underscores the contrast between those who—in their success in understanding the "mysteries of transgression"—fail to grasp the "mystery that is to be" and therefore forfeit any claim they might have to salvation at the moment of judgment. The contrast between those who have access to the רז נהיה and those who do not is set in relief against other dualistic formulations in the text: wickedness and righteousness; darkness and light; and (later) knowledge and folly. Like in other esoteric trends of antiquity, knowledge of special revelation is a key to redemption. And like in other esoteric trends, the rhetoric of special knowledge affirms a social boundary-marker intended not only to exclude the unworthy but also to gird up the self-understanding of the in-group as the elect whose understanding will be vindicated.

Elsewhere in *Mysteries*, we see a similar dichotomy between those who are "skilled in transgression" and those who apparently are learned in the "eternal mysteries," and in this passage there are the added

---

[78] Contrary to the reading given by Milik in DJD 1 (רזי פלא), Schiffman suggests that פלא here be emended to בליעל (in both parallels), which certainly makes more sense of the context. See his treatment in DJD 20:37, 105–106. I propose, however, that פשע may be the most suitable reconstruction given both context and available space, and given the fact that this construct also occurs elsewhere in *Mysteries*, e.g. 1Q27 1 i 2 (cf. 1QH[a] 13:38, 24:9).

elements of hidden wisdom and a sealed, secret vision, all of which seem to be equated with the "mysteries."

4Q300 1a ii-b

1 [ת] [ ] החר[ט]מים מלמדי פשע אמרו המשל והגידו החידה בטרם נדבר ואז
תדעו אם הבטתם

2 ותעודות השמ[י]ם -- [בסלכמה כי חתום מכם] ח[תם החזון וברזי עד לא
הבטתם ובבינה לא חשכלתם

3 א[ז]תאמרו ל] [--] ה והמי[ן --] [כי לא הבטתם בשורש חוכמה ואם תפתחו
החזון

4 תסת[ם מכם --]כל חוכמת[כ]ס כי לכם המ [--] [שמו כי] מ[ה היא חכמה

5 נכחדת[--]עו[ד לא תהיה] [--]

6 [ה]זון[--]

1 […] [the mag]icians who are skilled in transgression utter the parable and relate the riddle before it is discussed, and then you will know whether you have considered,

2 and the signs of the heav[ens …] your foolishness, for the [s]eal of the vision is sealed from you, and you have not considered the eternal mysteries, and you have not come to understand wisdom.

3 The[n]you will say […] for you have not considered the root of wisdom,[79] and if you open the vision

4 it will be kept secr[et from you …]all [yo]ur wisdom, for yours is the […] his name, for [wh]at is wisdom (which is)

5 hidden[… sti]ll there will not be […]

6 the [vis]ion [of …]

As I discuss in the next chapter, I see good reason to relate the "magicians" in this passage with those who "understand the mysteries of transgression" in the text cited above.[80] The specific use of the language of "magicians" (חרטמים) connects this passage also to the

---

[79] The term "root of wisdom" can also be found in the first chapter of Ben Sira: "The root of wisdom—to whom has it been revealed?" (1:6). It is probable that here Ben Sira is situating his text—and the kind of wisdom it represents—vis-à-vis both apocalyptic schools of thought and the Greek scientific traditions of Aristotle, Aristarchus, Archimedes, and Eratosthenes; see Jeremy Corley, "Wisdom Versus Apocalyptic and Science in Sirach 1, 1–10," in *Wisdom and Apocalypticism in the Dead Sea Scrolls and in the Biblical Tradition* (ed. Florentino García Martínez; BETL 168; Leuven: Leuven University Press, 2003), 269–85. See also the term שורשי בינה "roots of understanding" in 4Q301 1 2, 4Q301 2b 1, and 4Q418 55 9.

[80] See also my "'Riddled' with Guilt."

apocalyptic scenarios in Daniel and *1 Enoch* in which illegitimate revelations are contrasted with those of the respective protagonists (see, for example, Dan 2:2, 10, 27; 4:4, 6; 5:11; *1 En* 8:3 [4Q201 1 iv 2]).

Of course, we may also note that the theme of special "mysteries" revealed to the elect figures prominently in each of these apocalyptic texts, and that in each case these "mysteries" are contrasted with divinatory or interpretive practices of those in opposition to the hero. In the case of *Mysteries*, however, the foil group appears likely to be not from a foreign guild but from among Israel itself. The "magicians" of *Mysteries* thus represent the wayward interpreters of Israel's own sacred traditions. The author(s) of *Mysteries* define themselves by reference to an internal "other" whose distance from the in-group is highlighted with the use language normally reserved for the interpretive agents of "the nations." The רז נהיה is not simply a container of content—or a way of referring to a specific body of teaching—but is also a way of insinuating a boundary by appeal to a highly figured pattern of speech.

There is emerging consensus that 4QInstruction and *Mysteries* are not, strictly speaking, sectarian texts.[81] While the fragmentary nature of *Mysteries* (and 4Q301) might ultimately foreclose a definitive conclusion regarding its sectarian status, it is rather clear that 4QInstruction assumes a social situation that is different from the majority of the Qumran rule texts and associated literature like the *pesharim*. Even so, there is much in both texts that would have likely been appealing to a sectarian reader, including notions of special revelation entrusted to the elect and post-mortem reward for the righteous, and the role of pedagogy in the transmission of sacred teachings.

Armin Lange has argued that the *Treatise on the Two Spirits*, a free-standing work which was later incorporated into the *Community Rule* (1QS 3:13–4:26),[82] was based in part on *Mysteries* and other related dualistic sapiential traditions.[83] The *Treatise* also uses the language of

---

[81] For a review of the relevant issues and scholarship, see Goff, *Discerning Wisdom*, esp. 61–68 and 99–103.

[82] The *Treatise* was incorporated only into two extant manuscripts of the *Serekh*—1QS and 4QSᶜ (4Q257). There are no significant extant variants between the two manuscripts.

[83] Lange, *Weisheit und Prädestination*, 168; idem, "Wisdom and Pre-destination in the Dead Sea Scrolls"; idem, "Die Weisheitstexte aus Qumran: Eine Einleitung," in *The Wisdom Texts from Qumran and the Development of Sapiential Thought* (ed. Charlotte Hempel, Armin Lange, and Hermann Lichtenberger; BETL 159; Leuven: Leuven University Press, 2002), 13.

"mystery"[84] and other shared terminology, and reflects an important development in the ideology of the Yaḥad. It serves as a reference point for the teaching of the Maskil, who probably also figures prominently in the final column of 1QS in a series of first-person declarations that closely mirrors material from the "Teacher Hymns" of the *Hodayot* and also from the composition known as *Barkhi Nafshi* (both of which also use רז terminology). It is in the context of this passage in 1QS 11 that the phrase רז נהיה is incorporated.

The use of the phrase רז נהיה in 1QS is somewhat analogous to its appearance in 4QInstruction and *Mysteries*, though in this different context it also takes on a distinct function as the object of a special claim made by the speaker to have gazed upon the "mystery that is to be":

1QS 11:3–4

3 ... כיא ממקור דעתו פתח אורי ובנפלאותיו הביטה עיני ואורת לבבי ברז
4 נהיה ...

> 3 ... For from the fount of [God's] knowledge my light has gone forth;
>   upon his wonders my eye has gazed, and the light of my heart upon
>   the mystery
> 4 that is to be. ...

This bold assertion marks an crucial aspect of the Yaḥad's ideas about "mystery," as the speaker goes on to claim that his special access to the divine reality gives him wisdom, knowledge, and prudence hidden from others (נסתרה מאנוש) (1QS 11:6). All this is given as an "eternal possession" to those united in assembly with the angels, those of the special covenant, the "Council of the Yaḥad" (עצת יחד) (1QS 11:7–8). But for good measure—as if to back off just a little from these bold assertions—the column concludes with a soliloquy on the smallness of the human being and the statement that no one born of flesh can hope to penetrate the *full* depth of God's "mysteries" (1QS 11:19).

"MYSTERIES" OF KNOWLEDGE

Deutero-Isaiah makes the claim that the God of Israel will perform wonderful deeds "so that all may see (יראו) and know (וידעו), all may

---

[84] For example רזי דעת; see discussion below. According to the *Treatise on the Two Spirits*, even the promptings of the Angel of Darkness (מלאך חושך) are "allowed" to occur in keeping with the "mysteries of God" (לפי רזי אל) until "his era" begins (1QS 3:21–23). This passage is discussed in more detail in chapter 5.

consider (וישימו) and understand (וישכילו), that the Lord has done this, the Holy One of Israel has created it" (Isa 41:20). This passage appears to subsume all the possible varieties of human knowledge under the banner of God's redemptive mastery over creation: "Seeing, knowing, considering, and understanding ... do not always point to a deliberate distinction between sensory and intellectual apperception; more generally the totality of human knowledge is addressed," and, according to Isaiah, is only available by way of revelation from God.[85]

The emphasis on knowledge in the Qumran Scrolls has been noted since the earliest stages of research.[86] As we have already seen, the claim of possession of special knowledge is a hallmark of esoteric discourse, and for its part the Yaḥad apparently had a keen interest in accessing, mastering and controlling the available sources of authoritative knowledge. There are several different combinations of רז + X wherein X is a word with connotations of knowledge: דעת (knowledge), שכל (understanding), חכמה (wisdom), מחשבה (thought), and ערמה (prudence). While some differences can be detected among these various combinations, there is enough conceptual overlap that we may consider them together under the same heading. Nevertheless, we should not lose sight of the fact that different modes of perception may be connoted by the choice of one word or another.

רזי דעת

The phrase רזי דעת finds expression in two interesting and possibly related texts from Qumran.[87] In general, forms of ידע in the Dead Sea Scrolls refer to "special knowledge in the realm of anthropology, cosmology, and especially soteriology. Since sôd̲ and rāz often appear as objects [of the verb], yd῾ frequently stands for the secret esoteric knowledge of the sect."[88] This is in line with what we may observe about the use of דעת generally and in its more specific combination with רז in the Scrolls.

---

[85] Botterweck, "ידע," TDOT 5.462.

[86] For example see André Dupont-Sommer, The Dead Sea Scrolls: A Preliminary Survey (Oxford: Oxford University Press, 1952), 42 and 65 n. 1.

[87] On the use of דעת in the Hebrew Bible and in Qumran texts see Botterweck, "ידע"; W. D. Davies, "'Knowledge' in the Dead Sea Scrolls and Matthew 11:25–30," in Christian Origins and Judaism (London: Darton, Longman & Todd, Ltd., 1962), 120–44, esp. 124–34.

[88] Botterweck, "ידע," 475. Botterweck also cites the opinion of K. G. Kuhn, who understands all this to be an incipient form of "Gnosticism" introduced into late Jewish apocalypticism. See Kuhn, "Die in Palästina gefundenen Hand-

As noted in the section on רז נהיה, the phrase רזי דעת is part of a larger meditation on the character of sectarian knowledge in the *Treatise on the Two Spirits*. In this passage, the "paths in the world" of the sons of light are described according to what this knowledge allows them to discern. The knowledge is rooted in, or perhaps provides the possibility for, true understanding of the commandments (משפטים) and of one's disposition toward God. The text reads in full as follows:

1QS 4:2–8

2 ואלה דרכיהן בתבל להאיר בלבב איש ולישר לפניו כול דרכי צקד אמת
ולפחד לבבו במשפטי

3 אל ורוח ענוה ואׄרכ אפים ורוב רחמים וטוב עולמים ושכל ובינה וחכמת
גבורה מאמנת בכול

4 מעשי אל ונשענת ברוב חסדו ורוח דעת בכול מחשבת מעשה וקנאת
משפטי צדק ומחשבת

5 קודש ביצר סמוכ ורוב חסדים על כול בני אמת וטהרת כבוד מתעב כול גלולי
נדה והצנע לכת

6 בערמת כול וחבא לאמת רזי דעת ...

2 And these are (to be) their paths in the world: to enlighten the heart of man, straighten out in front of him all the paths of true justice, establish in his heart respect for the precepts

3 of God; it is a spirit of meekness, of patience, generous compassion, eternal goodness, intelligence, understanding, potent wisdom which trust in all

4 the works of God and depends on his abundant mercy; a spirit of knowledge in all the plans of action, of enthusiasm for the decrees of justice,

5 of holy plans with firm purpose, of generous compassion with all the sons of truth, of magnificent purity which detests all unclean idols, of careful behavior

6 in prudence concerning everything, of concealment concerning the truth of the mysteries of knowledge. ...

This recitation of the various purposes and values of hallowed knowledge uses poetic repetition and variation to describe the contours of the sectarian "spirit." Different terms are called forth to underline the notion that the sectarian has multifaceted access to all those things worth knowing, and to reinforce the identification between knowledge and goodness. This short passage, which is largely about "intelligence,

schriften und das NT," *ZThK* 47 (1950): 203–205; idem "Die Sektenschrift und die iranische Religion," 306–315.

understanding, potent wisdom," declares that the sons of truth have prudence concerning every relevant matter, and culminates with the statement that they keep hidden the "mysteries of knowledge." This presentation may be contrasted with that of *1 En* 8:1–3, which catalogs the various forms of illicit knowledge taught by the named Watchers and culminates with the summary that these were the "mysteries" that the heavenly beings revealed to their wives. The contraband "mysteries" are revealed unlawfully, and the "mysteries of knowledge" proper to the elect must be carefully guarded.

This notion of keeping the "truth of the mysteries of knowledge" hidden can be compared to expressions found in other sectarian texts. In a characteristically self-deprecating passage of the *Hodayot*, the speaker confesses that "in the mystery of your wisdom (ברז חכמתכה) you have reproved me, you have hidden the truth (תחבא אמת) until the period of [… until] its appointed time" (1QHᵃ 17:23–24). This statement seems to infer that the truth has been hidden *from* the speaker until the appointed time, i.e. that the hiding of knowledge is something God also does—even hiding it from the righteous.

These two passages reflect views about esoteric knowledge from an anthropological perspective (there are good and evil people, and the good possess knowledge and truth that is superior to the evil ones) and from a theological perspective (God knows things that even the members of the Yaḥad do not know). Yet another passage from the *Hodayot* implies the synthesis of these two kinds of knowledge and concealment, namely that the knowledge of the sect is superior and yet still only partial until the eschatological unfolding of God's universal plan has been accomplished:

1QHᵃ 16:5–9, 11–14

5 I g[ive thanks to you, my Lord, for] you placed me by a source of flowing (waters) in a dry land, a spring in a parched territory, a watered 6 garden [and a pool …] You [plan]ted a stand of juniper and elm along with cypress for your glory, trees

7 of life in the spring of mystery, hidden in the midst of all the trees by the water in order that a shoot might spring forth as an eternal planting (מטעת עולם).

8 Taking root before they shoot up, they extend their roots to the strea[m] that its trunk might be open to the waters of life

9 and become an eternal source. …

11 The shoot of holiness springs forth as a planting of truth (מטעת אמת), hiding (סותר)

12 and not accounted. And not being known, its mystery is sealed (ובלא
נודע חותם רזו). *Vacat* But you, [G]od, protect its fruit by the mystery
of warriors of strength (ברז גבורי כוח),
13 holy spirits, and whirling flames of fire. No one will [come to] the
spring of life and with the trees of eternity
14 drink the waters of holiness. ...

Here the sealed mystery is understood to exist hidden within the
"planting of truth," which itself is a "shoot of holiness" which is also
eternal. It is not clear whether in this passage the "mystery" is "not
known" to the sect itself, to the broader society, or to humanity in
general. It seems likely, given the broader context of the passage, that
knowledge of this "mystery" is indeed available to the sect, and that
"hiding," the "eternal shoot" keeps it sealed from those outside the
group. This passage alludes to a cultic context with references to garden
imagery, flaming fire, waters of holiness, and holy spirits—language that
is reminiscent of other sectarian texts such as the *Damascus Document*, the
Songs of the Sabbath Sacrifice, and other compositions.

The other passage in which the phrase רזי דעת is attested bears a
connotation that is, at first glance, quite different from its use in the
Treatise. In one of the cave 4 manuscripts of the *Songs of the Sabbath
Sacrifice* (4Q403 1 ii 27), the phrase occurs in the context of the song for
the eighth Sabbath:

4Q403 1 ii 23–27[89]

23 ... ודעת בינתם לשבע [--]
24 רוש מכוהן קורב לראשי עדת המלך בקהל [--]
25 ותשבחות רומם למלך הכבוד ומגדל [א]ל[ל]והי -- [
26 לאל אלים מלך הטהור ותרומת לשוניהם [--]
27 שבע רזי דעת ברז הפלא לשבעת גבולי קוד[ש קדשים -- [

23 And the insightful knowledge of the seven [...]
24 chief, from the priest of the inner sanctum. And the chiefs of the
congregation of the King in the assembly [...]
25 and praises of exaltation to the King of glory, and magnification of
the [G]o[d of ...]
26 to the God of the elim, King of purity. And the offering of their
tongues [...]
27 seven mysteries of knowledge in the wondrous mystery of the
seven [most] holy precincts [...]

---

[89] Text and translation are from Newsom, *Songs of the Sabbath Sacrifice*, 226–
27; English translation, 230.

Several commentators have wrestled with this passage and found it to be obscure. Carol Newsom states that "the text aptly describes the passage as a 'mystery,' for it is extremely difficult to construe."[90] At first glance the reference to the "seven mysteries of knowledge" is difficult to place, but the following "in the mystery of the wonder of the seven regions of the holy of holies" does qualify the phrase in an intriguing way. The latter "mystery" is perhaps a reference to the "wonder" of the heavenly temple, in which case the former "mysteries"—of knowledge—correspond to the kinds of knowledge proper to the seven different regions of the holy of holies.

The word דעת occurs with marked preponderance in the *Songs of the Sabbath Sacrifice*. Elliot Wolfson has presented a wide-ranging treatment of the theme of knowledge in the *Songs* and in the sectarian literature, especially as it pertains to the kind of "transformational mysticism" he sees in these texts. He correctly notes that

> To explicate this passage responsibly, and particularly the key expression *razei da'at*, it is obviously necessary to consider the meaning of two terms, *raz*, "mystery," and *da'at*, "knowledge." What kind of knowledge, what kind of mystery? ... Before approaching these philological and philosophical clarifications, it would be beneficial to situate the text better in its literary setting, a move that will shed light on the symbolic significance of the number seven, which will, in turn facilitate a better understanding of the mysteries of knowledge.[91]

Wolfson goes on to conclude that this term for knowledge (דעת) should be understood most accurately as a technical onto-theosophic designation for the contemplative meditation on "God's knowledge" (דעת אלוהים) performed by the priests of the Yaḥad (whom he refers to as *maśkîlim*) in the desert of Judah.[92] Accordingly, the "seven mysteries of knowledge" ought to be interpreted as "seven potencies that constitute the substance of *da'at 'elyon*."[93]

---

[90] Newsom, *Songs of the Sabbath Sacrifice*, 243.

[91] Wolfson, "Seven Mysteries of Knowledge," 194. For the term "transformational mysticism," and additional discussion of the *Sabbath Songs*, see Christopher R. A. Morray-Jones, "Transformational Mysticism and the Apocalyptic-Merkabah Tradition," *JJS* 43 (1992): 1–31; William F. Smelik, "On Mystical Transformation of the Righteous into Light in Judaism," *JSJ* 26 (1995): 122–44.

[92] Wolfson, "Seven Mysteries of Knowledge," 203.

[93] Ibid., 204.

Though his argument is much more complex than is fitting to review here, and though several of his assertions seem to derive from the framework of later Jewish mysticism through which he interprets the *Songs of Sabbath Sacrifice*,[94] Wolfson offers a compelling (if not always entirely clear) way to understand the phrase רזי דעת. These seven "mysteries" or "potencies" may well reflect a broader tradition about the number seven in ancient Jewish and early Christian thought,[95] but the use of this phrase in the *Sabbath Songs* highlights some important connections among the *Songs*, the *Community Rule*, and the *Hodayot* regarding the acquisition and use of esoteric knowledge of the "mysteries." Citing two important passages, Wolfson argues that in these compositions we can see that "knowledge of divine truth is equated with visually gazing at the glory, which occasions the recitation of God's mysteries."[96] These two texts are the following:

1QHᵃ 18:22–23

22 ואני לפי דעתי באמת[כה --]ובהביטי בכבודכה אספרה

23 נפלאותיכה ...

22 And I, according to my knowledge of [your] truth [...] and when I gaze upon your glory, I recount
23 your wonders. ...

1QS 11:3–4

3 ... כיא ממקור דעתו פתח אורי[97] ובנפלאותיו הביטה עיני ואורת לבבי ברז

4 נהיה ...

---

[94] For brief discussion of this problem, see Newman, "Priestly Prophets at Qumran," 33 n. 9.

[95] See Smelik, "Mystical Transformation," for a helpful review of this tradition.

[96] Wolfson, "Seven Mysteries of Knowledge," 208.

[97] The manuscript appears here to read אורו "his light," though the *vav* and *yod* are sometimes indistinguishable in some Qumran manuscripts, and the reading אורי "my light" probably makes better sense of the passage. Compare 1QHᵃ 17:26–27: "and through your glory, my light (אורי) becomes visible, for from darkness you make a light shine for [me]." In 1QHᵃ 23:1–2 there are two instances in which אורכה "your light" seems to refer to the notion that God established the luminaries out of his own light.

3 . . . For from the fount of [God's] knowledge my light has gone forth;
upon his wonders my eye has gazed, and the light of my heart upon
the mystery
4 that is to be. ...

Wolfson wishes finally to end up at the following statement, which
deserves to be quoted in full:

> [The priests] come to know the seven mysteries of divine knowledge
> through the exercise of their own knowledge though the actualization of
> their own knowledge is facilitated by apprehension of the seven
> mysteries of knowledge. The duty to discourse poetically about the
> splendor of divine kingship is predicated on being incorporated into
> this kingship, to become god-like and glorious, to be illumined by the
> soteric esotericism that affords one the opportunity to be assimilated
> into the divine potencies.[98]

Being assimilated into the divine potencies—or "mysteries"—is another
way of talking about what it means to "gaze upon" the "mystery of
wonder" (רז פלא) in the 4Q403 lines adduced above. The "seven
mysteries of wonder" are apparently, according to Wolfson, to be
understood in direct relation to a parallel passage in the same text that
depicts the presence of priests in the "seven wonderful regions" and
refers to "the comprehensive knowledge of the seven" (4Q403 1 ii 21–23).

This passage occurs within the broader context of the middle section
of the thirteen *Sabbath Songs*, namely songs 6–8.[99] This central section
exhibits a "formulaic and repetitive literary structure which stresses the
number seven."[100] Songs 6–8 serve as a fulcrum for the progression of the
entire sequence of songs from the first, more concrete and uniform
section (songs 1–5) to the final, climactic thirteenth song in which "the
angel-like priests with the *maskil* at their head [are] fully vested and
equipped for their oracular performance."[101] By this progression the

---

[98] Wolfson, "Seven Mysteries of Knowledge," 207.

[99] The *Sabbath Songs* are usually thought to comprise three major sections
consisting of columns 1–5, 6–8, and 9–13. These sections may be differentiated in
terms of both content and style. For discussion see Newman, "Priestly Prophets
at Qumran," 35–37.

[100] Newman, "Priestly Prophets at Qumran," 38.

[101] Ibid., 39; cf. Arnold, *The Social Role of Liturgy*, 146–48. According to
Newman, the eighth song is the point "in which the divine King and Creator is
made manifest in the throne room of the Temple" ("Priestly Prophets at
Qumran," 48).

priests themselves are gradually initiated into the divine presence and thereby appropriate divine knowledge as a priestly prerogative gained through ritual transformation. According to Newman's reading of the text (with which I largely concur), the priests are thus prepared to issue new revelation after a climactic moment in the liturgical cycle, namely the festival of Shavuʿot which memorialized both the Sinaitic revelation and the renewal of the covenant and provided the annual occasion for evaluation and initiation of new members to the Yaḥad.[102]

רזי שכל

The phrase רזי שכל "mysteries of understanding" which is found in the *Community Rule*, the *Hodayot*, and in the *Songs of the Sabbath Sacrifice*, carries connotations of both "knowledge" and of "wisdom."[103] The noun שכל "understanding" is fairly common in Qumran texts, especially in the explicitly sectarian (or sect-composed) literature. It is from the same root as the titular well-known from various rule scrolls, the משכיל who is known throughout this literature as the Instructor (or Maskil) who causes learning or insight to increase.[104] Some commentators have seen

---

[102] See James C. VanderKam, "Shavuʿot," *EDSS* 2.871–72. Newman's suggestion that the "new scriptural interpretation through oracular means" possibly took place especially in the "calendrical cultic aftermath" between the end of Shavuʿot and the summer solstice is plausible and compelling ("Priestly Prophets at Qumran," 30).

[103] See Koenen, "שכל," *TDOT* 14.112–28 for a full discussion of the use of the word שכל in biblical and Qumran Hebrew and Aramaic. Wolfson suggests that שכל and דעת are interchangeable in the Qumran Scrolls, and this does seem to be more or less the case. He states that "both [terms] refer to the cognitive faculty by means of which the enlightened priest apprehends divine truth" ("Seven Mysteries of Knowledge," 200).

[104] References to the Maskil can be found in the *Damascus Document*, the *Community Rule*, the *Rule of the Congregation*, the *Songs of the Sabbath Sacrifice*, the *Hodayot*, and other texts. For important discussions of this term and its referent see especially Carol A. Newsom, "The Sage in the Literature of Qumran: The Functions of the Maśkîl," in *The Sage in Israel and the Ancient Near East* (ed. John G. Gammie and Leo G. Perdue; Winona Lake, Ind.: Eisenbrauns, 1990), 373–82; Sarianna Metso, *The Textual Development of the Qumran Community Rule* (STDJ 21; Leiden: Brill, 1997), 135–40; Dwight D. Swanson, "4QCrypA Words of the Maskil to All the Sons of Dawn: The Path of the Virtuous Life," in *Sapiential, Liturgical, and Poetical Texts from Qumran: Proceedings of the Third Meeting of the International Organization for Qumran Studies, Oslo 1998* (ed. Daniel K. Falk, Florentino García Martínez, and Eileen M. Schuller; STDJ 35; Leiden: Brill, 2000), 49–61; L. Kosmala, "Maskil," *JANESCU* 5 (1973): 235–41; Lawrence Schiffman, "Utopia and Reality:

here some kind of connection with the book of Daniel—or at least its final redactors—whose background protagonists seem to be the משכילים "Maskilim" mentioned in the latter chapters of the book (11:33; 12:3).[105] In any case, Maskil in the Qumran Scrolls is most likely a technical term for the leader of the group whose primary responsibility is to lead members into knowledge and wisdom pertaining especially to spiritual matters, and also to conduct certain liturgical enactments of the Yaḥad.

The *Community Rule* states about the Maskil that "he should acquire all the understanding (שכל) that has been gained according to the periods (לפי העתים)" (1QS 9:13). Not only should the Instructor acquire this understanding, but he should make it known to (at least some of) the members of the Yaḥad. This broader passage about the role of the Instructor culminates with the statement that "he should lead them with knowledge and in this way teach them (להשכילם) the mysteries of

---

Political Leadership and Organization in the Dead Sea Scrolls Community," in *Emanuel: Studies in the Hebrew Bible, Septuagint, and Dead Sea Scrolls in Honor of Emanuel Tov* (ed. Shalom M. Paul et al; VTSup 94; Leiden: Brill, 2003), 423; Nathan Jastram, "Hierarchy at Qumran," in *Legal Texts and Legal Issues: Proceedings of the Second Meeting of the International Society for Qumran Studies, Cambridge 1995* (ed. Moshe Bernstein, Florentino García Martínez, and John Kampen; STDJ 23; Leiden: Brill, 1997), 358–60. The precise function of the Maskil and his relationship to other religious leaders at Qumran (e.g. the פקיד, the מבקר) remains a matter of some dispute. The sources (especially the extant copies of the *Damascus Document* and the *Community Rule*) do not present a clear and consistent picture. For the word משכיל in 4QInstruction, see Tigchelaar, *To Increase Understanding for the Learning Ones*, 245–46, where he discusses his proposal that it may be possible to locate this word in the first column of the composition.

[105] For example F. F. Bruce, "The Book of Daniel and the Qumran Community," in *Neotestamentica et Semitica: Studies in Honor of Matthew Black* (ed. E. Earle Ellis and Mat Wilcox; Edinburgh: T&T Clark, 1969), 221–39, esp. 228–30; P. Wernberg-Moeller, *The Manual of Discipline Translated and Annotated with an Introduction* (STDJ 1; Leiden: Brill, 1957), 66; Otto Plöger, *Das Buch Daniel* (KAT 18; Gütersloher Verlagshaus, 1965), 165; Friedrich Nötscher, *Zur theologischen Terminologie der Qumran-Texte* (BBB 10; Bonn: P. Hanstein, 1956), 56–57. Bruce states most directly that the "Qumran community appears to have stood in the direct succession of those faithful *maśkīlīm* [of the book of Daniel]" (228). There is another interesting connection here with the book of Daniel, 4QFlorilegium (4Q174) and the *Community Rule*: there seems to be a corresponding word play between the roots שכל and כשל, one which possibly reflects the social situation of the Yaḥad and its opponents. See James E. Harding, "The Wordplay between the Roots שכל and כשל in the Literature of the Yaḥad," *RevQ* 19 (1999): 69–82.

wonder and of truth (רזי פלא ואמת) in the midst of the men of the Community, so that they walk perfectly, one with another, in all that has been revealed to them" (1QS 9:18–19). Here the understanding and knowledge attained by the Maskil is indirectly equated with "mysteries," knowledge of which leads to perfection of "the way." We should not fail to note here the concluding claim that all of this "has been revealed to them," presumably by some special process of revelation to which only they have access.[106] The nominal and verbal forms of שכל in the sectarian texts most often connote the idea that "God has established the plan of history in the mysteries of his understanding (1QS 4:18; 1QH[a] 13:13; 4Q405 23 ii 13) and reveals to the Maskil the mysteries of that understanding (1QH[a] 9:31; 12:13)."[107] All this is another reflection of the notion that the members of the Yaḥad participated in a brand of wisdom that held a place for special revelation alongside the general human capacity to observe and understand the natural world—a wisdom of *numina* and of *phenomena*.[108]

In the *Community Rule*, the degree to which a member of the Yaḥad has gained or increased in שכל determines, at least in part, whether and to what degree he will advance within the ranks of the community.[109] At times this sort of knowledge or wisdom is mentioned in parallel with the phrase מעשיו בתורה, as in the following statement:

1QS 5:20–22

20 ... וכיא יבוא בברית לעשות ככול החוקים האלה להיחד לעדת קודש ודרשו
21 את רוחום ביחד בין איש לרעהו לפי שכלו ומעשיו בתורה על פי בני אהרון
המתנדבים ביחד להקים

---

[106]   An alternative reading might be that what has been "revealed to them" is precisely what the Maskil has taught them, or in other words it is his teaching itself that is the thing being revealed. This strikes me as a possibility, but is probably not the best way to understand the passage.

[107]   Koenen, "שכל," 127.

[108]   Rylaarsdam asserted long ago that Jewish wisdom was always, at some fundamental level, concerned with "the manner and means in and by which men come to possess a knowledge both of the true goals of life and of the way by which they can attain them," and that this was itself rooted in sorting out the complex relationship between the "aid or grace of a special nature" and the "natural creaturely endowments" (*Revelation in Jewish Wisdom Literature*, vi).

[109]   Compare 1QH[a] 18:27–28: עד ולפי דעתם [--] ולבני אמתכה נתתה שכל יכבדו איש מרעהו "but to the sons of your truth you have given understanding, [...] everlasting; and to the extent of their knowledge they are honored, one more than another."

22 את בריתו ולפקוד את כול חוקיו אשר צוה לעשות ועל פי רוב ישראל
המתנדבים לשוב ביחד לבריתו

20 ... When anyone enters the covenant to live according to these
statutes proper to the Yaḥad, to the congregation of holiness, they
will investigate

21 his spiritual qualities as a community, each of them (participating).
(They shall investigate him) according to his understanding and his
works in *torah*, in accordance with the sons of Aaron who together
have freely offered to uphold

22 his covenant and to observe all the statutes that he commanded to do,
and in accordance with the multitude of Israel, who have freely
offered to return as a community to his covenant.

The gaining of wisdom is here, as in other texts from this period,
associated with the proper understanding, interpretation, and practical
application of *torah*.[110] However, with respect to the רזי שכל, there is no
clear association with proper knowledge of *torah* as the sole underlying
content of the "mysteries." In fact, as several scholars have pointed out,
the esoteric teachings of the Yaḥad on matters of *torah* interpretation are
usually referred to not as "mysteries" but as "secrets" (נסתרות).[111]

As Lawrence Shiffman has observed, the Maskil, as the presumed
medium or locus of שכל within the community, was both master of the
sectarian legal tradition and the one who was responsible for teaching
the broader ideology and theology of the Yaḥad to its various
members.[112] In addition to these responsibilities, he also apparently had
liturgical leadership roles, as seen in the *Sabbath Songs* and in the *Songs of
the Maskil* (or *Songs of the Sage*, 4Q510–11). Overall, "even though the
search for the true interpretation of the Torah was central to the life of
the community, that quest did not take place in a vacuum but in a social
and cosmological context" which included understanding "something
about the origin, nature, and destiny of human existence in the world."[113]
Perhaps in this broader context we can better understand the use of the
phrase רזי שכל in Qumran texts. While these "mysteries of
understanding" may indeed have dealt with matters of *torah* and its

---

[110] In some traditions *torah* and wisdom are identified with one another, for
example in Sirach 24; see Collins, *Jewish Wisdom in the Hellenistic Age*, 23–61.

[111] See pages 134–36 above for discussion.

[112] Shiffman, "Utopia and Reality," 423; Schiffman, *The Halakhah at
Qumran*, esp. chapter 1.

[113] Newsom, "The Sage in the Literature from Qumran," 377.

proper interpretation and application, the range of sectarian knowledge went beyond what might be satisfactorily accounted for as "*torah*-study."

With recourse to the book of Nehemiah it is possible to make another suggestion about the connection between שכל and *torah*. In a famous scene Ezra stands atop a wooden tower accompanied by elders and Levites, and, in Mosaic fashion, reads from the book of the *torah* of Moses. With an apparently innovative twist, however, the elders and the Levites offer an interpretation (or translation) of the text, too:

Nehemiah 8:7–8

7 וישוע ובני ושרביה ימין עקוב שבתי הודיה מעשיה קליטא עזריה יוזבד חנן
פלאיה והלוים מבינים את־העם לתורה והעם על־עמדם
8 ויקראו בספר בתורת האלהים מפרש ושום שכל ויבינו במקרא

7 Also Jeshua, Bani, Sherebiah, Jamin, Akkub, Shabbethai, Hodiah, Maaseiah, Kelita, Azariah, Jozabad, Hanan, Pelaiah, the Levites, helped the people to understand the law, while the people remained in their places.

8 So they read from the book, from the law of God, with interpretation. They gave the sense,[114] so that the people understood the reading.

If, as John Levison has suggested, the שכל in this passage can be related to the gift of the spirit להשכילם "in order to instruct them" in Neh 9:20a, it becomes possible to see the whole scenario as a description of the process of inspired interpretation of authoritative text.[115] Such an idea also appears to have been operative among the Yaḥad, as the famous passage about the Teacher of Righteousness in the Habakkuk *pesher* attests. That text claims about this figure that God has made known to him "all the mysteries of the words of his servants the prophets"

---

[114] The word here for "sense" is מפרש, "which was equivalent to the Persian term (*h*)*uvarisûn* and describes the unique method invented in the Persian chanceries for translating a document [i.e. from Hebrew to Aramaic]" (William M. Schniedewind, "Aramaic, the Death of Written Hebrew, and Language Shift in the Persian Period," in *Margins of Writing, Origins of Cultures* [ed. Seth L. Sanders; OIS 2; Chicago: Oriental Institute of the University of Chicago, 2006], 139). See also J. Naveh and J. C. Greenfield, "Hebrew and Aramaic in the Persian Period," in *The Cambridge History of Judaism 1: Introduction: The Persian Period* (ed. W. D. Davies and L. Finkelstein; Cambridge: Cambridge University Press, 1984), 116.

[115] John R. Levison, *The Spirit in First-Century Judaism* (Leiden: Brill, 2002), 195–96.

(1QpHab 7:4–5) which pertain to the "men of truth, the doers of *torah* whose hands will not cease from the service of truth" (1QpHab 7:10–12).

רז חכמה

In one instance the phrase רז חכמה appears in the *Hodayot* (1QHᵃ 17:23) to refer to God's wisdom in "reproving" the speaker in the right ways and at the right times. Here the "mystery" appears to refer to God's own patterns of revelation and concealment, which are made known to the speaker in due time. The reproofs become for the speaker the mechanism by which God instructs him and delivers him from the sufferings of his soul. This "mystery" is also related to deliverance from the speaker's opponents and adversaries, who plot and complain against him.

1QHᵃ 17:23–25

23 כי אתה אלי ˡמוע]ד   [ריבי כי ברז חכמתכה הוכחתה בי
24 ויחבא אמת לקץ]   [מועדו ותהי תוכחתכה לי לשמחה וששון
25 ונגיעי למרפא ע]ולם ושלום [נצח ובוז צרי לי לכליל כבוד וכשלוני להבורת
26 עולם

23 For you, my God, at the appointed t[ime] you defend my cause. For in the mystery of your wisdom you reprove me,

24 and you conceal truth until (its) time[ ] its appointed time. Your reproof will become a matter for joy and rejoicing to me,

25 and my afflictions a matter of et[ernal] healing [and] everlasting [well-being], and the contempt of my foes will become a crown of glory for me, and my stumbling, (26) eternal strength.

While the "mystery" here does not appear to carry overtly esoteric connotations, it conveys a sense of theological concealment whose revelation will be known—in due time—only to the speaker and those with whom he participates in the covenant community.

רזי ערמה

There is a passage in the *Self-Glorification Hymn* that mentions רזי ערמתו "mysteries of his cunning" (4Q491c 11 i 3), referencing the means by which God has determined His truth throughout the generations.[116] The

---

[116] For a more extensive discussion of this composition, see chapter 5, pages 218–21.

word עָרְמָה/עָרוֹם/עָרֵם has a range of connotations in the Hebrew Bible, signifying prudence, cleverness, or shrewdness.[117] Yet there are also several instances in which the word is applied to express a negative connotation of craftiness: in Gen 3:1 the serpent is more "crafty" than all the other animals; and in Job (5:12; 15:5) God frustrates the aims of those who are crafty in deed and in speech. In the *Self-Glorification Hymn*, however, the word is used in its positive sense to indicate God's fashioning of truth and distribution of righteousness:

4Q491c 11 i 3–4[118]

3]‏‏י[שראל הכינה מאז אמתו ורזי ערמתו בכו]ל דור ודור -- [
4]מים ועצת אביונים לעדת עולמים[-- [

3 [... I]srael. He established his truth of old, and the mysteries of his prudence throughout all [generations ...]
4 [...]and the council of the humble for an everlasting congregation.

As the text continues, it becomes clear that the "mysteries" of prudence here are related to the speaker taking his seat in heaven, being reckoned "among the angels (אלים)" and issuing a steady, unequalled flow of righteous teaching.

רזי מחשבת

The phrase רזי מחשבת "mysteries of the thought (or plan) [of God]" is attested only once in the Qumran Scrolls in 1QH^a 5:17. In contrast to the more varied Semitic connotations of the root חשב in earlier literature, all related to the general meaning "to think," in the Qumran literature it takes the primary meaning of "plan" or "purpose," i.e. purposeful thought.[119] The use of the nominal forms of חשב in these texts refers to the purposes or plans of human beings, God, and, in some cases, the evil plans of Belial and his lot (1QM 13:4). When it is conjoined with the deity the word bears eschatological overtones that perhaps have roots in earlier prophetic traditions that deal with God's plans of judgment, punishment, and deliverance (Isa 55:8; Jer 29:11).

In the relevant passage the "mysteries of the thought (or plan)" are cited in the context of a *Song for the Maskil* (מזמור למשכיל) which recounts

---

[117] This is especially the case throughout the book of Proverbs.
[118] Numbering and text according to Eshel, "4Q471b: A Self-Glorification Hymn," *RevQ* 17 (1997): 184.
[119] Seybold, "חשב," *TDOT* 5.228–45.

the various and glorious features of the created order, all of which God has established "before the centuries" and apportioned "by the mysteries of your [his] understanding" (ברזי שכלכה) in order that his "glory may be known" (1QHᵃ 5:17–19). All this has been made available to the elect in the form of esoteric knowledge:

1QHᵃ 5:17–21

17 [--]ת כול בינה ומ[וסר] ורזי מחשבת וראשית[-- ה]כינותה
18 [--] קודש מקדם ע[ולם ו]לעולמי עד אתה הואל[תה --] קדושים
19 [--] וברזי פלאך הודע[תני בע]בוד כבודך ובעומק [-- מעין]בינתך לא
20 [--]אתה גליתה דרכי אמת ומעשי רע חוכמה ואולת[--] צדק
21 [--] מעשיהם אמת [--]ה ואולת ...

6 [...]t all insight and in[struction] and the mysteries of the plan, and the beginning [...] you [God] have established

7 [...] holiness from before the a[ges] of old [and] to everlasting ages you resolved [...]holy ones

8 [...] And in the mysteries of your wonder [you] have taught [me for the s]ake of your glory and in the depth of [... from the source of] your insight not

9 [...] You have revealed the paths of truth and the works of evil, wisdom, and folly [...]righteousness

10 [...] their works, truth [--]h and folly ...

"Mysteries" of Evil

Given the dualistic disposition of the Yaḥad, it is not surprising that there are references to malevolent or evil "mysteries" in several Qumran texts.[120] This is part of a much larger scope of ideas about the agents of evil or destruction in Second Temple Jewish literature, ideas that grew at least in part out of biblical traditions. There are primarily two related ways in which "mysteries" are associated with evil in Qumran literature. The first, the רזי בליעל "mysteries of Belial," probably reflects a broader development in late Second Temple Judaism in which evil becomes personified by characters such as Belial, Mastema, Melkireshaʿ, and others.[121] The second, the רזי פשע "mysteries of transgression," usually

---

[120] Brown, *Semitic Background*, 13–14; Bockmuehl, *Revelation and Mystery*, 40–41.

[121] See Philip S. Alexander, "The Demonology of the Dead Sea Scrolls," in *The Dead Sea Scrolls after Fifty Years: A Comprehensive Assessment, Volume 2* (ed.

refers to a similar set of ideas in the abstract, and is perhaps at some points interchangeable with the other formulation.

In biblical texts the dominant use of the word בליעל connotes the idea of "worthlessness" and does not appear to represent a personification of evil.[122] In some cases, the word retains this sense in Qumran usage, though the personified sense is more common.[123] Some scholars have suggested a gradual development from abstract to concrete sense during the life of the Yaḥad, a supposition which cannot really be proven one way or the other given the ambiguous nature of some of the references and the unlikelihood that such a development would have taken place during such a short period of time.[124] The most clear and consistent use of the term in Qumran texts is with respect to a personified figure whose actions and *raison d'être* are cast in anthropomorphic terms. This is especially true in the securely sectarian texts (even when compositional history is taken into consideration).

For example, many texts refer to the rule or dominion (ממשלת) of Belial (1QS 1:18, 2:19; 1QM 14:9; 4Q177 1–4, 8, 12–13 i 6; 4Q491 8–10 i 6); the lot (גורל) of Belial (1QS 2:5; 1QM 1:5); or the counsel (עצת) of Belial (4QMMT [4Q398] 14-17 ii 5). Elsewhere the word בליעל is placed in

---

Peter W. Flint and James C. VanderKam; Leiden: Brill, 1999), 331–53; Maxwell J. Davidson, *Angels at Qumran: A Comparative Study of 1 Enoch 1–36, 72–108 and Sectarian Writings from Qumran* (JSPSup 11; Sheffield: Sheffield Academic Press, 1992), 293–300; Paul J. Kobelski, *Melchizedek and Melchireša'* (CBQMS 10; Washington, D. C.: Catholic Biblical Association of America, 1981), 75–83. We may detect this tendency in texts like *T. Levi* 19:1, *T. Ash.* 1:8, *T. Jos.* 7:4, *T. Dan* 1:7, where the character is often referred to as Beliar or the Spirit of Beliar. Belial is the only character who appears in conjunction with "mysteries" in the Qumran Scrolls (and is by far the most frequently attested personification of evil in those texts).

[122] See D. Winton Thomas, "*beliyya'al* in the Old Testament," in *Biblical and Patristic Studies in Memory of Robert Pierce Casey* (Freiburg: Herder, 1963), 11–19; Victor Maag, "Belija'al im Alten Testament," *TZ* 21 (1965): 287–99; von der Osten-Sacken, *Gott und Belial*; J. A. Emerton, "Sheol and the Sons of Belial," *VT* 37 (1987): 214–19; S. D. Sperling, "Belial," *DDD*, 323; Benedikt Otzen, "בליעל," *TDOT* 2.131–36.

[123] Corrado Martone, "Evil or Devil? Belial Between the Bible and Qumran," *Henoch* 26 (2004): 115–27, esp. 110; see also Annette Steudel, "God and Belial," in *The Dead Sea Scrolls Fifty Years after Their Discovery. Proceedings of the Jerusalem Congress, July 20–25, 1997* (ed. Lawrence Schiffman, Emanuel Tov, and James C. VanderKam; Jerusalem: Israel Exploration Society in Cooperation with the Shrine of the Book, Israel Museum, 2000), 332–40; Michael Mach, "Demons," *EDSS* 1.189-92.

[124] Davidson, *Angels at Qumran*, 196.

juxtaposition with other known agents and is given a personified, active role (and a personal pronoun to go along with it), as in the *Damascus Document*:

CD 5:17–19

17 ... כי מלפנים עמד
18 משה ואהרן ביד שר האורים ויקם בליעל את יחנה ואת
19 אחיהו במזמתו בהושע ישראל את הראשונה

17 ... For in ancient times arose
18 Moses and Aaron by the hand of the Price of Lights, and Belial raised Jannes and
19 his brother by his cunning during the first deliverance of Israel.

As Corrado Martone observes, "in this text Belial appears and acts at a crucial point of the history of Israel, and is explicitly quoted as the counterpart of the Prince of Lights (*śr h'wrim*), another evidence [*sic*] toward an identification of the Prince of Darkness of 1QS with Belial."[125] This association hints at the degree to which various epithets for a *figure du mal* seem to be united under the banner of Belial or Mastema, who may themselves be identified with one another in certain compositions among the Qumran remains.[126]

The *War Rule* is the composition in which Belial's character is most consistently and vividly rendered as the malevolent ringleader of the sect's heavenly and earthly opponents. For example:

1QM 13:11–12

11 (ואתה) עשיתה בליעל לשחת מלאך משטמה ובחוש[ך ממשל]תו ובעצתו
להרשיע ולהאשים וכול רוחי
12 גורלו מלאכי חבל בחוקי חושך יתהלכו ואליו [תשו]קתמה יחד ...

11 (And you) have made Belial to corrupt,[127] an angel of malevolence; in dark[ness is his domin]ion, and his counsel is to cause wickedness and guilt. All the spirits

---

[125] Martone, "Evil or Devil?" 124.

[126] Mach states: "The functional equivalence of Belial and Mastemah can be seen by comparing *Jubilees* 15.33 (Belial [or Beliar]) with the Damascus Document (CD xvi.3–6; the angel of Mastemah)" ("Demons," 190).

[127] לשחת may also be read as a reference to "the Pit"; see Martínez and Tigchelaar, *Dead Sea Scrolls Study Edition*, 1.135: "You have made Belial for the

12 of his lot are angels of destruction; they walk in accordance with the
statutes of darkness, and it is their sole [de]sire ...

Here Belial acts not only in isolation but commands an army of wicked
spirits whose corrupting tendencies are seen as a direct foil to the spirits
of the "lot of [God's] truth" (1QM 13:12–13). Elsewhere in this scroll, the
final confrontation between those of Belial's lot and the armies of God's
elect is described in vivid detail (1QM 1:5; 15:2–3).

The personification of evil in the figure of Belial functions not only as
a locus for the sect's thinking about the efficacy and effects of evil (and I
will have more to say about this), but it also serves as a way to explain
the presence of sin in the context of a larger, overarching narrative about
the justification of the righteous and the consummation of God's
covenant with Israel through the activity of the elect.[128] In other words,
ideas about personified evil become part of the sect's theodicy, its way of
understanding the relationship between God and sin in the world. The
answer is that the work of evil—of Belial and related characters—is
subsumed under the broader category of God's plan for the universe and
is allowed by special provision within the created order.[129] But God has
also provided the sect solely with the means of avoiding the snares of
Belial and his associates (cf. CD 4:12–19). A new covenant in the form of

---

Pit. ..." See also Isa 51:14. It seems to me that it makes more sense to read this as
an infinitive rather than a preposition + noun. In other texts Belial is associated
with "the Pit," though different terminology is used. See CD 4:12–19, and below
for discussion.

[128] "CD attests the idea that Belial is loosed against Israel for a period
which overlaps that of the existence of the sect" (John J. Collins, "Was the Dead
Sea Sect and Apocalyptic Movement?" in *Archaeology and History in the Dead Sea
Scrolls: The New York University Conference in Memory of Yigael Yadin* [ed.
Lawrence Schiffman; JSOTSup 8. Sheffield: Sheffield Academic Press, 1990], 43).
This has been identified by Devorah Dimant as "the very heart of sectarian
thought" ("Qumran Sectarian Literature," 493).

[129] This is in part an extension of the already well-developed ideas about
theodicy that came about in wisdom circles as a response to the so-called "crisis
of wisdom" reflected in writings like the books of Job and Qohelet. On this
development see for example H. -P. Müller, "Tun-Ergehens-Zusammenhang,
Klageerhörung und Theodizee im biblischen Hiobbuch und in seinen
babylonischen Parallelen," in *The Wisdom Texts from Qumran and the Development
of Sapiential Thought* (ed. C. Hempel, A. Lange and H. Lichtenberger; BETL 159;
Leuven: Leuven University Press, 2002), 373–93; Shannon Burkes, *God, Self,
Death: The Shape of Religious Transformation in the Second Temple Period* (JSJSup 79;
Leiden: Brill, 2003); Jack T. Sanders, "Wisdom, Theodicy, Death and the
Evolution of Intellectual Traditions," *JSJ* 36 (2005): 263–77.

the community is established with strict guidelines for the avoidance of transgression. This community is bound to a certain way of living that alone can counteract the effects of sin and evil.

In a passage that very likely deals with the annual covenant renewal ceremony performed by the members of the Yaḥad, the *Community Rule* states:

1QS 1:16–20[130]

16 וכול הבאים בסרך היחד יאבורו בברית לפני אל לעשות
17 ככול אשר צוה ולוא לשוב מאחרו מכול פחד ואימה ומצרף
18 נסוים בממשלת בליעל ובעוברם בברית יהיו הכוהנים
19 והלויים מברכים את אל ישועות ואת כול מעשי אמתו וכול
20 העוברים בברית אומרים אחריהם אמן אמן *vacat*

16 All who enter the rule of the Yaḥad will be initiated into the covenant before God, in order to act
17 according to everything he has commanded and not to turn away from him because of any fear, terror, and persecution
18 that test (them)[131] during the dominion of Belial.[132] And when they pass into the covenant, the priests
19 and the Levites will bless the God of deliverance and all the words of his truth. All
20 those passing into the covenant will say after them, "Amen, amen."
vacat

And in the manifesto whose *raison d'ecrire* seems to have been to persuade authorities in Jerusalem to reconsider their errant ways, the author of 4QMMT implies that Belial stands behind the violations of the sect's opponents: "Consider well all these things and seek from him (his presence) so that he may support your counsel, and keep far from you the evil plans and the counsel of Belial—so that at the end of time you may rejoice in finding that some of our words are confirmed" (4Q398 14–

---

[130] There are a few places in these lines where the scribe has used medial forms instead of final forms for some letters (cf. 4QS^b [4Q256], where this is not the case); I have reverted to the final forms. There is also a letter marked by the scribe for deletion, which I have not included here.

[131] Another possibility here is to read נהיים instead of נסוים, and some editions prefer this option; see Martínez and Tigchelaar, *Dead Sea Scrolls Study Edition*, 1.70; Martone, "Evil or Devil?" 120.

[132] See CD 6:11–14 for a passage that uses slightly different language to express a similar point.

17 ii 4–6). Taken together, all of these prominent references to Belial underscore the way in which evil functioned for the Yaḥad as a reified presence or force in the world with its own kind of "mysteries."

As indicated above, the "mysteries of Belial" are presented as efficacious, or at least potentially so, save for the opposition of God who overcomes the works of evil in his adherence to the covenant relationship, which itself is acknowledged in at least one way by the community in the form of *torah*-regulated daily worship. The *War Scroll* is explicit about this, as the "mysteries of Belial" are contrasted with the divine "mysteries of God's wonders":

1QM 14:8–10, 12–15

8 [... ברוך] שמכה אל החסדים השומר ברית לאבותינו ועם

9 כול דורותינו הפלתה חסדיכה לשאר[ית עמכה] בממשלת בליעל ובכול
רזי שטמתו לוא הדיחונ[ו]

10 מבריתכה ...

12 ... ואנו עם קודשכה במעשי אמתכה נהללה שמכה

13 ובגבורותיכה נרוממה תפ[ארתכה בכול] עתים ומועדי תעודות עולמים עם
מ[בו]א יומם ולילה

14 ומוצאי ערב ובוקר כיא גדולה מ[חשבת כבו]דכה ורזי נפלאותיכה
במרומי[כה] ל[הרי]ם לכה מעפר

15 ולהשפיל מאלים *vacat*

8 [... Blessed] is your name, O God of kindness, the one who kept the
covenant of our fathers, and with

9 all our generations you have made your mercies wondrous for the
remnant of your people during the dominion of Belial. With the
mysteries of his enmity they have not driven us away

10 from your covenant. ...

12 ... We, your holy people, will praise your name by your works of
truth.

13 Because of your mighty acts we will exalt [your] spl[endor in all] eras
and appointed times of eternity, with the coming of day, night,

14 and the going of evening and morning. For great is the p[lan of]your
glor]y, and the mysteries of your wonders are in [your] heights—to
raise up for yourself from the dust

15 and to bring low from the divine beings.

The main issue here seems to be that there is an ever-present danger that those who participate in the covenant will be led astray, but that God has provided for this contingency. One implication of the second part of this quote is that this provision for staying on the "path" during the reign of Belial involves correct worship (which surely extends beyond the *Tamid* services alluded to in lines 13–14) and a humble disposition toward the "God of mercies." The reference to the מועדי תעודות "appointed times" has a parallel in the *Community Rule* (1QS 1:9) and likely has calendrical or cultic significance.[133] There is a similar idea at work in 4QWords of the Maskil to All the Sons of Dawn (4Q298 3–4 ii 8)—a sectarian composition written in Cryptic A script—which declares that the Sons of Dawn are to "add knowledge of the days of the appointed time" (ימי תעודה) whose interpretation (פתריהם) the Maskil will make known to them in order that they may give proper heed to the end (קץ).[134]

Taking all of the elements of this passage together, and switching fully to a cultic frame of reference, it might also be the case that the phrase "mysteries of Belial" is an allusion to the *improper* application of cultic regulations of an oppositional priestly group, i.e. in the Jerusalem temple, whereas the members of the (renewed) covenant participate in "mysteries" that are a legitimate expression of the cosmically-ordained order of worship. They are separated from the temple, but not from proper worship—and thus not from the covenant.

This connection of "mysteries"—both in positive and negative terms—with the issue of calendar and cultic performance is to be seen elsewhere as well, and is perhaps related also to the "mysteries" of various creation phenomena which are discussed below. The "mysteries" are then not only the phenomena themselves but also consist in the ways in which these phenomena are understood or interpreted by the knowing community.

In other passages the association with evil is expressed by the formulation רזי פשע "mysteries of transgression." As discussed earlier, a similar phrase occurs in Aramaic in the *Genesis Apocryphon*, a text that may have served as an important source of ideas for members of the Yaḥad. The passage, which is very fragmentary, appears to occur in the context of an introduction to the story of Noah's birth. The reference to the רז רשעא "mystery of wickedness" follows the (fragmentary) statement הוו[א נחת]ין ועם נקבתא --] "[... wer]e descend[in]g, and with

---

[133] Schiffman argues that this phrase in the *Community Rule* does not refer to a sectarian calendar but "to the changing of the law in accord with the stages of history" (*Halakhah at Qumran*, 27). In other words the law changes in its rightful stages as it is received and interpreted properly by the community. In the case of the passage in the *War Scroll*, however, the context makes it clear that liturgical and calendrical issues are behind the statement.

[134] See S. Pfann in his official edition of 4Q298, DJD 20:1–30; here 25–28; cf. Dwight Swanson, "4QCrypA Words of the *Maskil*," 49–61.

women" (1:2), which suggests that the passage is concerned with the Watchers (or "sons of God") and their illicit "mystery." This fits well with other roughly contemporaneous manifestations of the Enochic tradition (cf. *1 En* 6–7; *Jub* 4:15; 6:1–3).

In addition to these examples, the book of *Mysteries* includes several mentions of illicit "mysteries" in its juxtaposition of and differentiation between the righteous and unrighteous. I have discussed these passages above and in chapter 5. It is clear from all these examples that both good and evil kinds of "mysteries" are effectual—they *matter*—but what is less clear is just how they are to be understood relative to one another. The relationship between these two kinds of "mysteries" is clarified to a degree by a passage in the *Treatise on the Two Spirits*:

1QS 3:20–23

20 ביד שר אורים ממשלת כול בני צדק בדרכי אור יתהלכו וביד מלאך

21 חושך כול ממשלת בני עול ובדרכי חושך יתהלכו ובמלאך חושך תעות

22 כול בני צדק וכול חטאתם ועונותם ואשמתם ופשעי מעשיהם בממשלתו

23 לפי רזי אל עד קצו ...

20 And in the hand of the Prince of Darkness is dominion over all the sons of justice; they walk along paths of light. And in the hand of the Angel of
21 Darkness is total dominion over the sons of deceit; they walk along paths of darkness. From the Angel of Darkness stems the corruption of
22 all the sons of justice, and all their sins, their iniquities, their guilts, and their offensive deeds are under his dominion
23 in compliance with the mysteries of God until his time. ...

This last phrase is remarkable in many ways, not least of which is its claim that God has organized the world in such a way that the Angel of Darkness rules in his realm in accordance with God's overall "plan" for the universe. The activities of personified evil and all its functionaries thus find their rightful place within the broader economy of salvation as it was conceived by the members of the Yaḥad. This broader economy is referred to as the "mysteries of God," which is evidently at the same time both hidden and manifest to the members of the community.

"MYSTERIES OF GOD"

In addition to the specialized ways in which רז is joined with other terms to form adjunct concepts in Qumran texts, there are also instances of a generalized usage in which the category of "mystery" expresses, essentially, the will and knowledge of God. These references usually involve some action on the part of God that is related to his "mysteries"—in other words, the "mysteries of God" are effectual, they are active and real, and are not merely things about God that the human mind does not comprehend.

For example, in the *War Scroll* there is a command that "on the trumpets of ambush they shall write God's mysteries to destroy wickedness" על חצוצרות המארב יכתובו רזי אל לשחת רשעה (1QM 3:8–9). This command is part of the series of statements involving the use of trumpets (and later, banners)[135] in the formation for war, and it reflects both the influence of Roman military convention and, probably by extension, some association with the military practices of the Maccabees in the revolt against the Seleucids.[136] Thus, the reference here to God's "mysteries" participates in the kind of dualistic framework elucidated above, and here "mysteries" are—as elsewhere—associated with an eschatological reality that is to come (or was already then underway). It is apparently the "mysteries" that are themselves to destroy wickedness, and the statement operates as some kind of slogan for the triumph of God's purposes for Israel.

It is interesting here that the act of writing is also efficacious—or perhaps prophetic—in a way that is reminiscent of the prophetic traditions in which an inscription functions as a proleptic enactment or realization of the future reality being envisioned. Such an idea is met in Isa 8:1–4, where God commands the prophet to "Get yourself a large table and write on it in ordinary script, 'concerning *Mahēr-Shālāl-Ḥāsh-Baz*,'" which inscription serves as a forecasting of both the name of Isaiah's child and the message the child represents to Israel—that

---

[135] These are likely called respectively the "rule for the trumpets" and the "rule for the banners." Though the beginning of the "trumpets" section is missing, the series of "banners" regulations begins with "Rule of the banners of the whole congregation according to their formations" סרך אותות כול העדה למסורותם (1QM 3:13); thus by analogy the introduction to the "trumpets" series can plausibly be restored as "Rule of the trumpets" סרך החצוצרות (1QM 2:16).

[136] See especially Russell Gmirken, "The War Scroll and Roman Weaponry Reconsidered," *DSD* 3 (1996): 89–129, esp. 125–26; idem, "Historical Allusions in the War Scroll," *DSD* 5 (1998): 174–214; Jean Duhaime, "The War Scroll from Qumran and Graeco-Roman Tactical Treatises," *RevQ* 13 (1988): 135–51. On the use of trumpets by the Maccabeans see 1 Macc. 4:13; 5:31, 33; 7:45; for different kinds of trumpet calls that correspond to Maccabean military operations see 1QM 3:1–11; 7:12–13; 8:1–19; 9:1–6; 16:3–13).

Assyria will soon overtake Syria and Samaria. We also see this basic pattern in other texts like Isa 30:8–11, Hab 2:2–4, Ezek 4:1–3, and Jer 36.[137]

We may also pause to note that there appear to be 13 successive trumpets whose inscriptions together comprise a movement in the direction of eschatological fulfillment. The number 13 is important liturgically because of its connection to other texts like the *Songs of the Sabbath Sacrifice* and the use of the solar calendar among the Yaḥad—a calendar which was evidently perceived to reflect both the cosmic structures of creation and the eschatological alignment of heaven and earth.

Elsewhere God's "mysteries" regulate the behavior of the Angel of Darkness whose "guilt and offensive deeds" are "in compliance with the mysteries of God" (1QS 3:23), a statement that is reminiscent of the general theodicy of the Qumran Scrolls. According to *Pesher Habakkuk*, these divine "mysteries" stand behind the prophecy of Hab 2:3 ("For the vision has an appointed time, it will have an end and not fail"): it proclaims that the proper understanding of this verse is כיא רזי אל להפלה "the mysteries of God cause wonderful things" (1QpHab 7:8),[138] which will come to pass at the right moment—a moment apparently understood by the sect to be imminent.

VERBS USED IN CONJUNCTION WITH *RAZ*

An assessment of the semantic range of "mystery" in the Qumran Scrolls requires some attention to its verbal associations. The following verbs accompany the use of רז, demonstrating further that it was a

---

[137] Hindy Najman, "The Symbolic Significance of Writing in Ancient Judaism," in *The Idea of Biblical Interpretation: Essays in Honor of James L. Kugel* (ed. Hindy Najman and Judith Newman; JSJSup 83; Leiden: Brill, 2004), 139–73.

[138] García Martínez and Tigchelaar (*Dead Sea Scrolls Study Edition*, 1.17) translate this as "the mysteries of God are wonderful." The verb, however, is likely a *hiphil* infinitive construct, and thus should retain a causative sense. The spelling here is anomalous: it is the only instance in which a ה substitutes for an א in all occurrences of this word. This kind of substitution is otherwise a common feature of Qumran Hebrew; see Y. Kutscher, *The Language and Linguistic Background of the Isaiah Scroll (1QIsaa)* (STDJ 6; Leiden: Brill, 1974), 174. See also Maurya P. Horgan, *Pesharim: Qumran Interpretations of Biblical Books* (CBQMS 8; Washington, D.C.: Catholic Biblical Association of America, 1979), 38; Horgan takes the form to be a *niphal* infinitive construct (which appears to be a relatively common way to read this word). It does seem to me, however, that a causative meaning is not only possible but is the preferable reading given the overall context of the passage.

multifaceted construct that was a locus for ideas about revelation, wisdom, cultic practice, and the proper location of esoteric knowledge. The verbs employed in conjunction with רז include the following:

Category	Verb	Citations
Verbs of Revealing	גלה	1QHᵃ 9:21; 1Q26 1 4; 4Q270 (4QDᵉ) 2 ii 13; 4Q416 2 iii 18 [4Q418 10a-b 1]; 4Q418 123 ii 4; 184 2; 190 2
	ידע (hiphil)	1QpHab 7:5; 1QHᵃ 12:27
	פרש	4Q417 1 i 8
	פתח	1QHᵃ 20:13
Verbs of Concealing	חבא	1QS 4:6; 1QHᵃ 13:25
	חתם	1QHᵃ 26:1 [4Q427 7 i 9]; 4Q428 11 2
	סתר	1QHᵃ 16:11
	שמר	1QHᵃ 3:7; 1Q36 16 2; 4Q416 2 ii 8
	תמך	1Q27 1 i 7; 4Q300 8 5; 4Q301 1 2
Verbs of Perceiving or Knowing	בחן	4Q415 6 4
	בין	4Q417 1 i 25
	הגה	4Q418 43–45 i 4
	ידע	1QHᵃ 15:27; 1Q27 1 i 3; 4Q405 3 ii 9; 4Q417 1 i 13; 4Q418 177 7a; 4Q511 2 ii 6
	ליץ	1QHᵃ 10:13
	לקח	4Q418 77 4
	נבט	1QS 11:3 (5), 19; 4Q300 1aii-b 2; 4Q416 2 i 5; 4Q417 1 i 2, 18 [4Q418 43–45 i 14]
	שכל	1QS 9: 18 [4QSᵈ8:3; 4QSᵉ 3:17]; 1QHᵃ 19:10; 20:20
	שמע	1QM 16:16 [4Q491 11 i 13]
Other	יכה	1QHᵃ 17:23
	כפר	CD 3:18 (רז is indirect object)
	מלט	1Q27 1 i 4 [4Q300 3 4]
	שחת	1QM 3:9

By a rather wide margin the majority of verbal formulations attests to the fact that the conceptual field of רז is associated with the contents of esoteric knowledge—with the unveiling, knowing, and concealing matters of ultimate concern. Verbs of perceiving or knowing tend to predominate in wisdom-oriented compositions like 4QInstruction, whereas verbs of revealing and concealing have a slightly wider distribution in sectarian texts. Each of these verbal uses deserves a detailed study in its own right, though for reasons of space such discussion will not be offered here.

SUMMARY AND CONCLUSION

In this chapter I have attempted to establish the overall semantic range of the word רז in the Qumran Scrolls by means of a detailed examination of its various contexts, constructs, and verbal associations. The results of this investigation have demonstrated that the use of "mystery" in the Scrolls is multifaceted, and that it is used with cosmological, eschatological, and theological connotations. It typically denotes something that falls within the domain of esoteric knowledge— something that is known to the elect and hidden to those outside the group—and reflects the dynamic interaction of revelation, knowledge, and concealment. The range of texts in which רז occurs corresponds rather well with the broader sectarian interests, and many of these texts appear to have played a central role in the life of the Yaḥad at one point or another in the several stages of its existence. We have already begun to see how the various motifs and tropes that are clustered around the word רז are suggestive of the various discourses that will provide the framework for interpretation in the next chapter.

CHAPTER FIVE

PROPHETIC, SAPIENTIAL, AND PRIESTLY "MYSTERIES"

> In the first place, one form of specialization clearly occurs in those religious organizations which have an establishment of learned men, especially when these practitioners in some sense control knowledge derived from the book, at least from the religious Book. ... With writing a new situation arises since the priest has privileged access to the sacred texts of which he is the custodian and prime interpreter. As a mediator he has a unique link to God, whose Word only he is often able to read.
>
> Jack Goody

The previous chapters have addressed the uses and dimensions of mystery language in Jewish texts of the Second Temple period and especially in the Qumran Scrolls. In what follows, I offer an account of how mystery language functions within the prophetic, sapiential, and priestly discourses that together constitute the "community of discourse" of the Yaḥad.[1] For each of these I provide an interpretation of how we might characterize the discourse and the ways in which it fits into the broad social, religious, and intellectual contours of Second Temple Judaism. I should reiterate that this framework is not meant to imply some real, on-the-ground, and absolute differentiation between the different discourses, but instead my purpose is to construct a heuristic device for exploring the ways in which appeals to these discourses may have contributed to the rhetorical shaping of the Yaḥad's presentation of its ideas, ideals, and practices.

The epigraph is from Jack Goody, *The Logic of Writing and the Organization of Society* (Cambridge: Cambridge University Press, 1986), 155–56.

[1] See chapter 2 for a more detailed discussion of the Yaḥad as a "community of discourse."

PROPHETIC DISCOURSE AND "MYSTERY"

This part of the study will take for granted that there was in fact some notion of continued "prophecy" or prophetic authority and activity in the Judaism of the late Second Temple period.[1] Despite earlier traditional and scholarly assertions about the cessation of prophecy in ancient Israel or early Judaism, it has become quite clear in recent years that—however transformed by and adapted to the changing circumstances of Jewish life in the exilic and post-exilic periods—prophetic activity continued as an operative mode of religious authority and as a resource for religious creativity within certain strands of Second Temple Judaism.[2] Likewise,

---

[1] This position appears to have gained ground and is perhaps now the dominant position in the relevant scholarship. See especially John Barton, *Oracles of God: Perceptions of Ancient Prophecy in Israel After the Exile* (Oxford: Oxford University Press, 1986; Rebecca Gray, *Prophetic Figures in Late Second Temple Jewish Palestine: The Evidence from Josephus* (Oxford: Oxford University Press, 1993); David Aune, *Prophecy in Early Christianity and the Ancient Mediterranean World* (Grand Rapids, Mich.: Eerdmans, 1983); Louis H. Feldman, "Prophets and Prophecy in Josephus," *JTS* 41 (1990): 386–422; Y. Gitay, *Prophecy and Prophets: The Diversity of Contemporary Issues in Scholarship* (Semeia Studies 33; Atlanta: Scholars Press, 1997); Lester Grabbe, *Priests, Prophets, Diviners, Sages: A Socio-Historical Study of Religious Specialists in Ancient Israel* (Valley Forge, Penn.: Trinity Press International, 1995); and most recently, Alex P. Jassen, *Mediating the Divine: Prophecy and Revelation in the Dead Sea Scrolls and Second Temple Judaism* (STDJ 68; Leiden: Brill, 2007). Jassen's book is the most comprehensive treatment of prophecy in the Dead Sea Scrolls, and drawing on some of the same material I discuss in the present work, he makes a similar and convincing case that prophecy was an ongoing activity among the Yaḥad.

[2] For the traditional rabbinic view regarding the cessation of prophecy, see *t. Sota* 13:2; *y. Sota* 24b; *b. Sota* 48b; *b. Sanh.* 11a; *b. Yoma* 9b. The rabbinic locution for the drying up of prophecy is usually that "the spirit withdrew from Israel" after the death of Haggai, Zechariah and Malachi (though after this point, according to this tradition, the *Bath-kol*, an "echo/daughter of a voice" was still an available source of revelation, even if it did not carry the same weight as previous revelation [see the well-known story of the *tanur Achnai, b. Baba Metzia* 59b]). On this point there is some variation, though in general the cessation is linked to the distinction between the first and second temples (in some texts Jeremiah is the last of the prophets). The texts usually marshaled to explain or corroborate the rabbinic views include 1 Macc 4:46; 9:27; 14:41; Josephus *Ag. Ap.* 1.40–41; 2 *Bar* 85:3. For a summary of older scholarly views about the demise of prophecy see Rex Mason, "The Prophets of the Restoration," in *Israel's Prophetic Tradition: Essays in Honour of Peter R. Ackroyd* (ed. R. Coggins, A. Phillips and M. Knibb; Cambridge: Cambridge University Press, 1982), 137–54; E. Urbach, "When Did Prophecy Cease?" *Tarbiz* 17 (1955): 1–11 (Hebrew). Recent scholarly

prophecy or prophetic activity—contrary to some early sources—was not universally imagined to be in a latent phase until the coming of the eschatological age, during which the prophetic gift would be restored and even consummated.[3] (And even if a consummate prophetic figure was thought to herald the coming of the Messiah, such a claim does not inherently require the cessation of prophecy in the meantime.) In other words, even if older models of prophecy did cease to function in this period, new forms emerged to take their place.

Even within scriptural texts, interpretative writing had already made purchase as a mode of receiving and articulating divine revelation,[4] and early apocalypticism was at least in part a recipient of the mantle of Israelite prophecy in the Persian and Hellenistic periods. Thus it is perhaps most appropriate to think in the terms offered by Thomas Overholt: "We cannot correctly say that prophecy ended with the exile, either in the sense that it ceased or that it was transformed into something else" but "we ought to conceive of prophecy as a continuing potentiality in a given society."[5]

This point about the continuation of prophetic activity is extremely important for understanding the intellectual and religious world of mid-late Second Temple Judaism. Bracketing for the moment any sort of agonistic theories about the struggle for power among various Jewish

---

work has successfully challenged the older view by reevaluating the relevant material. In addition to those works list above in n. 39, see for example Frederick Greenspahn, "Why Prophecy Ceased," *JBL* 108 (1989): 37–49; John Levison, "Did the Spirit Withdraw from Israel? An Evaluation of the Earliest Jewish Data," *NTS* 43 (1997): 35–57; William Schniedewind, *The Word of God in Transition*; Naomi Cohen, "From *Nabi* to *Mal'ak* to 'Ancient Figure,'" *JJS* 36 (1985): 12–24; and the recent volume edited by Michael Floyd and Robert Haak, *Prophets, Prophecy, and Prophetic Texts in Second Temple Judaism* (LHBOTS 427; London: T&T Clark, 2006). See also Jacob Neuser, "What 'the Rabbis' Thought: A Method and a Result. One Statement on Prophecy in Rabbinic Judaism," in *Pursuing the Text: Studies in Honor of Ben Zion Wacholder on the Occasion of His Seventieth Birthday* (ed. J. C. Reeves and J. Kampen; JSOTSup 184; Sheffield: JSOT Press, 1994), 303–20.

[3] On this see, for example, Kobelski, *Melchizedek*, passim.

[4] Michael Fishbane, *Biblical Interpretation in Ancient Israel*, esp. the section on "Mantological Exegesis," 443–505; Hindy Najman, "The Symbolic Significance of Writing,"; Schniedewind, *The Word of God in Transition*.

[5] Thomas Overholt, *Channels of Prophecy: The Social Dynamics of Prophetic Activity* (Minneapolis: Fortress, 1989), 161; cf. Stephen B. Reid, "The End of Prophecy in Light of Contemporary Social Theory," *SBLSP* 24 (1985): 515–23; David Petersen, "Israelite Prophecy: Change Versus Continuity," in *Congress Volume Leuven 1989* (ed. J. A. Emerton; VTSup 43; Leiden: Brill, 1991), 190–203.

groups in the Second Temple period[6]—and the corollary claims to authority rooted in appeals to right knowledge and praxis—the prophetic tradition (if not exactly the *figure* of the prophet *per se*) seems to have played a major role in the restoration of the exilic community, the shaping of the biblical canon,[7] and the emergence of apocalypticism, not to mention the self-understanding of John the Baptist, Jesus, and other early Christian figures.[8] Though the ancient sources offer a portrait of prophetic activity in the post-exilic period that is less clearly drawn than we might wish, and thus they do not allow for a final and definitive conclusion to the issue, they allow at the very least for the provisional assumption that in the minds of some religious Jews of the Second Temple period God continued to make known his will, his "plans," by means of some modified forms of prophetic activity.[9]

It will be helpful at this point to clarify the definition of "prophetic activity" or "prophecy" under consideration here, and why it might be appropriate to speak in this way about certain material found in some biblical and pseudepigraphical works and in the Qumran Scrolls. If older scholarly distinctions between "classical" and other forms of prophetic behavior still have any purchase in our imaginations,[10] there is good reason to be cautious in this area, especially since prophecy, properly speaking, was thought in some circles to have ceased with the last of the classical or "writing" prophets. To be sure, we do not find in the mid-late

---

[6] For example those theories posited by Plöger, *Theocracy and Eschatology*, and Hanson, *Dawn of Apocalyptic*.

[7] Joseph Blenkinsopp, *Prophecy and Canon: A Contribution to the Study of Jewish Origins* (Notre Dame, Ind.: University of Notre Dame Press, 1977), esp. 124–52.

[8] Otto Plöger, with some justification, reflects that the canonization of the prophetic corpus was related to an apocalyptic, eschatological group associated with the conventicle behind the production of the book of Daniel: "I [have come] to regard it as increasingly probable that the gradual collection of the products of the prophetic spirit into a canon parallel to the Pentateuch was not led primarily by the representatives of the official Jewish community; rather—to express it somewhat vaguely in the first place—it was directed by groups that had a definite eschatological interest and lived on the spirit of prophecy into paths which may perhaps be regarded as an earlier stage of the *Hasidim*" (*Theocracy and Eschatology*, 23). Blenkinsopp, on the other hand, sees in the later redactional stages of Isaiah the precursors to the *maśkîlîm* and the *rabbîm* of the book of Daniel and the Qumran community (Isa 52:11, 13; Dan 11:32–33; *Damascus Document, Community Rule*); see his *Opening the Sealed Book*, 18–28.

[9] Philo, *Cher.* 27; *Migr.* 34–35; Josephus, *J.W.* 1.68–69; *Ant.* 20.97.

[10] See for example S. Paul, "Prophets and Prophecy," *EncJud* 10.1150–76.

Second Temple period the kinds of prophetic figures and their associated roles as once existed in the earlier life of Israelite society,[11] and again we must emphasize the fluid nature of prophetic activity and be clear about what we do find in the period under investigation. Even while we do this we must bear in mind that during the earlier life of ancient Israel, prophets came in many forms and under varying circumstances.[12] In any case, it is clear that for some groups during the Second Temple period, the Spirit did *not* depart from Israel.

In his book *The Word of God in Transition: From Prophet to Exegete in the Second Temple Period*, William Schniedewind demonstrates several ways in which Israel's prophetic tradition experienced a dramatic shift after the Babylonian Exile. Focusing on the work of the Chronicler, Schniedewind traces the transition from prophet to "inspired messenger" to show how various messengers, "moved by the spirit, become prophetically inspired exegetes."[13] He applies this model of transition also to the evolution and growth of prophetic literature such as Jeremiah and Isaiah, arguing that "it is through the inspired voice (or inspired messenger) who collects and edits that we hear the voice of the historical Isaiah."[14] About the book(s) of Chronicles he argues that it is *"an interpretation of prophecy* [that is, the Deuteronomistic History] and, on the other hand, *a reflection of postexilic prophecy itself."*[15] Perhaps the same could be said of, say, the Qumran *pesharim* or the rewritten biblical texts among the Qumran Scrolls, a point to which we will return below.

The idea that prophecy continued in the form of inspired interpretation of existing texts has been well documented. Armin Lange and others have called this *Schriftprophetie*, by which the exegetical creation of new meaning "can be described as an act of prophecy in

---

[11] See for example Robert R. Wilson, *Prophecy and Society in Ancient Israel* (Philadelphia: Fortress, 1980); Joseph Blenkinsopp, *A History of Prophecy in Israel* (rev. and enl. ed.; Louisville, Ky.: Westminster John Knox, 1996), 26–72.

[12] Even the nomenclature assigned to biblical prophetic figures underlines this point (even if there was some functional overlap among the different titles). See David L. Petersen, *The Prophetic Literature: An Introduction* (Louisville, Ky.: Westminster John Knox, 2002), 5-8; Wilson, *Prophecy and Society in Ancient Israel*, 21–28; idem, "Prophecy and Ecstasy: A reexamination," *JBL* 98 (1979): 321–37. The variety of types of prophecy is also emphasized by VanderKam in "The Prophetic-Sapiential Origins of Apocalyptic Thought."

[13] Schniedewind, *Word of God in Transition*, 238.

[14] Ibid., 241. Schniedewind perhaps has the work of Michael Fishbane in mind here. See Fishbane's treatment of what he calls "mantological exegesis" in his *Biblical Interpretation in Ancient Israel*, 441–524.

[15] Schniedewind, *Word of God in Transition*, 22 (italics his).

itself."[16] This is, of course, but one trajectory of prophetic activity as it continues into the Second Temple period. In addition to this kind of *Schriftprophetie* we might also say something about apocalypticism, mantic wisdom, and priestly forms of divination and revelation—and again, we must keep in mind the dynamic and interpenetrating nature of the various religious discourses and practices under consideration here. (For example, while we may discuss prophetic and priestly dimensions as separate categories, they may also at times overlap in interesting ways, as in the broad category of "divination.")

With respect to the views about prophecy and prophetic activity among the inhabitants of Qumran, there are two primary types of sources for this question: the texts recovered from Qumran, and the Greek historiographical accounts of Josephus, Philo, and Hippolytus. Given that the members of the Qumran group were Essenes of one kind or another, the ancient Greek sources indicate that prophetic activity would have been part of the normal course of community life. Josephus corroborates this possibility in several places in his writings. He seems to have no problem assuming that prophecy was in some way ongoing, and that it even flourished among the Essenes.[17] Josephus appears to make some important distinctions among different kinds of prophets or prophetic figures, and is somewhat sparing in his application of the term προφήτης to noncanonical prophets of the Second Temple period.[18] But

---

[16] Armin Lange, "Reading the Decline of Prophecy," in *Reading the Present in the Qumran Library: The Perception of the Contemporary by Means of Scriptural Interpretations* (ed. Kristin De Troyer and Armin Lange; SBLSymS 30; Atlanta: Society of Biblical Literature, 2005), 190; idem, *Vom prophetischen Wort zur prophetischen Tradition: Studien zur Traditions- und Redaktionsgeschichte innerprophetischer Konflikte in der Hebräischen Bibel* (FAT 34; Tübingen: Mohr Siebeck, 2002); see also O. H. Steck, *Die Prophetenbücher und ihr theologisches Zeugnis: Wege der Nachfrage und Fährten zur Antwort* (Tübingen: Mohr Siebeck, 1996), 166–86.

[17] For an especially lucid and helpful account see Gray, *Prophetic Figures in Second Temple Jewish Palestine*; cf. Todd S. Beall, *Josephus' Description of the Essenes Illustrated by the Dead Sea Scrolls* (Cambridge: Cambridge University Press, 1988); George J. Brooke, "Prophecy," *DSSE* 2.694–700; Millar Burrows, "Prophecy and Prophets at Qumrân," in *Israel's Prophetic Heritage: Essays in Honor of James Muilenburg* (ed. Bernhard W. Anderson and Walter Harrelson; New York: Harper, 1962), 223–32.

[18] As David Aune points out in a short note ("The Use of ΠΡΟΦΗΤΗΣ in Josephus," *JBL* 101 [1982]: 419–21), scholars have in recent years tended to accept the assertion that Josephus applies the term only to canonical OT prophets. Aune, however, goes on to demonstrate that there are at least two cases in which

given the widespread use of this term in other Jewish and Christian literature of the period, it was probably not generally restricted to the technical designation of a "canonical prophet," even if Josephus seems to prefer the distinction.[19] Furthermore, Hippolytus says in his *Refutation of All Heresies* that the Essenes cultivated "the practice of prophecy and the prediction of future events" τὸ προφητεύειν καὶ προλέγειν τὸ ἐσόμενα.[20] It is not clear here whether Hippolytus means to be redundant, or whether we may take his words as an indication that there was an important distinction to be made between "prophesying" and "predicting," between prophecy and divination, or whether he means to employ hendiadys to suggest that prophesying is inherently the foretelling of the things to come.

In any case, it is true that Josephus's depictions of Essene prophecy fall solely into the category of *predictive* pronouncements; the figures he portrays do not generally go about the business of proclaiming the will of God in the way of the early canonical prophets, namely by bringing forth the covenant traditions to bear witness to the contemporary social, political, and religious situation. Instead, they predict what will happen within the social, political, and military spheres of Jewish and Roman life, and do not, as Josephus tells it, deal with the ethical and religious demands of the covenant. With respect to the Essenes, Josephus uses only μάντις-terminology in connection with the prophetic figures he mentions (Judas, Menahem and Simon), a fact which is intriguing for what it might suggest about Essene divinitory practices, at the same time that it does little to clarify just how Josephus thought about these figures and their practices.[21]

Josephus uses προφήτης to refer to "persons in the late second temple period whom he describes as prophetically gifted (or so regard themselves). ..." In one of these (*Ant.* 1.15), Josephus seems to accept the appellation given to one "Kleodemos the prophet, also called Malchos," whose prophetic authority was apparently linked to his status as a historian (also *Ag. Ap.* 1.37–38). Josephus also apparently considered his own historiographical work to be in line with the tradition that identified history-writing with prophecy. Interestingly, Josephus also makes the claim that from an early age Samson, who in Judg 13:5 is called a נזיר (a "Nazirite"), "clearly was to be a prophet" δῆλος ἦν προφητεύσων (*Ant.* 5.285). I have Eugene Ulrich to thank for this reference. See his *The Qumran Text of Samuel and Josephus* (HSM 19; Cambridge, Mass.: Harvard University Press, 1978), 165–66.

[19] See Aune, *Prophecy in Early Christianity*, 103–52.

[20] *Refutatio* 27; this reference is taken from VanderKam, "Mantic Wisdom in the Dead Sea Scrolls," 340.

[21] It is also of interest that Josephus recounts an episode concerning a dream

The Hebrew texts from Qumran would appear to align at least in part with Josephus's distinctions between προφήτης- and μάντις-terminology, especially regarding the possible distinctions between different forms of prophetic activity. As Blenkinsopp notes, "the men of Qumran avoid using the word *nābî'* while clearly claiming for themselves, and for the *mōreh hassedeq* in superlative measure, the gift of prophecy in the sense of direct access to revelation."[22] In other words, the *activity* of prophecy is present even if the dominant biblical term for prophet (*nābî'*) is not.[23] To affirm his conclusion Blenkinsopp marshalls texts such as the *Hodayot* (passim), the *Community Rule* (1QS 9:3), and *Pesher Habakkuk* (1QpHab 2:9; 7:5), most of which present the prophetic figure as one who somehow has access to "mysteries." Since the present work is on "mystery" in the Qumran Scrolls, and not strictly the question of prophecy among the Qumran group, it would be helpful if a more direct link could be established between the use of mystery language vis-à-vis the Essenes and the status and nature of prophetic activity among them.

---

of Archelaus, an episode that closely resembles the dream-interpretation sequences found in the Joseph cycle and in the Danielic court-tales. In this passage (*J.W.* 2.111–13), Josephus claims that Simon the Essene, with "various interpretations being given," offered his own (presumably correct) view of the dream and its interpretation. Elsewhere (*J.W.* 3.352) Josephus presents himself in a similar fashion, namely as a priest with knowledge of scripture and the ability to interpret dreams.

[22] Joseph Blenkinsopp, "Prophecy and Priesthood in Josephus," *JJS* 25 (1974): 245. Of course this may also be due to the general trend away from the use of the term נביא in the post-exilic period. As Naomi Cohen demonstrates, "though this is perhaps often overlooked, in the exilic and post-exilic prophetic works the term *mal'ak* ["messenger"] comes to be used as a synonym for the word *nabi*, eventually virtually replacing it completely" ("From *Nabi* to *Mal'ak* to 'Ancient Figure,'" 13).

[23] See also George Brooke, "Prophets and Prophecy in the Qumran Scrolls and in the New Testament" (paper presented at the Ninth Annual Orion Symposium, Hebrew University, Jerusalem, Israel, January 2004), http://orion.mscc.huji.ac.il/symposiums/9th/papers/BrookePaper.html: "The weight of explicit use of the terms [for prophets and prophecy] is in the past, but there is enough to suggest that continuities with scriptural prophets and prophecy were maintained in the community's present and for the future. The strength of identifying and describing those continuities rests chiefly in a more phenomenological approach in which it is possible to see that the communities [sic] interest in the exposition of the law, its interpretation of the prophets and its creative poetic activities were very much consistent, coherent, and continuous with the activities of prophets of earlier generations."

One helpful way to clarify this issue is to appeal to the category of mantic wisdom that has received an increasing amount of attention in recent years.[24] This broad category provides a useful conceptual framework for understanding the development of prophecy and apocalypticism in the late Second Temple period—or in other words how apocalyptic ways of thinking and writing were extended from earlier notions of both Israelite prophecy and wisdom. As VanderKam has shown, "certain kinds of mantic wisdom and late prophecy were closely related phenomena, and both clearly contributed to the thinking of the apocalyptists,"[25] of which the Qumran group appears to have been a good example.[26]

While there was likely at least a partial association between prophecy and divination at Qumran, there were clearly preferred forms of divination that were licit and authoritative means of deriving the kinds of esoteric knowledge specific to the Yaḥad. And there were also perhaps forms of prophetic activity that would not properly be classified as "divination" in the context of the contemporary ancient Near Eastern and Hellenistic cultures, as well as forms of divination that were not historically associated with the prophetic mode of revelation—such as casting of lots, which was a divinatory practice restricted to the priestly domain.[27]

George Brooke advocates a full view of prophetic activity reflected in the Qumran Scrolls. Though for the sake of the structure of my argument I discuss priestly divination in a separate section, I am in substantial agreement with Brooke's assessment:

Once the term *prophecy* is not narrowly restricted to those in the Bible who are labeled as prophets (especially *navi'*), then the study of

---

[24] Müller, "Mantische-Weisheit"; VanderKam, "Mantic Wisdom in the Dead Sea Scrolls"; Lange, "The Essene Position on Magic and Divination."

[25] VanderKam, "Mantic Wisdom in the Dead Sea Scrolls," 338.

[26] But see Carol Newsom, "Apocalyptic and the Discourse of the Qumran Community," *JNES* 49 (1990): 135–44. In this article (which seems to lay the groundwork for her later book, *The Self As Symbolic Space*), Newsom cautions against making the straightforward assumption that the Qumran community was an "apocalyptic community": "Judgment about the role of apocalyptic should be reserved until we can assess the specific ways in which apocalyptic motifs figure in that discourse [about what most interests the Qumran sectarians] and are combined with other distinctive vocabularies of motive and meaning" (136). Also Collins, "Was the Dead Sea Sect an Apocalyptic Movement?"

[27] Burke O. Long, "The Effect of Divination upon Israelite Literature," *JBL* 92 (1973): 489–97.

prophecy in the Dead Sea Scrolls should consider all the means of divine communication that are hinted at in the scrolls: the transmission and interpretation of visions and dreams (as in the Enoch literature and Daniel), the use of lots and priestly means of divination, such as the Urim and Thummim, the writing down of angelic discourse (as in *Jubilees*), inspired interpretation of authoritative oracles (as in the *pesharim*), and the symbolic activity of the community as a whole and of its individual members.[28]

In the category of divinatory literature from Qumran we may place, along with VanderKam, those texts that deal with astronomical and astrological phenomena on the one hand, and on the other hand those texts that present other divinatory methods rooted in dream interpretation and the "mantic manipulation of prophetic texts (understood broadly)."[29] The former category includes texts like 4QHoroscope (4Q186), 4QPhysiognomy/Horoscope ar (4Q561), 4QBrontologion ar (4Q318), and perhaps 4QBirth of Noah (or "Elect of God") ar (4Q534–36), though only the last of these employs the word רז in its extant portions and is a non-sectarian text. In the latter category we find a broader range of texts, including those that preceded (or were, in VanderKam's words, "inherited by") the Yaḥad as well as those that were composed by the Qumran group or its predecessors, texts like *1 Enoch*, Daniel, *Aramaic Levi*, *Jubilees*, the *Genesis Apocryphon*, and the Qumran *pesher* literature. Again, because this is a study of "mystery" and not of the full range of divinatory practices among the Qumran group,[30] we shall limit the investigation to those texts that employ רז while referring to others where appropriate.

Returning to the discussion of prophetic discourse, there are essentially two different ways to characterize prophetic aspects of the use of רז in the Qumran Scrolls: the experiential, including those texts in which a speaker (an "I") recounts or celebrates the revelation of "mystery" or "mysteries" to him by God; and the exegetical, including those texts which participate in the kind of *Schriftprophetie* mentioned above, the inspired reinterpretation ("mantic manipulation") of existing prophetic texts. Both of these prophetic modes were revelatory insofar as

---

[28] Brooke, "Prophecy," *DSSE*, 2.695.

[29] "Mantic Wisdom in the Dead Sea Scrolls," 350. By "mantic manipulation" VanderKam means a kind of divination that derives new (inspired) meaning from the authoritative exegesis of existing texts—meaning that often has a predictive value.

[30] For a detailed and lengthy study of magic and divination at Qumran, see Lange, "The Essene Position on Magic and Divination."

they resulted in what the Yaḥad took to be new understanding of the nature of the cosmos and God's purposes, as well as the transmission of that new understanding to those "in the know." As we will see, however, because of the complex nature of the relationship between textuality, performance, and experience, it is often difficult to distinguish between the exegetical and the experiential in the texts we will address. Perhaps the present study will contribute to an increasing appreciation for the ways in which both textual traditions and ritual experiences are often simultaneous and mutually informing and reinforcing.

EXEGETICAL PROPHECY AND "MYSTERY"

The exegetical interests of the Qumran community are well known and have been studied with great care. The Qumran library exhibits not only pluriform biblical text-types with possibly different, independent exegetical tendencies,[31] but also newly discovered forms of biblical interpretation such as the *pesher* literature,[32] rewritten biblical texts,[33] and

---

[31] This is the most recent theory along the trajectory of the "text-type" theory initiated by W. F. Albright ("New Light on Early Recensions of the Hebrew Bible," *BASOR* 140 [1955]: 27–33) and championed by Frank Moore Cross ("The History of the Biblical Text in the Light of the Discoveries in the Judaean Desert," *HTR* 57 [1964]: 281–99; idem, "The Contribution of the Qumrân Discoveries to the Study of the Biblical Text," *IEJ* 16 [1966]: 81–95). This theory has been modified and developed over the past couple decades by Eugene Ulrich in a series of articles and books on the "successive literary editions" of biblical texts. See *The Dead Sea Scrolls and the Origins of the Bible*; "The Dead Sea Scrolls and the Hebrew Scriptural Texts," in *Scripture and the Scrolls* (ed. James H. Charlesworth; vol. 1 of *The Bible and the Dead Sea Scrolls: The Princeton Symposium on the Dead Sea Scrolls*, ed. James H. Charlesworth; Waco, Tex.: Baylor University Press, 2006), 77–99; "The Qumran Scrolls and the Biblical Text," in *The Dead Sea Scrolls Fifty Years after Their Discovery: Proceedings of the Jerusalem Congress, July 20–25, 1997* (ed. L. H. Schiffman, E. Tov and J. C. VanderKam; Jerusalem: Israel Exploration Society and the Shrine of the Book Museum, 2000), 51–59. Flint and VanderKam have offered a concise summary of this theory: "[T]hese different [successive] literary editions occurred later in the compositional process of the Scriptures, which took place in several stages that were different for each book or set of books. Each new edition resulted from the creative efforts of some author or scribe who intentionally revised the edition (or passages) current in his time in the light of a new religious outlook or national challenge. ... As they developed over time (i.e. *diachronically*) Ulrich labels the variant editions *text traditions*, and when considered at the same time (i.e. *synchronically*), he calls them *text types*" (*The Meaning of the Dead Sea Scrolls*, 144).

[32] In addition, J. J. M. Roberts has noted the similarities and continuities

other types of commentary whose aim is to interpret, update, harmonize, and correct or otherwise to interact with the emerging body of authoritative scriptures.[34] The type of exegesis most germane here is the

---

between "inner-biblical exegesis" and Qumran exegesis, taking the development of Isaiah and its Qumran *pesher* as an illustration: "[O]ne should recognize that there are many points of continuity between Qumran exegesis and the internal development of the very biblical texts that the Qumran exegetes were interpreting" ("The Importance of Isaiah at Qumran," in *Scripture and the Scrolls* [ed. James H. Charlesworth; vol. 1 of *The Bible and the Dead Sea Scrolls: The Princeton Symposium on the Dead Sea Scrolls*, ed. James H. Charlesworth; Waco, Tex.: Baylor University Press, 2006], 280).

[33] The category of "rewritten Bible" has received a notable share of scholarly attention in recent years, in part because of the important contribution these texts make to textual criticism and to understanding the canonical history of the Bible, methods of biblical interpretation and transmission, and the literary and hermeneutical creativity of religious Jews in the Second Temple period. But the category is also the subject of some terminological controversy, given the fact that during the period concerned there was not yet a "Bible" and that there were multiple editions of scriptural texts in circulation. It is thus anachronistic to use such a term, because there was as yet no "consensus text"; the "Bible" that had apparently been *re*written was not itself established until centuries later. The term "rewritten Bible" was first coined by Geza Vermes in the second chapter of his *Scripture and Tradition in Judaism: Haggadic Studies* (SPB 4; Leiden: Brill, 1974). For subsequent discussion see George J. Brooke, "Rewritten Bible," *EDSS* 2.777–81; Moshe Bernstein, "4Q252: From Re-Written Bible to Biblical Commentary," *JJS* 45 (1994): 1–27; George W. E. Nickelsburg, "The Bible Rewritten and Expanded," in *Jewish Writings of the Second Temple Period: Apocrypha, Pseudepigrapha, Qumran Sectarian Writings, Philo, Josephus* (ed. Michael E. Stone; CRINT 2.2; Philadelphia: Fortress, 1984), 89–156; Craig Evans, "The Genesis Apocryphon and the Rewritten Bible," *RevQ* 13 (1988): 153–65; Devorah Dimant, "Use and Interpretation of Mikra in the Apocrypha and Pseudepigrapha," in *Mikra: Text, Translation, Reading and Interpretation of the Hebrew Bible in Ancient Judaism and Early Christianity* (ed. Martin J. Mulder; CRINT 2.1; Minneapolis: Fortress, 1990), 379–419. For discussion about the terminological infelicities, see Sidnie White Crawford, "The Rewritten Bible at Qumran," *Scripture and the Scrolls* (ed. James H. Charlesworth; vol. 1 of *The Bible and the Dead Sea Scrolls: The Princeton Symposium on the Dead Sea Scrolls*, ed. James H. Charlesworth; Waco, Tex.: Baylor University Press, 2006), 131–47, esp. 131–34. See recently Crawford, *Rewriting Scripture in Second Temple Times* (SDSSRL; Grand Rapids, Mich.: Eerdmans, 2008); Daniel K. Falk, *The Parabiblical Texts: Strategies for Extending the Scriptures among the Dead Sea Scrolls* (LSTS 63; T&T Clark, 2007).

[34] See Moshe Bernstein, "Interpretation of Scriptures," *EDSS* 1.376–83; George J. Brooke, *Exegesis at Qumran: 4QFlorilegium in Its Jewish Context* (JSOTSup 29; Sheffield: JSOT Press, 1985); William Brownlee, "Biblical Interpretation

pesher, though other forms are also relevant in an indirect way insofar as they attest to the capacity of the Qumran group to produce and guard esoteric knowledge based on its own exegetical activities. Thus, while I will discuss only the texts directly dealing with the use of "mystery," perhaps we may consider the whole body of Qumran exegetical literature to exist within the community's domain of special (secret) knowledge.[35] The overall task of interpretation seems to have been directly related to the community's self-understanding as true guardians of *torah* in terms of both belief and practice; "the books of what is now known as the Hebrew scriptures frequently functioned as both the source and the framework for what the Qumran writers wanted to say and the way in which they said it."[36]

The *pesher* genre is one of the more interesting and frequently employed forms of interpretative writing found in the Qumran caves.[37] It is a specific, Qumranic adaptation of a divinatory form that was evidently widespread in the ancient Near Eastern world, and that was

---

among the Sectaries of the Dead Sea Scrolls," *BA* 14 (1951): 54–76; Michael Fishbane, "Use, Authority, and Interpretation of Mikra at Qumran," in *Mikra: Text, Translation, Reading, and Interpretation of the Hebrew Bible in Ancient Judaism and Early Christianity* (ed. Martin J. Mulder; CRINT 2.1; Minneapolis: Fortress, 1988), 339–77; Henri Gabrion, "L'Interprétation de l'Ecriture dans la littérature de Qumrân," *ANRW* 19.1 (1979): 779–848; Matthias Henze, ed., *Biblical Interpretation at Qumran* (SDSSRL; Grand Rapids, Mich.: Eerdmans, 2005); Daniel Patte, *Early Jewish Hermeneutic in Palestine* (SBLDS 22; Missoula, Mont.: Scholars Press, 1975); Otto Betz, *Offenbarung und Schriftforschung in der Qumransekte* (WUNT 6; Tübingen: Mohr Siebeck, 1960); J. Maier, "Early Jewish Biblical Interpretation in the Qumran Literature," in *Hebrew Bible/Old Testament: The History of Its Interpretation*, vol. 1: *From the Beginnings to the Middle Ages (Until 1300)* (ed. M. Sæbø; Göttingen: Vandenhoeck & Ruprecht, 1996), 108–29; Geza Vermes, "Bible Interpretation at Qumran," in *Yigael Yadin Memorial Volume* (ed. A. Ben-Tor, J. C. Greenfield, and A. Malamat; Jerusalem: Israel Exploration Society, 1989), 184–91.

[35] The compositions included in the *Exegetical Texts* volume of Brill's genre-specific Dead Sea Scrolls Reader are almost entirely sectarian texts. The volume includes both the "thematic" and the "continuous" *pesharim*, the commentaries on Genesis (4Q252–54a) and Malachi (4Q253a), the so-called 4QTanhumim (4Q176) and 4QTestimonia (4Q175), the *Midrash Sefer Moshe* (4Q249) written in the Cryptic A script, and several other *pesher*-like texts. See Donald W. Parry and Emanuel Tov, eds., *Exegetical Texts* (DSSR 2; Leiden: Brill, 2004).

[36] Moshe Bernstein, "Interpretation of Scriptures," 1.376.

[37] Horgan, *Pesharim*; Shani Berrin, "Qumran Pesharim," in *Biblical Interpretation at Qumran* (ed. Matthias Henze; SDSSRL; Grand Rapids, Mich.: Eerdmans, 2005), 110–33; George Brooke, "Qumran Pesher: Toward the Redefinition of a Genre," *RevQ* 10 (1981): 483–503.

used, in perhaps its most famous example, in the Danielic court tales to provide the dream-interpretation sequence with its core structure and rationale. The word *pesher* itself is related to the Akkadian *pašāru*, which was used in the context of omen-interpretation to signify interpretations of enigmatic and symbolic vision-dreams, which often had the therapeutic and even prophylactic function of dissipating the evil consequences revealed in the dream.[38]

It is worth noting that in the ancient material—and especially in Dan 2 and 4—the interpretation or *pesher* is as much a part of the revelation as is the sign which it interprets.[39] The interpretation "is not *an exposition* but is *the revelation* of the message of the deity addressed to the dreaming person concerning the future."[40] Thus, in a text roughly contemporaneous to the Qumran literature, we find that revelation and interpretation are intertwined in such a way that the latter becomes part of the former—a reflex not unlike the scripture-interpretation scenario described in the "visions" section of the book of Daniel (Dan 9:2–27). There, after Daniel reads and reflects upon the writings of Jeremiah and the meaning of the "seventy weeks" (Jer 25:11, 12; 29:10), the angelic interpreter Gabriel comes to him "at the time of the evening sacrifice" and reveals the "true" meaning of Jeremiah's prophecy.[41] The

---

[38] A. Leo Oppenheim, *The Interpretation of Dreams in the Ancient Near East. With a Translation of an Assyrian Dream-Book* (*TAPS* 46; Philadelphia: The American Philosophical Society, 1956), 217–25; Horgan, *Pesharim*, 231–37.

[39] Anne Marie Kitz calls attention to the relationship between Israelite and Mesopotamian divination that leads her to the conclusion that "in general, Mesopotamian texts do not distinctly state that diviners ever provided interpretations that were themselves divinely inspired. By the Neo-Assyrian period, competing interpretations were of such concern that the kings began to work out their own explanations. ... Those responsible for the received texts of the Hebrew Bible prefer a different emphasis. Sometime during the evolution of Israel's religion, the interpretation of a divine sign became its *divinely inspired* interpretation, which, in turn, became an integral element of the initial sign itself, whether this was received as word, vision, dream, or deed" ("Prophecy as Divination," *CBQ* 65 [2003]: 41). Strangely, she does not include Daniel among the biblical texts she treats in her essay.

[40] Horgan, *Pesharim*, 231; italics mine.

[41] The *angelus interpres*, or an angelic mediator in general, is a common feature of late prophetic and apocalyptic writing, and has been studied at length in the scholarly literature. What is noteworthy here is that in the prophetic writings of the post-exilic period, the angelic mediator becomes an element almost *sine qua non* for revelatory experience. See for example James L. Kugel and Rowan A. Greer, *Early Biblical Interpretation* (LEC 3; Philadelphia: Westminster Press, 1986), 13–39; Hindy Najman, "Angels at Sinai: Exegesis, Theology and

interpretation of the prophecy (by means of an angelic mediator) becomes the new prophecy.

The *pesharim* represent one way in which prophecy—or a prophetic statement—could be "updated" using the analogy of the Danielic *raz-pesher* sequence, in which both the "mystery" and its interpretation were considered inseparable parts of the revelation as a whole. The mechanics of this comparison have been studied at some length,[42] and it is not necessary to recapitulate the arguments here. As I discussed in chapter 3, we must note that *both the dream and its interpretation* are part of the "mystery": Dan 2:28 states that "there is a God in heaven who reveals mysteries, and He has made known to King Nebuchadnezzar what is to be at the end of days. This is your dream. ..." Daniel must recount both the dream and its meaning—not simply interpret a dream narrative that has already been recounted. Daniel goes on in the story to claim that "not because my wisdom is greater than that of other creatures has this mystery been revealed to me, but in order that the meaning should be made known to the king ..." (Dan 2:30). It is built into the logic of the story that both the thing to be interpreted and its interpretation are given together to Daniel, who is uniquely qualified (despite his own humility about his wisdom[43]) to receive and understand the message and its true meaning. This appears also to be the principle underlying the Danielic updating of Jeremiah's "seventy weeks" prophecy (Dan 9:2–27).

All this can help us to understand the hermeneutical reasoning behind the task of *pesher* interpretation, namely that in the minds of the Qumran community members the prophetic scriptures were always subject to authoritative interpretation based on the special, esoteric knowledge of the Teacher of Righteousness and his inheritance.[44] While

---

Interpretive Authority," *DSD* 7 (2000): 313–33; James C. VanderKam, "The Angel of the Presence in the Book of Jubilees," *DSD* 7 (2000): 378–93.

[42] Asher Finkel, "The Pesher of Dreams and Scriptures," *RevQ* 4 (1963–64): 357–70; Blenkinsopp, *Opening the Sealed Book*, 14–27.

[43] This is itself perhaps a reflex of the convention of prophetic humility—i.e. that the prophet is not a specialist or a technician, but one who is chosen for his lack of preparation. See, for example, Exod 3:11, 4:10–13; Isa 6:4–7; and Jer 1:6–7. Alternatively, it may simply be attributable to the fact that by the mid-Second Temple period certain strands of Jewish wisdom had embraced the notion that the only true wisdom comes by revelation from God, and thus Daniel's humility serves to underscore that point.

[44] See S. D. Fraade, "Interpretative Authority in the Studying Community at Qumran," *JJS* 44 (1993): 46–69; C. Hempel, "Interpretative Authority in the Community Rule Tradition," *DSD* 10 (2003): 59–80. In recent years it has become more and more clear that we should think in terms of the evolution or

there is only one *pesher* from Qumran (1QpHab) that employs in extant portions the word רז, it does so in a way which appears to include the interpretive activity found in the other *pesharim*. In a famous passage in the seventh column of *Pesher Habakkuk*, the text declares the true meaning of the lemma in Hab 2:2, "So that the one who runs[45] may read it" למען ירוץ הקורא בו:

1QpHab 7:4–5

4 פשרו על מורה הצדק אשר הודיעו אל את

5 כול רזי דברי עבדיו הנבאים

4 Its interpretation concerns the Teacher of Righteousness, to whom God has made known
5 all the mysteries of the words of his servants, the prophets.

In a gloss on Habakkuk, in other words, the writer claims for the Teacher "all the mysteries" of the *words* of the *prophets*.[46] Perhaps we may take the series of plurals here to refer to all those writings that for the Qumran community would have fallen into the category of "the prophets."[47] In

---

development of the Qumran community over time, beginning with the early stages of the Yaḥad before the Qumran settlement and ending with the Roman destruction of the site. The redactional history of the *Community Rule* traditions, for example, suggests such a development over the life of the Yaḥad. In any case, 1QS states that it is the *Maskil* who takes on the task of guiding the people of the community "with knowledge and thus instruct them in the wonderful and true mysteries … in all that has been revealed to them" (1QS 9:18–19).

[45] MT does not include the definite article prefixed to the participle קורא. The phrase ירוץ קורא has been interpreted in different ways; while "one who runs [or a runner] may read it" is a common enough translation (e.g. NRSV), others have rendered it along the lines of "so that a reader may run with it," which may be a specific reference to a social category of the "town crier"—i.e. one who announces crucial information in a public setting.

[46] Elsewhere in *Pesher Habakkuk* it states, "when they hear all that is going to come upon the last generation from the mouth of the priest into whose heart God has put understanding to interpret all the words of his servants the prophets" (1QpHab 2:7–10; Horgan, *Pesharim*, 229).

[47] George Brooke notes an interesting discrepancy in the treatment of the prophetic literature at Qumran, one that may have interesting implications which I will take up in a later study. Brooke points out that only Isaiah and the Twelve are the subject of sectarian *pesher*-like commentaries in extant works, and that Jeremiah and Ezekiel evidently did not receive such treatment. On the other hand, the latter two exist in several (non-sectarian) *rewritten* forms (Apocryphon of Jeremiah A-E; Pseudo-Ezekiel[a-c]), but Isaiah and the Twelve do not. Brooke

any case, it is especially interesting here that the implied subject of ירוץ in Hab 2:2 *can* "read" the vision the prophet has "written on the tablets." Elsewhere in a prophetic text, the same word is used to suggest the inauthenticity of *false* prophets who do not hear a genuine word of God but who "run" all the same: "I did not send the prophets, yet they ran; I did not speak to them, yet they prophesied. But if they had stood in my council (סוד), then they would have proclaimed my words to my people ..." (Jer 23:21–22).

Though it may constitute a rumination from silence (or material degradation), I have wondered why the word רה occurs in column 7 of *Pesher Habakkuk* and yet has not surfaced in any of the other *pesharim*. One possible answer is that unlike any other biblical passages that are the objects of *pesher* interpretation in the Qumran corpus, the lemmata being glossed here deal fairly explicitly with reading what is written and then awaiting or seeking additional revelation. It seems to be understood almost as a brief manifesto of at least one aspect of prophetic revelation at Qumran. The text of Habakkuk states that the prophet is to "write the vision and make it plain upon the tablets so that the one who runs may read it" (Hab 2:2), but that "there is yet a vision (עוד חזון) for the appointed time; it speaks of the end and does not lie ..." (Hab 2:3a). In the same way for the members of the Yaḥad, perhaps they understood their own interpretations to be an inherent part of the revelation that was initiated with the "biblical" prophets, and that their own readings of the "written vision" constituted the עוד חזון of Habakkuk's prophecy—not just the continued vision of Habakkuk but all the legitimate interpretations of all the prophets.

---

forms the following conclusion, which I quote in full: "The rewritten forms of *Jeremiah* and *Ezekiel* include both narrative and visionary material, the former perhaps suggesting that they were viewed as legendworthy men of God like Elijah and Elisha, the latter indicating that subsequent scribal transmission and adjustment of the earlier prophetic text was considered part of prophetic activity. The lack of rewritten forms of *Isaiah* and the Twelve Minor Prophets may be entirely accidental, since it does not mirror what was previously known [about other rewritten forms of these books]. ... Or it may be that the remains of the prophetic literature at Qumran signal something particular about the place of *Isaiah* and the Twelve in the community's self-understanding" (Brooke, "Prophecy," 2.696). Blenkinsopp makes the interesting observation that the book of Isaiah, as a *book*, "as a collection of many 'scraps' and several compilations differing in linguistic character and theme," has more in common with the *Dodekapropheton* than with Jeremiah and Ezekiel (*Opening the Sealed Book*, 6).

Pesher Habakkuk continues to expound Habakkuk's statement, declaring that the additional "vision" that "speaks of the end" suggests that the "last end-time will be prolonged, and it will be greater than anything of which the prophets spoke, for the mysteries of God are wonderful" רזי אל להפלא (1QpHab 7:8). This is an extraordinary statement that makes a rather strong claim not only about the unfolding eschatological drama, but also about the capacity of the Teacher of Righteousness (and his group) to have *even greater* insight into God's "mysteries" than the earlier prophets themselves had.

The next scriptural text in the running commentary advises the reader that "if it tarries, wait for it, for it will surely come, and it will not be late" (Hab 2:3b), a passage that the Qumran sect easily related to itself and its contemporaneous context. The interpretation of the passage makes yet another striking claim about its ultimate meaning:

1QpHab 7:10–14

10... פשרו על אנשי האמת
11 עושי התורה אשר לוא ירפו ידיהם מעבודת
12 האמת בהמשך עליהם הקץ האחרון כיא
13 כול קיצי אל יבואו לתכונם כאשר חקק
14 להם ברזי ערמתו ...

10 ... Its interpretation concerns the men of truth,
11 the doers of the law, whose hands do not drop away from the service
12 of the truth when the last end-time drags on for them—for
13 all of God's ends will come according to their measure, as he decreed
14 for them by the mysteries of his prudence. ...[48]

---

[48] Compare 4Q491c 11 i 10, which states, "He established his truth from of old, and the mysteries of his prudence in eve[ry...]" הכינה מאז אמתו ורזי ערמתו [-- בכו]ל. The context of this passage is difficult to discern, and the fragment itself has been assigned to different compositions such as the *War Rule* and also the *Hodayot*. For a history of the scholarship on this text, see Michael Wise, "מי כמוני באלים: A Study of 4Q491c, 4Q471b, 4Q427 7 and 1QH^a 25:35–26:10," *DSD* 7 (2000): 173–219. See also Morton Smith, "Ascent to the Heavens and Deification in 4QM^a" in *Archaeology and History in the Dead Sea Scrolls* (ed. Lawrence Schiffman; Sheffield: Sheffield Academic Press, 1990), 181–88; M. Abegg, "4Q471: A Case of Mistaken Identity?" in *Pursuing the Text: Studies in Honor of Ben Zion Wacholder on the Occasion of His Seventieth Birthday* (ed. J. C. Reeves, and J. Kampen; JSOTSup 184; Sheffield: JSOT Press, 1994), 136–47; Eshel, "4Q471b: A Self-Glorification Hymn"; D. Dimant, "A Synoptic Comparison of Parallel Sections in 4Q427 7, 4Q491 11 and 4Q471B," *JQR* 85 (1994): 157–61. We will return to a discussion of this text below.

The text reassures its audience that despite appearances to the contrary, God's plan is unfolding according to the pre-existent pattern he has established for the world, a pattern that the Teacher of Righteousness has come to understand so that his interpretation fulfills (even supplants!) the prophecy of Habakkuk.

In spite of what we have observed so far about the hermeneutical strategies in play here and what they accomplish for the authorization of inspired interpretation among the Yaḥad, these observations do not get us much closer to understanding the precise *content* of the "mysteries" and how the Teacher of Righteousness (and anyone else) came to know them. In other words, if we may say that the exegetical work of the Qumran group was a prophetic activity because of its being rooted in, or bringing to light, the "mysteries" of God, whence the knowledge of those "mysteries"? Maurya Horgan puts it this way: "These texts do not give any clues as to how the Qumran interpreters characterized or experienced this revelation."[49] Perhaps a slightly more nuanced way to formulate the problem is this: there are no extant texts which clearly spell out the process or experience of revelation or the precise contents of the resulting knowledge, and so the difficulty is in ascertaining the direction of flow.

Does knowledge of "mysteries" follow from revelatory experience, and then provide the basis for authoritative interpretation? Or does knowledge follow from the interpretative task, which eventually becomes authoritative and provides the basis for (or becomes) new revelation? I agree with Horgan that this is not evident in the *pesharim*, but I suggest that we may look elsewhere to gain a better understanding of the relationship between the experience of revelation and the act of interpretation among the Yaḥad. In the end, though the sources do not allow for a crystal clear picture of the dynamics of this relationship, we may say more about it than so far has been said.

Although we may not hope to resolve this difficulty definitively, it serves to point out again the role that interpretation has played in the long history of biblical revelation,[50] and the fact that we must be wary of positing too great a distinction between the experiential moment of revelation and the act of textual interpretation—as if there was always a pristine moment of "revelation" that later gave way to a derived text

---

[49] Horgan, *Pesharim*, 229. See also Betz, *Offenbarung und Schriftforschung in der Qumransekte*, 82–86.

[50] Michael Fishbane, "Hermeneutics of Scripture in Formation," in *The Garments of Torah: Essays in Biblical Hermeneutics* (ISBL; Bloomington, Ind.: Indiana University Press, 1989), 3–46; idem, *Biblical Interpretation in Ancient Israel*.

which could then be "interpreted." As Hindy Najman noted in her paper "Revelation as Interpretation,"

> in recent years some scholars have taken steps to reject the dichotomy between interpretation and the production of scripture by demonstrating that scripture production is part of a long and ancient process of biblical interpretation so that interpretation is already active or effective within scripture production.[51]

While the present task is not further to illuminate the process of scripture production, but to understand the relationship between revelation and interpretation among the Qumran sectarians, the former may help us with the latter. By dispensing with the dichotomy between revelation and interpretation, we are able to sidestep the problem—at least for the moment—of the direction of flow among revelatory experience, knowledge of the "mysteries," and exegetical work.

With some risk of anachronistically applying a later development in Jewish tradition to an earlier time, I quote Elliot Wolfson's remarks about revelation and interpretation in Medieval kabbalistic texts:

> It is sometimes assumed by scholars of Jewish thought that the modalities of revelation and interpretation are mutually exclusive. An appeal to exegesis thus arises specifically in a situation wherein access to divine revelation has ceased, for were such a revelation forthcoming there would be no need to derive truths out of a fixed canon. *Midrash*, in a word, presupposes a distance from God due to the cessation of prophetic or revelatory states. Yet, it can be shown that within the Judaic tradition, particularly in the apocalyptic and mystical literature, that there is an intrinsic connection between the study of a text and visionary experience. Far from being mutually exclusive, the visionary experience itself may be interpretative in nature, drawing upon prior visions recorded in a written document, while the exegetical task may originate and eventuate in a revelatory state of consciousness.[52]

---

[51] "Revelation as Interpretation" (paper presented at the annual meeting of the Association for Jewish Studies, Los Angeles, Calif., December 15–17, 2002), 1.

[52] Elliot R. Wolfson, "The Hermeneutics of Visionary Experience: Revelation and Interpretation in the Zohar," *Religion* 18 (1988): 312. See also his *Through a Speculum that Shines: Vision and Imagination in Medieval Jewish Mysticism* (Princeton, N.J.: Princeton University Press, 1994). I have Hindy Najman to thank for calling my attention to Wolfson's work. See her "Revelation as Interpretation," 2. Wolfson's comments also serve to call to mind that *midrash*, as an exegetical or hermeneutical phenomenon, only becomes possible at the

Such a relationship between revelation and exegesis has already been posited from both directions by some scholars of the Qumran Scrolls, i.e. that there is possibly a revelatory aspect to *pesher*-type exegesis, and that there is likely a textual basis for the kinds of mystical or visionary experiences described in some of the Qumran liturgical texts.[53] If knowledge of "mystery" seems to be related both to exegesis and to visionary experience in the Qumran (especially sectarian) literature, Wolfson's suggestion may indeed be a helpful way of characterizing what we find to be the case among the Yaḥad.

EXPERIENCE OF "MYSTERY" REVELATION

In a number of sectarian compositions there are indications of a prophetic kind of visionary or otherwise revelatory experience. As might be expected, these are found especially in some of the first-person statements in texts associated with the Teacher of Righteousness and/or the *Maskil*, texts such as the "Teacher Hymns" of the *Hodayot*,[54] *Barkhi*

---

moment at which a text becomes "fixed"—and as such can no longer be changed, elaborated, or adapted to new circumstances—and in this way perhaps it is anachronistic to speak of *midrash* in the Qumran literature. The advances that have been made in the understanding of both the history of the biblical text/canon and the hermeneutical strategies of *midrash* provide a corrective to earlier ways of characterizing the Qumran finds, such as William Brownlee's designation of *Pesher Habakkuk* as a *midrash* (*The Midrash Pesher to Habakkuk*; SBLMS 24; Missoula, Mont.: Scholars Press, 1979). This is not to denigrate earlier scholarship on the Qumran Scrolls, but to suggest that the contours of early Judaism look different with several decades of new perspective and research.

[53] On the one hand see George Brooke, "Qumran Pesher"; idem, *Exegesis at Qumran*, esp. 149–56. On the other hand see Seth Sanders, "Performative Exegesis," in *Paradise Now: Essays on Early Jewish and Christian Mysticism* (ed. April DeConick; SBLSymS 11; Atlanta: Society of Biblical Literature, 2006), 57–82.

[54] I do not intend to enter into the controversies surrounding either the differentiation between Teacher Hymns and Hymns of the Community, or the relationships among the various copies and recensions, of the *Hodayot*. While I recognize that the identity of the first person subject, and thus perhaps also the purpose and genre, of these hymns may vary, the important thing for the present argument is *that* certain statements are made about the "mysteries." For recent work on the editorial history and shaping of the *Hodayot* see Angela Kim Harkins, "Observations on the Editorial Shaping of the So-Called Community Hymns from 1QH^a and 4QH^a (4Q427)," *DSD* 12 (2005): 233–56; eadem, "The Community Hymns Classification: A Proposal for Further Differentiation," *DSD* 15 (2008): 121–54.

Nafshi (4Q434–38), and in the final column of the *Community Rule*.[55] These texts display a significant amount in common with some of the liturgical texts that witness to a kind of "performative exegesis"[56]—and thus what we observe here may also be of some use in the following discussion about the priestly aspects of "mystery" discourse.

The first-person figures of several of these works employ prophetic tropes to relate experience and revelation. According to several passages in the *Hodayot*, the speaker, like the prophets before him, makes reference to having participated in a heavenly gathering which has resulted in his apprehension of the "mysteries," which in turn has prepared him to "illumine the face of many":

1QH³ 12:28–30

28 ... ובי האירותה פני רבים ותגבר עד לאין מספר כי הודעתני רזי

29 פלאכה ובסוד פלאכה הגברתה עמדי והפלא לנגד רבים בעבור כבודכה ולהודיע

30 לכול החיים גבורותיכה ...

28 Through me you have illumined the faces of many [or the Many],
and you have increased them beyond number. For you have made
me understand the mysteries of
29 your wonder, and in the council of your wonder you have shown

---

[55] Émile Puech places most of these texts in a long list of compositions that should be seen "in comparison with one another": "1Q36–40, 3Q6, 6Q18, 8Q5, 11Q15–16, the end of 1QRule of the Community ix.26–xi, the Hymns that are scattered throughout the War Scroll (1QM xii–xix) and the parallels in War Scroll[b] (4Q492), War Scroll[c] (4Q495) and particularly War Scroll[a] (4Q491 11), which attest to some overlaps with 4QHodayot[a], the Prayer of Michael, and 1QHodayota xxvi. More broadly, they ought to be related to the Songs of the Sage[a-b] (4Q510–511), the Songs of the Sabbath Sacrifice[a-h] (4Q400–407, as well as 11Q17), the Words of the Luminaries[a-c] (4Q504–506), the Blessings (*Berakhot*), and the Noncanonical Psalms (4Q380–381, 11Q5[a], 4Q88[f], 4Q448, 4QPsAp[a] among the most notable Qumran compositions), as well as to the *Psalms of Solomon*, the *Psalms*, and Song of the Hebrew Scriptures, as well as the *Benedictus* and *Magnificat* (*Lk.* 1) or some passages from the *Gospel of John* (the Prologue of *Jn.* 1) in the New Testament" ("Hodayot," *EDSS* 1.367). It is of some interest that among the Qumran texts listed here, most employ the word רז in some fashion or another.

[56] Seth Sanders defines this term as having to do with a "process that is quintessentially exegetical, yet turns the stereotypical relationship of exegete to text inside out. Rather than reading elements of life into a sacred text, elements of preexisting texts are used to forge new roles in ritual and thus lay the foundation for new experiences in life" ("Performative Exegesis," 79).

yourself strong to me and working wonders before many for the sake
of your glory and in order to make known
30 to all the living your mighty deeds. ...

Here the hymnic figure draws upon the older notion of the prophet
"standing" in God's council and thereby roots his authority in the
prophetic idiom. The structure of the passage underlines its overall
message: the reception of "mysteries" is set off in parallel to the
"council," and "understanding" is identified with "standing." This
parallel is offered as a proof or explanation ("for/because you have ...")
for the speaker's religious and moral authority in the community, where
his "standing" is thus also affirmed.

This entire passage is juxtaposed to the earlier part of col. 12 in
which the opponents of the speaker are described using language
reminiscent of Jer 23. These opponents do not properly understand the
חזון דעת "vision of knowledge" and will be judged accordingly by God
who will cut them off from the covenant. In their error they are in league
with Belial and his corrosive plans. The text states:

1QHª 12:14–18

14 ... והמה נעלמים זמות בליעל
15 יחשובו וידרשוכה בלב ולב ולא נכונו באמתכה שורש פורה רוש ולענה
במחשבותם
16 ועם שרירות לבם יתורו וידרשוכה בגלולים ומכשול עוונם שמו לנגד פניהם
ויבאו
17 לדורשכה מפי נביאי כזב מפותי תעות והם [ב]ל[ו]עג שפה ולשון אחרת
ידברו לעמך
18 להולל ברמיה כול מעשיהם ...

14 But they, the deceivers, hatch the plans of Belial
15 and seek you with a divided heart. And they are not established in
    your truth. The root growing poison and wormwood is in their
    thoughts,
16 and with a stubbornness of their heart they look around and seek you
    among idols. The stumbling block of their iniquity they have placed
    before themselves, and they come
17 to seek you by the mouth[s] of lying prophets, those corrupted by
    error. With mocking lips and a strange tongue they speak to your
    people
18 only to mock with deceit all their works. ...

Elsewhere in the *Hodayot* the protagonist is called upon to translate or
interpret his own experience to those under his tutelage. In one passage,
the speaker characterizes himself using an intriguing turn of phrase to

capture a double meaning which differentiates him from his enemies: "For you have set me up as a standard for the elect of righteousness, as a mediator of knowledge (מליץ דעת) in mysteries of wonder" (1QHᵃ 10:15). This word, מליץ, a *hiphil* participle of the root ליץ, is deployed several times in the surrounding context with its other connotation in mind: the same word can also mean "one who scorns or scoffs," or may be combined with negative words like תעות or כזב or רמיה to yield "mediators of error" or the like, and it is with this in mind that the composer of the hymn contrasts the first-person speaker with his enemies.[57] It is especially interesting that in biblical usage the word is found generally to have a negative sense, even when it carries the sense of "mediator/interpreter,"[58] and yet here, the author claims that his superior intermediation—his interpretation—is a function of his place within the community and is directly opposed to the other מליצים, the ones who "mediate error" or "scorn."

Such a sentiment is mirrored in the *pesher* to the Psalms (4Q171/4QpPsᵃ), in which the lemma "Be silent before the LORD and wait for him, do not be annoyed with the one who has success, with someone who hatches plots" (Ps 37:7) is interpreted in the following way:

4QpPsᵃ 1–2 i 18–19

18 ... [פשר]ו על איש הכזב אשר התעה רבים באמרי
19 שקר כיא בחרו בקלות ולוא שמ[עו] למליץ דעת ...

18 ... Its [interpretation] concerns the Man of the Lie, who deceived many with words

19 of falsehood, for they have chosen dishonorable things and did not listen to the mediator of knowledge. ...

This "mediator of knowledge" may be a reference to the same figure represented as the speaker in many of the *Hodayot*, which is a further indication that we should read these passages alongside one another.

---

[57] BDB proposes an etymology that might explain both meanings: that the word is related to the Phoenician word for "interpreter," as well as an Arabic cognate that means "to turn aside"; "hence, perh. prop. *speak indirectly* or *obliquely*" (539).

[58] See Isa 43:27: "Your first ancestor sinned, and your ambassadors (?) transgressed against me" אביך הראשון חטא ומליציך פעשו בי. An exception is in the Joseph cycle, in which Joseph and his brothers communicate through an interpreter, כי המליץ בינתם (Gen 42:23).

Despite the speaker's elevated status in the council, and his duty to mediate the "mysteries of knowledge" to the elect, he complains about those around him and their inability to follow him in acting justly:

1QHª 13:25–28

25 ... ג]ם א[וכלי לחמי
26 עלי הגדילו עקב ויליזו עלי בשפת עול כול נצמדי סודי ואנשי עצתי סוררים
27 ומליבים סביב וברז חבתה בי ילכו רכיל לבני הוות ובעבור הגבי[רכה] בי ולמען
28 אשמתם סתרת מעין בינה וסוד אמת ...

25 ... Ev[en those] who eat my bread
26 have lifted the heel against me, and all who joined my council have mocked me with evil lips. And the men of my congregation are stubborn,
27 and they go around muttering. And about the mystery you have hidden in me they go slandering to the sons of destruction. Because [you] have exal[ted yourself] in me, and for the sake
28 of their guilt you have hidden [in me?] the spring of understanding and the foundation of truth. ...[59]

Nevertheless, the "I" of these hodayot knows that God "will soon raise up survivors among Your people ... and refine them so that they may be cleansed from guilt" (1QHª 14:8). The text continues with an intriguing reference to the "men of Your council and in the lot together with the angels of the presence":

1QHª 14:16–18

16 לכול אנשי עצתכה ובגורל יחד עם מלאכי פבים ואין מליץ בנים לק] -- ל[השיב
17 כרוח כי] -- [ ] ישובו בפי כבודכה ויהיו שריכה בגור[ל עולם וגזע]ם
18 פרח כציץ] יציץ ל[הוד עולם לג‏̇ל נצר לעופי מטעת עולם ...

16 (to) all the men of Your council, in the lot together [or of the Yaḥad] with the angels of the presence and without a mediator for your [holy ones?] [to] return [or to answer?]

---

[59] See also 4QAges of Creation B, which reflects perhaps a similar recognition that there were those in the ranks who had betrayed the covenant as it was conceived by the Yaḥad leadership: "[...] for guilt in the Yaḥad with the coun[cil] of shame[fulness] ([סו]ד ער[וה) to wa[l]low in the sin of humankind, and for great judgments and severe diseases in their flesh ... according to their uncleanness caused by the council of the sons of h[eaven] and earth, as a wicked Yaḥad (ליחד רשעה) until the end" (4Q181 1 3–4). For discussion of the interpretation of this text see Peters, *Noah Traditions in the Dead Sea Scrolls*, 154–58.

17 according to the spirit, for [...] They will return [repent?] according
to your glory, and they will be your rulers in the [everlasting] lo[t.]
Their [stem]

18 sprouts like a flower [that blooms for] eternal splendor, to raise up a
shoot as branches of an eternal planting. ...[60]

In this striking image, the men of the council are bound up with the
angels of the presence, but *there is no mediator* for (between?) the "holy
ones." It is not exactly clear how the word מליץ is to be understood here,
but it shows up in a similar context in another copy (or recension) of the
Hodayot from cave 4. In this case, the text appears to draw upon the
tradition found in some of the creation Psalms (Pss 8, 92, 104) and in the
book of Job (Job 26, 38–41), in which the vast chasm that separates the
creature ("of dust") from God is emphasized. This text acknowledges
that separation, and yet affirms that God has chosen "the poor" to join
with the "sons of heaven" in some kind of union:

4Q427 7 ii 16–22 (partial overlap with 1QHᵃ 26:35–38)[61]

16 ... ומה יחש[ב עפר ואפר]
17 לספר אלה מקץ לקץ ולהתיצב במעמד] לפניכה ולבוא ביחד עם]
18 בני שמים ואין מליץ להשיב] דבר כפיכה -- [
19 לכה כיא העמדתנו לרצ[ונכה -- ונעצור]
20a שמע נפלאותיכה] -- [62]

---

[60] The trope "eternal planting" is fairly common in the sectarian literature as
a reference to the Yaḥad, but is found in other, related literature such as
4QInstruction (4Q418 81 13); *1 En* 10:16 ("plant of truth"), 84:6 ("plant of the
eternal seed"), 93:5, 10; *Jub* 1:16, 16:26, 21:24, and 36:6. See Patrick Tiller, "The
'Eternal Planting' in the Dead Sea Scrolls," *DSD* 4 (1997): 312–35, and the
bibliography he provides. Tiller concludes that the phrase "eternal planting" is
"a relatively fixed metaphor which functions within certain variable limits of
meaning and application, and that we must therefore assume a common cultural
matrix in which the documents were first composed and transmitted" (313). See
also Paul Swarup, *The Self-Understanding of the Dead Sea Scrolls Community* (LSTS
59; London: T&T Clark, 2006) and his discussion of the "eternal planting" motif.

[61] This is possibly the "missing beginning" of a composition called the
Canticle of Michael (4Q491) by Maurice Baillet in his *editio princeps* in DJD 7; for
discussion see Wise, "מי כמוני באלים," 173–193, 205–16. This composition is
perhaps related to the "Self-Glorification Hymn"; see below for additional
discussion.

[62] Lines 20a–20 reflect scribal corrections in 4QHᵃ. Eileen Schuller explains
as follows: "As far as the process can be reconstructed: in 4QHᵃ 7 ii 20, after כוח,
the scribe wrote להשיב לכה; this was expunctuated by dots above all the letters.
The scribe corrected with an interlinear addition, שמע נפלאותיכה. Having written

20 להשיב לכה כ]אלה -- [
21 דברנו לכה ולוא לאיש בי]נים -- והטיתה[
22 אוז]ן [למוצא שפיתנו ...

16 ... How is [dust and ashes to be reckoned]
17 in order to recount these things continually, and take a stand in place[before You, and come into community with]
18 the sons of heaven? There is no mediator to ans[wer at Your command ...]
19 to You. For You have established us at [your good]pleas[ure ... and we possess strength
20 to hear wonders such as [these ...]
21 We speak to you and not to an inter[mediary ... You have inclined
22 an ear to the utterance of our lips. ...[63]

It is difficult to reconcile the statements made here with those of the previous citations. Perhaps the latter two texts describe an unmediated communal kind of visionary experience in which there is no need for a mediatory figure, or they reflect a time in the life of the community when there was in fact no מליץ and yet the community still spoke to God and not to an איש בינים.[64] While these two statements pose a challenge to understanding the mediatorial function of the מליץ דעת attested in the *Hodayot* and the Psalms *pesher*, they do not necessarily undermine the claim that the Teacher and his followers understood his participation in God's council—however construed—to instill in him the knowledge that informed the community's interpretative work, which in turn undergirded his experience and knowledge of the true nature of God and God's creation. This notion is reinforced elsewhere in the *Hodayot*:

נפלאותיכה, the form of the word that is most common in the *Hodayot*, the scribe then changed this to נפלאות with dots above יכה to delete these letters. In 4QH[b] 21 1, כוח לשמוע[is preserved. In 4QH[a], we could read לשמיע, a *Hip'il* infinitive, which fits perhaps better with נפלאות, but in the 4QH[a] interlinear correction, שמע seems to be a *Qal* infinitive." Schuller suggests that given all the evidence the phrase should be restored to read ונעצור כוח לשמוע נפלאות כאלה "and we possess strength to hear wonders such as these" (Schuller, DJD 40:299–307).

[63] See 1QS 11:8, where a similar scenario is envisioned: "He unites their assembly to the sons of the heavens in order (to form) the council of the Community and a foundation of the building of holiness to be an eternal plantation throughout all time to come."

[64] The only biblical use of this phrase is with reference to Goliath in 1 Sam 17:4, 23, where it is often translated as "champion." There it appears as איש־ הבנים, which BDB defines as "the man of the space between two armies" (108).

1QHᵃ 23:11–14

11 [...] כיא מק[ור פתחתה בפי עבדכה ובלשוני
12 חקקתה על קו מ[שפט למ[שמיע ליצר מבינתו ולמליץ באלה
13 לעפר כמוני ותפתח מק[ור [להוכיח ליצר חמר דרכו ואשמ{ו}ת ילוד
14 אשה כמעשיו ולפתח מ[קו]ר אמתכה ליצר אשר סמכתה בעוזכה

11 [For] you open [a foun]tain in the mouth of your servant, and upon my tongue
12 you have engraved ju[dgment] according to the measuring line [for the one who pro]claims his understanding to a creature, and for one who interprets [or mediates] these things
13 to a being of dust like me. You open a foun[tain]in order to reprove a creature of clay with respect to his way and the guilt of the one born
14 of woman according to his deeds, and (you) open the f[oun]tain of your truth to the creature whom you have sustained by your strength . ...

The מליץ is appointed to stand before God, and his tongue has been "engraved with a measuring line" so that he will know how to declare to the "human vessel" some of his understanding—"that he might open a fountain of truth" to the one who receives the reproving. This "measuring line"[65] is apparently installed to guide the interpreter in his "choice" of words, so that what he speaks will be in precise conformity with the predetermined order of the cosmos. This image, perhaps as much as any notion of prophecy found in the Hebrew Bible, depicts the speaker as one who has no choice *but* to speak the words pre-ordained for him to convey (Amos 3:8: "the Lord has spoken—who can but prophesy?"), and picks up on the presentation of (for example) Moses, who receives the words to speak which he otherwise would be incapable of uttering (Exod 4:10–16). In an earlier column such speech is also associated with knowing and recounting the "mysteries":

1QHᵃ 9:29–33

29 ... אתה בראתה
30 בלשון ותדע דבריה ותכן פרי שפתים בטרם היותם ותשם דברים על קו

---

[65] The word קו is used in interesting ways in the Hebrew Bible, often in reference to the "measuring" involved in creation—either of the world or of the (real or imagined) temple (1 Kgs 7:23; Ezek 47:3; Zech 1:16; Jer 31:39; Job 38:5)—or to the marking off distribution land (Isa 34:17), or even for marking an area for destruction (2 Kgs 21:13; Isa 34:11). In any case, it is a word that always connotes the task of measuring in preparation for some kind of constructive or destructive activity.

31 ומבע רוח שפתים במדה ותוצא קוים לרזיהם ומבעי רוחות לחשבונם להודיע
32 כבודכה ולספר נפלאותיכה בכול מעשי אמתכה ומ[ש[פ]ט]י צדקכה
ולהלל שמכה
33 בפה כול יודעיכה לפי שכלם יברכוכה לעולמי ע[ולמי]ם ...

29 ... You yourself created
30 breath for the tongue. You know its words, and you determine the
fruit of the lips before they exist. You set the words according to a
measuring line
31 and the utterance of the breath of the lips by measure. You bring
forth the line according to their mysteries and the utterances of the
breath according to their calculus, in order to make known
32 your glory and to recount your wonders in all your faithful deeds
and your righteous j[ud]gm[ents], and to praise your name
33 with the mouth of all who know you. According to their insight they
bless you for ev[erlasti]ng ages. ...[66]

This passage is part of a larger and magnificent soliloquy in which the
speaker meditates on the total mastery of God over creation, drawing on
biblical creation language and emphasizing the predetermined nature of
everything—not only "everything under the sun" but the sun (perhaps
especially the sun) as well. The luminaries, stars, and the heavenly
storehouses—all of these have been established "according to their
mysteries," which the speaker also has come to know and understand. In
fact he declares that he knows these things through God's knowledge,
and addressing God, says that it is "because you have opened my ears to
the mysteries of wonder" (1QHª 9:9–21).[67]

This phrase "opened my ears to the mysteries" גליתה אוזני לרזי פלא
brings us to one more way in which the apprehension of "mysteries" is
cast in terms reminiscent of the prophetic tradition, as it links the
moment of understanding with a revelatory function.[68] The phrase גלה
אוזן is an idiomatic expression that has the sense of "to reveal," perhaps
in an auditory fashion, and is found in passages dealing with the
receiving of a prophetic word (1 Sam 9:15; 2 Sam 7:27).

Yet in one passage, in the context of Elihu's rebuke of Job for
(apparently) not understanding God's ways, the book of Job declares,
"For God speaks in one way, and in two, though people do not perceive
it. In a dream, in a vision of the night ... then he opens their ears ..." (Job

---

[66] Compare 1QS 9:9, 25–26.
[67] See 1QHª 5:5–8.
[68] Primarily in 4QInstruction and related texts: 4Q416 2 iii 18; 4Q418 123 ii 4;
4Q418 184 2; 4Q423 4 4; 4Q423 5 1; and 4Q423 7 6.

33:15–16). This passage is intriguing for the way in which it combines vision and hearing into a description of the reception of divine reality. Even though the book itself is usually characterized as a wisdom composition, this is an example of how it occasionally reflects apocalyptic and even prophetic kinds of language and structure.[69]

One final way in which we might consider the prophetic aspects of the use of "mystery" language in the Qumran texts is through the use of the phrase "to gaze upon the mysteries." The word נבט is used in several cases in the Hebrew Bible in connection with Moses and his encounters with the God of Israel, as well as in (at least) one instance in which the word is associated with (presumably licit) magical practice. In Moses' first encounter with God at the burning bush, Moses "hid his face, for he was afraid to look at God" משה פניו כי ירא מהביט אל־האלהים (Exod 3:6); but in the famous passage in Num 12 in which Moses' prophetic authority is asserted over that of Miriam and Aaron, a rather bold claim is made about him: "With him I speak mouth to mouth, plainly and not in riddles, and he gazes upon the likeness of the Lord" פה אל־פה אדבר־בו ומראה ולא בחידת ותמנת יהוה יביט (Num 12:8). In a strikingly different episode, when the people have suffered God's punishment for their complaint in the wilderness—a punishment of *seraph* serpents with fatal bites—Moses is commanded to fashion such a *seraph* figure and attach it to a standard as a kind of salubrious antidote (and perhaps as an apotropaic device?). "And when anyone was bitten by a serpent, he would look at (נבט) the copper serpent and recover" (Num 21:4–9).[70]

In these texts the function of "gazing" has a certain performative quality, and it seems to be efficacious in some way or another. The act of "gazing" itself comes with certain results, which explains both Moses' reluctance to look at God in the burning bush episode (he was afraid of what might happen) as well as the superiority of his prophetic status (he is the only human who is allowed to see God). The implication of his "gazing upon the likeness of the Lord" is that he *knows* more and thus his authority is not to be questioned. As a result of his authority, his

---

[69] See the interesting paper by Timothy J. Johnson, which is derived from his recent Marquette University dissertation: "Job as Proto-Apocalypse: A Fresh Proposal for Job's Governing Genre" (paper presented at the annual meeting of the Society of Biblical Literature, San Antonio, Tex., 22 November, 2004).

[70] The copper or (often) bronze serpent is an interesting artifact from the ancient Israelite cult. See 2 Kgs 18:4, in which Hezekiah, as part of his cultic reforms, broke into pieces the "bronze serpent that Moses had made, for until those days the people of Israel had made offerings to it. …" See Karen Randolph Joines, "The Bronze Serpent in the Israelite Cult," *JBL* 87 (1968): 245–56.

mediatorial function also involves crafting the figure of the serpent whose power was also to transform the state of the gazer. While all this may seem to have but marginal relevance to the present study, it helps at least to make the point that in the Qumran texts we find the adoption of a similar use for נבט, one that is also performative, efficacious, and transformative.

The final column of the *Community Rule* states: "By his righteousness my transgression is blotted out. For from the fountain of his knowledge my light has gone forth (opened up), and upon his wonders my eyes have gazed—the light of my heart upon the mystery that is to be" ובצדקותו ימח פשעי כיא ממקור דעתו פתח אורי ובנפלאותיו הביטה עיני ואורת לבבי ברז נהיה (1QS 11:3–4). The subject here claims that there is a direct causal relationship between the reversal of his transgressions, his gazing upon the wonders and mysteries, and his "light" going forth from the source of God's knowledge. It is interesting here that it is the "light of his heart" that does the gazing upon the "mystery that is to be," insofar as such language of "light" is a typical element of apocalyptic and mystical discourses in which the "righteous ones" are transformed into light by a process of angelification or deification.[71] Of course, this reflex also calls Moses to mind as the one who, in his close encounter with God, descends the mountain with a "mask of light" which itself becomes a source of "enlightenment" for his followers.

Such a possibility for mystical transformation reaches its ultimate expression in a text whose genre, title, and affiliation have been a matter of some dispute, but one that is intimately related to other sectarian liturgical hymns like the *Hodayot* and the *Songs of the Sabbath Sacrifice*. In this so-called *Self-Glorification Hymn* (which has at least two different recensions[72]) there is yet another association between the "mysteries"

---

[71] This motif is complex, widespread in ancient Judaism and Christianity, and has been treated in a number of important studies. See Smelik, "On Mystical Transformation of the Righteous," 122–44; Sanders, "Performative Exegesis," 64–79; Crispin T. Fletcher-Louis, "Heavenly Ascent or Incarnational Presence? A Revisionist Reading of the Songs of the Sabbath Sacrifice," and Christopher Morray-Jones, "The Temple Within: The Embodied Divine Image and Its Worship in the Dead Sea Scrolls and Other Early Jewish and Christian Sources," both published in *Society of Biblical Literature Seminar Papers* (SBLSP 37; Atlanta: Scholars Press, 1998), 367–99 and 400–431, respectively.

[72] According to Eshel, "4Q471b: A Self-Glorification Hymn," Recension A is reflected in 4Q471b (= 4Q431—see Wise, "מי כמוני באלים," 194–203), 4Q427 7 i 5–23, and 1QHᵃ 26:6–16; and Recension B is reflected in 4Q491c. It is difficult at this stage to be certain about the redactional history and relationship of these

and the claim that the subject has taken his place in God's heavenly council. The presumed answer to the series of rhetorical questions is "no one else but God." In this text, the speaker—perhaps modeled on the Teacher of Righteousness, if not that very figure himself[73]—issues several astonishing statements whose effect is to elevate his status beyond the normal limits of humanity.[74] I present here the two most salient passages from the different recensions:

---

recensions, but both possibly derive from an earlier hymn that circulated independently of its inclusion in other contexts like the *Hodayot*.

[73] The identity of the speaker of this hymn has long been debated since Baillet first identified him as the archangel Michael. Morton Smith critiqued Baillet's view and concluded that the speaker was a human being (and not an angel) who had ascended to heaven ("Ascent to the Heavens," 181–88; "Two Ascended to Heaven—Jesus and the Author of 4Q491" in *Jesus and the Dead Sea Scrolls* [ed. J. H. Charlesworth; New York: Doubleday, 1992], 290–300); Eshel ("4Q471b: A Self-Glorification Hymn"), John Collins (*The Scepter and the Star* [New York: Doubleday, 1995], 136–53), and Devorah Dimant (J. J. Collins and D. Dimant, "A Thrice-Told Hymn: A Response to Eileen Schuller," *JQR* 85 [1994]: 154) agree that the speaker is to be understood as a human being; Émile Puech argues that there is a collective use of the text in which each member of the sectarian community speaks for himself or herself (Puech, "Une apocalypse messianique (4Q521)," *RevQ* 15 [1992]: 489–90). While the question must remain open given the inconclusive nature of the textual evidence, I side with those who see this as a human speaker, and I tend to agree with Alexander's comment that "if we assume that the original Self-Glorification Hymn was composed by the Teacher of Righteousness, who, in the manner of his ancestor Levi, established his priestly and prophetic credentials within the community by an ascent to heaven, then it would make sense to see each successive Maskil as reaffirming the Teacher's experience, and as demonstrating in his own right his fitness to lead the community" (*The Mystical texts,* 89). I would add to this conclusion a reference to the *Songs of the Sage* (4Q511 8 6–8), lines presumably spoken by the Maskil: "God [has made] me [dwell] in the shelter (בסתר = "in the secret place") of the Most High […] [in the shadow of] his [hand]s He hid me […] [He has concea]led me with His holy ones […] [togeth]er (יחד) with [His] holy ones […]." Eshel reconstructed the first word in line 6 (הושי[בני), which is missing in Baillet's edition in DJD 7; see "4Q471b: A Self-Glorification Hymn," 197.

[74] The text and translation are from Eshel, "4Q471b: A Self-Glorification Hymn," 184. The text is from 4Q491c, which has parallels with 4Q471b, 4Q427 7, and 1QH[a] 26; the history of reconstruction and interpretation of these fragments is also discussed by Wise, "מי כמוני באלים."

Recension A—4Q471b (= 4Q431) 1–2 (par. 4Q427 7 i; 1QHᵃ 26:6–16)[75]

1 [*vacat* אני עם אלים א]תחש[ב ומעוני בעדת]
2 קודש מ[י לבוז נחשב בי ומי]נבזה כמונ[י ומי]
3 כמוני חדל[אישים ומי יסבול]רע ידמה ב[י והוריה לוא]
4 תדמה בהרותי [כי]אני ישב[תי -- כשמים]
5 מי כמוני באלים [מי ינודני בפתחי פי ומזל]
6 שפתי מי יכיל מי [בלשון יועדני וידמה במשפטי כי אני]
7 ידיד המלך רע לקד[ושים ולוא יבא בי ולכבודי]
8 לוא ידמה כי א[ני עם אלים מעמדי וכבודי עם בני המלך לוא]
9 בפז (א)(כת]יר לי וכתם אופירים לוא[
10 [ ] זמרו[ן ידידים ...

1 [*vacat* I am]recko[ned with the angels, my dwelling is in] the holy
2 [council.] Wh[o has been accounted despicable like me? And who] has been despised like m[e? And who]
3 has been shunned [by men] like me? [And who] compares to [me in enduring] evil? [No teaching]
4 compares with my teaching. [For]I sit [in heaven]
5 Who is like me among the angels? [Who would cut me off when I open my mouth? And] who
6 could measure [the flow] of my lips? Who [can associate with me in speech, and thus compare with my judgment? For I]
7 am the beloved of the King, a companson of the ho[ly ones, and no one can accompany me. And to my glory]
8 no one can compare, for I [have my station with the angels, and my glory with the sons of the King. Neither]
9 with gold will (I) cro[wn myself, nor with refined gold]
10 [ ] Sing, [O beloved ones ...

Recension B—4Q491c 6–8[76]

5 [... לו]א דומי
6 [ל]כבודי ליא {{ ידמה }} ולוא ירומם זולתי ולוא יבוא ביא כיא אני ישכתי
ב[רום נשא בשמ]ים ואין
7 [סב]יבים אני עם אלים איחשב ומכוני בעדת קודש לוא כבשר תאו]תי כיא אם
נוד[לי בכבוד
8 [מע]ו[ן הקודש [מ]י[א לבוז נחשב ביא ומיא בכבודי ידמה ליא ...

5 [... No]ne can compare
6 [to] my glory; none has been exalted save myself, and none can oppose me. I sit on [high, exalted in hea]ven, and none

---

[75] Text from Eshel, DJD 29:428.
[76] Text and translation are from Wise, "מי כמוני באלים," 182–83.

7 [su]rround (me). I am reckoned with the angels, my dwelling is in the
holy council. [My] desi[re] is not of the flesh; [rather,] my [por]tion
lies in the glory of

8 the holy [hab]itation. [W]ho has been accounted contemptible like me,
yet who is like me in my glory?

These fascinating texts push to the extreme what other Qumran texts
suggest in a more circumspect manner, namely the experience of the
process of deification or angelification that accompanies participation in
the heavenly liturgy. In such a context the speaker of this hymn comes
(apparently) to know the "mysteries of his devising/plan," which
includes knowledge of the heavens and the council, and thus his
teaching attains superlative status so that he can claim, somewhat in the
manner of Job's God, "who can measure my speech?"

These passages have important thematic and linguistic parallels in
other Qumran texts such as *Berakhot* (4Q286–90), the *Songs of the Sage*
(4Q510–11), 4QMysteries[c] (4Q301), 11QMelchizedek (11Q13), and the
Songs of the Sabbath Sacrifice (4Q400-407; 11Q17; Mas1k).[77] There are
doubtless additional texts one might adduce to reinforce the fact that one
of the important aspects of the use of "mystery" language in the Qumran
scrolls was the use of prophetic tropes and motifs. I have tried to present
a sufficiently clear argument that this was the case. Even if it has been
difficult at times to differentiate the prophetic from the priestly or
sapiential in this regard, I hope to have contributed to at least two
current scholarly discussions: (1) the nature of prophetic activity attested
in the Qumran scrolls and (2) one function of the concept of "mystery"
therein.[78]

---

[77] Alexander has discussed these at length in *The Mystical Texts*, 13–72; see
also Esther Eshel, "The Identification of the 'Speaker' of the Self-Glorification
Hymn," in *The Provo International Conference on the Dead Sea Scrolls: Technological
Innovations, New Texts, and Reformulated Issues* (ed. D. W. Parry and E. Ulrich;
STDJ 30; Leiden: Brill, 1999), 619–35.

[78] Several scholarly works on the nature of prophecy and mystery in the
Dead Sea Scrolls have been published too recently for me to incorporate them
here. I wish it would have been possible to interact with them in this section,
especially Martti Nissinen's "Transmitting Divine Mysteries: The Prophetic Role
of Wisdom Teachers in the Dead Sea Scrolls," in *Scripture in Transition: Essays on
Septuagint, Hebrew Bible, and Dead Sea Scrolls in Honour of Raija Sollamo* (ed. Anssi
Voitila and Jutta Jokiranta; JSJSup 126; Leiden: Brill, 2008), 513–33; and George
Brooke's "The Place of Prophecy in Coming out of Exile: The Case of the Dead
Sea Scrolls," in the same volume, pages 535–50.

SAPIENTIAL ASPECTS OF "MYSTERY"

The presence of wisdom-related compositions at Qumran has been a topic of great interest to scholars of early Judaism and the Dead Sea Scrolls. In terms of the longstanding question about the relationships among wisdom, prophecy, and apocalypticism and their corresponding literary genres, the strong interest in wisdom themes among several of the Qumran texts—and often in the context of apocalyptically-oriented compositions—has been frequently noted, and has helped to establish a kind of "missing link" in discussions about the generic and ideological relationships among wisdom, prophecy, and apocalyptic worldviews.

Because so much scholarly attention has been paid in recent years to the wisdom compositions from Qumran—and especially to the "revealed wisdom" of 4QInstruction and related texts—this section will not dwell at length on them. As I have indicated throughout the present work, the primary locus for expressions of "mystery" in the wisdom-oriented compositions is in the term רז נהיה. Such a "mystery that is to be" itself becomes the object of revelation, study, and contemplation, as well as the subject matter for pedagogical instruction. Often the verb accompanying the phrase רז נהיה is a form of גלה, and in the Qumran Scrolls the subject of the verb is most often God, so that it is God who does the "uncovering" or "revealing," with the result that the recipient of the revelation comes to know the "mystery" in the process. Not as frequent, though equally interesting, are the cases in which the one doing the "uncovering" is a human being, for example in 4QInstruction:

4Q416 2 iii 17–19 (par. 4Q418 10 1–2)

17 ... כאשר המשילמה בכה ויצר על הרוח כן עובדם וכאשר

18 גלה[79] אוזנכה ברז נהיה כבדם למען כבודכה וב] [הדר פניהמה

19 למען חייכה וארוך ימיכה *vacat*

---

[79] According to the editors of this text (Strugnell and Harrington, DJD 34.122), the singular גלה is to be read as a plural: "The structure and thought here ... do not require 'God' as subject of the verb, or 'one,' but demand a plural subject instead, 'they' (sc. the parents); therefore correct to גלו (cf. כבדם, עובדם, etc. and ויצוו in line 17 *supra*). But the fixed use of a singular subject may have attracted the גלו, needed here, into an easier גלה; the parents' actions are compared with God's, as in the context." I am not sure that the context demands this emendation; the recipient of the רז נהיה, having had his ears uncovered *by* God, may simply then be able to direct his attention in the proper way toward his parents.

17 ... And just as He has set them [parents] in authority over you and fashioned you according to the Spirit, so you should serve them. And as

18 they have uncovered your ear to the mystery that is to be, honor them for the sake of your own honor and with [reverence] before them,

19 for the sake of your life and the length of your days. *vacat*

In this case, then, it is apparently the parents who have the divinely appointed task of uncovering the רז נהיה to their offspring, who himself is evidently counted among the elect. It is somewhat difficult to understand the role of the parents depicted here, in part because the social arrangement presumed by the composition as a whole is not family-oriented but rather seems to reflect a school-like setting involving sage and disciple or student. Indeed, elsewhere in this composition it is clear that the רז נהיה is esoteric knowledge appropriated or available only to those among the in-group of 4QInstruction.

Benjamin G. Wright III attempts to resolve this problem by noting that elsewhere in this composition God is compared to one's parents ("For as God is to a man, so is his own father; and as the Lord is to a person, so is his mother" [4Q416 2 iii 16]), and that by directly address-ing the *mevin* [the instructee] as "son," the sage inserts himself into that relationship, effectively claiming the same authority that he has urged between the *mevin* and his "real" parents. At the same time, the linkage of the sage to the *mevin's* parents and to God essentially grounds the sage's teaching in the divine order. "Your father is like God to you, and I am a father to you," says the sage. How could one fail to listen?[80] Thus even if the addressee's parents—or the *mevin*—are said to be involved in "revealing" the רז נהיה to the instructee, it is ultimately God who is understood to be the source of the content of such a "mystery." Both the divine and mundane uses of the phrase are here employed simultaneously.

The other verbs that are associated with the phrase רז נהיה include הגה, לקח, דרש, and פרש, all of which are found in compositions with prominent wisdom themes and associations. It is interesting that each of these terms may presuppose an already existing form of revelation (something that is amenable to "searching" or "interpreting"), but that the results of such activities are often characterized as additional

---

[80] "From Generation to Generation: The Sage as Father in Early Jewish Literature," in *Biblical Traditions in Transmission: Essays in Honour of Michael A. Knibb* (ed. Charlotte Hempel and Judith M. Lieu; JSJSup 111; Leiden: Brill, 2006), 383.

revelation, or at the very least as constituting an epistemological transformation that is accompanied by new forms and objects of knowledge which are somehow divinely inspired. Some passages, however, do appear to reflect a more experiential and even mystical connotation.

Regarding the first of these verbs, נבט, which occurs in the *Community Rule* (1QS 11:3 and 19—a section often thought to have some affinities with 4QInstruction and other wisdom compositions), *Mysteries* (4Q300 1aii–b2), and 4QInstruction (4Q416 2 i 5; 4Q417 1 i 2), the action of "gazing" is related in some way to the רז נהיה and its contents. It is possible, however, that this referent is understood or applied in slightly different ways in these texts. In the *Community Rule* passage, the speaker claims that "from the source of [God's] knowledge (ממקור דעתו) he has opened up my light, and my eye has gazed upon his wonders and the light of my heart (has gazed) upon the mystery that is to be" ובנפלאותיו הביטה עיני ואורת לבבי ברז נהיה (1QS 11:3). And later in the same column the speaker declares, in a somewhat parallel fashion, that "my eye has gazed upon what is eternal—even the wisdom hidden from men, the knowledge and wise prudence hidden from humanity" (1QS 11:5–6). Even "in 4QInstruction the frequency of נבט with regard to the mystery that is to be underscores a more visual understanding [and] ... this suggests that gazing upon the mystery that is to be might have been a type of visionary experience."[81] But in this passage, the broader context often suggests that "contemplation of the mystery that is to be probably involved reflection upon teachings that had already been given."[82] This is also true of the other passages in which the "mystery that is to be" is studied, searched, interpreted, grasped, and so forth.

In other passages there are more direct appropriations of sapiential discourse in the form of combinations of רז + words denoting wisdom, knowledge, and prudence. The *Hodayot* hymnist claims that "by the mysteries of your wonder you have given insight" (1QH^a 19:10), and "in the mystery of your wisdom (ברז חכמתכה) you have reproved me" (1QH^a 17:23). And as I have demonstrated in chapter 4, throughout the Qumran Scrolls the use of "mystery" is entirely bound up with concepts and terms pertaining to knowledge and wisdom, all of which might be described as being part of the sapiential discourse of the Yaḥad. Of course, if we are to speak about a sapiential discourse in the Qumran literature, it must be with full awareness of the fact that by this time in the Second Temple period certain strains of Jewish thought had already

---

[81] Goff, *Worldly and Heavenly Wisdom*, 38.
[82] Ibid., 39.

transformed the notion of "wisdom" into something like what we encounter in the Qumran Scrolls themselves.

Wisdom had already been linked to revelation, which itself was only available to sage-like figures whose moral and religious dispositions were pure enough to merit divine favor—ideal figures like Daniel and Enoch—so that we are not surprised to find important "Qumranic" figures like the Maskil and the Teacher of Righteousness presented in an analogous fashion.[83] The use of "mystery," then, is one way in which the Qumran texts participate in this broader discourse, and in the process they make their own contribution to the array of depictions of how the fullness of divine wisdom can be revealed to select people whose righteousness makes them worthy to receive it and whose capacity for understanding makes the whole proposition worthwhile.

1Q/4QMysteries[84]

One particularly good example of a text that brings together many of the themes developed in the present study is *Mysteries* (1Q27; 4Q299–300 [301][85]).[86] As Lawrence Schiffman stated in one of his preliminary publications of 4QMysteries,

---

[83] For discussion of "revealed wisdom" in the Second Temple period see George W. E. Nickelsburg, "Revealed Wisdom as a Criterion for Inclusion and Exclusion: From Jewish Sectarianism to Early Christianity," in *To See Ourselves as Others See Us* (ed. J. Neusner and E. S. Frerichs; Atlanta: Society of Biblical Literature, 1985), 73–91; Argall, *1 Enoch and Sirach*, 15–98; Collins, *Jewish Wisdom in the Hellenistic Age*; A. Rofe, "Revealed Wisdom from the Bible to Qumran," in *Sapiential Perspectives: Wisdom Literature in Light of the Dead Sea Scrolls. Proceedings of the Sixth International Symposium of the Orion Center for the Study of the Dead Sea Scrolls and Associated Literature, 20–22 May 2001* (ed. J. J. Collins, G. E. Sterling, and R. Clements; STDJ 51; Leiden: Brill, 2004), 1–12; Grant Macaskill, *Revealed Wisdom and Inaugurated Eschatology in Ancient Judaism and Early Christianity* (JSJSup 115; Leiden: Brill, 2007).

[84] The following section is adapted from my article "'Riddled' with Guilt."

[85] There is some scholarly disagreement regarding whether 4Q301 is part of—or is a different recension of—the same composition as the other *Mysteries* manuscripts; in any case, it contains some important parallels and is related in some way to them. For discussion of this issue see E. Tigchelaar, "Your Wisdom and Your Folly: The Case of 1–4QMysteries," in *Wisdom and Apocalypticism in the Dead Sea Scrolls and in the Biblical Tradition* (ed. F. G. Martínez; BETL 168; Leuven: Leuven University Press, 2003), 69–73.

[86] Ibba has argued that *Mysteries* is not a wisdom text in his "Il 'Libro dei Misteri,'"; but see Matthew J. Goff, "Discerning Trajectories: 4QInstruction and the Sapiential Background of the Sayings Source," *JBL* 124 (2005): 666.

The mysteries texts ... open before us a new genre of wisdom literature. Hidden secrets spell out the future based on the proper understanding of the past. But these secrets are available only to a select group of people who are endowed with an ability to interpret the signs. What we have here is a wedding of wisdom and prophecy, not only a new literary genre, but further testimony to the religious creativity of Second Temple Judaism.[87]

The following passage from 4Q300 is especially germane in the way that it blends "wisdom" and "prophecy" into a "new literary genre" and also a new ideological mode of expression:

4Q300 1a ii–b 1–6[88]

1 [ ] ת[ ] החר[טמים מלמדי פשע אמרו המשל והגידו החידה בטרם נדבר ואז
תדעו אם הבטתם

2 ותעודות השמ[ים -- [בסלכמה כי חתום מכם[ח[תם החזון וברזי עד לא
הבטתם ובבינה לא השכלתם

3 א[ז [תאמרו ל[-- [ה והמי[-- [כי לא הבטתם בשורש חוכמה ואם
תפתחו החזון

4 תסת[ם מכם -- [כל חוכמת[כ[ם כי לכם המ[-- [שמו כי[מ[ה היא חכמה
5 נכחדת[-- עו[ד לא תהיה[-- [
6 ח[זון [--]

1 [ ] [the mag]icians who are skilled in transgression utter the parable and relate the riddle before it is discussed, and then you will know whether you have considered,

2 and the signs of the heav[ens   ]your foolishness, for the [s]eal of the vision is sealed from you, and you have not considered the eternal mysteries, and you have not come to understand wisdom.

3 The[n]you will say [   ] for you have not considered the root of wisdom, and if you open the vision

4 it will be kept secr[et from you   ]all [yo]ur wisdom, for yours is the [   ] his name, for [wh]at is wisdom (which is)

5 hidden[sti]ll there will not be [   ]

6 the [vis]ion [of   ]

---

[87] Schiffman, "4QMysteries: A Preliminary Edition," 235.

[88] Text and translation are from the official publication by Schiffman in DJD 20:102–103. In this study I focus my attention on 4Q300 not to the exclusion of the other *Mysteries* manuscripts, but simply because 4Q300 is the manuscript that contains the passages most relevant to my purpose. The text above represents a composite of frags 1a ii and 1b, for which see Schiffman, DJD 20:100–103.

Several prominent questions (among many) readily emerge from a reading of this text: (1) Who are these "magicians," or whom do they represent? (2) What is this "vision" and in what way is it sealed? (3) What are the "mysteries" and how do they come to be known? And in what ways are these "mysteries" related to the "root of wisdom"?

As Schiffman pointed out in his DJD publication of this text, the language of 4Q300 is strongly reminiscent of the book of Daniel, especially in its use of the "sealed vision" motif (חתם החזון), in its reference to "magicians" (חרטמים), and in the notion of revealed wisdom associated with the apprehension of "mysteries" by a worthy figure.[89] There are additional scriptural reflexes in *Mysteries*, such as from the Pentateuch and the book of Isaiah, and these have been explored by T. Elgvin in a recent publication on *Mysteries*.[90] What has not been adequately registered in the literature, however, is the affinity that *Mysteries* has with the book of Habakkuk and its Qumran *pesher* (1QpHab), as well as other Qumran sectarian literature such as the *Hodayot*.[91]

THE MAGICIANS In the book of Daniel the magicians are those whose skill and knowledge prove inadequate to the task of recounting and interpreting the dreams of the king (Dan 1:20; 2:2, 10, 2:27; 4:4, 6; 5:11). Daniel's knowledge is a foil to that of the חרטמין/חרטמים; he has the requisite understanding and wisdom to do what the king requests, though he defers to God as the source of his knowledge—to the "God in heaven who reveals mysteries" אלה בשמיא גלא רזין (Dan 2:28). In the ancient Near East and in Egypt, these חרטמים are related to a certain class of diviners whose primary task was to interpret dream-signs or dream-visions and, in some cases, to preempt the realization of the dream with the use of therapeutic magic.[92] Where they are not explicitly denounced in the biblical tradition, they are at best ineffective and unreliable.[93]

---

[89] Schiffman, DJD 20:102; Tigchelaar, "Your Wisdom and Your Folly," 75.

[90] T. Elgvin, "The Use of Scripture in 1Q/4QMysteries," in *New Perspectives on Old Texts: Proceedings of the Tenth Annual International Orion Symposium, January 9–11, 2005* (ed. E. Chazon et al; STDJ; Leiden: Brill, forthcoming).

[91] A. Lange points out some of the parallels between *Mysteries* and the *Hodayot* in chapter 3 of his *Weisheit und Prädestination*, but does not draw the same conclusions as I offer below.

[92] See discussions and bibliographies in Collins, *Daniel*, 128, 145, 155–56; Nickelsburg, *1 Enoch*, 198–99.

[93] Other biblical texts using this root include Exod 32:4 (in which Aaron uses a חרטם ["graving-tool"] to fashion the molten calf); Gen 41:8, 24; Exod 7:11; 8:3,

In addition to 4Q300, the only other texts from Qumran that witness to the use of the word חרטם are the *Book of the Watchers* of *1 Enoch* (4Q201 1 iv 2), 4QReworked Pentateuch^c (4Q365 2, 3–4 [Exod 8:14–15]), as well as an unidentified fragment from cave 4 (PAM 43.676 23 1). In the case of the Aramaic fragments of *1 Enoch* (4Q201 1 iv 2), the word (חרטמו, a noun) represents one of the illicit practices taught by the watcher Hermoni, though the textual data are rather jumbled for this passage.[94] At any rate, it is likely that here *1 Enoch* attests to a tradition, also found in Daniel and in the Joseph stories of the book of Genesis, that distinguishes different kinds of dream interpretation: those authorized and inspired ones of the divinely-sanctioned expositors, and those of the transgressive, unauthorized, or simply lame imposters. In all cases including *1 Enoch*, the revelations given to the protagonist are contrasted with the bankrupt divinations of the foil group.[95] If one of the purposes of the Watchers story is to provide an etiology for the presence of sin and evil in the world, surely another purpose is to provide a suitable antithesis to the true nature of Enoch's knowledge, and the knowledge of the group associating itself with him. As we know from other parts of *1 Enoch* and the biblical accounts,[96] divination in the form of dream interpretation is not inherently evil in the minds of their authors—only when the wrong people are doing the divining does it become anathema.[97] Indeed, as Armin Lange has demonstrated, dream interpretation was likely among the forms of "magic" or divination performed among the Yaḥad.[98]

To return to 4Q300: the magicians or interpreters are said to be skilled *in transgression* (מלמדי פשע); their activities (divinations) are bankrupt and in the end amount to sins. This charge would indeed correspond with what we have already adduced from other sources, and

14, 15; 9:11. As Nickelsburg points out (*1 Enoch*, 198–99), in the Joseph story "LXX translates [חרטמים] with ἐξεγήται" ("interpreters"). In the Exodus story חרטם denotes the magicians who attempt to explicate Moses' and Aaron's miracles.

[94] See Nickelsburg, *1 Enoch*, 189; 198–99; J. T. Milik, *The Books of Enoch: Aramaic Fragments from Qumran* (Oxford: Clarendon Press, 1976), 160.

[95] For pertinent discussion of the dream visions in *1 Enoch* see Nickelsburg, *1 Enoch*, 32; 198–201.

[96] *1 En* 13:7–16:4; 83–84, 85–90.

[97] As VanderKam expresses it, "biblical opposition to certain mantic arts was based less on qualms about divination itself than on the pagan milieu within which Israel's neighbors and conquerors practiced them" ("Prophetic-Sapiential Origins of Apocalyptic Thought," 247).

[98] Lange, "Essene Position on Magic and Divination."

might suggest that a similar literary and social strategy is here at work.[99] If we may take a clue from other parts of *Mysteries*, (1Q27 1 i 2–3, 7; 4Q299 43 2; 4Q300 8 5; 4Q301 1 2) it is likely that these magicians/ interpreters are the same ones who participate in the "mysteries of transgression" (רזי פשע) or "mysteries of Belial" (רזי בליעל), terms found also in other compositions stemming from the Yaḥad.[100] To quote Schiffman again, the magicians are challenged to explain the hidden meaning of the parable or riddle to see whether they have properly understood the signs. The text makes clear that they cannot, since the true vision, perhaps that of prophecy, is hidden from them, and they do not understand the mysteries of God.[101]

This identification of the "true vision" with an esoteric prophetic insight is an important key for understanding this text. Indeed, according to *Mysteries*, because they grasp the wrong kind of "mysteries," which are in turn related to transgression, these interpreters do not understand the signs and are unable to unlock the riddle: they are "riddled with guilt."[102]

THE VISION—DREAM OR TEXT? The word חזון "vision" is often used in the special sense of seeing some revelation from God; it occurs most often in the context of a prophetic witness account, and is perhaps a technical term proper to the domain of a נביא. In his entry "Visions" in the *Dead Sea Scrolls Encyclopedia*, Erik Larson draws the same conclusion, asserting that the word retains this specialized meaning in the Qumran corpus.[103] Nevertheless, it is interesting that typically what is "seen" or received by a prophet is not a visual image but a word from God. As for why this Aramaic word may have entered into and been retained by Hebrew usage, it is possible that it was a technical term for a particular kind of experience of the divine word: a nocturnal vision or seeing of the word,

---

[99] See also A. Klostergaard Peterson, "Wisdom as Cognition: Creating the Others in the Book of Mysteries and 1 Cor 1–2," in *The Wisdom Texts from Qumran and the Development of Sapiential Thought* (ed. C. Hempel, A. Lange and H. Lichtenberger; BETL 159; Leuven: Leuven University Press, 2002), 410–20.

[100] 1QM 14:9; 1QHª 13:36; 24:5; cf. 1QGenAp 1:2 (רז רשעא).

[101] Schiffman, DJD 20:102.

[102] The use of the word חידה "riddle" also poses several interesting questions, but they will not be elaborated here. For the use of this word in other contexts, see A. Yadin, "Samson's ḤÎDÂ," *VT* 52 (2002): 407–26.

[103] Larson, "Visions," *EDSS* 2.957–58.

but one that is distinct from other kinds of visions like a מראה/ראה or a חלום.[104]

The book of Habakkuk begins המשא אשר חזה חבקוק הנביא ("The oracle which the prophet Habakkuk envisioned"); here the prophet "sees" or envisions a משא or an oracle/utterance. In Hab 2:2, the prophet declares ויענני יהוה ויאמר כתוב חזון ובאר על־הלחות למען ירוץ קורא בו ("Then the Lord answered me and said, 'Write the vision, engrave it on the tablets so that the one who runs may read it'"). These passages suggest that the oracle, or the utterance, is, or at least becomes, the vision, and that the vision is *text*, or at least has the capacity to become text. As we know from the *pesher* to Habakkuk, the "one who runs" is identified by Qumran sectarians as the Teacher of Righteousness who, knowing the "mysteries of the words of the prophets," is endowed with the authority to read and understand that vision/text in its truest sense. He is capable, in other words, of interpreting a vision-as-text instead of a vision-as-dream. Though there is not necessarily a direct or continuous sociological relationship between *Mysteries* and *Pesher Habakkuk*, it is at least somewhat clear that they display a similar understanding of the dynamic that involves prophetic "vision," the ability to "read the signs," and the esoteric knowledge that leads to wisdom.

The book of Isaiah offers additional help in making some sense out of what we find in 4Q300:

Isaiah 29:10–12

For the Lord has poured out upon you a spirit of deep sleep; he has closed your eyes, you prophets, and covered your heads, you seers. *The vision of all this* [חזות הכל] *has become for you like the words of a sealed document.* If it is given to those who can read, with the command, "Read this," they say, "We cannot, for it is sealed." And if it is given to those who cannot read, saying, "Read this," they say, "We cannot read."

Joseph Blenkinsopp has recently suggested that we should understand verses 11–12 to be an editorial comment on the *reception* of the book of Isaiah in the form in which it existed at the time these verses were

---

[104]   A. Jepsen, however, suggests that by the time of the mid-late second temple period and the composition of the book of Daniel, the distinction between a night vision (חזון/חזות) and a dream (חלום) had been somewhat eroded ("Chazah, Chozeh, Chazon," *TDOT* 4.280–90); but such a change in usage does not foreclose the possibility that an earlier distinction might have been deliberately retained in some writings.

included—a book described here as the "vision of all these things."[105] As he further notes, it is the committing to writing and then sealing of the prophecies that are acts of authentication. Those who are unable or unwilling to read properly will not be able to "open the vision." But presumably Isaiah, and those who are the inheritors of his prophetic legacy, *can* read the vision, and accordingly they *can* understand the true nature of what is inscribed there, much like the "one who runs" may read and understand the vision of Habakkuk.[106]

Perhaps the חרטמים of *Mysteries* perform an analogous function with respect to a vision—however we might construe it—as did those magicians in the context of the dream scenarios in the book of Daniel. The magicians of 4Q300 fail in their foolishness to interpret the vision correctly. In other words, the same language is used to make a similar point, but the referent has changed: it is not a dream but a vision—or the text of a vision, or perhaps the vision-report itself. The objects of scorn in 4Q300—the diviners who are unable to open and properly interpret the vision—do not only lack comprehension, but they are also "guilty" insofar as they undertake interpretations (of the parables and riddles) without proper access to the vision. They know only the "mysteries of transgression"; because they lack access to the vision, the mysteries they understand are not the eternal mysteries contained in the vision, the ones identified with the roots of true wisdom. While this may not get us any closer to knowing exactly what the *content* of those mysteries was conceived to be,[107] at least we can say something about the social dynamic of the rights and denial of access to special knowledge. The way this is expressed in *Mysteries* is rather analogous to what we find in much of the Qumran sectarian literature.

Those magicians who are skilled in transgression, according to the text, also seem to have trouble comprehending correctly the "signs of the heavens"—the תעודות השמים. It is possible that this is a reference to the proper interpretation of heavenly bodies as a function of esoteric knowledge in the form of celestial divination or astronomical/

---

[105]   Most recently, Blenkinsopp, *Opening the Sealed Book,* 11–14.

[106]   Another famous passage comes to mind: "But you, Daniel, keep the words secret, and seal the book until the time of the end. Many will range far and wide and knowledge will increase" (Dan 12:4).

[107]   Lange posits that the term רז in Mysteries designates the "hidden preexistent order of the world," and thus that the תומכי רזים (the opposition group in *Mysteries*) use divination in an attempt to discover this preexistent order. See his *Weisheit und Prädestination,* 57–69; 103–109; "Wisdom and Predestination," 343–46; "Essene Position on Magic and Divination," 405–408.

astrological studies for the purpose of predicting the future.[108]
Alternatively, this could allude to the proper interpretation of heavenly
bodies for the purpose of the correct reckoning of the calendar. Both
possibilities are perhaps reinforced by 4Q298 (4QWords of the Maskil to
the Sons of Dawn)—certainly a sectarian composition written in the
Cryptic A script[109]—which declares that the Sons of Dawn are to "add
knowledge of the ימי תעודה," whose interpretation (פתריהם) the Maskil
will recount in order that proper heed may be given to the end (קץ).[110]
Was such knowledge itself also derived from a proper reading of the
contents of the "vision"?[111]

There is another possibility regarding the character of this "vision"
and its relationship to another crux of Qumran studies, the ספר הגי
familiar from the *Damascus Document* (CD 10:6; 13:2–3; 14:6–8), and the
Rule of the Congregation (1QSa 1:6–7).[112] In most cases where this term
occurs, it is in one of the forms given above (i.e. in construct with ספר).
But in one instance in 4QInstruction, the reference is to חזון ההגו (4Q417 1
i 16). If we are to equate the two different constructions based on the
presence of the word הגו/י, it might serve to reinforce the notion that the
"vision" referred to in 4Q300 is in fact a book, perhaps even that of הגו/י
whatever that may have been.[113] Or possibly it is a vision that has
become a book, as the context of 4Q417 1 i 13–18 may also imply:

---

[108]   Lange, "The Essene Position on Magic and Divination," 387–92; 399–
408.

[109]   See Pfann, DJD 29:1–30, esp. 25–28; Swanson, "4QCrypA Words of the
Maskil to All Sons of Dawn," 49–61.

[110]   1QpHab 7:5–8: "'For the vision has an appointed time, it will have an
end and will not fail' [Hab 2:3]. Its interpretation: the last age will be extended
and go beyond everything the prophets have said, for the mysteries of God are
wondrous" כיא עוד חזון למועד יפיח לקץ ולוא יכזב פשרו אשר יארוך הקץ האחרון
ויתר על כול אשר דברו הנביאים כיא רזי אל להפלה.

[111]   There is of course the added complexity—and interest—that the use of
the word תעודה/תעודות brings to any discussion. For a survey and discussion of
this word see C. Werman, "The תורה and the תעודה Engraved on the Tablets,"
DSD 9 (2002): 75–103.

[112]   For discussions of this term see esp. Goff, *Worldly and Heavenly Wisdom*,
82–94, and the bibliographies given in 82 n. 8 and 83 n. 10; D. Steinmetz, "Sefer
HeHago: The Community and the Book," *JJS* 52 (2001): 40–58; C. Werman, "What
is the Book of Hagu?" in *Sapiential, Liturgical, and Poetical Texts from Qumran:
Proceedings of the Third Meeting of the International Organization for Qumran Studies,
Oslo 1998* (ed. D. Falk et al; STDJ 35; Leiden: Brill, 2000), 125–40.

[113]   Contra Werman ("What is the Book of Hagu?") who argues that
4QInstruction does not know anything such as a *book* of Hago/u, but rather the
"meditated vision" found there later becomes written down and is known to the

4Q417 1 i 14–16

Engraved is the statute, and ordained is all the punishment, because engraved is that which has been ordained by God against all the in[iquities of] the sons of Sheth. The book of remembrance [ספר זכרון] is written before him for those who keep his word—that is, the vision of Hagu for the book of remembrance.

The fact that this "book" or "vision" is called upon in 4QInstruction, the *Damascus Document*, and the *Rule of the Congregation* would serve to link the ideas in these texts to the sectarian worldview even more, and underscore the points made above, even if it gets us no closer to knowing for certain what the "vision" or "book" of הגו/י may have contained.[114]

As a final note on this issue, though the word חזון is relatively rare in the Qumran texts, we do find a couple of curious phrases in the *Hodayot* that would seem to corroborate the previous suggestions. In col. 6 of 1QHᵃ there is a reference to the "men of your vision," whose "ears have been opened" to the truth (1QHᵃ 6:2–7). These are later contrasted in col. 12 with those men of Belial who say that the "the vision of knowledge is not certain!" (1QHᵃ 12:17–20). Once again, it is difficult not to relate such passages to the ones we have considered in 4Q300. In light of all the above, I would characterize the "vision" of the Yaḥad as an esoteric insight that integrates prior notions of prophecy and wisdom and is connected also to a set of ritual practices (not now well understood) by which the reflexive relationship between exegesis (or study) and experience generates authentic and authoritative knowledge (or "wisdom") for the members of the group.

KNOWLEDGE OF THE "MYSTERIES" Perhaps the most persistently intriguing part of *Mysteries* and related texts is the word רז and its various

---

Yaḥad as a book or *sefer*. This strikes me as no *more* likely than the possibility that it was already known in 4QInstruction as a written source.

[114] Though I agree with Goff's caution in discussing the sectarian affiliation of 4QInstruction and *Mysteries*, the important thing here is that they were obviously important to the Qumran community and helped to shape communal self-understanding and expression; see his *Worldly and Heavenly Wisdom*, 219–28; *Discerning Wisdom*, 69–103. "Mysteries has affinities with the Treatise on the Two Spirits, and the latter probably appropriated and elaborated motifs in the former. Although Mysteries was not written by a member of the movement associated with the Teacher of Righteousness, the text has a sectarian mindset. ... The book of Mysteries can be understood as a wisdom text with an apocalyptic worldview" (*Discerning Wisdom*, 103).

associations. One of the frequent phrases involving רז in the Qumran sectarian literature states that God has "uncovered the ears" to the "mystery." This is sort of a curious phrase, insofar as uncovering (from גלה) uses language of revelation; but it is in any case either a reference to some kind of auditory communication or to a general opening of the mind. Elsewhere, however, and primarily in the context of didactic literature like 4QInstruction and the *Community Rule*, one is called to gaze upon (נבט) the "mystery" to internalize its contents in a way that apparently involves seeing.[115] Whether hearing or seeing, one cannot help but wonder whether the implied object of either phrase is the חזון, the prophetic word that is open and unsealed to those who are worthy to receive it, the prophetic word that has become text, whose internalization leads to wisdom, and whose interpretation in turn becomes a new prophetic—or sapiential—act.[116]

Like other texts from Qumran, 4Q300 seems to posit identification between the "eternal mysteries" and the "roots of wisdom" (both objects of the verb נבט in this case), and perhaps the easiest way to summarize the point being made by 4Q300 1a ii–b is this: the root of wisdom = the eternal "mysteries" = the vision. In other words, there is a prophetic kind of revelation, namely the חזון, which provides access to the eternal "mysteries" which in turn are the basis for all legitimate wisdom. The other mysteries—those of transgression, or of Belial—do not derive from the authorized vision, and thus do not lead to wisdom.

Thus what we can begin to see in *Mysteries* is one way in which the prophetic and sapiential discourses have been woven into a rhetorical tapestry by which the group associated with the text expresses its claim to true wisdom and constructs boundaries around those who possess it. With its language of concealment and "mysteries," and its interest in ultimate matters and speculative wisdom, it conveys a clearly esoteric point of view. While many of its particular expressions derive from prophetic modes of speech, these have been adapted to a new context in which revealed wisdom is the main object of commentary.

There are several other related passages in which sapiential discourse is employed in connection with "mystery." They all revolve around the theme of God's wisdom, which God has used to predetermine the order of creation and the unfolding of the divine plan and has communicated in some way to the members of the sect. They can be roughly summarized by citing *Pesher Habakkuk*: "for all the times

---

[115] 1QHᵃ 9:21; 1Q26 1 4; 4Q416 2 iii 18 [4Q418 10a–b 1]; 4Q418 123 ii 4.
[116] 1QS 9:3, 19; 4Q300 1a ii–b 2; 4Q416 2 i 5; 4Q417 1 i 2, 18.

fixed by God will come at their proper time just as he has decreed for them by the mysteries of his insight (ברזי ערמות)" (1QpHab 7:13–14).

PRIESTLY ASPECTS OF "MYSTERY"

In any discussion of the sectarian literature from Qumran there is a very real sense in which *everything* found there is "priestly," insofar as it was in the domain of a group made up of, or at least led by, priests. But for the purpose of discerning the particular priestly inheritance of the Qumran use of "mystery," I will limit the following discussion. Also, because I have already addressed elsewhere a number of texts which could be qualified as liturgical texts that depict priestly kinds of activities (esp. *Berakhot*, the *Songs of the Sabbath Sacrifice*, and the *War Scroll*), the following will deal with (1) those passages that display concern with issues of calendar and cosmology, cultic festivals, ritual impurity, or atonement for iniquity and (2) the use of רז in compositions that otherwise show a keen interest in priests or the priesthood.

Priestly issues are also related to the dynamics of revelation and interpretation. As James VanderKam has noted,

> revelation and scriptural interpretation ... communicated the true calendar and the properly ordered times in which to celebrate the festivals. Sun and moon operated according to strict, schematic laws that the covenanters understood, but others, who followed the ways of the gentiles, did not.[117]

Many of the priestly concerns, in other words, were expressed in terms of esoteric, sectarian knowledge about the true nature of the cosmos, the correct meaning of authoritative texts, and the proper application of human effort to God's plan for the universe, most of which was wrapped up in a complex system that seems to have sewn the sources for correct knowledge and practice into a rather seamless religious garment. Many of these things we have already discussed in connection with the prophetic and sapiential dimensions of "mystery" in the Qumran texts, and yet we may still look at them profitably from the perspective of the priestly dimension.

---

[117] James C. VanderKam, *The Dead Sea Scrolls Today* (Grand Rapids, Mich.: Eerdmans, 1994), 114. As VanderKam goes on to note, several texts deal with related issues such as the coordination of the *mishmarot* and the celebration of three extra (Qumranic?) festivals of New Wine, New Oil and Wood, which "appear to have been a product of biblical interpretation" (114–115).

CALENDAR AND COSMOLOGY, FESTIVALS, AND ATONEMENT

One is not surprised to find in many of the texts from Qumran a marked interest in issues of calendar, cosmology, the proper observance of festivals, purity laws, and practices of atonement. These are all stock-in-trade of priests and the priesthood, and are part of a long priestly tradition in the life of ancient Israel and Second Temple Judaism. What has not been noted in the scholarly literature is the several associations between these loci of religious knowledge and practice and concepts of "mystery" in the Qumran scrolls. In several texts, there are connections being made—either explicitly or implicitly—between knowledge (or experience) of "mysteries" and the proper understanding and observance of proper cultic practices. Some of these texts are somewhat fragmentary, and thus in some cases we may venture only brief speculations about the significance of the passage in question.

As was evident in some of the passages above, such as the *Hodayot*, the *Community Rule*, and others, there was a rather profound interest in the correct understanding of the order of the cosmos. We saw how the kind of determinism that informed the self-understanding, organization, and language of the Yaḥad was also extended to (or was an extension of) their understanding of cosmic order, of both the visible and invisible celestial realms. One effect of such a way of thinking about the various phenomena of creation was to link the activity of the empyrean with that of the earthly realm, so that the proper conduct of priestly affairs was in perfect correspondence with the order governing all of the cosmos. Such harmony between the celestial and cultic spheres was understood also to be associated with the "mysteries," and often with the רזי פלא. Given the broader associations of this phrase as discussed in chapter 4, this comes as little surprise.

Though the exact nature and function of the calendar at Qumran is a matter of continuing dispute,[118] what *is* clear is that many of the texts from Qumran witness to the high value placed upon structuring the liturgical life of the community (and of Israel) according to the solar calendar, or perhaps more precisely, a sabbath-oriented calendar of 364 days. What is more, such a conformity to the pre-ordained structure of

---

[118] James C. VanderKam, *Calendars in the Dead Sea Scrolls: Measuring Time* (London: Routledge, 1998); S. Talmon, "The Calendar of the Covenanters of the Judean Desert," in *The World of Qumran from Within: Collected Studies* (Jerusalem: Magnes Press, 1989), 147–85; Uwe Glessmer, "Calendars in the Qumran Scrolls," in *The Dead Sea Scrolls after Fifty Years, Volume 2* (ed. Peter Flint and James C. VanderKam; Leiden: Brill, 1999), 213–74; Ben Dov, *Head of All Years.*

the universe is understood as a matter of esoteric knowledge that God has revealed to those who "remained steadfast in his precepts: his holy sabbaths and his glorious feasts, his just stipulations and his truthful paths, and the wishes of his will ..." (CD 3:13–15). But even these "defiled themselves with human sin and unclean paths ... but God, in the mysteries of his wonder, atoned for their iniquity and pardoned their sins" (CD 3:17–18).

It is not clear from the text exactly in what the "human sin and unclean paths" consisted, but their effacement is accomplished by God in the "mysteries of his wonder," which are, as the passage continues to relate, somehow associated with the "safe home" in which those who remain steadfast will live perpetually and will gain "all the glory of Adam" (CD 3:18–20).[119] Such a future reality is justified by appeal to Ezekiel's prophecy that the "priests and the levites and the sons of Zadok who maintained the service of my temple when the children of Israel strayed far away from me—they shall offer me the fat and the blood" (Ezek 44:15). It is possible that here we have encountered a motif that has some affinity with that found in the *Songs of the Sabbath Sacrifice* and in the *War Rule*, namely that the "mystery of wonder," as a function or expression of a liturgical and cosmic reality, efficaciously atones for the misguided application of human effort toward religious ends, and the ones responsible for understanding and participating in the "mystery" of the cosmic order are the ones the text seeks to grant ultimate knowledge and authority (cf. 1QM 3:9; 16:11–16; 4Q403 1 ii 27).

In a text affiliated with a Qumran covenantal ceremony,[120] the "mysteries of wonder(s)" are tied to the strict divisions, dates, and festivals of the proper cultic calendar:

4Q286 1 ii 8–11

8 ... ורזי פל[אים]

[ ] 9 בהר[אותמ]ה ושבועי קודש בתכונמה ודגלי חודשים [   ]

---

[119] For a lengthy and comprehensive treatment of this phrase and its broader Qumranic context, see Crispin T. Fletcher-Louis, *All the Glory of Adam: Liturgical Anthropology in the Dead Sea Scrolls* (STDJ 42; Leiden: Brill, 2002).

[120] Compare 1QS 1:16–3:12. See Bilhah Nitzan, *Qumran Prayer and Religious Poetry* (trans. Jonathan Chipman; STDJ 12; Leiden: Brill, 1994), 119–71; eadem, "Blessings and Curses," *EDSS* 1.95–100; eadem, "4QBerakhot (4Q286–90): A Preliminary Report"; Sarianna Metso, "Shifts in Covenantal Discourse in Second Temple Judaism," in *Scripture in Transition: Essays on Septuagint, Hebrew Bible, and Dead Sea Scrolls in Honour of Raija Sollamo* (ed. Anssi Voitila and Jutta Jokiranta; JSJSup 126; Leiden: Brill, 2008), 497–512.

10 [ ] ראשי ש[נ]ים בתקופותמה ומועדי כבוד בתעודות[מה]
11 [ ] [ושבתות ארץ במחל[קותמה ומו[עדי דרו[ר]

8 ... And mysteries of won[ders]
9 when th[ey app]ear and holy weeks in their fixed order, and divisions of months, [...]
10 [beginnings of y]ears in their cycles and glorious festivals in [their] ordained times
11 [...]and the sabbatical years of the land in [their] divi[sions and appo]inted times of relea[se]

The notice about "mysteries of wonder(s) *when they appear*" is an intriguing turn of phrase, and it is difficult to know what it means in this context. But it is possible that here again a correlation is being made between the "mysteries" and the celestial bodies (beings) that govern, reflect, and participate in the structures of the created world. The "mysteries when they appear" may thus be a somewhat oblique reference to the cycles of the supernal array, the knowledge of which has profound relevance to the activities and cycles of Qumran cultic life.

PRIESTLY DIVINATION AND "MYSTERY"

One final text to consider is the so-called 4QTanhumim commentary (4Q176), the bulk of which contains sections of the book of Isaiah interspersed with comments that are intended to provide words of "divine comfort" "to a readership distressed by the present downtrodden state of the holy city Jerusalem and its Temple ... in a day when the Temple stood defiled (in their eyes) by an illegitimate priesthood and the land continued to chafe under pagan domination."[121]

---

[121] Stanley, "The Importance of *4QTanhumim*, 576–77; Jesper Høgenhaven, "The Literary Character of 4QTanhumim," *DSD* 14 (2007): 99–123. Stanley says further about this composition, "What we see ... is a written record of one person's progressive reading through a limited portion of Scripture (*Second Isaiah*) in which certain passages that appeared to speak to the concerns of the reader and/or his broader community were copied down for later reference. So far as I am aware, this is the only document of its kind in the Qumran corpus" (576). Høgenhaven has demonstrated the textual affinity of 4Q176 with 1QIsaᵃ, which might suggest, if Tov is correct that the latter is characteristic of the "Qumran scribal school" (Emanuel Tov, "The Text of Isaiah at Qumran," in *Writing and Reading the Scroll of Isaiah: Studies of an Interpretive Tradition. Volume 2* [ed. C. C. Broyles and C. A. Evans; VTSup 70.2; Leiden: Brill, 1997], 477–80), that 4Q176 has a Qumran sectarian provenance.

In the surviving portions of the fragmentary text, the quotations from and musings on Second Isaiah are preceded by a prayer "calling upon God to perform his wonder, and to act vigorously on behalf of his sanctuary."[122] In the section that is of present concern, in the fifth column of the composition, we encounter a phrase that is *sui generis* in the Qumran corpus: "mysteries of the casting of the lot" רזי הפיל גורל (4Q176 16 2). The phrase occurs within the broader context of a statement about the creation of "eternal generations," a "holy house" (ב[י]ת קודש), and a reward for those who keep the commandments and the covenant. In other fragments of the composition there are references to an angel (17 4), the temple (?—ב[י]קדוש), and Zion ציון.

These themes reflect a mythological characterization of a divinatory practice, in which God is (presumably) imagined to predetermine the fates of human beings which become known by casting the lot, the "mystery" of which, according to the logic of priestly divination, is also knowable. This is a cluster of motifs similar to what we have already seen in the texts we have analyzed, and the determinism of the phrase הפיל גורל is reminiscent of other Qumran texts in which the fate of each individual is weighed according to his "lot," which has been assessed according to the authority of the priests and of the Many.[123]

The phrase הפיל גורל is a reflex of a more ancient application in priestly divination, namely the "oracle of the lot," in which lots were cast as a way of discerning the divine will.[124] In other Qumran texts, it is clearly established that the lot is a constituent part of the process by

---

[122]   Høgenhaven, "The Literary Character," 107.

[123]   See esp. 1QS 5:1–4 and 1QS 6:16–23.

[124]   See J. Lindblom, "Lot-Casting in the Old Testament," *VT* (1962): 164–78; Edward Robertson, "The 'Ûrîm and Tummîm; What Were They?" *VT* 14 (1964): 67–74; A. Lange, "The Determination of Fate by the Oracle of the Lot in the Dead Sea Scrolls, the Hebrew Bible and Ancient Mesopotamian Literature," in *Sapiential, Liturgical and Poetical Texts from Qumran: Proceedings of the Third Meeting of the International Organization for Qumran Studies, Oslo 1998, Published in Memory of Maurice Baillet* (ed. Daniel K. Falk, Florentino García Martínez and Eileen Schuller; STDJ 35; Leiden: Brill, 2000), 39–48. As Lange notes ("Essene Position," 395), the oracle of the lot was still in practice during the Second Temple period, as attested in texts such as Lev 16:8–11; 1 Chr 24–26; Ezra 2:63; 11QT^a 58:18–21; Sir 14:15; and *Jub* 8:11, 10:30. It is interesting that in Neh 11:1 the very phrase הפיל גורלות is used to describe the selection process by which residents of the restored Jerusalem were to be chosen: "Now the leaders of the people lived in Jerusalem; and the rest of the people cast lots to bring one out of ten to live in the holy city Jerusalem, while nine-tenths remained in the other towns."

which the novice was allowed to remain and to advance within the community (1QS 6:16–23): "Thus in addition to the examination stipulated in 1QS 6:15–16 the *yahad*'s administrating body ascertained how to act according to the will of God concerning whether or not an applicant was to be accepted as a new member of the *yahad* by means of the oracle of the lot."[125]

Such a practice, it was believed, was a way to reveal the manner in which each individual fit into the predetermined structure of the universe and thus either belonged to the עדת קודש or to the יחד רשעה (4Q181 1 5; cf. the *Treatise on the Two Spirits*, 1QS 4:26).[126] And as Lange summarizes, the "preponderance of priestly elements in the organizational pattern of the *yahad* may suggest that the use of the oracle of the lot by the Essenes was of priestly origins."[127] In column 5 of the *Community Rule*, the ultimate authority in such matters appears to fall to the "sons of Zadok," who, presumably, were the priestly leaders of the entire community, the ones "who safeguard the covenant" (1QS 5:2–3). Thus what we have in this small, fragmentary reference to casting the lot "according to his mysteries" is part of a larger, priestly discourse that reflects the practice of determining by divination the divine will for humanity and for the cosmos, a practice that is used for the structuring and patterning of the community. It is a point of overlap between sapiential ideas about the pre-existent order of the universe and a priestly commitment to discerning and applying such knowledge to the maintenance of the sacred regulations

---

[125]   Lange, "Essene Position," 409.

[126]   Perhaps also association with this assessment of the "lot" of each individual member of the community was the astrological/physiognomical descriptions found in the so-called *Horoscope*, 4Q186. P. S. Alexander says about this text that "strictly speaking the text is not a horoscope, or series of horoscopes, but a piece of astrological physiognomy based on the common astrological doctrine that a person's temper, physical features, and luck are determined by the configuration of the heavens at the time of his birth" ("Incantations and Books of Magic," in *The History of the Jewish People in the Age of Jesus Christ (175 B.C - A.D. 135) by Emil Schürer. A New English Version Revised and Edited* [ed. G. Vermes, F. Millar, and M. Goodman; 3 vols.; Edinburgh: T&T Clark, 1973–87], 3.1.369). See also Francis Schmidt, "Ancient Jewish Astrology: An Attempt to Interpret 4QCryptic (4Q186)," in *Biblical Perspectives: Early Use and Interpretation of the Bible in Light of the Dead Sea Scrolls* (ed. Michael Stone and Esther Chazon; STDJ 28; Leiden: Brill, 1998), 189–205; and more recently Popović, *Reading the Human Body*.

[127]   Lange, "Essene Position," 423.

SUMMARY AND CONCLUSIONS

There are three primary modes or discourses of religious authority in which concepts of "mystery" operate in the Qumran Scrolls. Though there is much more that could be said about these different discourses and their broader associations and implications for understanding the function of esoteric knowledge in the Qumran Scrolls, I hope to have sketched out the contours for a fruitful path of additional study.

The functions of esoteric knowledge in the Qumran Scrolls have been addressed in terms of the general strategies for claiming religious authority, but it is perhaps another thing to relate such functions to a concrete historical reality (or a series of concrete historical realities), in which such claims to knowledge can help us to understand the inter-group dynamics of the Second Temple period.

It is also important to point out that our talk here of "discourses" brings the speech practices of the Yaḥad (or any discursive community) into the foreground, thereby potentially downplaying the fact that "communities" are much more than their habits of language. While I have focused here on the discursive world of the Yaḥad, we may well expect to find that textual representations of certain forms of religious speech do in fact presuppose corresponding activities. The Yaḥad did not merely speak in priestly terms but also embodied priestly practice—which as we have seen included more than the observance of cultic ritual. Likewise, participation in sapiential discourse was not simply a co-option of wisdom language but a product of the active cultivation of effective wisdom, and so on.

Finally, it is also likely that the contents, and therefore the use, of ideas about "mystery" changed over time, and thus it may be possible, in a different project, to chart the evolution of the use of "mystery" over the life of the Yaḥad. One might begin, for example, by noting the general use of the word רז in the *Damascus Document*, in which "God, in the mysteries of his wonder, atoned for their iniquity" (CD 3:18); i.e. the רזי פלא are understood at this point to refer to God's grace in delivering the community to a "safe home in Israel," a deliverance which itself is understood and presented in the paradigmatic terms of Exodus and Exile. Later, perhaps, once the community was well-established and inhabiting the site of Qumran, they may have developed the notion of the רזי פלא with its more cultic and eschatological associations (4Q403 1 ii 27; 1QM 3:9; 14:8; and other texts). To make a compelling case for such developments, however, would require a more stable scholarly assessment of the dates of composition and redaction of the relevant texts, as well as the relationships among the different texts.

CHAPTER SIX

CONCLUSION: VISION, KNOWLEDGE, AND WORSHIP

I will begin to end this book where it started, with a quote from Elliot Wolfson on the nature of the "mystery" or the secret:

> What is so engaging about the secret is that it remains enigmatic in spite of the concerted effort on the part of many very fine scholars to clarify the issue through logical analysis. To be what it is the secret must persist as a secret. In many different cultural settings, the notion of secrecy structurally embraces the paradox of the hidden and the manifest even though the specific content of these may vary from one tradition to another. In the lived experience of encountering the mystery, the disclosure and the concealment are not polar opposites. On the contrary, what is disclosed is disclosed because it is concealed, and what is concealed is concealed because it is disclosed.[1]

While this kind of paradoxical language itself can conceal more than it reveals, it suggests something important about the relationship between any "objective" construction of knowledge about a long-lost group in a bygone era and their own experience of the lives they lived—or at least the experience from which they composed and transmitted the texts that mattered to them. Their "lived experience" was much more than we might ever hope to enter into and describe, and their living interaction with their own practices and symbols was a complex cultural reality that conceals much of itself from the gaze of the modern scholar of religion. As they encountered the "mystery" so central to their own under-standing of reality, the members of the Yaḥad left only traces of this encounter—but traces they left!

I have tried in this study to crystallize a salient feature of the discursive world of the Yaḥad, if only long enough to say something helpful about the ways in which members of this group constructed social boundaries, characterized the knowledge they possessed, and interpreted their received traditions through their intellectual work,

---

[1] Wolfson, "Introduction," 10.

communal and ritual practice, and scribal activity. The object of my attention here has been to construct a heuristic frame by which we can meaningfully organize an approach to understanding not simply the contents of "mysteries"—*what* they thought they *knew* (or did not know)—but also the effective functions of appeals to "mystery" in the social and ideological world of the Yaḥad. I have been interested all along in exempting myself from the charge made by Timothy Fitzgerald that modern scholars of religion

> construct a notion of human relations divorced from power. One of the characteristics of books produced in the religion sector is that they present an idealized world of so-called faith communities—of worship, customs, beliefs, doctrines, and rites entirely divorced from the realities of power in different societies.

In some loose sense we might speak of the Yaḥad as a "faith community" and attempt to describe all these aspects of its "religious life." But any such description will fall short if it fails to appreciate the ways in which the particular manifestations of the Yaḥad's religiosity were tied to its own power relationships—both internal and external. The use of "mystery" language is one way its members went about claiming priority and authority, and such use reflects also the boundary-making activities of the Yaḥad and its attempts to assert control over its members and its world. I have argued that the discourses in which it participated—and by which its members fashioned their own new discursive world—included the prophetic, sapiential, and priestly modes of speech. Each of these discourses was the language of a particular kind of religious authority that made normative claims over its constituents, and by the mid-late Second Temple period the elements of these discourses were being fashioned into new ways of speaking, writing, and acting religiously.

Of course, for the Yaḥad control rested ultimately with the God of Israel, who in their view concealed and disclosed certain matters and constructed divinely-ordained boundaries. With the proper kinds of insight, the "men of the vision" understood themselves to be capable of possessing and cultivating diverse and esoteric knowledge about the reality of God, the order of the cosmos, and the meaning of historical time—things normally beyond the ken of the average human and therefore "mysterious."

But this knowledge did not exist in a vacuum. The "Qumran library" was neither a warehouse of dust-collecting scrolls (at least not while in use) nor a container of free-floating "information." Rather, the contents of the Qumran Scrolls reflect a concrete and active engagement with the traditional material of Israel and other cultures, as well as a kind of reflexivity between knowledge, ritual practice, and other forms of communal life. Interpretation, ritual, "magic" and other religious activities were thoroughly bound up with one another into a set of practices that were informed by the ideological persuasions of the Yaḥad even as their actions in turn shaped their "beliefs." The discourses out of which they fashioned their own peculiar modes of speech were—to some degree or another—pre-existing conceptual patterns that became situated in the particular context of the Yaḥad, which I take to have been a priestly scribal group that understood itself to be the locus for transmitting and transforming scriptural traditions (torah), cultivating esoteric knowledge for the purpose of ritual application, and receiving or even generating divine revelation in various forms. The deposit of all this was for the Yaḥad a kind of priestly-prophetic wisdom that was limited to and guarded by the group as its own unique inheritance.

I have described how the precursors to the Yaḥad's use of mystery language could be found in Israel's prophetic and sapiential traditions, especially as these coalesce in the Second Temple period and find expression in the later stages of composition and redaction of the book of Isaiah, the court-tales of Daniel, and the Book of the Watchers of 1 Enoch. It is at this stage in the textual record (roughly the third–second centuries B.C.E.) that we begin to encounter use of the word רז in Jewish texts, and especially in compositions of an apocalyptic orientation.

If we may understand apocalypticism and apocalyptic literature as entailing an attempt to synthesize the "horizontal" march of historical time with the "vertical" or cosmic realm of eternal and divine being—as a way of grappling with the intellectual, social, political and theological problems of the day—then we may begin to see why "mystery" became an important expression in the context of apocalyptically-oriented groups like the Yaḥad and its predecessors. In this way, too, we may see how such a useful and dynamic concept, in the context of the mid-late Second Temple period, may have become associated with the priestly domain, which had its own well-developed notions about the derivation and application of revealed knowledge.

It is by appeal to special, esoteric knowledge of God's true nature and purposes—and of the correct manner in which to worship God in order to vouchsafe his continued favor and self-disclosure—that the members of the Yaḥad grounded their own claims to special status within the community of Israel. It has been important in this study to investigate the related social constructs of esotericism and sectarianism, especially since one of the conditions of knowledge of the "mysteries" appears to have been secrecy. Such knowledge was almost invariably characterized as divinely revealed wisdom, and thus the integrity and authority of the knowledge—and its knowers—could hardly be questioned or undermined by its opponents.

Esoteric knowledge usually functions at least in part to grant a kind of symbolic power to those "in the know," and in the life of the Yaḥad it also contributed to the establishment of boundaries between itself and the broader world, undergirded the structure and rationale of the group, and reinforced the self-understanding of the group as the "eternal planting," the "men of the vision" who alone understood the ways of God and the world, the order of the universe, and the proper application of knowledge to the ritual life of the community. The Yaḥad grasped and guarded their "mysteries," and like so many esoteric groups from antiquity they did not leave a systematic account of what this meant to them.

Scholarship on the Dead Sea Scrolls has always dealt in fragments and reconstructions. The present effort has proven no different, yet perhaps out of the many pieces a broader view has begun to take shape. This book has addressed some questions about "mystery" in the Qumran Scrolls—and perhaps raised many more without definitively answering them—and more work remains to be done on this elusive, enigmatic, and persistently alluring problem. The concealment of the Yaḥad and the opacity of its writings have not yet deterred us from striving to understand them.

APPENDIX: ON THE PERSIAN ETYMOLOGY OF *RAZ*

The prevailing scholarly opinion regarding the etymology of רז is that it is ultimately of Persian origin, and that its meaning in Aramaic and Hebrew is akin to what we may find in ancient Iranian compositions. In general, and despite the fact that questions of dating remain rather open, there has been a rather lively scholarly literature on the nature of the ancient Zoroastrian belief system and its relationship to other religious worldviews with which it came into contact. In particular, the influence of Zoroastrian ideas on the development of early Judaism and Christianity has been a subject of investigation and debate, especially in light of the prolonged contact between Judeans and Persians of the Achaemenid Empire and the continued interaction between Zoroastrians, Jews, and Christians into the Parthian period.[1] Scholars have most often noted the affinities between the Avestan material and early Jewish apocalyptic texts, especially in the areas of dualism, eschatology, and cosmology. Even more specifically, the question of

---

[1] The relationships among Zoroastrianism, Judaism and Christianity have been topics of debate for two centuries. For recent contributions see, for example, Mary Boyce and F. Grenet, *A History of Zoroastrianism. III, Zoroastrianism under Macedonian and Roman Rule* (Leiden: Brill, 1991); Shaul Shaked and A. Netzer, *Irano-Judaica: Studies Relating to Jewish Contact with Persian Culture throughout the Ages* (5 vols.; Jerusalem: Ben-Zvi Institute Press, 1982–2003); John R. Hinnells, "Zoroastrian Influence on Judaism and Christianity: Some Further Reflections," in *Zoroastrian and Parsi Studies: Selected Works of John R. Hinnells* (Aldershot: Ashgate, 2000) 73–92; Norman Cohn, *Cosmos, Chaos, and the World to Come: The Ancient Roots of Apocalyptic Faith* (2nd ed.; New Haven: Yale University Press, 1993), 77–104; Shaul Shaked, "Iranian Influence on Judaism: First Century B.C.E to Second Century C.E.," in *The Cambridge History of Judaism* (ed. W. D. Davies and L. Finkelstein; 2 vols.; Cambridge: Cambridge University Press, 1984), 1.308–25; James Barr, "The Question of Religious Influence: The Case of Zoroastrianism, Judaism and Christianity," *JAAR* 53 (1985): 202–35; Edwin M. Yamauchi, *Persia and the Bible* (Grand Rapids, Mich.: Baker Book House, 1990); J. Duchesne-Guillemin, "Apocalypse juive et apocalypse iranienne," in *La Soteriologia dei Culti Orientali nell' Impero Romano* (ed. U. Bianchi and M. Vermaseren; Leiden: Brill, 1982), 753–59; and most recently A. Hultgård, "Persian Apocalypticism," in *The Continuum History of Apocalypticism* (ed. Bernard McGinn, John J. Collins, and Stephen J. Stein; New York: Continuum, 2003), 30–63, which contains a summary statement of Hultgård's work on the topic.

Persian influence among the manuscript remains of Qumran—and the groups represented by them—has been quietly but consistently addressed by a handful of scholars.[1] In short, the Persian (or more properly Avestan) etymology of רז is part of a broader issue, namely the question of Zoroastrian influence on early Judaism and Christianity.

With respect to the Persian background of the word, M. Ellenbogen states the following:

> It is generally recognized that this word is a borrowing from Iranian. Scheftelowitz assumes an Old Persian *raz* "secret," a cognate of Avestan *razah* and Sanskrit *rahas* "solitariness, secret," as the word from which the Aramaic רז ... arose. No such Old Persian word occurs, however, in the extant texts, but some such form would seem to be guaranteed by the existence of Pahlavi *râz*, Parthian *r'z*, beside the Modern Persian *râz*, and which would be the source also of the Samaritan רז and the Mandaean ראזא.[2]

As Ellenbogen indicates, though there is somewhat ample later attestation of the word in Persian literature, especially in Pahlavi, Parthian and Modern Persian, the word does not occur, or is not extant, in the largely secular language of the Old Persian.[3] The earliest extant textual attestation of *raz* in any language is thus in a copy of an Aramaic

---

[1] See especially K. G. Kuhn, "Die Sektenschrift und die iranische Religion," *ZT(h)K* 49 (1952): 296–316; A. Dupont-Sommer, "Le problème des influences étrangères sur la secte juive de Qumrân," *RHPR* 35 (1955): 75–94; R. J. Jones, "The Manual of Discipline (1QS), Persian Religion, and the Old Testament," in *The Teacher's Yoke: Studies in Memory of Henry Trantham* (ed. E. J. Vardeman and J. L. Garret, Jr.; Waco, Tex.: Baylor University Press, 1964), 94–108; David Winston, "The Iranian Component in the Bible, Apocrypha, and Qumran: A Review of the Evidence," *HR* 5 (1966): 183–216; Shaul Shaked, "Qumran: Some Iranian Connections," in *Solving Riddles and Untying Knots: Biblical, Epigraphic, and Semitic Studies in Honor of Jonas C. Greenfield* (ed. Ziony Zevit, Solomon Gitin and Michael Sokoloff; Winona Lake, Ind.: Eisenbrauns, 1995), 277-81; Geo Widengren, Anders Hultgård and Marc Philonenko, *Apocalyptique iranienne et dualisme qoumrânien* (RI 2; Paris: Adrien Maisonneuve, 1995); Jörg Frey, "Different Patterns of Dualistic Thought in the Qumran Library: Reflections on Their Background and History," in *Legal Texts and Legal Issues: Proceedings of the Second Meeting of the International Organization for Qumran Studies, Cambridge 1995* (ed. Moshe Bernstein, Florentino García Martínez and John Kampen; STDJ 23; Leiden: Brill, 1997), 275–335.

[2] M. Ellenbogen, *Foreign Words in the Old Testament: Their Origin and Etymology* (London: Luzac & Company, 1962), 153.

[3] See R. G. Kent, *Old Persian: Grammar, Texts, Lexicon* (New Haven: Yale University Press, 1953).

text stemming from the third century B.C.E., namely the *Book of the Watchers* of *1 Enoch*.[4]

In a way, this is exactly what we might expect given the fact that the word *raz* has invariably religious or cosmological connotations in Persian texts. Old Persian—the language of the Achaemenid Empire—was essentially a secular language which has been preserved in only a handful of inscriptions, and Persian "religious works were handed down orally; it was not until probably the fifth century [C.E.] that they were at last committed to writing, in the 'Avestan' alphabet, especially invented for the purpose."[5] We do not find religious texts, and thus any mention of *raz*, during the Achaemenid period, because those texts did not exist *as written texts* until much later.

Indeed, while this does not foreclose the possibility—or even the likelihood—that the word crossed over into Aramaic as a result of religious interaction, or by the adoption of a foreign word to express a Jewish idea in a new way, there is no evidence that can verify how and when this may have happened. How the word might have entered into use in Aramaic, and just what connotations it carried, remain open questions.

All this makes it considerably more difficult to be certain whether the conceptual value or semantic range of the Persian *raz* was the same during the first half of the Second Temple period as it was later during the Parthian period (third century B.C.E. to third century C.E.), or whether its meaning drifted from one context to another. It is at least conceivable that the semantic value "mystery" is an undue projection of a later meaning upon an earlier usage. For that matter, it is at least conceivable that this connotation was in fact influenced by the use of רז as it was taken up in Jewish (and possibly Christian, esp. Syriac) literature before the Iranian sages went about their work of recording in writing the ancient traditions of Zoroaster.[6]

---

[4] The *Book of the Watchers* and the *Astronomical Book* are usually dated to the third c. B.C.E. Milik dated 4Q201 (4QEnᵃ), which contains *1 En* 1–10/12, to the first half of the second century B.C.E., but thought it may possibly have been copied from a third century manuscript (*The Books of Enoch*, 140–141); see also Nickelsburg, *1 Enoch*, 9.

[5] Mary Boyce, *Textual Sources for the Study of Zoroastrianism* (Totowa, N.J.: Barnes & Noble, 1984), 3. Old Persian and Avestan are the two preserved Old Iranian languages, Avestan being primarily the religious language of the Zoroastrian tradition.

[6] Hultgård states that there is a "growing tendency to argue that Hellenistic, Jewish, and Gnostic ideas have influenced anthropological,

Moreover, "we do not know to what extent the Zoroastrian priests composed new texts in Avestan during the Parthian and Sassanian periods," i.e. during a time after Zoroastrianism had already come into contact with early Judaism (and Christianity). However appealing and correct it may be to assume considerable antiquity for the Persian traditions in which *raz* occurs, the fact that the earliest Iranian *textual* witnesses date from the Sassanian period ought to encourage a bit of caution.

Despite these reservations, we may indeed see some important parallels between the use of רז in early Jewish apocalyptic literature and in Zoroastrian texts. Perhaps the most relevant material is to be found in the Denkard (Madau), a tenth century C.E. summary of the now lost Great Avesta, itself the canonical product of seventh century C.E. Sassanian high priests.[7] Many of the traditions of the Great Avesta are presumed to be pre-Pahlavi and perhaps reflect the most ancient Zoroastrian works. In his work on 4QInstruction,[8] Matthew Goff called our attention to two important passages:

Denkard 598.20

pad nimez i az waxš ewarzed o razig gyag ku padiš amarg daštar <i> tan ta frašgird pad dadar kam.

By order of the spirit, his immortal preserver moves his body to a secret place (where it is kept) until the (eschatological) Renovation, according to the Creator's will.

Denkard 6.214

arzanig bawišn pad harw raz [i pay] gar i yazd ud yazdan 'dyn'y . . . 'dynyx i yazdan ud raz i paygar i xweš az kas-ez nihan nest . . . ud raz i xir i xweš aweš nimayend.

One ought to be worthy with regard to every mystery of the battle of the gods and with regard to the gods' secrecy (?) . . . The secrecy (?) of the gods and the mystery of their battle are not hidden from any one . . . and they [the gods] show him the mystery of their things.

---

cosmological, and apocalyptic ideas of the Pahlavi books" ("Persian Apocalypticism," 59).

[7] Boyce, *Textual Sources*, 3.

[8] The text and translation of these citations comes from Goff, *Worldly and Heavenly Wisdom*, 30–31. Goff does not discuss the problem of the date of these texts, but simply offers them as extant witnesses to the occurrence of the word *raz* in Iranian texts.

At first glance one can see the affinities these texts have with Jewish apocalyptic texts of the late Second Temple period. The first text seems to describe the (hidden) process by which resurrection takes place at the eschaton, emphasizing the work of the spirit in accordance with the will of the Creator. The second text displays the themes of divine battles, secrecy, and the necessity to be "worthy" of divine matters. While the first text indicates that the word *raz* can in fact have the meaning of "secret" (*razig* = adj. "secret"), a place that is hidden from view, the second text is perhaps the richer one for the present study. There the *raz* is nominal—it signifies a thing or a concept, something to be grasped and known. Beyond this, however, there are only marginal associations with early Jewish texts (such as, for example, "the mystery of the battle of the gods," which may share some ideas with the *War Rule* from Qumran). Unlike in Jewish apocalyptic texts, the mysteries here are said *not* to be hidden—they are available to everyone, and thus one might wonder in what way they are secrets or mysteries.[9] In this last respect, these passages differ markedly from what we find in the Qumran texts concerning the relationship between divine election and access to esoteric knowledge.

To the passages cited above I would add another excerpt discussed by Shaul Shaked in his article "Esoteric Trends in Zoroastrianism,"[10] a passage that is even more germane to the present inquiry. In this text and others, as Shaked demonstrates, there are references to a certain restricted element of religious knowledge, an aspect of teaching that was accessible only by "a small group of reliable people" who are capable of grasping and remembering it.[11] The relevant text is as follows:

Denkard 6.254

u-šān ēn-ez a'ōn dāšt ku āštīh ud mihr andar harw dām dahišn, kirbag ō harw kas gōwišn, ud zand pad šabestān cāšišn, ud rāz ō ōstwārān gōwišn. Ud

---

[9] Shaul Shaked ("Esoteric Trends in Zoroastrianism," in *Proceedings of the Israel Academy of Sciences and Humanities* [1969]: 175–200) notes that the word *raz* "does not necessarily designate in many of its occurrences a secret piece of knowledge or a doctrine which must be kept hidden; it seems often to denote a hidden cause, a latent factor, a connection which is not immediately evident. Such is the use of the term, for example, when it is said that the 'secret' why the Jews rest on the Sabbath is the fact that God rested on the seventh day of creation" (193; here he cites *ŠGV* xiii:14).

[10] See note 92.

[11] Shaked notes several Avestan texts that already display an interest in secret doctrines; e.g. *Yasna* xlviii:3; *Yašt* iv:9; and xiv:46.

srōšīgīh ud dādestānīgīh andar anjaman dārišn, ud rāmišn andar myazd gāh, ud yazišn ī yazdān pad škōyišn kunišn.

They held this, too, thus: One should instruct peace and love in every creature, speak good deeds to every person, teach *Zand* in the household, and tell the secret (*rāz*) to reliable people. One should keep obedience and lawfulness in the assembly, joy in the place of the *myazd* [ritual], and perform the worship of the gods in confinement (?).[12]

As Shaked goes on to discuss, "the word *rāz* is used several times in the Pahlavi books in connection with a group of religious mysteries, which seem to be usually related to the fields of creation and eschatology as well as to the knowledge of the proper way of fighting the demons."[13] While wishing to avoid the implication that there is an obligatory genealogical connection between "Qumran and Iran" in this regard, this statement could well apply also to the use of "mystery" in the Scrolls. When coupled with our earlier observations about the esoteric tendencies—indeed, the esotericism—reflected in the Qumran texts, there is perhaps good reason to assume a connection of some kind between Persian and Jewish religious specialists during the Second Temple period.

In any case, the Persian origin of the word seems likely given the fact that the oldest attestations of רז in Aramaic are in texts clearly associated with neo-Babylonian and Persian cultural and religious traditions.[14] The

---

[12] Text and translation from Shaked, "Esoteric Trends," 185.

[13] Ibid., 193.

[14] A. E. Cowley has reconstructed a lacuna in the Aramaic *Wisdom of Ahiqar* to read [רז]יך אל תגלי קדם [רה]מיך "thy *secrets* reveal not before thy *friends*" (*Aramaic Papyri of the 5ᵗʰ Century B.C.* [Oxford: Oxford University Press, 1923; repr. Osnabrück: Otto Zeller, 1967], 243). This decision derives in part from Cowley's assertion that the Aramaic version was translated from Persian, or was under Persian influence, a conclusion which is based on the stylistic and idiomatic similarity between *Ahiqar* and, e.g., the *Behistun Inscription*. As J. M. Lindenberger ("Ahiqar," *OTP* 2.482) notes, however, "Since the Imperial Aramaic of the Persian period and later shows a great many Persian words, the absence of such Persian loans in *Ahiqar* suggests a date of composition before the mid-sixth century." In the other words, he sees little or no Persian influence in this text, and thus disagrees with Cowley that a Persian translation serves as the source for the Aramaic *Ahiqar*. I am not a specialist in this area of research, but it seems to me that here Lindenberger's arguments are persuasive. The absence of Persian loan words is better evidence than stylistic and idiomatic similarity, especially when reconstructing missing words as in the present case. While Lindenberger also suggests the translation "your secrets," he does so on the basis

book of Daniel and the *Book of the Watchers*—both very important texts for the Yaḥad—provide the only *known* bridges for this word from Persian to Aramaic (and, subsequently, Hebrew).[15] These texts hold a key place in the discussion of mystery language in the Second Temple period, and are treated at substantial length above.

To summarize, there is in fact very little historical evidence to demonstrate a clear Persian etymology of the Aramaic/Hebrew word רז. Later Persian texts, however, do deploy the word in a way that is somewhat compatible with its use in early Jewish apocalyptic literature, though not it a way that is perfectly parallel or exhaustive. We are therefore left to take up the general—and more or less prevailing— position that while the Persian "background" cannot be proven definitively, neither can it be denied that the existing parallels are compelling, and that the problem rests in deciding upon the direction and degree of "influence" of one tradition on another. While some connection with ancient Iranian religious concepts and vocabulary does seem plausible, a functional *meaning* of רז cannot be derived from it. To assert that it has something to do with "secrecy" or "mystery" is not to say very much at all, and thus we have been pressed to look to other sources to refine our understanding of the use of רז in early Jewish texts.

---

of the reconstructed Aramaic סתרין. Indeed, other proposals have been made for the lacuna which also do not presuppose Persian influence: for example, M. Seidel suggests reading חטא[ך] "your sins," a reading that is perhaps even more suitable to the context than "thy secrets" ("Bemerkungen zu den aramaïschen Papyrus und Ostraka aus Elephantine," *ZAW* 32 [1912]: 292). The desire to read "secrets" in some form is probably due to the assumption that there is a parallel here with Prov 25:9b and Sir 8:18–19. In any case, this usage would be secular and would not necessarily have sociological or theological ramifications.

[15] Daniel 2:18, 19, 27, 28, 29, 30, 47 (2x); 4:6; 1 *En* 8:3 (and other instances are likely, though not extant; see below). On the Babylonian/Persian background of the Daniel and Enoch traditions, see esp. Collins, *Daniel*, 12–71; and VanderKam, *Enoch and the Growth of an Apocalyptic Tradition*, passim. Elgvin states that "The word *raz*, 'mystery,' enters the Jewish and apocalyptic tradition through the book of Daniel. Both books [Daniel and 4QInstruction] could derive from related circles which characterized divine mysteries with this Aramaic word" ("The Mystery to Come," 138). But it is not clear to me that Daniel (or 1 *Enoch*, for that matter) constitutes the *necessary* vehicle by which רז comes into use in Jewish apocalyptic literature. These are simply the earliest extant texts that employ this term in Aramaic.

BIBLIOGRAPHY

Abegg, Martin G. Jr. "4Q471: A Case of Mistaken Identity?" Pages 136–47 in *Pursuing the Text: Studies in Honor of Ben Zion Wacholder on the Occasion of His Seventieth Birthday*. Edited by John C. Reeves and John Kampen. Journal for the Study of the Old Testament: Supplement Series 184. Sheffield: JSOT Press, 1994.

——. "The Messiah at Qumran: Are We Still Seeing Double?" *Dead Sea Discoveries* 2 (1995): 125–44.

Abegg, Martin et al. *The Dead Sea Scrolls Concordance: The Non-Biblical Texts from Qumran*. 2 vols. Leiden: Brill, 2003.

Adams, Samuel. *Wisdom in Transition: Act and Consequence in Second Temple Instructions*. Journal for the Study of Judaism: Supplement Series 125. Leiden: Brill, 2008.

Albright, William F. "New Light on Early Recensions of the Hebrew Bible." *Bulletin of the American Schools of Oriental Research* 140 (1955): 27–33.

Alexander, Philip S. "The Demonology of the Dead Sea Scrolls." Pages 331–53 in *The Dead Sea Scrolls after Fifty Years: A Comprehensive Assessment, Volume 2*. Edited by Peter W. Flint and James C. VanderKam. Leiden: Brill, 1999.

——. "Enoch and the Beginnings of Jewish Interest in Natural Science." Pages 223–42 in *The Wisdom Texts from Qumran and the Development of Sapiential Thought*. Edited by Charlotte Hempel, Armin Lange, and Hermann Lichtenberger. Bibliotheca Ephemeridum Theologicarum Lovaniensium 159. Leuven: Leuven University Press, 2002.

——. "Incantations and Books of Magic." Pages 1.342–79 in *The History of the Jewish People in the Age of Jesus Christ (175 B.C – A.D. 135) by Emil Schürer. A New English Version Revised and Edited, Vol. 3*. Edited by Geza Vermes, Fergus Millar, and Martin Goodman. Edinburgh: T&T Clark, 1973–87.

——. *The Mystical Texts*. Library of Second Temple Studies 61. London: T&T Clark, 2006.

——. "Physiognomy, Initiation, and Rank in the Qumran Community." Pages 385–94 in *Geschichte—Tradition—Reflexion: Festschrift für Martin Hengel zum 70 Geburtstag*. Edited by H. Cancik, Herman Lichtenberger, and Peter Schäfer. Tübingen: Mohr Siebeck, 1996.

——. "Wrestling against Wickedness in High Places: Magic in the Worldview of the Qumran Community." Pages 318–37 in *The Scrolls and the Scriptures: Qumran Fifty Years After*. Edited by Stanley E. Porter and Craig A. Evans. Journal for the Study of Old Testament: Supplement Series 26. Sheffield: Sheffield Academic Press, 1997.

Anderson, Francis I. and David Noel Freedman. *Amos: A New Translation with Introduction and Commentary*. Anchor Bible 24A. New York: Doubleday, 1989.

Arbel, Vita Daphna. *Beholders of Divine Secrets: Mysticism and Myth in the Hekhalot and Merkavah Literature*. Albany: State University of New York Press, 2003.

Argall, Randall. *1 Enoch and Sirach: A Comparative Literary and Conceptual Analysis of the Themes of Revelation, Creation and Judgment*. Society of Biblical Literature Early Judaism and Its Literature 8. Atlanta: Scholars Press, 1995.

Arnold, Russell C. D. *The Social Role of Liturgy in the Religion of the Qumran Community*. Studies on the Texts of the Desert of Judah 60. Leiden: Brill, 2006.

Aune, David. *Prophecy in Early Christianity and the Ancient Mediterranean World*. Grand Rapids, Mich.: Eerdmans, 1983.

———. "The Use of ΠΡΟΦΗΤΗΣ in Josephus." *Journal of Biblical Literature* 101 (1982): 419–21.

Bakhtin, Mikhail. *The Dialogic Imagination*. Translated by C. Emerson and M. Holquist. Vol. 1. Austin: University of Texas Press, 1981.

Bar–Ilan, Meir. "Reasons for Sectarianism According to the Tannaim and Josephus' Allegation of the Impurity of Oil for the Essenes." Pages 587–99 in *The Dead Sea Scrolls Fifty Years After Their Discovery, 1947–1997*. Edited by Lawrence Schiffman, Emanuel Tov and James C. VanderKam. Jerusalem: Israel Exploration Society in Cooperation with the Shrine of the Book, Israel Museum, 2000.

Barkun, Michael. *A Culture of Conspiracy: Apocalyptic Visions in Contemporary America*. Berkeley: University of California Press, 2003.

———. "Religion and Secrecy After September 11," *Journal of the American Academy Religion* 74 (2006): 275–301.

Barr, James. "The Question of Religious Influence: The Case of Zoroastrianism, Judaism, and Christianity." *Journal of the American Academy of Religion* 53 (1985): 202–35.

———. *The Semantics of Biblical Language*. Oxford: Oxford University Press, 1961.

Barton, John. *Oracles of God: Perceptions of Ancient Prophecy in Israel After the Exile*. Oxford: Oxford University Press, 1986.

Baumgarten, Albert. "Ancient Jewish Sectarianism." *Judaism* 47 (1998): 387–403.

———. "He Knew that He Knew that He Knew that He Was an Essene." *Journal of Jewish Studies* 48 (1997): 53–61.

———. *The Flourishing of Jewish Sects in the Maccabean Era: An Interpretation*. Journal for the Study of Judaism: Supplement Series 55. Leiden: Brill, 1997.

———. "Greco-Roman Voluntary Associations and Jewish Sects." Pages 93–111 in *Jews in a Greco-Roman World*. Edited by Martin Goodman. Oxford: Clarendon Press, 1998.

Beall, Todd S. *Josephus' Description of the Essenes Illustrated by the Dead Sea Scrolls*. Cambridge: Cambridge University Press, 1988.

Bedenbender, Andreas. "Jewish Apocalypticism: A Child of Mantic Wisdom?" *Henoch* 24 (2002): 189–96.

Ben Dov, Jonathan. *Head of All Years: Astronomy and Calendars at Qumran in Their Ancient Context*. Studies on the Texts of the Desert of Judah 77. Leiden: Brill, 2008.

———. "Scientific Writings in Aramaic and Hebrew at Qumran: Translation and Concealment." In Aramaic Qumranica: The Aix-en Provence Colloquium on the Aramaic Dead Sea Scrolls. Edited by Katell Berthelot and Daniel Stökl ben Ezra. Studies on the Texts from the Judean Desert. Leiden: Brill, forthcoming.

Bernstein, Moshe. "4Q252: From Re-Written Bible to Biblical Commentary." Journal of Jewish Studies 45 (1994): 1–27.

———. "Interpretation of Scriptures." Pages 376–83 in vol. 1 of Encyclopedia of the Dead Sea Scrolls. Edited by James C. VanderKam and Lawrence Schiffman. Oxford: Oxford University Press, 2000.

———. "Noah and the Flood at Qumran." Pages 199–231 in The Provo International Conference on the Dead Sea Scrolls: Technological Innovations, New Texts, and Reformulated Issues. Edited by Donald W. Parry and Eugene Ulrich. Studies on the Texts of the Desert of Judah 30. Leiden: Brill, 1999.

Berrin, Shani. "Qumran Pesharim." Pages 110–33 in Biblical Interpretation at Qumran. Edited by Matthias Henze. Studies in the Dead Sea Scrolls and Related Literature. Grand Rapids, Mich.: Eerdmans, 2005.

Betz, Otto. Offenbarung und Schriftforschung in der Qumransekte. Wissenschaftliche Untersuchungen zum Neuen Testament 6. Tübingen: Mohr Siebeck, 1960.

Beaulieu, Paul-Alain. "The Descendants of Sîn-lēqi-unnini." Pages 1–16 in Assyriologica et Semitica: Festschrift für Joachim Oelsner Edited by J. Marzahn and H. Neumann. Alter Orient und Altes Testament 252. Münster: Ugarit-Verlag, 2000.

———. "New Light on Secret Knowledge in Late Babylonian Culture." Zeitschrift für Assyriologie und Vorderasiatische Archäologie 82 (1992): 98–99.

———. The Reign of Nabonidus King of Babylon, 556–539 B.C. Yale Near Eastern Researches 10. New Haven: Yale University Press, 1989.

Bietenhard, Hans. Die himmlische Welt im Urchristentum und Spätjudentum. Wissenschaftliche Untersuchungen zum Neuen Testament 2. Tübingen: Mohr Siebeck, 1951.

Blanchot, Maurice. The Book to Come. Translated by Charlotte Mandel. Stanford, Calif.: Stanford University Press, 2003.

Blenkinsopp, Joseph. A History of Prophecy in Israel. Revised and enlarged edition. Louisville, Ky.: Westminster John Knox, 1996.

———. "Interpretation and the Tendency Toward Sectarianism: An Aspect of Second Temple History." Pages 1–26 in Jewish and Christian Self–Definition, Vol. 2: Aspects of Judaism in the Graeco–Roman Period. Edited by E. P. Sanders, A. I. Baumgarten and A. Mendelson. Philadelphia: Fortress, 1981.

———. Isaiah 1–39: A New Translation with Introduction and Commentary. Anchor Bible 19. New York: Doubleday, 2000.

———. "A Jewish Sect of the Persian Period." Catholic Biblical Quarterly 52 (1990): 5–20.

———. Opening the Sealed Book: Interpretations of the Book of Isaiah in Late Antiquity. Grand Rapids, Mich.: Eerdmans, 2006.

———. Prophecy and Canon: A Contribution to the Study of Jewish Origins. Notre Dame, Ind.: University of Notre Dame Press, 1977.

———. "Prophecy and Priesthood in Josephus." *Journal of Jewish Studies* 25 (1974): 239–62.

———. *Sage, Priest, Prophet: Religious and Intellectual Leadership in Ancient Israel.* Louisville, Ky.: Westminster John Knox, 1995.

Bloom, Maureen. *Jewish Mysticism and Magic: An Anthropological Perspective.* London: Routledge, 2007.

Boccaccini, Gabriele. *Beyond the Essene Hypothesis: The Parting of the Ways between Qumran and Enochic Judaism.* Grand Rapids, Mich.: Eerdmans, 1998.

———. "Enochians, Urban Essenes, Qumranites: Three Social Groups, One Intellectual Movement." Pages 301–28 in *The Early Enoch Literature.* Edited by Gabriele Boccaccini and John J. Collins. Journal for the Study of Judaism: Supplement Series 121. Leiden: Brill, 2007.

———. *Roots of Rabbinic Judaism: An Intellectual History, from Ezekiel to Daniel.* Grand Rapids, Mich.: Eerdmans, 2002.

Boccaccini, Gabriele, ed. *Enoch and Qumran Origins: New Light on a Forgotten Connection.* Grand Rapids, Mich.: Eerdmans, 2005.

Böck, Barbara. "An Esoteric Babylonian Commentary, Revisited." *Journal of the American Oriental Society* 120 (2000): 615–20.

Bockmuehl, Markus. *Revelation and Mystery in Ancient Judaism and Pauline Christianity.* Wissenschaftliche Untersuchungen zum Neuen Testament 36. Tübingen: Mohr Siebeck, 1990. Repr., Grand Rapids, Mich.: Eerdmans, 1997.

Bohak, Gideon. *Ancient Jewish Magic: A History.* Cambridge: Cambridge University Press, 2008.

Böhlig, A. *Mysterion und Wahrheit: Gesammelte Beiträge zur spätantiken Religionsgeschichte.* Arbeiten zur Geschichte des späteren Judentums und des Urchristentums 6. Leiden: Brill, 1968.

Bok, Sisela. *Secrets: On the Ethics of Concealment and Revelation.* New York: Vintage, 1989.

Bolle, Kees, ed. *Secrecy in Religions.* Studies in the History of Religions 49. Leiden: Brill, 1987.

———. "Secrecy in Religion." Pages 1–24 in *Secrecy in Religions.* Edited by Kees W. Bolle. Studies in the History of Religion 49. Leiden: Brill, 1987.

Botterweck, G. J., H. Ringgren, and H. -J Fabry, eds. *Theological Dictionary of the Old Testament.* Translated by J. T. Willis, G. W. Bromiley, and D. E. Green. 15 vols. Grand Rapids, Mich.: Eerdmans, 1974–

Bourdieu, Pierre. *Language and Symbolic Power.* Translated by Gino Raymond and M. Adamson. Cambridge, Mass.: Harvard University Press, 1995.

Boustan, Ra'anan. *From Martyr to Mystic: Rabbinic Martyrology and the Making of Merkavah Mysticism.* Tübingen: Mohr Siebeck, 2005.

Boyce, Mary. *Textual Sources for the Study of Zoroastrianism.* Totowa, N.J.: Barnes & Noble, 1984.

Boyce, Mary and F. Grenet. *A History of Zoroastrianism. III, Zoroastrianism under Macedonian and Roman Rule.* Leiden: Brill, 1991.

Brayer, Menachem. "Psychosomatics, Hermetic Medicine, and Dream Interpretation in the Qumran Literature (Psychological and Exegetical Considerations)." *Jewish Quarterly Review* 60 (1969): 112–127.

Bremmer, Jan. "Religious Secrets and Secrecy in Classical Greece." Pages 61–78 in *Secrecy and Concealment: Studies in the History of Mediterranean and Near Eastern Religions*. Edited by H. Kippenberg and Guy G. Stroumsa. Studies in the History of Religions (Supplement to *Numen*) 65. Leiden: Brill, 1995.

Brooke, George. *The Dead Sea Scrolls and the New Testament*. Minneapolis: Fortress, 2005.

———. *Exegesis at Qumran: 4QFlorilegium in Its Jewish Context*. Journal for the Study of the Old Testament: Supplement Series 29. Sheffield: JSOT Press, 1985.

———. "Miqdash Adam, Eden, and the Qumran Community." Pages 285–301 in *Gemeinde ohne Tempel*. Edited by B. Ego et al. Tübingen: Mohr Siebeck, 1999.

———. "The Place of Prophecy in Coming out of Exile: The Case of the Dead Sea Scrolls." Pages 535–50 in *Scripture in Transition: Essays on Septuagint, Hebrew Bible, and Dead Sea Scrolls in Honour of Raija Sollamo*. Edited by Anssi Voitila and Jutta Jokiranta. Journal for the Study of Judaism: Supplement Series 126. Leiden: Brill, 2008.

———. "Prophecy." Pages 694–700 in vol. 2 of *Encyclopedia of the Dead Sea Scrolls*. Edited by James C. VanderKam and Lawrence Schiffman. Oxford: Oxford University Press, 2000.

———. "Prophets and Prophecy in the Qumran Scrolls and in the New Testament." Paper presented at the Ninth annual Orion Symposium, Hebrew University. Jerusalem, Israel, January, 2004. http://orion.mscc.huji.ac.il/symposiums/9th/papers/BrookePaper.html

———. "Qumran Pesher: Toward the Redefinition of a Genre." *Revue de Qumran* 10 (1981): 483–503.

———. "Rewritten Bible." Pages 777–81 in vol. 2 of *Encyclopedia of the Dead Sea Scrolls*. Edited by James C. VanderKam and Lawrence Schiffman. Oxford: Oxford University Press, 2000.

Brown, Francis, Samuel R. Driver and Charles Briggs. *A Hebrew and English Lexicon of the Old Testament*. Oxford: Oxford University Press, 1952.

Brown, Raymond. "The Pre-Christian Semitic Concept of 'Mystery.'" *Catholic Biblical Quarterly* 20 (1958): 417–43.

———. "The Semitic Background of the Pauline *Mystérion*." Ph.D. diss., Johns Hopkins University, 1958.

———. "The Semitic Background of the New Testament *Mysterion*." *Biblica* 39 (1958): 426–48.

———. *The Semitic Background of the Term 'Mystery' in the New Testament*. Facet Books Biblical Series 21. Philadelphia: Fortress, 1968.

Brownlee, William. "Biblical Interpretation among the Sectaries of the Dead Sea Scrolls." *The Biblical Archaeologist* 14 (1951): 54–76.

———. *The Midrash Pesher of Habukkuk*. Society of Biblical Literature Monograph Series 24. Missoula, Mont.: Scholars Press, 1979.

Bruce, F. F. "The Book of Daniel and the Qumran Community." Pages 221–39 in *Neotestamentica et Semitica: Studies in Honor of Matthew Black*. Edited by E. Earle Ellis and Mat Wilcox. Edinburgh: T&T Clark, 1969.

———. *Biblical Exegesis in the Qumran Texts*. London: Tyndale Press, 1959.

Burkes, Shannon. *God, Self, Death: The Shape of Religious Transformation in the Second Temple Period.* Journal for the Study of Judaism: Supplement Series 79. Leiden: Brill, 2003.

Burns, Joshua Ezra. "Practical Wisdom in 4QInstruction." *Dead Sea Discoveries* 11 (2004): 12–42.

Burrows, Millar. "Prophecy and Prophets at Qumrân." Pages 223–32 in *Israel's Prophetic Heritage: Essays in Honor of James Muilenburg.* Edited by Bernhard W. Anderson and Walter Harrelson. New York: Harper, 1962.

Burstein, Stanley. *Berossus the Chaldean.* Studies in the Ancient Near East 1,3. Malibu, Calif.: Undena, 1977.

Callendar, Dexter E. Jr. *Adam in Myth and History: Ancient Israelite Perspective on the Primal Human.* Harvard Semitic Studies 48. Winona Lake, Ind.: Eisenbrauns, 2000.

Cansdale, Lena. *Qumran and the Essenes: A Re-Evaluation of the Evidence.* Tübingen: Mohr Siebeck, 1997.

Carmignac, J. "Qu'est-ce que l'Apocalyptique? Son emploi à Qumrân." *Revue de Qumran* 10 (1979): 3–33.

Chalcraft, David, ed. *Sectarianism in Early Judaism: Sociological Advances.* London: Equinox, 2007.

Charlesworth, James H. "Jewish Interest in Astrology during the Hellenistic and Roman Period." *ANRW* 20.2: 926–51. Part 2, *Principat*, 20.2. Edited by H. Temporini and W. Haase. New York: de Gruyter, 1987.

———, ed. *Old Testament Pseudepigrapha.* 2 vols. New York: Doubleday, 1983.

Clifford, Richard J. *The Cosmic Mountain in Canaan and the Old Testament.* Harvard Semitic Monographs 4. Cambridge, Mass.: Harvard University Press, 1972.

Clines, David. *Job 1–20.* Word Biblical Commentary. Dallas: Word, 1989.

Cohen, Chaim. "Was the P Document Secret?" *Journal of the Ancient Near Eastern Society of Columbia University* 1/2 (1968/69): 39–44.

Cohen, Naomi. "From *Nabi* to *Mal'ak* to 'Ancient Figure.'" *Journal of Jewish Studies* 36 (1985): 12–24.

Cohen, Shaye D. *The Beginnings of Jewishness: Boundaries, Varieties, Uncertainties.* Berkeley: University of California Press, 1999.

Cohn, Norman. *Cosmos, Chaos, and the World to Come: The Ancient Roots of Apocalyptic Faith.* New Haven: Yale University Press, 1993.

Collins, Adela Yarbro. *Cosmology and Eschatology in Jewish and Christian Apocalypticism.* Journal for the Study of Judaism: Supplement Series 50. Leiden: Brill, 1996.

———. Review of *The Open Heaven* by Christopher Rowland. *Journal of Biblical Literature* 103 (1984): 465–67.

Collins, John J. "Apocalypse: Toward the Morphology of a Genre." *Semeia* 14 (1979): 1–21.

———. "Apocalyptic Eschatology as the Transcendence of Death." *Catholic Biblical Quarterly* 36 (1974): 21–42.

———. *The Apocalyptic Imagination: An Introduction to Jewish Apocalyptic Literature.* Second Edition. Grand Rapids: Eerdmans, 1998.

———. *Apocalypticism in the Dead Sea Scrolls.* London: Routledge, 1997.

———. *Between Athens and Jerusalem: Jewish Identity in the Hellenistic Diaspora.* Grand Rapids, Mich.: Eerdmans, 2000.

———. "The Court-Tales in Daniel and the Development of Apocalyptic." *Journal of Biblical Literature* 94 (1975): 218–34.

———. *Daniel: A Commentary.* Hermeneia. Minneapolis: Fortress, 1993.

———. *Daniel with an Introduction to Apocalyptic Literature.* Forms of Old Testament Literature 20. Grand Rapids: Eerdmans, 1984.

———. "'Enochic Judaism' and the Sect of the Dead Sea Scrolls." Pages 283–300 in *The Early Enoch Literature.* Edited by G. Boccaccini and J. J. Collins. Journal for the Study of Judaism: Supplement Series 121. Leiden: Brill, 2007.

———. "Forms of Community in the Dead Sea Scrolls." Pages 97–111 in *Emanuel: Studies in Hebrew Bible, Septuagint, and Dead Sea Scrolls in Honor of Emanuel Tov.* Edited by S. M. Paul et al. Supplements to Vetus Testamentum 94. Leiden: Brill, 2003.

———. "Genre, Ideology and Social Movements in Jewish Apocalypticism." Pages 11–32 in *Mysteries and Revelations: Apocalyptic Studies since the Uppsala Colloquium.* Edited by John J. Collins and James H. Charlesworth. Journal for the Study of the Pseudepigrapha: Supplement Series 9. Sheffield: Sheffield Academic Press, 1991.

———. *Jewish Wisdom in the Hellenistic Age.* Louisville, Ky.: Westminster John Knox, 1997.

———. "The Meaning of 'the End' in the Book of Daniel." Pages 91–98 in *Of Scribes and Scrolls: Studies on the Hebrew Bible, Intertestamental Judaism, and Christian Origins.* Edited by Harold W. Attridge et al. Lanham: University Press of America, 1990.

———. "The Mysteries of God: Creation and Eschatology in 4QInstruction and the Wisdom of Solomon." Pages 287–305 in *Wisdom and Apocalypticism in the Dead Sea Scrolls and in the Biblical Tradition.* Edited by Florentino García Martínez. Bibliotheca ephemeridum theologicarum lovaniensium 168. Leuven: Leuven University Press, 2003.

———. "Prophecy, Apocalypse, and Eschatology: Reflections on the Proposals of Lester Grabbe." Pages 44–52 in *Knowing the End from the Beginning: The Prophetic, the Apocalyptic, and Their Relationships.* Edited by Lester L. Grabbe and Robert D. Haak. London: T&T Clark, 2003.

———. "Response: The Apocalyptic Worldview of Daniel." Pages 59–66 in *Enoch and Qumran Origins: New Light on a Forgotten Connection.* Edited by Gabriele Boccaccini. Grand Rapids, Mich.: Eerdmans, 2005.

———. Review of *The Self as Symbolic Space: Constructing Identity and Community at Qumran,* by Carol Newsom. *Journal of Biblical Literature* 124 (2005): 170–73.

———. *The Scepter and the Star: The Messiahs of the Dead Sea Scrolls and Other Ancient Literature.* Anchor Bible Reference Library. New York: Doubleday, 1995.

———. "Sectarian Consciousness in the Dead Sea Scrolls." Pages 177–92 in *Heavenly Tablets: Interpretation, Identity and Tradition in Ancient Judaism.* Edited by L. LiDonnici and A. Lieber. Journal for the Study of Judaism: Supplement Series 119. Leiden: Brill, 2007.

————. "Was the Dead Sea Sect an Apocalyptic Movement?" Pages 25–51 in *Archaeology and History in the Dead Sea Scrolls: The New York University Conference in Memory of Yigael Yadin*. Edited by Lawrence Schiffman. Journal for the Study of the Old Testament: Supplement Series 8. Sheffield: Sheffield Academic Press, 1990.

————. "Wisdom Reconsidered, in Light of the Scrolls," *Dead Sea Discoveries* 4 (1997): 265–81.

————. "The Yahad and 'the Qumran Community.'" Pages 81–96 in *Biblical Traditions in Transmission: Essays in Honor of Michael A. Knibb*. Edited by Charlotte Hempel and Judith M. Lieu. Journal for the Study of Judaism: Supplement Series 111. Leiden: Brill, 2006.

———— and Devorah Dimant. "A Thrice-Told Hymn: A Response to Eileen Schuller." *Jewish Quarterly Review* 85 (1994): 151–55.

Cooke, G. "The Sons of (the) God(s)." *Zeitschrift für die alttestamentliche Wissenschaft* 76 (1964): 22–47.

Corbin, Henry. *Spiritual Body and Celestial Earth: From Mazdean Iran to Shi'ite Iran*. Princeton, N.J.: Princeton University Press, 1977.

Corley, Jeremy. "Wisdom Versus Apocalyptic and Science in Sirach 1, 1–10." Pages 269–85 in *Wisdom and Apocalypticism in the Dead Sea Scrolls and in the Biblical Tradition*. Edited by Florentino García Martínez. Bibliotheca ephemeridum theologicarum lovaniensium 168. Leuven: Leuven University Press, 2003.

Cotton, Hannah. "Greek." Pages 324–26 in vol. 1 of *Encyclopedia of the Dead Sea Scrolls*. Edited by James C. VanderKam and Lawrence Schiffman. Oxford: Oxford University Press, 2000.

Cowley, A. E. *Aramaic Papyri of the Fifth Century B.C.* Oxford: Oxford University Press, 1923. Repr., Osnabrück: Otto Zeller, 1967.

Crawford, Sidney White. *Rewriting Scripture in Second Temple Times*. Studies on the Dead Sea Scrolls and Related Literature. Grand Rapids, Mich.: Eerdmans, 2008.

————. "The Rewritten Bible at Qumran." Pages 131–47 in *Scripture and the Scrolls*. Edited by James H. Charlesworth. Vol. 1 of *The Bible and the Dead Sea Scrolls: The Princeton Symposium on the Dead Sea Scrolls*. Edited by James H. Charlesworth. Waco, Tex.: Baylor University Press, 2006.

Crenshaw, James L. *Old Testament Wisdom: An Introduction*. Atlanta: John Knox, 1981.

Cross, Frank Moore. *Canaanite Myth and Hebrew Epic*. Cambridge, Mass.: Harvard University Press, 1973.

————. "The Contribution of the Qumrân Discoveries to the Study of the Biblical Text." *Israel Exploration Journal* 16 (1966): 81–95.

————. "The Council of Yahweh in Second Isaiah," *Journal of Near Eastern Studies* 12 (1953): 274–77.

————. "The History of the Biblical Text in the Light of the Discoveries in the Judaean Desert." *Harvard Theological Review* 57 (1964): 281–99.

Davidson, Maxwell J. *Angels at Qumran: A Comparative Study of 1 Enoch 1–36, 72–108 and Sectarian Writings from Qumran*. Journal for the Study of the

Pseudepigrapha: Supplement Series 11. Sheffield: Sheffield Academic Press, 1992.

Davies, Philip R. "Eschatology at Qumran." *Journal of Biblical Literature* 104 (1985): 39 55.

———. "Reading Daniel Sociologically." Pages 345–61 in *The Book of Daniel in the Light of New Findings*. Edited by A. S. van der Woude. Bibliotheca ephemeridum theologicarum lovaniensium 106. Leuven: Leuven University, 1993.

———. *Scribes and Schools: The Canonization of the Hebrew Scriptures*. Louisville, Ky.: Westminster John Knox, 1998.

———. "Sect Formation in Early Judaism." Pages 133–55 in *Sectarianism in Early Judaism: Sociological Advances*. Edited by David Chalcraft. London: Equinox, 2007.

Davies, W. D. "'Knowledge' in the Dead Sea Scrolls and Matthew 11:25–30." Pages 120–44 in *Christian Origins and Judaism*. London: Darton, Longman & Todd Ltd., 1962.

Davila, James R. "The Dead Sea Scrolls and Merkavah Mysticism." Pages 249–64 in *The Dead Sea Scrolls in their Historical Context*. Edited by Timothy Lim et al. Edinburgh: T&T Clark, 2000.

———. *Descenders to the Chariot: The People behind the Hekhalot Literature*. Journal for the Study of Judaism: Supplement Series 70. Leiden: Brill, 2001.

———. "The Flood Hero as King and Priest." *Journal of Near Eastern Studies* 54 (1995): 199–214.

———. "The Peril of Parallels." No pages. Cited 5 February 2006. Online: http://www.st–andrews.ac.uk/~www_sd/parallels.html.

———. "Scripture as Prophetically Revealed Writings." Paper presented at the Annual Meeting of the Society of Biblical Literature. Washington, D.C., November 18, 2006.

DeConick, April D., ed. *Paradise Now: Essays on Early Jewish and Christian Mysticism*. Society of Biblical Literature Symposium Series 11. Atlanta: Society of Biblical Literature, 2006.

Dimant, Devorah. "4QFlorilegium and the Idea of the Community as Temple." Pages 165–89 in *Hellenica et Judaica: Homage à Valentin Nikiprowetsky*. Edited by A. Caquot, M. Hadas–Lebel and J. Riaud. Paris: Peeters, 1986.

———. "Noah in Early Jewish Literature." Pages 123–50 in *Biblical Figures Outside the Bible*. Edited by Michael E. Stone and Theodore A. Bergren. Harrisburg, Penn.: Trinity Press International, 1998.

———. "The Qumran Manuscripts: Contents and Significance." Pages 23–58 in *Time to Prepare a Way in the Wilderness*. Edited by D. Dimant and L. Schiffman. Studies on the Texts of the Desert of Judah 16. Leiden: Brill, 1995.

———. "Qumran Sectarian Literature. " Pages 483–550 in *Jewish Writings of the Second Temple Period: Apocrypha, Pseudepigrapha, Qumran Sectarian Writings, Philo Josephus*. Edited by Michael E. Stone. Compendia Rerum Iudaicarum ad Novum Testamentum 2.2. Philadelphia: Fortress, 1984.

———. "A Synoptic Comparison of Parallel Sections in 4Q427 7, 4Q491 11 and 4Q471B." *Jewish Quarterly Review* 85 (1994): 157–61.

————. "Use and Interpretation of Mikra in the Apocrypha and Pseudepigrapha." Pages 379–419 in *Mikra: Text, Translation, Reading and Interpretation of the Hebrew Bible in Ancient Judaism and Early Christianity.* Edited by Martin J. Mulder. Compendia Rerum Ioudaicarum Novum Testamentum 2.1. Minneapolis: Fortress, 1990.

Donceel, Robert. *Synthèse des observations faites en fouillant les tombes des necropolis de Khirbet Qumrân et des environs. Qumran Chronicle* 10. Kraków: Enigma Press, 2002.

Drawnel, Henryk. *An Aramaic Wisdom Text from Qumran: A New Interpretation of the Levi Document.* Journal for the Study of Judaism: Supplement Series 86. Leiden: Brill, 2004.

————. "Moon Computation in the *Aramaic Astronomical Book* (1)." *Revue de Qumran* 23 (2007): 3–41.

————. "Some Notes on Scribal Craft and the Origins of the Enochic Literature." Paper presented at the Fourth Enoch Seminar. Camaldoli, Italy, July 2007.

————. "Priestly Education in the *Aramaic Levi Document* (*Visions of Levi*) and *Aramaic Astronomical Book* (4Q208–211)." *Revue de Qumran* 22 (2006): 547–74.

Duchesne-Guillemin, J. "Apocalypse juive et apocalypse iranienne." Pages 753–59 in *La Soteriologia dei Culti Orientali nell' Impero Romano.* Edited by U. Bianchi and M. Vermaseren. Leiden: Brill, 1982.

Duhaime, J. "The War Scroll from Qumran and Graeco-Roman Tactical Treatises." *Revue de Qumran* 13 (1988): 135–51.

Duhm, Bernhard. *Das Buch Jesaja.* Göttingen: Vandenhoeck & Ruprecht, 1922.

Duncan, Ann Williams. "Religion and Secrecy: A Bibliographic Essay." *Journal of the American Academy of Religion* 74 (2006): 469–82.

Dupont-Sommer, A. *The Dead Sea Scrolls: A Preliminary Survey.* Oxford: Oxford University Press, 1952.

————. "Le problème des influences étrangères sur la secte juive de Qumrân." *Revue d'histoire et de philosophie religieuses* 35 (1955): 75–94.

Eaton, John. *Vision in Worship: The Relation of Prophecy and Liturgy in the Old Testament.* London: SPCK, 1981.

Ebeling, Florian. *The Secret History of Hermes Trismegistus: Hermeticism from Ancient to Modern Times.* Translated by David Lorton. Ithaca, N.Y.: Cornell University Press, 2007.

Eisenman, Robert and Michael O. Wise. *The Dead Sea Scrolls Uncovered: The First Complete Translation and Interpretation of 50 Key Documents Withheld for Over 35 Years.* Shaftesbury: Element Books, 1992.

Elgvin, Torleif. "Admonition Texts from Qumran Cave 4." Pages 179–96 in *Methods of Investigation of the Dead Sea Scrolls and the Khirbet Qumran Site: Present Realities and Future Prospects.* Edited by Michael O. Wise, Norman Golb, John J. Collins, and Dennis G. Pardee. Annals of the New York Academy of Sciences 722. New York: New York Academy of Sciences, 1994.

————. "An Analysis of 4QInstruction." Ph.D. diss., Hebrew University of Jerusalem, 1997.

————. "Early Essene Eschatology: Judgment and Salvation According to Sapiential Work A." Pages 126–65 in *Current Research and Technological*

Developments on the Dead Sea Scrolls: Conference on the Texts from the Judean Desert, Jerusalem, 30 April 1995. Edited by D. W. Parry and S. D. Ricks. Studies on the Texts of the Desert of Judah 20. Leiden: Brill, 1996.

——. "'The Mystery to Come': Early Essene Theology of Revelation." Pages 113–50 in *Qumran between the Old and New Testaments.* Edited by F. H. Cryer and T. L. Thompson. Journal for the Study of the Old Testament: Supplement Series 290. Sheffield: Sheffield Academic Press, 1998.

——. "Priestly Sages? The Milieus of Origin of 4QMysteries and 4QInstruction." Pages 67–88 in *Sapiential Perspectives: Wisdom Literature in Light of the Dead Sea Scrolls. Proceedings of the Sixth International Symposium of the Orion Center, 2001.* Edited by J. J. Collins, G. E. Sterling and R. A. Clements. Studies on the Texts of the Desert of Judah 51. Leiden: Brill, 2003.

——. "The Use of Scripture in 1Q/4QMysteries." In *New Perspectives on Old Texts: Proceedings of the Tenth Annual International Orion Symposium, January 9–11, 2005.* Edited by E. Chazon et al. Studies on the Texts of the Desert of Judah. Leiden: Brill, forthcoming.

——. "Wisdom and Apocalypticism in the Early Second Century B.C.E.: The Evidence of 4QInstruction." Pages 226–47 in *The Dead Sea Scrolls: Fifty Years After Their Discovery: Proceedings of the Jerusalem Congress, July 20–25, 1997.* Edited by Lawrence Schiffman, Emanuel Tov and James C. VanderKam. Jerusalem: Israel Exploration Society, in collaboration with The Shrine of the Book, Israel Museum, 2000.

——. "Wisdom, Revelation, and Eschatology in an Early Essene Writing." Pages 440–63 in *Society of Biblical Literature Seminar Papers, 1995.* Atlanta: Scholars Press, 1995.

Eliade, Mircea. *The Myth of the Eternal Return: Or, Cosmos and History.* Princeton, N.J.: Princeton University Press, 1954.

——. *Occultism, Witchcraft, and Cultural Fashions: Essays in Comparative Religions* Chicago: University of Chicago Press, 1978.

Elior, Rachel. *The Three Temples: On the Emergence of Jewish Mysticism.* Oxford: Littman Library of Jewish Civilization, 2004.

Ellenbogen, M. *Foreign Words in the Old Testament: Their Origin and Etymology.* London: Luzac & Company, 1962.

Emerton, J. A. "Sheol and the Sons of Belial," *Vetus Testamentum* 37 (1987): 214–19.

Eshel, Esther. "4Q471b: A Self-Glorification Hymn." *Revue de Qumran* 17 (1997): 175–203.

——. "Genres of Magical Texts in the Dead Sea Scrolls." Pages 395–415 in *Demons: The Demonology of Israelite-Jewish and Early Christian Literature in Context of their Environment.* Edited by A. Lange, H. Lichtenberger, and K. F. D. Römheld. Tübingen: Mohr Siebeck, 2003.

——. "The Identification of the 'Speaker' of the Self-Glorification Hymn." Pages 619–35 in *The Provo International Conference on the Dead Sea Scrolls: Technological Innovations, New Texts, and Reformulated Issues.* Edited by D. W. Parry and E. Ulrich. Studies on the Texts of the Desert of Judah 30. Leiden: Brill, 1999.

Evans, Craig. "A Note on the 'First-Born Son' of 4Q369." *Dead Sea Discoveries* 2 (1995): 185–201.

Fabry, Heinz-Josef. "סוד. Der himmlische Thronrat als ekklesiologisches Modell." Pages 99–126 in *Bausteine biblischer Theologie: Festgabe für G. Johannes Botterweck zum 60 Geburtstag dargebracht von seinen Schülern*. Edited by H. -J. Fabry. Bonner biblische Beiträge 50. Cologne: Hanstein, 1977.

———. "סוד." *TDOT* 12.171–78.

Faivre, Antoine. *The Eternal Hermes: From Greek God to Alchemical Magus*. York Beach, Maine: Phanes Press, 1995.

Falk, Daniel. *The Parabiblical Texts: Strategies for Extending the Scriptures among the Dead Sea Scrolls*. Library of Second Temple Studies 63. T&T Clark, 2007.

Feldman, Louis. "Prophets and Prophecy in Josephus." *Journal of Theological Studies* 41 (1990): 386–422.

Festugière, A. -J. *La revelation dHermès Trismégiste*. 3 vols. Paris: Les Belles Lettres, 1981.

Finkel, Asher. "The Pesher of Dreams and Scriptures." *Revue de Qumran* 4 (1963–64): 357–70.

Fishbane, Michael. *Biblical Interpretation in Ancient Israel*. Oxford: Oxford University Press, 1985.

———. "The Hermeneutics of Scripture in Formation." Pages 3–46 in *The Garments of Torah: Essays in Biblical Hermeneutics*. Indiana Studies in Biblical Literature. Bloomington, Ind.: Indiana University Press, 1989.

———. "Use, Authority, and Interpretation of Mikra at Qumran." Pages 339–77 in *Mikra: Text, Translation, Reading, and Interpretation of the Hebrew Bible in Ancient Judaism and Early Christianity*. Edited by Martin J. Mulder. Compendia Rerum Iudaicarum ad Novum Testamentum 2.1. Minneapolis: Fortress, 1988.

Flannery-Dailey, Frances. *Dreamers, Scribes, and Priests: Jewish Dreams in the Hellenistic and Roman Eras*. Journal for the Study of Judaism: Supplement Series 90. Leiden: Brill, 2004.

Fletcher-Louis, Crispin H. T. *All the Glory of Adam: Liturgical Anthropology in the Dead Sea Scrolls*. Studies on the Texts of the Desert of Judah 42. Leiden: Brill, 2002.

———. "Heavenly Ascent or Incarnational Presence? A Revisionist Reading of the Songs of the Sabbath Sacrifice." Pages 367–99 in *Society of Biblical Literature Seminar Papers*. Society of Biblical Literature Seminar Papers 37. Atlanta: Scholars Press, 1998.

Flint, Peter W. *The Bible at Qumran: Text, Shape and Interpretation*. Studies in the Dead Sea Scrolls and Related Literature. Grand Rapids: Eerdmans, 2001.

Floyd, Michael and Robert Haak, eds. *Prophets, Prophecy and Prophetic Texts in Second Temple Judaism*. Library of Hebrew Bible/Old Testament Studies 427. London: T&T Clark, 2006.

Fowden, Garth. *The Egyptian Hermes: A Historical Approach to the Late Pagan Mind*. Cambridge: Cambridge University Press, 1986.

Fraade, Steven. "Interpretative Authority in the Studying Community at Qumran." *Journal of Jewish Studies* 44 (1993): 46–69.

Frerichs, Ernst and Jacob Neusner, eds. *Goodenough on the History of Religion and on Judaism*. Brown Judaic Studies 121. Atlanta: Scholars Press, 1986.

Frey, Jörg. "Different Patterns of Dualistic Thought in the Qumran Library: Reflections on their Background and History." Pages 275–335 in *Legal Texts and Legal Issues: Proceedings of the Second Meeting of the International Organization for Qumran Studies, Cambridge 1995*. Edited by Moshe Bernstein, Florentino García Martínez and John Kampen. Studies on the Texts of the Desert of Judah 23. Leiden: Brill, 1997.

———. "The Notion of 'Flesh' in 4QInstruction and the Background of Pauline Usage." Pages 197–226 in *Sapiential, Liturgical, and Poetical Texts from Qumran: Proceedings of the Third Meeting of the International Organization for Qumran Studies, Oslo 1998*. Edited by D. K. Falk, F. G. Martínez, and E. M. Schuller. Studies on the Texts of the Desert of Judah 34. Leiden: Brill, 2000.

Frey, Jörg and Michael Becker. *Apokalyptik und Qumran*. Einblicke 10. Paderborn: Bonifatius, 2007.

Gabrion, Henri. "L'Interprétation de l'Ecriture dans la littérature de Qumrân." *ANRW* 19.1: 779–848. Part 2, *Principat*, 19.1. Edited by H. Temporini and W. Haase. New York: de Gruyter, 1979.

Galor, K., J. -B. Humbert, and J. Zangenberg, eds. *Qumran: The Site of the Dead Sea Scrolls: Archaeological Interpretation and Debates. Proceedings of a Conference Held at Brown University, November 17–19, 2002*. Studies on the Texts of the Desert of Judah 57. Leiden: Brill, 2006.

Gammie, John G. "Spatial and Ethical Dualism in Jewish Wisdom and Apocalyptic Literature." *Journal of Biblical Literature* 93 (1974): 365–85.

García Martínez, Florentino. "4QMes. Aram. y el libro de Noé." *Salmanticensis* 28 (1981): 195–232.

———. "Apocalypticism in the Dead Sea Scrolls." Pages 195–226 in *Qumranica minora I: Qumran Origins and Apocalypticism*. Edited by Eibert J. C. Tigchelaar. Studies on the Texts of the Desert of Judah 63. Leiden: Brill, 2007.

———. "*Aramaica qumranica apocalyptica?*" In Aramaica Qumranica: *The Aix-en-Provence Colloquium on the Aramaic Dead Sea Scrolls*. Edited by Katell Berthelot and Daniel Stökl Ben Ezra. Studies on the Texts of the Desert of Judah. Leiden: Brill, forthcoming.

———. "Conclusion: Mapping the Threads." Pages 329–36 in *The Early Enoch Literature*. Edited by Gabriele Boccaccini and John J. Collins. Journal for the Study of Judaism: Supplement Series 121. Leiden: Brill, 2007.

———. *The Dead Sea Scrolls Translated: The Qumran Texts in English*. Translated by Wilfred G. E. Watson. 2nd ed. Leiden and Grand Rapids: Brill and Eerdmans, 1996.

———. "Magic in the Dead Sea Scrolls." Pages 13–33 in *The Metamorphosis of Magic from Late Antiquity to the Early Modern Period*. Edited by Jan N. Bremmer and J. R. Veenstra. Leuven: Peeters, 2002.

———. "Marginalia on 4QInstruction." *Dead Sea Discoveries* 13 (2006): 24–37.

———. "Qumran Origins and Early History: A Groningen Hypothesis." *Folia orientalia* 25 (1988): 113–36.

————. *Qumran and Apocalyptic: Studies on the Aramaic Texts from Qumran*. Studies on the Texts of the Desert of Judah 9. Leiden: Brill, 1992.

————. "¿Sectario, no-sectario, o qué? Problemas de una taxonomía correcta de los textos qumránicos." *Revue de Qumran* 23 (2008): 383–394.

————. "Wisdom at Qumran: Worldly or Heavenly?" Pages 1–15 in *Wisdom and Apocalypticism in the Dead Sea Scrolls and in the Biblical Tradition*. Edited by Florentino García Martínez. Bibliotheca ephemeridum theologicarum lovaniensium 168. Leuven: Leuven University Press, 2003.

García Martínez, Florentino and Eibert J. C. Tigchelaar. *The Dead Sea Scrolls Study Edition*. 2 vols. Leiden: Brill, 1997.

García Martínez, Florentino and Julio Trebolle Barrera, *The People of the Dead Sea Scrolls*. Translated by Wilfrid G. E. Watson. Leiden: Brill, 1995.

García Martínez, Florentino and Adam S. van der Woude. "A 'Groningen' Hypothesis of Qumran Origins and Early History." *Revue de Qumran* 14 (1990): 521–41.

Geller, M. "New Documents from the Dead Sea: Babylonian Science in Aramaic." Pages 224–29 in *Boundaries in the Ancient Near Eastern World: A Tribute to Cyrus H. Gordon*. Edited by Meir Lubetski, Claire Gottlieb and Sharon Keller. Journal for the Study of the Old Testament: Supplement Series 273. Sheffield: Sheffield Academic Press, 1998.

George, A. R. *The Babylonian Gilgamesh: Introduction, Critical Edition, and Cuneiform Texts*. 2 volumes. Oxford: Oxford University Press, 2003.

Gibson, Arthur. *Biblical Semantic Logic: A Preliminary Analysis*. New York: St. Martin's Press, 1981.

Gitay, Y. *Prophecy and Prophets: The Diversity of Contemporary Issues in Scholarship*. Semeia Studies 33. Atlanta: Scholars Press, 1997.

Gladd, Benjamin. *Revealing the* Mysterion*: The Use of* Mystery *in Daniel and Second Temple Judaism and Its Bearing on First Corinthians*. Beihefte zur Zeitschrift für die neuestestamentliche Wissenschaft 160. Berlin: de Gruyter, 2008.

Glessmer, Uwe. "Calendars in the Qumran Scrolls." Pages 213–74 in *The Dead Sea Scrolls after Fifty Years, Volume 2*. Edited by Peter Flint and James C. VanderKam. Leiden: Brill, 1999.

Gmirken, Russell. "Historical Allusions in the War Scroll." *Dead Sea Discoveries* 5 (1998): 174–214.

————. "The War Scroll and Roman Weaponry Reconsidered." *Dead Sea Discoveries* 3 (1996): 89–129.

Goff, Matthew. "Discerning Trajectories: 4QInstruction and the Sapiential Background of the Sayings Source." *Journal of Biblical Literature* 124 (2005): 657–73.

————. *Discerning Wisdom: The Sapiential Literature of the Dead Sea Scrolls*. Vetus Testamentum: Supplement Series 116. Leiden: Brill, 2007.

————. "The Mystery of Creation in 4QInstruction." *Dead Sea Discoveries* 10 (2003): 163–86.

————. "Reading Wisdom at Qumran: 4QInstruction and the Hodayot." *Dead Sea Discoveries* 11 (2004): 263–88.

————. *The Worldly and Heavenly Wisdom of 4QInstruction*. Studies on the Texts of the Desert of Judah 50. Leiden: Brill, 2003.

———. "The Worldly and Heavenly Wisdom of 4QInstruction." Ph.D. diss., University of Chicago, 2002.

Golb, Norman. *Who Wrote the Dead Sea Scrolls? The Search for the Secret of Qumran.* New York: Scribner, 1995.

Goldstein, Jonathan A. "Review of Goodenough." Pages 57–66 in *Semites, Iranians, Greeks, Romans: Studies in Their Interactions.* Brown Judaic Studies 217. Atlanta: Scholars Press, 1990.

Goodenough, Erwin R. *By Light, Light: The Mystic Gospel of Hellenistic Judaism.* New Haven: Yale University Press, 1935.

———. *Jewish Symbols in the Greco-Roman Period.* 13 vols. New York: Pantheon, 1953–68.

Goody, Jack. *The Logic of Writing and the Organization of Society.* Studies in Literacy, Family, Culture and the State. Cambridge: Cambridge University Press, 1986.

Gordon, Robert. "From Mari to Moses: Prophecy at Mari and in Ancient Israel." Pages 63–79 in *Of Prophets' Visions and the Wisdom of Sages: Essays in Honour of R. Norman Whybray on His Seventieth Birthday.* Edited by Heather McKay and David Clines. Journal for the Study of the Old Testament: Supplement Series 162. Sheffield: JSOT Press, 1993.

Grabbe, Lester L. *Priests, Prophets, Diviners, Sages: A Socio-Historical Study of Religious Specialists in Ancient Israel.* Valley Forge, Penn.: Trinity Press International, 1995.

———. "Prophetic and Apocalyptic: Time for New Definitions—and New Thinking." Pages 107–33 in *Knowing the End from the Beginning: The Prophetic, the Apocalyptic, and Their Relationships.* Edited by Lester L. Grabbe and Robert D. Haak. London: T&T Clark, 2003.

Gracián, Baltasar. *The Art of Worldly Wisdom.* Translated by Christopher Maurer. New York: Doubleday, 1991.

Graf, Fritz. *Magic in the Ancient World.* Revealing Antiquity 10. Cambridge, Mass.: Harvard University Press, 1997.

Gray, George Buchanan. *A Critical and Exegetical Commentary on the Book of Isaiah Volume 1.* International Critical Commentary. Edinburg: T&T Clark, 1912.

Gray, Rebecca. *Prophetic Figures in Late Second Temple Jewish Palestine: The Evidence from Josephus.* Oxford: Oxford University Press, 1993.

Green, W. S. "Ancient Judaisms: Contours and Complexity." Pages 293–310 in *Language, Theology and the Bible.* Edited by Samuel E. Balentine and John Barton. Oxford: Clarendon Press, 1994.

Greenfield, Jonas. "The Words of Levi Son of Jacob in Damascus Document IV.15-19." *Revue de Qumran* 13 (1988): 319–22.

Greenfield, Jonas and Michael Sokoloff. "Astrological and Related Omen Texts in Jewish Palestinian Aramaic." *Journal of Near Eastern Studies* 48 (1989): 201–214.

Greenfield, Jonas, Michael Stone and Esther Eshel. *Aramaic Levi Document: Text, Translation and Commentary.* Studia in Veteris Testamenti pseudepigraphica 19. Leiden: Brill, 2004.

Greenspahn, Frederick. "Why Prophecy Ceased." *Journal of Biblical Literature* 108 (1989): 37–49.

Greenspoon, Leonard. "The Dead Sea Scrolls and the Greek Bible." Pages 101–27 in *The Dead Sea Scrolls after Fifty Years: A Comprehensive Assessment, Vol. 1.* Edited by Peter Flint and James C. VanderKam. 2 vols. Leiden: Brill, 1999.

Grelot, Pierre. "L'Eschatologie des Esséniens et le Livre D'Hénoch." *Revue de Qumran* 1 (1958): 113–31.

———. "La géographie mythique d'Hénoch et ses sources orientales." *Revue Biblique* 65 (1958): 33–69.

———. "La légende d'Hénoch dans les apocryphes et dans la Bible: Origine et significance." *Recherches de science religieuse* 46 (1958): 5–26.

Grossman, Maxine. "Cultivating Identity: Textual Virtuosity and 'Insider' Status." Pages 1–11 in *Defining Identities: We, You, and the Other in the Dead Sea Scrolls: Proceedings of the Fifth Meeting of the IOQS in Groningen.* Edited by Florentino García Martínez. Studies on the Texts of the Desert of Judah 70. Leiden: Brill, 2008.

———. "Priesthood as Authority: Interpretive Competition in First-Century Judaism and Christianity." Pages 117–31 in *The Dead Sea Scrolls as Background to Postbiblical Judaism and Early Christianity: Papers from an International Conference at St. Andrews in 2001.* Edited by James Davila. Studies on the Texts of the Desert of Judah 46. Leiden: Brill, 2002.

———. "Reading for Gender in the Damascus Document." *Dead Sea Discoveries* 11 (2004): 212–39.

———. *Reading for History in the Damascus Document: A Methodological Method.* Studies on the Texts of the Desert of Judah 45. Leiden: Brill, 2002.

Gruenwald, Ithamar. *Apocalyptic and Merkavah Mysticism.* Leiden: Brill, 1980.

———. *From Apocalypticism to Gnosticism: Studies in Apocalypticism, Merkavah Mysticism and Gnosticism.* Beiträge zur Erforschung des Alten Testaments und des antiken Judentum 14. Frankfurt: Peter Lang, 1988.

———. "The Jewish Esoteric Literature in the Time of the Mishnah and Talmud." *Immanuel* 4 (1974): 37–46.

Halbertal, Moshe. *Concealment and Revelation: Esotericism in Jewish Thought and Its Philosophical Implications.* Translated by Jackie Feldman. Princeton, N.J.: Princeton University Press, 2007.

Hamilton, M. "Who Was a Jew? Jewish Ethnicity during the Achaemenid Period." *Restoration Quarterly* 37 (2001): 102–17.

Hanson, Paul. *The Dawn of Apocalyptic: The Historical and Sociological Roots of Jewish Apocalyptic Eschatology.* Philadelphia: Fortress, 1975.

———. "Jewish Apocalyptic Against Its Near Eastern Environment." *Revue Biblique* 78 (1971): 31–58.

———. "Rebellion in Heaven, Azazel, and Euhemeristic Heroes in 1Enoch 6–11." *Journal of Biblical Literature* 96 (1977): 195–233.

Harding, James E. "The Wordplay between the Roots כשל and שכל in the Literature of the Yahad." *Revue de Qumran* 19 (1999): 69–82.

Harkins, Angela Kim. "The Community Hymns Classification: A Proposal for Further Differentiation." *Dead Sea Discoveries* 15 (2008): 121–54.

———. "Observations on the Editorial Shaping of the So-Called Community Hymns from 1QH[a] and 4QH[a]." *Dead Sea Discoveries* 12 (2005): 233–56.

Harrington, Daniel, S.J. "The *Rāz Nihyeh* in a Qumran Wisdom Text (1Q26, 4Q415–18, 4Q423)." *Revue de Qumran* 17 (1996): 549–53.

———. "Recent Study of 4QInstruction." Pages 105–23 in *From 4QMMT to Resurrection: Mélanges qumraniens en hommage à Émile Puech*. Edited by Florentino García Martínez, Annette Steudel, and Eibert J. C. Tigchelaar. Studies on the Texts of the Desert of Judah 61. Leiden: Brill, 2006.

———. "Wisdom and Apocalyptic in 4QInstruction and 4 Ezra." Pages 343–55 in *Wisdom and Apocalypticism in the Dead Sea Scrolls and in the Biblical Tradition*. Edited by Florentino García Martínez. Bibliotheca ephemeridum theologicarum lovaniensium 168. Leuven: Leuven University Press, 2003.

———. "Wisdom at Qumran." Pages 137–52 in *The Community of the Renewed Covenant: The Notre Dame Symposium on the Dead Sea Scrolls*. Edited by Eugene Ulrich and James C. VanderKam. Christianity and Judaism in Antiquity 10. Notre Dame, Ind.: University of Notre Dame Press, 1994.

———. *Wisdom Texts from Qumran*. New York: Routledge, 1996.

Harvey, A. E. "The Use of Mystery Language in the Bible." *Journal of Theological Studies* N. S. 31 (1980): 320–36.

Heger, Paul. "The Development of Qumran Law: *Nistarot, Niglot*, and the Issue of 'Contemporization.'" *Revue de Qumran* 23 (2007): 167–206.

Hempel, Charlotte. "Interpretative Authority in the Community Rule Tradition." *Dead Sea Discoveries* 10 (2003): 59–80.

Hengel, Martin. *Judaism and Hellenism: Studies in Their Encounter During the Early Hellenistic Period*. 2 vols. Philadelphia: Fortress, 1974.

Henze, Matthias. *Biblical Interpretation at Qumran*. Studies in the Dead Sea Scrolls and Related Literature. Grand Rapids, Mich.: Eerdmans, 2005.

Herbert, A. S. *The Book of the Prophet: Isaiah 1–39*. Cambridge Bible Commentary. Cambridge: Cambridge University Press, 1973.

Hinnells, John R. "Zoroastrian Influence on Judaism and Christianity: Some Further Reflections." Pages 73–92 in *Zoroastrian and Parsi Studies: Selected Works of John R. Hinnells*. Aldershot: Ashgate, 2000.

Hirschfeld, Yizhar. *Qumran in Context: Reassessing the Archaeological Evidence*. Peabody, Mass.: Hendrickson, 2004.

Høgenhaven, Jesper. "The Literary Character of 4QTanhumim." *Dead Sea Discoveries* 14 (2007): 99–123.

Holst, Søren and Jesper Høgenhaven. "Physiognomy and Eschatology: Some More Fragments of 4Q561." *Journal of Jewish Studies* 57 (2006): 26–43.

Horgan, Maurya. *Pesharim: Qumran Interpretations of Biblical Books*. Catholic Biblical Quarterly Monograph Series 8. Washington, D.C.: The Catholic Biblical Association of America, 1979.

Huggins, R. V. "Noah and the Giants: A Response to John C. Reeves." *Journal of Biblical Literature* 114 (1995): 103–10.

Hultgård, A. "Persian Apocalypticism." Pages 30–63 in *The Continuum History of Apocalypticism*. Edited by Bernard McGinn, John J. Collins, and Stephen J. Stein. New York: Continuum, 2003.

Hultgren, Stephen. *From the Damascus Covenant to the Covenant of the Community: Literary, Historical, and Theological Studies in the Dead Sea Scrolls.* Studies on the Texts of the Desert of Judah 66. Leiden: Brill, 2007.

Hunger, H. *Babylonische und assyrische Kolophone.* Neukirchen-Vluyn: Neukirchener Verlag, 1968.

Huppenbauer, Hans-Walter. "Belial in den Qumrantexten." *Theologische Zeitschrift* 15 (1959): 81–89.

Ibba, Giovanni. "Il 'Libro dei Misteri' (1Q27, f.1); testo escatologico." *Henoch* 21 (1999): 73–84.

Janowitz, Naomi. *Icons of Power: Ritual Practices in Late Antiquity.* University Park: Pennsylvania State University Press, 2002.

Jansen, H. Ludin. *Die Henochgestalt: Eine vergleichende religionsgeschichtliche Untersuchung.* Oslo: Dybwad, 1939.

Jassen, Alex. *Mediating the Divine: Prophecy and Revelation in the Dead Sea Scrolls and Second Temple Judaism.* Studies on the Texts of the Desert of Judah 68. Leiden: Brill, 2007.

Jastram, Nathan. "Hierarchy at Qumran." Pages 349–76 in *Legal Texts and Legal Issues: Proceedings of the Second Meeting of the International Organization for Qumran Studies, Cambridge 1995.* Edited by Moshe Bernstein, Florentino García Martínez and John Kampen. Studies on the Texts of the Desert of Judah 23. Leiden: Brill, 1997.

Jefferies, D. *Wisdom at Qumran: A Form-Critical Analysis of the Admonitions in 4QInstruction.* Gorgias Dissertations/Near Eastern Studies 3. Piscataway, N.J.: Gorgias Press, 2002.

Johnson, Timothy. "Job as Proto–Apocalypse: A Fresh Proposal for Job's Governing Genre." A paper presented for the Wisdom and Apocalypticism in Early Judaism and Early Christianity Group at the Annual Meeting of the SBL, San Antonio, Tex., 22 November, 2004.

Joines, Karen Randolph. "The Bronze Serpent in the Israelite Cult." *Journal of Biblical Literature* 87 (1968): 245–56.

Jokiranta, Jutta. "'Sectarianism' of the Qumran 'Sect': Sociological Notes." *Revue de Qumran* 20 (2001): 223–40.

Jones, R. J. "The Manual of Discipline (1QS), Persian Religion, and the Old Testament." Pages 94–108 in *the Teacher's Yoke: Studies in Memory of Henry Trantham.* Edited by E. J. Vardeman and J. L. Garret, Jr. Waco, Tex.: Baylor University Press, 1964.

Kanagaraj, Jey. *Mysticism in the Gospel of John: An Inquiry into Its Background.* Journal for the Study of the New Testament: Supplement Series 158. Sheffield: Sheffield Academic Press, 1998.

Kelber, Werner. "Narrative and Disclosure: Mechanisms of Concealing, Revealing, and Reveiling." *Semeia* 43 (1988): 1–20.

Kent, R. G. *Old Persian: Grammar, Texts, Lexicon.* New Haven: Yale University Press, 1953.

Kingsbury, E. C. "Prophets and the Council of Yahweh." *Journal of Biblical Literature* 83 (1964): 279–86.

Kippenberg, Hans A. and Guy Stroumsa, eds. *Secrecy and Concealment: Studies in the History of Mediterranean and Near Eastern Religions*. Studies in the History of Religions 65. Leiden: Brill, 1995.

Kitz, Anne Marie. "Prophecy as Divination." *Catholic Biblical Quarterly* 65 (2003): 22–42.

Klauck, H. -J. *The Religious Context of Early Christianity: A Guide to Graeco-Roman Religions*. Translated by Brian McNeil. Minneapolis: Fortress, 2003.

Kleingünther, A. *ΠΡΩΤΟΣ ΕΥΡΗΤΕΣ: Untersuchungen zur Geschichte einer Fragestellung*. Leipzig: Dietrich, 1933. Repr. New York: Arno, 1976.

Klinghardt, M. "The Manual of Discipline in the Light of Statutes of Hellenistic Associations." Pages 251–70 in *Methods of Investigation of the Dead Sea Scrolls and the Khirbet Qumran Site: Present Realities and Future Prospects*. Edited by Michael O. Wise et al. Annals of the New York Academy of Sciences 722. New York: The New York Academy of Sciences, 1994.

Klostergaard Peterson, A. "Wisdom as Cognition: Creating the Others in the Book of Mysteries and 1 Cor 1–2." Pages 410–20 in *The Wisdom Texts from Qumran and the Development of Sapiential Thought*. Edited by C. Hempel, A. Lange and H. Lichtenberger. Bibliotheca ephemeridum theologicarum lovaniensium 159. Leuven: Leuven University Press, 2002.

Klutz, Todd E., ed. *Magic in the Biblical World: From the Rod of Aaron to the Ring of Solomon*. London: T&T Clark, 2003.

Knibb, Michael. "Eschatology and Messianism in the Dead Sea Scrolls." Pages 379–402 in *The Dead Sea Scrolls after Fifty Years, Volume 2*. Edited by Peter W. Flint and James C. VanderKam. Leiden: Brill, 1999.

———. *The Ethiopic Book of Enoch*. 2 vols. Oxford: Clarendon Press, 1978.

———. *The Qumran Community*. Cambridge: Cambridge University Press, 1987.

Knohl, Israel. "נגלות ונסתרות—Revealed and Hidden Torah." *Jewish Quarterly Review* 85 (1994): 103–108.

Kobelski, Paul J. *Melchizedek and Melchirešaʿ*. Catholic Biblical Quarterly Monograph Series 10. Washington, D.C.: Catholic Biblical Association of America, 1981.

Koch, Klaus. *The Rediscovery of Apocalyptic*. Studies in Biblical Theology 22. London: SCM Press, 1972.

Kosmala, L. "Maskil," *Journal of the Ancient Near Eastern Society of Columbia University* 5 (1973): 235–41.

Kugel, James and Rowan A. Greer. *Early Biblical Interpretation*. Library of Early Christianity 3. Philadelphia: Westminster, 1986.

Kugler, Robert. *From Patriarch to Priest: The Levi-Priestly Tradition from Aramaic Levi to Testament of Levi*. Society of Biblical Literature Early Judaism and Its Literature 9. Atlanta: Scholars Press, 1996.

———. "Whose Scripture? Whose Community? Reflections on the Dead Sea Scrolls Then and Now, By Way of Aramaic Levi." *Dead Sea Discoveries* 15 (2008): 5–23.

Kuhn, K. G. "Die in Palästina gefundenen Handschriften und das NT," *Zeitschrift für Theologie und Kirche* 47 (1950): 193–205.

———. "Die Sektenschrift und die iranische Religion." *Zeitschrift für Theologie und Kirche* 49 (1952): 296–316.

Kutscher, E. Y. *The Language and Linguistic Background of the Isaiah Scroll (1QIsaa)*. Studies on the Texts of the Desert of Judah 6. Leiden: Brill, 1974.

Kvanvig, Helge. *The Roots of Apocalyptic: The Mesopotamian Background of the Enoch Figure and of the Son of Man*. Wissenschaftliche Monographien zum Alten und Neuen Testament 61. Neukirchen-Vluyn: Neukirchener Verlag, 1988.

Lange, Armin. "The Determination of Fate by the Oracle of the Lot in the Dead Sea Scrolls, the Hebrew Bible and Ancient Mesopotamian Literature." Pages 39–48 in *Sapiential, Liturgical and Poetical Texts from Qumran: Proceedings of the Third Meeting of the International Organization for Qumran Studies, Oslo 1998, Published in Memory of Maurice Baillet*. Edited by Daniel K. Falk, Florentino García Martínez and Eileen Schuller. Studies on the Texts of the Desert of Judah 35. Leiden: Brill, 2000.

———. "In Diskussion mit dem Tempel: zur Auseinandersetzung zwischen Kohelet und weisheitlichen Kreisen am Jerusalemer Tempel." Pages 113–59 in *Qohelet in the Context of Wisdom*. Edited by Anton Schoors. Bibliotheca ephemeridum theologicarum lovaniensium 136. Leuven: Leuven University Press, 1998.

———. "Dream Visions and Apocalyptic Milieus." Pages 27–34 in *Enoch and Qumran Origins: New Light on a Forgotten Connection*. Edited by Gabriele Boccaccini. Grand Rapids, Mich.: Eerdmans, 2005.

———. "The Essene Position on Magic and Divination." Pages 377–435 in *Legal Texts and Legal Issues: Proceedings of the Second Meeting of the International Organization for Qumran Studies, Cambridge 1995*. Edited by Moshe Bernstein, Florentino García Martínez, and John Kampen. Studies on the Texts of the Desert of Judah 23. Leiden: Brill, 1997.

———. "Kriterien zur Bestimmung 'essenischer Ver-fasserschaft' von Qumrantexten." Pages 71–85 in *Qumran kontrovers: Beiträge zu den Textfunden vom Toten Meer*. Edited by Jörg Frey and Hartmut Stegemann, with the collaboration of Michael Becker and Alexander Maurer. Einblicke 6; Paderborn: Bonifatius, 2003.

———. "Kriterien essenischer Texte." Pages 59–69 in *Qumran kontrovers: Beiträge zu den Textfunden vom Toten Meer*. Edited by Jörg Frey and Hartmut Stegemann, with the collaboration of Michael Becker and Alexander Maurer. Einblicke 6; Paderborn: Bonifatius, 2003.

———. *Vom prophetischen Wort zur prophetischen Tradition: Studien zur Traditionsund Redaktionsgeschichte innerprophetischer Konflikte in der Hebräischen Bibel* Forschungen zum Alten Testament 34. Tübingen: Mohr Siebeck, 2002.

———. "Reading the Decline of Prophecy." Pages 181–91 in *Reading the Present in the Qumran Library: The Perception of the Contemporary by Means of Scriptural Interpretations*. Edited by Kristin De Troyer and Armin Lange. Society of Biblical Literature Symposium Series 30. Atlanta: Society of Biblical Literature, 2005.

———. *Weisheit und Prädestination: Weisheitliche Urordnung und Prädestination in den Textfunden von Qumran.* Studies on the Texts of the Desert of Judah 18. Leiden: Brill, 1995.

———. "Die Weisheitstexte aus Qumran: Eine Einleitung." Pages 3–30 in *The Wisdom Texts from Qumran and the Development of Sapiential Thought.* Edited by C. Hempel, A. Lange, and H. Lichtenberger. Bibliotheca ephemeridum theologicarum lovaniensium 159. Leuven: Leuven University Press, 2002.

———. "Wisdom and Predestination in the Dead Sea Scrolls." *Dead Sea Discoveries* 2 (1995): 340–54.

Larson, Erik. "Visions." Pages 957–58 in vol. 2 of *Encyclopedia of the Dead Sea Scrolls.* Edited by James C. VanderKam and Lawrence Schiffman. 2 vols. Oxford: Oxford University Press, 2000.

Leaney, A. R. C. "Greek Manuscripts from the Judaean Desert." Pages 283–300 in *Studies in New Testament Language and Text: Essay in Honour of George D. Kilpatrick on the Occasion of His Sixty-fifth Birthday.* Edited by J. K. Elliott. Leiden: Brill, 1976.

Lease, Gary. "Jewish Mystery Cults Since Goodenough." *ANRW* 20.2:858–80. Part 2, *Principat,* 20.2. Edited by H. Temporini and W. Haase. New York: de Gruyter, 1987.

Lefkovitz, Judah. *The Copper Scroll: 3Q15: A Reevaluation. A New Reading, Translation, and Commentary.* Studies on the Texts of the Desert of Judah 25. Leiden: Brill, 2000.

Lenzi, Alan. *Secrecy and the Gods: Secret Knowledge in Ancient Mesopotamia and Biblical Israel.* State Archives of Assyria Studies 19. Winona Lake, Ind.: Eisenbrauns, 2008.

———. "Secrecy, Textual Legitimation, and Inter-Cultural Polemics in the Book of Daniel." *Catholic Biblical Quarterly* 71 (2009): 330–48.

Lesses, Rebecca. *Ritual Practices to Gain Power: Angels, Incantations, and Revelation in Early Jewish Mysticism.* Harrisburg: Trinity Press International, 1998.

Levison, John R. "Did the Spirit Withdraw from Israel? An Evaluation of the Earliest Jewish Data." *New Testament Studies* 43 (1997): 35–57.

———. *The Spirit in First-Century Judaism.* Leiden: Brill, 2002.

Lim, T. *Holy Scripture in the Qumran Commentaries and Pauline Letters.* Oxford: Clarendon Press, 1997.

Limet, H. "Le Secret et Les Écrits: Aspects du L'Ésotericisme en Mésopotamie Ancienne." Pages 243–54 in *Les Rites d'Initiation: Actes du Colloque de Liege et de Louvain-la-Neuve, 20–21 Novembre 1984.* Edited by H. Limet and J. Ries. Louvain-la-Neuve: Centre d'Histoire des Religions, 1986.

Lindblom, Johannes. "Lot-Casting in the Old Testament." *Vetus Testamentum* 12 (1962): 164–78.

Lindenberger, J. M. "Ahiqar." Pages 479–508 in vol. 1 of *Old Testament Pseudepigrapha.* Edited by J. H. Charlesworth. 2 vols. New York: Doubleday, 1983.

Livingstone, Alisdair. *Mystical and Mythological Explanatory Works of Assyrian and Babylonian Scholars.* Oxford: Clarendon Press, 1986.

Long, Burke O. "The Effect of Divination upon Israelite Literature." *Journal of Biblical Literature* 92 (1973): 489–97.

Louw, J. P. *Semantics of Biblical Greek*. Philadelphia: Fortress, 1982.

Luke, K. "The Technical Term 'Raza.'" *Christian Orient* 4 (1983): 112–22.

Lyons, W. J. and A. M. Reimer. "The Demonic Virus and Qumran Studies: Some Preventative Measures." *Dead Sea Discoveries* 5 (1998): 16–32.

Maag, Victor. "Belija'al im Alten Testament." *Theologische Zeitschrift* 21 (1965): 287–99.

Mach, Michael. "Demons." Pages 189–92 in vol. 1 of *Encyclopedia of the Dead Sea Scrolls*. Edited by James C. VanderKam and Lawrence Schiffman. 2 vols. Oxford: Oxford University Press.

Magen, Yitzhak and Yuval Peleg. "The Qumran Excavations 1993–2004: Prelimary Report." Judea and Samaria Publications 6. Jerusalem: Israel Antiquities Authority, 2007.

Maier, Johann. "Early Jewish Biblical Interpretation in the Qumran Literature." Pages 108–29 in *Hebrew Bible/Old Testament: The History of Its Interpretation, Vol. 1: From the Beginnings to the Middle Ages (Until 1300)*. Edited by Magne Sæbø. Göttingen: Vandenhoeck & Ruprecht, 1996.

Macaskill, Grant. *Revealed Wisdom and Inaugurated Eschatology in Ancient Judaism and Early Christianity*. Journal for the Study of Judaism: Supplement Series 115. Leiden: Brill, 2007.

Malamat, A. "The Secret Council and Prophetic Involvement in Mari and Israel." Pages 231–36 in *Prophetie und geschichtliche Wirklichkeit im alten Israel: Festschrift für Siegfried Herrmann zum 65. Geburtstag*. Edited by Rüdiger Liwak and Siegfried Wagner. Stuttgart: Kohlhammer, 1991.

Mannheim, Karl. *Ideology and Utopia: An Introduction to the Sociology of Knowledge*. Translated by L. Wirth and E. Shils. New York: Harcourt Brace, 1936.

Mansoor, Menahem. "The Nature of Gnosticism in Qumran." Pages 389–400 in *Le origini dello gnosticismo: Colloquio di Messina 13–18 Aprile 1966*. Edited by U. Bianchi. Studies in the History of Religions (supplement to *Numen*) 10. Leiden: Brill, 1970.

Martone, Corrado. "Evil or Devil? Belial Between the Bible and Qumran." *Henoch* 26 (2004): 115–27.

Mason, Rex. "The Prophets of the Restoration." Pages 137–54 in *Israel's Prophetic Tradition: Essays in Honour of Peter R. Ackroyd*. Edited by Richard Coggins, A. Phillips and Michael Knibb. Cambridge: Cambridge University Press, 1982.

Mason, Steve. "What Josephus Says about the Essenes in His *Judean War*." Pages 423–52 in *Text and Artifact in the Religions of Mediterranean Antiquity: Essays in Honour of Peter Richardson*. Edited by Stephen G. Wilson and Michel Desjardins. Waterloo: Wilfrid Laurier University Press, 2000.

Mastrocinque, Attilio. *From Jewish Magic to Gnosticism*. Studien und Texte zu Antike und Christentum 24. Tübingen: Mohr Siebeck, 2005.

McCutcheon, Russell. *Manufacturing Religion: The Discourse on Sui Generis Religion and the Politics of Nostalgia*. Oxford: Oxford University Press, 1997.

McDonald, Lee Martin and James A. Sanders. *The Canon Debate*. Peabody, Mass.: Hendrickson, 2002.

McGinn, Bernard J., John J. Collins and Stephen J. Stein, eds. *The Continuum History of Apocalypticism*. New York: Continuum, 2003.

Metso, Sarianna. "Qumran Community Structure and Terminology as Theological Statement." *Revue de Qumran* 20 (2002): 429–44.

———. "Shifts in Covenantal Discourse in Second Temple Judaism." Pages 497–512 in *Scripture in Transition: Essays on Septuagint, Hebrew Bible, and Dead Sea Scrolls in Honour of Raija Sollamo*. Edited by Anssi Voitila and Jutta Jokiranta. Journal for the Study of Judaism Supplements 126. Leiden: Brill, 2008.

———. *The Textual Development of the Qumran Community Rule*. Studies on the Texts of the Desert of Judah 21. Leiden: Brill, 1997.

———. "Whom Does the Term Yaḥad Identify?" Pages 63–84 in *Defining Identities: We, You, and the Other in the Dead Sea Scrolls, Proceedings of the Fifth Meeting of the IOQS in Groningen*. Edited by Florentino García Martínez and Mladen Popović. Studies on the Texts of the Desert of Judah 70. Leiden: Brill, 2008.

Michalowski, P. "Adapa and the Ritual Process." Rocznik Orientalistyczny 41. (1980): 77–82.

Milik, J. T. *The Books of Enoch: Aramaic Fragments of Qumran Cave 4*. Oxford: Clarendon Press, 1976.

Miller, Patrick D. "Cosmology and World Order in the Old Testament: The Divine Council As Cosmic-Political Symbol." *Horizons in Biblical Theology* 9 (1987): 53–78.

Morgan, Michael. *Sefer ha-Razim: The Book of Mysteries*. Society of Biblical Literature Texts and Translations 25. Chico: Scholars Press, 1983.

Morray-Jones, Christopher R. A. "The Temple Within: The Embodied Divine Image and Its Worship in the Dead Sea Scrolls and Other Early Jewish and Christian Sources." Pages 400–431 in *Society of Biblical Literature Seminar Papers*. Society of Biblical Literature Seminar Papers 37. Atlanta: Scholars Press, 1998.

———. "Transformational Mysticism in the Apocalyptic Merkabah Tradition." *Journal of Jewish Studies* 43 (1992): 1–31.

Mullen, E. Theodore, Jr. *Assembly of the Gods: The Divine Council in Canaanite and Early Hebrew Literature*. Harvard Semitic Monographs 24. Chico, Calif.: Scholars Press, 1980.

Müller, H. -P. "Magisch-mantische Weisheit und die Gestalt Daniels." *Ugarit Forschungen* 1 (1969): 79–94.

———. "Mantische Weisheit und Apokalyptik." Pages 268–93 in *Congress Volume: Uppsala 1971*. Supplements to Vetus Testamentum 22. Leiden: Brill, 1972.

———. "Tun–Ergehens–Zusammenhang, Klageerhörung ud Theodizee im biblischen Hiobbuch und in seinen babylonischen Parallelen." Pages 373–93 in *The Wisdom Texts from Qumran and the Development of Sapiential Thought*. Edited by Charlotte Hempel, Armin Lange and Herman Lichtenberger. Bibliotheca ephemeridum theologicarum lovaniensium 159. Leuven: Leuven University Press, 2002.

Najman, Hindy. "Angels at Sinai: Exegesis, Theology, and Interpretive Authority." *Dead Sea Discoveries* 7 (2000): 313–33.

———. "Revelation as Interpretation." Paper presented at the Annual Meeting of the Association for Jewish Studies. Los Angeles, Calif., December 15–17, 2002.

———. *Seconding Sinai: The Development of Mosaic Discourse in Second Temple Judaism.* Journal for the Study of Judaism: Supplement Series 77. Leiden: Brill, 2003.

———. "The Symbolic Significance of Writing." Pages 139–73 in *The Idea of Biblical Interpretation: Essays in Honor of James L. Kugel.* Edited by Hindy Najman and Judith H. Newman. Journal for the Study of Judaism: Supplement Series 83. Leiden: Brill 2004.

Naveh, Joseph and J. C. Greenfield. "Hebrew and Aramaic in the Persian Period." Pages 115–29 in *The Cambridge History of Judaism 1: Introduction: The Persian Period.* Edited by W. D. Davies and L. Finkelstein. Cambridge: Cambridge University Press, 1984.

Naveh, Joseph and Shaul Shaked. *Amulets and Magic Bowls: Aramaic Incantations of Late Antiquity.* 2nd edition. Jerusalem: Magnes Press, 1987.

———. *Magic Spells and Formulae: Aramaic Incantations of Late Antiquity.* Jerusalem: Magnes Press, 1993.

Neef, Heinz-Dieter. *Gottes himmlischer Thronat: Hintergrund und Bedeutung von sôd JHWH im Alten Testament.* Stuttgart: Calwer, 1994.

Netz, R. "The First Jewish Scientist?" *Scripta Classica Israelica* 17 (1998): 27–33.

Neuser, Jacob. "What 'the Rabbis' Thought: A Method and a Result. One Statement on Prophecy in Rabbinic Judaism." Pages 303–320 in *Pursuing the Text: Studies in Honor of Ben Zion Wacholder on the Occasion of His Seventieth Birthday.* Edited by John C. Reeves and John Kampen. Journal for the Study of the Old Testament: Supplement Series 184. Sheffield: JSOT Press, 1994.

Newman, H. and R. Ludlam. *Proximity to Power and Jewish Sectarian Groups of the Ancient Period: A Review of Lifestyle, Values, and Halacha in the Pharisees, Sadducees, Essenes, and Qumran.* Leiden: Brill, 2006.

Newman, Judith. "Priestly Prophets at Qumran: Summoning Sinai through the Songs of the Sabbath Sacrifice." Pages 29–72 in *The Significance of Sinai: Traditions about Sinai and Divine Revelation in Judaism and Christianity.* Edited by G. J. Brooke, H. Najman, and L. T. Stuckenbruck. Themes in Biblical Narrative 13. Leiden: Brill, 2008.

Newsom, Carol. "Apocalyptic and the Discourse of the Qumran Community." *Journal of Near Eastern Studies* 49 (1990): 135–44.

———. "The Sage in the Literature of Qumran: The Functions of the *Maśkîl*." Pages 373–82 in *The Sage in Israel and the Ancient Near East.* Edited by John G. Gammie and Leo G. Perdue. Winona Lake, Ind.: Eisenbrauns, 1990.

———. "'Sectually Explicit' Literature from Qumran." Pages 167–87 in *The Hebrew Bible and Its Interpreters.* Edited by William H. Propp, Baruch Halpern and David Noel Freedman. Winona Lake, Ind.: Eisenbrauns, 1990.

———. *The Self as Symbolic Space: Constructing Identity and Community at Qumran.* Studies on the Texts of the Desert of Judah 52. Leiden: Brill, 2004.

———. *Songs of the Sabbath Sacrifice: A Critical Edition.* Harvard Semitic Studies 27. Atlanta: Scholars Press, 1985.

———. "What Do We Mean by Genre? A Report from Genology." Paper presented at the Annual Meeting of the SBL. San Antonio, Tex., November, 2004.

Newsom, Carol and Yigael Yadin. "The Masada Fragment of the Qumran Songs of the Sabbath Sacrifice." *Israel Exploration Journal* 34 (1984): 77–88.

Nickelsburg, George W. E. *1 Enoch: A Commentary on the Book of 1 Enoch Chapters 1–36; 81–108.* Hermeneia. Minneapolis: Fortress, 2001.

———. "Apocalyptic and Myth in 1 Enoch 6–11." *Journal of Biblical Literature* 96 (1977): 383–405.

———. "The Apocalyptic Construction of Reality in *1 Enoch.*" Pages 51–64 in *Mysteries and Revelations: Apocalyptic Studies since the Uppsala Colloquium.* Edited by J. J. Collins and J. Charlesworth. Journal for the Study of the Old Testament: Supplement Series 9. Sheffield: Sheffield Academic Press, 1991.

———. "The Bible Rewritten and Expanded." Pages 89–156 in *Jewish Writings of the Second Temple Period: Apocrypha, Pseudepigrapha, Qumran Sectarian Writings, Philo, Josephus.* Edited by Michael E. Stone. Compedia Rerum Ioudaicarum Novum Testamentum 2.2. Philadelphia: Fortress, 1984.

———. "The Epistle of Enoch and the Qumran Literature." *Journal of Jewish Studies* (1982): 333–48.

———. "The Nature and Function of Revelation in 1 Enoch, Jubilees, and Some Qumranic Documents." Paper presented at the annual symposium of the Orion Center. Jerusalem, Israel, 1997. Online: http://orion.mscc.huji.ac.il/orion/symposiums/2nd/papers/Nickelsburg.97

———. "Revealed Wisdom as a Criterion for Inclusion and Exclusion: From Jewish Sectarianism to Early Christianity." Pages 73–91 in *To See Ourselves as Others See Us.* Edited by J. Neusner and E. S. Frerichs. Atlanta: Society of Biblical Literature, 1985.

Nickelsburg, George W. E. and James C. VanderKam. *1 Enoch: A New Translation.* Minneapolis: Fortress, 2004.

Niditch, Susan and Robert Doran. "The Success Story of the Wise Courtier." *Journal of Biblical Literature* 96 (1977): 179–93.

Niehaus, Jeffrey. "*RĀZ-PEŠAR* in Isaiah XXIV." *Vetus Testamentum* 31 (1981): 376–77.

Nissinen, Marti. "Prophets and the Divine Council." Pages 4–19 in *Kein Land für sich allein: Studien zum Kulturdontakt in Kanaan, Israel/Palästina und Ebirnâri für Manfred Weippert zum 65. Geburtstag.* Edited by U. Hübner and E. A. Knauf. Orbis biblicus et orientalis 186. Freiburg: Universitätsverlag, 2002.

———. "Transmitting Divine Mysteries: The Prophetic Role of Wisdom Teachers in the Dead Sea Scrolls." Pages 513–33 in *Scripture in Transition: Essays on Septuagint, Hebrew Bible, and Dead Sea Scrolls in Honour of Raija Sollamo.* Edited by Anssi Voitila and Jutta Jokiranta. Journal for the Study of Judaism: Supplement Series 126. Leiden: Brill, 2008.

Nitzan, Bilhah. "4QBerakhot (4Q286–90): A Preliminary Report." Pages 53–71 in *New Qumran Texts and Studies: Proceedings of the First Meeting of the International Organization for Qumran Studies.* Edited by G. J. Brooke and F. G. Martínez. Studies on the Texts of the Desert of Judah 15. Leiden: Brill, 1994.

————. "Blessings and Curses." Pages 95–100 in vol. 1 of *Encyclopedia of the Dead Sea Scrolls*. Edited by James C. VanderKam and Lawrence Schiffman. 2 vols. Oxford: Oxford University Press, 2000.

————. "Harmonic and Mystical Characteristics in Poetic and Liturgical Writings from Qumran." *Jewish Quarterly Review* 85 (1994): 163–84.

————. "The Idea of Creation and Its Implications in Qumran Literature." Pages 240–64 in *Creation in the Jewish and Christian Tradition*. Edited by H. G. Reventlow and Y. Hoffman. Sheffield: Sheffield Academic Press, 2002.

————. "The Ideological and Literary Unity of 4QInstruction and Its Authorship." *Dead Sea Discoveries* 12 (2005): 257–79.

————. *Qumran Prayer and Religious Poetry*. Translated by Jonathan Chipman. Studies on the Texts of the Desert of Judah 12. Leiden: Brill, 1994.

Noegel, Scott. *Nocturnal Ciphers: The Allusive Language of Dreams in the Ancient Near East*. American Oriental Studies 89. New Haven, Conn.: American Oriental Society, 2007.

Nötscher, Friedrich. *Zur theologischen Terminologie der Qumran-Texte*. Bonner biblische Beiträge 10. Bonn: P. Hanstein, 1956.

Oppenheim, Leo. *The Interpretation of Dreams in the Ancient Near East*. Philadelphia: American Philosophical Society, 1956.

Orlov, Andrei. *From Apocalypticism to Merkabah Mysticism: Studies in the Slavonic Pseudepigrapha*. Journal for the Study of Judaism: Supplement Series 114. Leiden: Brill, 2007.

————. *The Enoch-Metatron Tradition*. Texte und Studien zum antiken Judentum 107. Tübingen: Mohr Siebeck, 2005.

Osten-Sacken, Peter von der. *Gott und Belial: Traditionsgeschichtliche Unter-suchungen zum Dualismus in den Texten aus Qumran*. Studien zur Umwelt des Neuen Testaments 6. Göttingen: Vandenhoeck & Ruprecht, 1969.

Ottley, Richard. *The Book of Isaiah According to the Septuagint*. 2 vols. Cambridge: Cambridge University Press, 1904–06.

Otzen, Benedikt. "Heavenly Visions in Early Judaism: Origin and Function." Pages 199–215 in *In the Shelter of Elyon: Essays on Ancient Palestinian Life and Literature in Honor of G. W. Ahlström*. Edited by W. B. Barrick and J. R. Spencer. Journal for the Study of the Old Testament: Supplement Series 31. Sheffield: JSOT Press, 1984.

Overholt, Thomas W. *Channels of Prophecy: The Social Dynamics of Prophetic Activity*. Minneapolis: Fortress, 1989.

Owen, Paul. "The Relationship of Eschatology to Esoteric Wisdom in the Jewish Pseudepigraphal Apocalypses." Pages 122–33 in *Of Scribes and Sages: Early Jewish Interpretation and Transmission of Scripture. Vol. 1: Ancient Versions and Traditions*. Edited by Craig A. Evans. Library of Second Temple Studies 50. London: T&T Clark, 2004.

Parpola, Simo. "The Assyrian Tree of Life: Tracing the Origins of Jewish Monotheism and Greek Philosophy." *Journal of the Near Eastern Society* 52 (1993): 161–208.

————. "Mesopotamian Astrology and Astronomy as Domains of the Mesopotamian 'Wisdom.'" Pages 47–59 in *Die Rolle der Astronomie in den*

Kulturen Mesopotamiens: Beiträge zum 3. Grazer Morgenländischen Symposium (23–27 September 1991). Edited by H. D. Galter. Grazer Morgenländischen Symposion 3. Graz, 1993.

———. "Monotheism in Ancient Assyria." Pages 165–209 in *One God or Many? Concepts of Divinity in the Ancient World.* Edited by Bezalel N. Porter. Transactions of the Casco Bay Assyriological Institute 1. Chebeague, Maine: Casco Bay Assyriological Institute, 2000.

Patte, Daniel. *Early Jewish Hermeneutic in Palestine.* Society of Biblical Literature Dissertation Series 22. Missoula, Mont.: Scholars Press, 1975.

Paul, Shalom. *Amos: A Commentary on the Book of Amos.* Hermeneia. Minneapolis: Fortress, 1991.

Pearson, Birger. "Gnosticism." Pages 313–17 in vol. 1 of *Encyclopedia of the Dead Sea Scrolls.* Edited by James C. VanderKam and Lawrence Schiffman. 2 vols. Oxford: Oxford University Press, 2000.

Penney, D. L. and Michael O. Wise. "By the Power of Beelzebub: An Aramaic Incantation Formula from Qumran (4Q560)." *Journal of Biblical Literature* 113 (1994): 627–50.

Perdue, Leo. "Revelation and the Problem of the Hidden God in Second Temple Wisdom Literature." Pages 201–222 in *Shall Not the Judge of the Earth Do What Is Right? Studies on the Nature of God in Tribute to James L. Crenshaw.* Edited by D. Penchansky and P. L. Redditt. Winona Lake, Ind.: Eisenbrauns, 2000.

Peters, Dorothy. *Noah Traditions in the Dead Sea Scrolls: Conversations and Controversies in Antiquity.* Society of Biblical Literature Early Judaism and Its Literature 26. Atlanta: Society of Biblical Literature, 2008.

Petersen, David L. "Israelite Prophecy: Change Versus Continuity." Pages 190–203 in *Congress Volume Leuven 1989.* Edited by J. A. Emerton. Supplements to Vetus Testamentum 43. Leiden: Brill, 1991.

———. *The Prophetic Literature: An Introduction.* Louisville, Ky.: Westminster John Knox, 2002.

Petuchowski, Jakob. "Judaism as 'Mystery'—The Hidden Agenda?" *Hebrew Union College Annual* 52 (1981): 141–52.

Peursen, Wido van. "Qumran Origins: Some Remarks on the Enochic/Essene Hypothesis." *Revue de Qumran* 20 (2001): 241–53.

Piovanelli, Perluigi. "Some Archaeological, Sociological, and Cross-Cultural Afterthoughts on the 'Groningen' and the 'Enochic/Essene' Hypotheses." Pages 95–106 in *Enoch and Qumran Origins: New Light on a Forgotten Connection.* Grand Rapids, Mich.: Eerdmans, 2005.

———. "Was There Sectarian Behaviour before the Flourishing of Jewish Sects? A Long-Term Approach to the History and Sociology of Second Temple Judaism." Pages 156–79 in *Sectarianism in Early Judaism: Sociological Advances.* Edited by David Chalcraft. London: Equinox, 2007.

Piper, Otto. "The 'Book of Mysteries' (Qumran I 27): A Study in Eschatology." *Journal of Religion* 38 (1958): 95–106.

Plöger, Otto. *Das Buch Daniel.* Kommentar zum Alten Testament 18. Gütersloher Verlagshaus, 1965.

———. *Theocracy and Eschatology*. Translated by S. Rudman. Richmond: John Knox, 1968.

Polley, Max. E. "Hebrew Prophecy Within the Council of Yahweh, Examined in Its Ancient Near Eastern Setting." Pages 141–56 in *Scripture in Context: Essays on the Comparative Method*. Edited by W. W. Hallo, J. B. White, C. D. Evans. Pittsburgh, Penn.: Pickwick, 1980.

Pongratz-Leisten, B. *Herrschaftwissen in Mesopotamien: Formen der Kommunikation zwischen Gott und König im 2. und 1. Jahrtausend v. Chr.* State Archives of Assyria Studies 10. Helsinki: The Neo-Assyrian Text Corpus Project, 1999.

Popović, Mladen. "Physiognomic Knowledge in Qumran and Babylonia: Form, Interdisciplinarity, and Secrecy." *Dead Sea Discoveries* 13 (2006): 150–76.

———. *Reading the Human Body: Physiognomics and Astrology in the Dead Sea Scrolls and Hellenistic-Early Roman Period Judaism*. Studies on the Texts of the Desert of Judah 67. Leiden: Brill, 2007.

Puech, Émile. "Une apocalypse messianique (4Q521)." *Revue de Qumran* 15 (1992): 475–519.

———. "Les Fragments eschatologiques de 4QInstruction (4Q416 I et 4Q418 69 ii, 81–81a, 127)." *Revue de Qumran* 22 (2005): 89–119.

———. "Hodayot." Pages 365–69 in vol. 1 of *Encyclopedia of the Dead Sea Scrolls*. Edited by James C. VanderKam and Lawrence Schiffman. 2 vols. Oxford: Oxford University Press, 2000.

———. "Le *Testament de Lévi* en araméen de la Geniza du Caire." *Revue de Qumran* 20 (2002): 511–66.

Qimron, Elisha and John Strugnell. "An Unpublished Halakhic Letter from Qumran." Pages 400–407 in *Biblical Archaeology Today*. Jerusalem: Israel Exploration Society, 1985.

Rabinowitz, I. "The Authorship, Audience and Date of the deVaux Fragment of an Unknown Work." *Journal of Biblical Literature* 71 (1952): 19–32.

———. "The Qumran Author's *spr hhgw/y*." *Journal of Near Eastern Studies* 20 (1961): 109–14.

Rad, Gerhard von. *Theologie des Alten Testaments*. 2 vols. Munich: C. Kaiser, 1960.

———. *Wisdom in Israel*. Nashville: Abingdon Press, 1972.

Radin, Max. *The Jews Among the Greeks and Romans*. Philadelphia: The Jewish Publication Society, 1915.

Ramírez, J. M. C. "El tema del 'Misterio' divino en la 'Regla de la Comunidad' de Qumran." *Scripta Theologica* 7 (1975): 481–97.

———. "Los 'Himnos' de Qumran y el 'Misterio' paulino." *Scripta Theologica* 8 (1976): 9–56.

———. "El 'Misterio' divino en los escritos posteriors de Qumran." *Scripta Theologica* 8 (1976): 445–75.

Reed, Annette Yoshiko. *Fallen Angels and the History of Judaism and Christianity: The Reception of Enochic Literature*. Cambridge: Cambridge University Press, 2005.

Reeves, John. *Jewish Lore and Manichaean Cosmogony: Studies in the Book of Giants Traditions*. Monographs of the Hebrew Union College 14. Cincinnati, Ohio: Hebrew Union College Press, 1992.

———. "Utnapishtim in the Book of Giants?" *Journal of Biblical Literature* 112 (1993): 110–15.

Regev, Eyal. "Abominated Temple and a Holy Community: The Formation of the Concepts of Purity and Impurity at Qumran." *Dead Sea Discoveries* 10 (2003): 243–78.

———. "Comparing Sectarian Practice and Organization: The Qumran Sect in Light of the Regulations of the Shakers, Hutterites, Mennonites and Amish." *Numen* 51 (2004): 146–81.

———. *Sectarianism in Qumran: A Cross-Cultural Perspective.* Religion and Society 45. Berlin: de Gruyter, 2007.

———. "The *Yaḥad* and the *Damascus Covenant*: Structure, Organization and Relationship." *Revue de Qumran* 21 (2003): 233–62.

Reicke, Bo. "The Knowledge Hidden in the Tree of Paradise." *Journal of Semitic Studies* 1 (1956): 193–201.

———. "Traces of Gnosticism in the Dead Sea Scrolls?" *New Testament Studies* 1 (1954): 137–41.

Reid, Stephen B. "The End of Prophecy in Light of Contemporary Social Theory." *Society of Biblical Literature Seminar Papers* 24 (1985): 515–23.

Reitzenstein, Richard. *Die hellenistischen Mysterien-religionen, ihre Grundgedanken un Wirkungen.* Leipzig: Tübner, 1910.

Rengstorf, Karl. *Hirbet Qumran und die Bibliothek vom Toten Meer.* Stuttgart: Kohlhammer, 1960.

Riedweg, Christoph. *Mysterienterminologie bei Platon, Philon und Klemens von Alexandrien.* Untersuchungen zur antiken Literatur und Geschichte 26. Berlin: de Gruyter, 1987.

Riffard, Pierre. *L'ésotérisme.* Paris: Payot, 1990.

Rigaux, B. "Révélation des Mystères et Perfection a Qumran et dans le Nouveau Testament." *New Testament Studies* 4 (1958): 237–62.

Ringgren, H. "Qumran and Gnosticism." Pages 379–84 in *Le origini dello gnosticismo: Colloquio di Messina 13–18 Aprile 1966.* Edited by U. Bianchi. Studies in the History of Religions (supplement to *Numen*) 10. Leiden: Brill, 1970.

Roberts, J. J. M. "The Importance of Isaiah at Qumran." Pages 273–86 in *Scripture and the Scrolls.* Edited by James H. Charlesworth. Vol. 1 of *The Bible and the Dead Sea Scrolls: The Princeton Symposium on the Dead Sea Scrolls.* Edited by James H. Charlesworth. Waco, Tex.: Baylor University Press, 2006.

Robertson, Edward. "The Urīm and Tummīm; What Were They?" *Vetus Testamentum* 14 (1964): 67–74.

Robinson, H. Wheeler. "The Council of Yahweh." *Journal of Theological Studies* 45 (1944): 151–57.

Rochberg, Francesca. *The Heavenly Writing: Divination, Horoscopy, and Astronomy in Mesopotamian Culture.* Cambridge: Cambridge University Press, 2004.

Rofe, A. "Revealed Wisdom from the Bible to Qumran." Pages 1–12 in *Sapiential Perspectives: Wisdom Literature in Light of the Dead Sea Scrolls. Proceedings of the Sixth International Symposium of the Orion Center for the Study of the Dead Sea Scrolls and Associated Literature, 20–22 May 2001.* Edited by J. J. Collins, G. E.

Sterling, and R. Clements. Studies on the Texts of the Desert of Judah 51. Leiden: Brill, 2004.

Ross, James. "The Prophet as Yahweh's Messenger." Pages 98–107 in *Israel's Prophetic Heritage: Essays in Honor of James Muilenburg*. Edited by Bernhard W. Anderson and Walter Harrelson. New York: Harper & Row, 1962.

Rowland, Christopher. *The Open Heaven: A Study of Apocalyptic in Judaism and Early Christianity*. New York: Crossroad, 1982.

Rylaarsdam, J. C. *Revelation in Jewish Wisdom Literature*. Chicago: University of Chicago Press, 1946.

Sæbø, Magne. *On the Way to Canon: Creative Tradition History in the Old Testament*. Journal for the Study of the Old Testament: Supplement Series. Sheffield: Sheffield Academic Press, 1998.

Sanders, E. P. *Judaism: Practice and Belief 63 B.C.E to 66 C.E.* London: SCM/Philadelphia: Trinity Press International, 1992.

———. *Paul and Palestinian Judaism: A Comparison of Patterns of Religion*. Philadelphia: Fortress, 1977.

Sanders, Jack T. "Wisdom, Theodicy, Death and the Evolution of Intellectual Traditions," *Journal for the Study of Judaism* 36 (2005): 263–77.

Sanders, Seth. "Performative Exegesis." Pages 57–82 in *Paradise Now: Essays on Early Jewish and Christian Mysticism*. Edited by April DeConick. Society of Biblical Literature Symposium Series 11. Atlanta: Society of Biblical Literature, 2006.

Sandmel, Samuel. "Parallelomania." *Journal of Biblical Literature* 81 (1962): 1–13.

Sapir, Edward. *Culture, Language and Personality*. Berkeley: University of California Press, 1970.

Sawyer, J. F. A. "'My Secret Is with Me' (Isaiah 24:16): Some Semantic Links between Isaiah 24–27 and Daniel." Pages 307–317 in *Understanding Poets and Prophets: Essays in Honor of George Wishart Anderson*. Edited by A. Graeme Auld. Journal for the Study of the Old Testament: Supplement Series 152. Sheffield: JSOT Press, 1993.

Schäfer, Peter, and Hans Kippenberg, eds. *Envisioning Magic: A Princeton Seminar and Symposium*. Studies in the History of Religions (supplement to *Numen*) 75. Leiden: Brill, 1975.

Schams, Christine. *Jewish Scribes in the Second-Temple Period*. Journal for the Study of the Old Testament: Supplement Series 291. Sheffield: Sheffield Academic Press, 1998.

Schaudig, H. *Die Inschriften Nabonids von Babylon und Kyros' des Großen samt den in ihrem Umfeld entstandenen Tendenzschriften: Textausgabe und Grammatik*. Alter Orient und Altes Testament 256. Münster: Ugarit, 2001.

Schiffman, Lawrence. "4QMysteries[a]: A Preliminary Edition and Translation." Pages 85–103 in *Solving Riddles and Untying Knots: Biblical, Epigraphic, and Semitic Studies in Honor of Jonas C. Greenfield*. Edited by Ziony Zevit et al. Winona Lake, Ind.: Eisenbrauns, 1995.

———. *The Eschatological Community of the Dead Sea Scrolls*. Atlanta: Scholars Press, 1989.

————. *The Halakhah at Qumran*. Studies in Judaism in Late Antiquity 16. Leiden: Brill, 1975.

————. "The King, His Guard, and the Royal Council in the *Temple Scroll*." *Proceedings of the American Academy of Jewish Research* 54 (1987): 237–59.

————. "The New Halakhic Letter (4QMMT) and the Origins of the Qumran Sect." *Biblical Archaeologist* 53 (1990): 64–73.

————. "Utopia and Reality: Political Leadership and Organization in the Dead Sea Scrolls Community." Pages 413–27 in *Emanuel: Studies in Hebrew Bible, Septuagint and Dead Sea Scrolls in Honor of Emanuel Tov*. Edited by Shalom M. Paul et al. Supplements to Vetus Testamentum 94. Leiden: Brill, 2003.

Schiffman, Lawrence and Michael Swartz. *Hebrew and Aramaic Incantation Texts: Selected Texts from Taylor-Schechter Box K1*. Sheffield: JSOT Press, 1992.

Schiffman, Lawrence and James C. VanderKam, eds. *Encyclopedia of the Dead Sea Scrolls*. 2 vols. Oxford: Oxford University Press, 2000.

Schmidt, Francis. "Ancient Jewish Astrology: An Attempt to Interpret 4QCryptic (4Q186)." Pages 189–205 in *Biblical Perspectives: Early Use and Interpretation of the Bible in Light of the Dead Sea Scrolls*. Edited by Michael E. Stone and Esther Chazon. Studies on the Texts of the Desert of Judah 28. Leiden: Brill, 1998.

Schmidt, Johann M. *Die jüdische Apokalyptik: die Geschichte ihrer Erforschung von den Anfängen bis zu den Textfunden von Qumran*. Second Edition. Neukirchen Vlyun: Neukirchener, 1976.

Schniedewind, William. "Aramaic, the Death of Written Hebrew, and Language Shift in the Persian Period." Pages 137–48 in *Margins of Writing, Origins of Cultures*. Edited by Seth L. Sanders. Oriental Institute Seminars 2. Chicago: Oriental Institute of the University of Chicago, 2006.

————. "Linguistic Ideology in Qumran Hebrew." Pages 245–55 in *Diggers at the Well: Proceedings of a Third International Symposium on the Hebrew of the Dead Sea Scrolls and Ben Sira*. Edited by T. Muraoka and J. F. Elwolde. Studies on the Texts of the Desert of Judah 36. Leiden: Brill, 2000.

————. "Qumran Hebrew As An Antilanguage." *Journal of Biblical Literature* 118 (1999): 235–52.

————. *The Word of God in Transition: From Prophet to Exegete in the Second Temple Period*. Journal for the Study of the Old Testament: Supplement Series 197. Sheffield: Sheffield Academic Press, 1995.

Schofield, Alison. *From Qumran to the Yahad: A New Paradigm of Textual Development for the Community Rule*. Studies on the Texts of the Desert of Judah 77; Leiden: Brill, 2008.

————. "The Wilderness Motif in the Dead Sea Scrolls." Pages 37–53 in *Themes in Biblical Narrative: Israel in the Wilderness*. Edited by K. Pomykala. Leiden: Brill, 2008.

————. "Rereading S: A New Model of Textual Development in Light of the Cave 4 *Serekh* Copies." *Dead Sea Discoveries* 15 (2008): 96–120.

Schwartz, S. "Language, Power and Identity." *Past and Present* 148 (1995): 21–31.

Scott, R. B. Y. "Priesthood, Prophecy, Wisdom, and the Knowledge of God." *Journal of Biblical Literature* 80 (1961): 1–15.

Segert, Stanislav. "Die Sprachenfragen in der Qumran Gemeinschaft." Pages 315–19 in *Qumran-Probleme: Vorträge des Leipziger Symposions über Qumran-Probleme vom 9. bis 14. Oktober 1961*. Edited by Hans Bardtke. Deutsche Akademie der Wissenschaften zu Berlin. Schriften der Sektion für Altertumswissenschaft 42. Berlin: Akademie-Verlag, 1963.

Seidel, M. "Bemerkungen zu den aramaïschen Papyrus und Ostraka aus Elephantine." *Zeitschrift für die alttestamentliche Wissenschaft* 32 (1912): 288–96.

Seitz, Christopher. *Isaiah 1–39*. Louisville, Ky.: John Knox, 1993.

Shaked, Shaul. "Esoteric Trends in Zoroastrianism." Proceedings of the Israel Academy of Sciences and Humanities 3 (1969): 193–213.

———. "Iranian Influence on Judaism: First Century BCE to Second Century CE." Pages 308–25 in *The Cambridge History of Judaism, Volume 1*. Edited by W. D. Davies and L. Finkelstein. 2 vols. Cambridge: Cambridge University Press, 1984.

———. "Qumran and Iran: Further Considerations." *Israel Oriental Society* 2 (1972): 433–46.

Shaked, S. and A. Netzer. *Irano-Judaica: Studies Relating to Jewish Contact with Persian Culture throughout the Ages*. 5 vols. Jerusalem: Ben-Zvi Institute Press, 1982–2003.

Shemesh, Aharon and Cana Werman. "The Hidden Things and Their Revelation." *Revue de Qumran* 18 (1998): 409–27.

Simmel, G. *The Sociology of Georg Simmel*. Translated and edited by K. H. Wolff. Glencoe, Ill.: Free Press, 1950.

Sjöberg, A. W. "In Praise of the Scribal Art." *Journal of Cuneiform Studies* 24 (1972): 126–27.

Skehan, Patrick and Alexander Di Lella. *The Wisdom of Ben Sira*. Anchor Bible 38. New York: Doubleday, 1987.

Smelik, Willem. "On Mystical Transformation of the Righteous into Light in Judaism." *Journal for the Study of Judaism* 26 (1995): 122–44.

Smith, Jonathan Z. *Drudgery Divine: On the Comparison of Early Christianities and the Religions of Late Antiquity*. Chicago: University of Chicago Press, 1990.

———. *Map is Not Territory: Studies in the History of Religions*. Chicago: University of Chicago Press, 1993.

Smith, Morton. "Ascent to the Heavens and Deification in 4QM^a." Pages 181–88 in *Archaeology and History in the Dead Sea Scrolls: A New York University Conference in Memory of Yigael Yadin*. Edited by Lawrence Schiffman. Sheffield: Sheffield Academic Press, 1990.

———. "Goodenough's Jewish Symbols in Retrospect." *Journal of Biblical Literature* 86 (1967): 53–68.

———. "Two Ascended to Heaven—Jesus and the Author of 4Q491." Pages 290–300 in *Jesus and the Dead Sea Scrolls*. Edited by J. H. Charlesworth. New York: Doubleday, 1992.

Smyth, H. W. *Aeschylus I*. Loeb Classical Library. Cambridge: Harvard University Press, 1922.

———. *Greek Grammar*. Cambridge: Harvard University Press, 1920.

Sokoloff, Michael. *A Dictionary of Jewish Palestinian Aramaic.* Ramat-Gan, Israel: Bar Ilan University Press, 1990.

Sperling, S. D. "Belial." Pages 169–71 in *Dictionary of Deities and Demons in the Bible.* Edited by K. van der Toorn, B. Becking, and P. van der Horst. 2nd ed. Grand Rapids, Mich.: Eerdmans, 1999.

Stanley, Christopher D. "The Importance of 4QTanḥumim (4Q176)." *Revue de Qumran* 15 (1992): 569–82.

Stark, Rodney and W. S. Bainbridge. *The Future of Religion: Secularization, Revival, and Cult Formation.* Berkeley: University of California Press, 1985.

Steck, Otto. *Die Prophetenbücher und ihr theologisches Zeugnis: Wege der Nachfrage und Fährten zur Antwort.* Tübingen: Mohr Siebeck, 1996.

Stegemann, Hartmut. "Die Bedeutung der Qumranfunde für die Erforschung der Apokalyptik." Pages 495–530 in *Apocalypticism in the Mediterranean World and the Near East: Proceedings of the International Colloquium on Apocalypticism, Uppsala, August 12–17, 1979.* Edited by David Hellholm. Tübingen: Mohr Siebeck, 1983.

Steinmetz, Devorah. "Sefer HeHago: The Community and the Book." *Journal of Jewish Studies* 52 (2001): 40–58.

Steudel, Annette. "אחרית הימים in the Texts from Qumran." *Revue de Qumran* 16 (1993): 225–46.

———. "God and Belial." Pages 332–40 in *The Dead Sea Scrolls: Fifty Years after Their Discovery. Proceedings of the Jerusalem Congress, July 20–25, 1997.* Edited by Lawrence Schiffman, Emanuel Tov and James C. VanderKam. Jerusalem: Israel Exploration Society in Cooperation with the Shrine of the Book, Israel Museum, 2000.

Stone, Michael E. "The Axis of History at Qumran." Pages 133–49 in *Pseudepigraphic Perspectives: The Apocrypha and Pseudepigrapha in Light of the Dead Sea Scrolls.* Edited by M. E. Stone and E. Chazon. Studies on the Texts of the Desert of Judah 31. Leiden: Brill, 1999.

———. "The Book of Enoch and Judaism in the Third Century B.C.E." *Catholic Biblical Quarterly* 40 (1978): 479–92.

———. "Enoch, Aramaic Levi, and Sectarian Origins." *Journal for the Study of Judaism* 19 (1988): 159–70.

———. "Levi, Aramaic." Pages 486–88 in vol. 1 of *Encyclopedia of the Dead Sea Scrolls.* Edited by James C. VanderKam and Lawrence Schiffman. 2 vols. Oxford: Oxford University Press, 2000.

———. "Lists of Revealed Things in the Apocalyptic Literature." Pages 414–54 in *Magnalia Dei: The Mighty Acts of God: Essays on the Bible and Archaeology in Memory of G. Ernest Wright.* Edited by Frank Moore Cross, Werner E. Lemke, and Patrick D. Miller, Jr. Garden City, N.Y.: Doubleday, 1976.

———. *Scriptures, Sects and Visions: A Profile of Judaism from Ezra to the Jewish Revolts.* Philadelphia: Fortress, 1980.

———. "Three Transformations in Judaism: Scripture, History, and Redemption." *Numen* 32 (1985): 218–35.

——— and E. Eshel. "The Holy Language at the End of Days in Light of a Qumran Fragment." *Tarbiz* 62 (1993): 169–77. Hebrew.

Stroumsa, Guy G. "From Esotericism to Mysticism in Early Christianity." Pages 289–309 in *Secrecy and Concealment: Studies in the History of Mediterranean and Near Eastern Religions*. Edited by Hans G. Kippenberg and Guy G. Stroumsa. Studies in the History of Religions (*Numen* Book Series) 65. Leiden: Brill, 1995.

———. *Hidden Wisdom: Esoteric Traditions and the Roots of Christian Mysticism*. Studies in the History of Religions (*Numen* Book Series) 70. Leiden: Brill, 1996.

Strugnell, John. "Notes en marge du Volume V des <<Discoveries in the Judaean Desert of Jordan>>." *Revue de Qumran* 7 (1970): 163–276.

———. "The Sapiential Work 4Q415ff. and the Pre-Qumranic Works from Qumran." Pages 595–608 in *The Provo International Conference on the Dead Sea Scrolls*. Edited by Donald W. Parry and Eugene Ulrich. Studies on the Texts of the Desert of Judah 30. Leiden: Brill, 1999.

Stuckenbruck, Loren T. "The 'Angels' and 'Giants' of Genesis 6:1–4 in Second and Third Century BCE Jewish Interpretation: Reflections on the Posture of Early Apocalyptic Traditions." *Dead Sea Discoveries* 7 (2000): 354–77.

———. *The Book of Giants from Qumran*. Tübingen: Mohr Siebeck, 1997.

———. "4QInstruction and the Possible Influence of Early Enochic Traditions: An Evaluation." Pages 245–61 in *The Wisdom Texts from Qumran and the Development of Sapiential Thought*. Edited by Charlotte Hempel, Armin Lange, and Herman Lichtenberger. Bibliotheca ephemeridum theologicarum lovaniensium 159. Leuven: Leuven University Press, 2002.

———. "Giant Mythology and Demonology: From the Ancient Near East to the Dead Sea Scrolls," Pages 318–38 in *Demons: The Demonology of Israelite-Jewish and Early Christian Literature in Context of their Environment*. Edited by Armin Lange, Hermann Lichtenberger, and K. F. Diethard Römheld. Tübingen: Mohr Siebeck, 2003.

Stuckrad, Kocku von. *Frömmigkeit und Wissenschaft. Astrologie in Tanach, Qumran und frührabbinischer Literatur*. Frankfurt: Peter Lang, 1996.

———. *Geschichte der Astrologie. Von den Anfängen bis zur Gegenwart*. Rev. ed. Munich: Beck, 2007.

———. "Jewish and Christian Astrology in Late Antiquity—A New Approach." *Numen* 47 (2000): 1–40.

———. "Reenchanting Nature: Modern Western Shamanism and Nineteenth-Century Thought." *Journal of the American Academy of Religion* 70 (2002): 771–99.

———. *Das Ringen um die Astrologie. Jüdische und christliche Beiträge zum antiken Zeitverständnis*. Religionsgeschichtliche Versuche und Vorarbeiten 49. Berlin: de Gruyter, 2000.

———. *Schamanismus und Esoterik. Kultur- und wissenschaftsgeschichtliche Betrachtungen*. Gnostica: Text and Interpretations 4. Leuven: Peeters, 2003.

———. *Western Esotericism: A Brief History of Secret Knowledge*. Translated by N. Goodrick-Clarke. London: Equinox, 2005. Translation of *Was ist Esoterik? Kleine Geschichte des geheimen Wissens*. Munich: Beck, 2004.

Swanson, Dwight. "4QCrypA Words of the *Maskil* to All the Sons of Dawn: The Path of the Virtuous Life." Pages 49–61 in *Sapiential, Liturgical and Poetical Texts from Qumran: Proceedings of the Third Meeting of the International Organization for Qumran Studies, Oslo 1998*. Edited by Daniel K. Falk, Florentino García Martínez and Eileen M. Schuller. Studies on the Texts of the Desert of Judah 35. Leiden: Brill, 2000.

Swartz, Michael. "The Dead Sea Scrolls and Later Jewish Magic and Mysticism." *Dead Sea Discoveries* 8 (2001): 182–93.

Swarup, Paul. *The Self-Understanding of the Dead Sea Scrolls Community*. Library of Second Temple Studies 59. London: T&T Clark, 2006.

Talmon, Shemaryahu. "The Calendar of the Covenanters of the Judean Desert." Pages 147–85 in *The World of Qumran from Within: Collected Studies*. Jerusalem: Magnes, 1989.

———. "The 'Desert Motif' in the Bible and in Qumran Literature." Pages 31–63 in *Biblical Motifs, Origins, and Transformations*. Edited by A. Altmann. Cambridge: Harvard University Press, 1966.

———. "The Emergence of Jewish Sectarianism in the Early Second Temple Period." Pages 587–616 in *Ancient Israelite Religion: Essays in Honor of Frank Moore Cross*. Edited by Patrick Miller, Paul Hanson and S. Dean McBride. Philadelphia: Fortress, 1987.

———. "The Internal Diversification of Judaism in the Early Second Temple Period." Pages 16–43 in *Jewish Civilization in the Hellenistic-Roman Period*. Edited by S. Talmon. Philadelphia: Trinity Press International, 1991.

Thomas, D. Winton. "*beliyya'al* in the Old Testament." Pages 11–19 in *Biblical and Patristic Studies in Memory of Robert Pierce Casey*. Freiburg: Herder, 1963.

Thomas, Samuel I. Review of Philip S. Alexander, *The Mystical Texts: Songs of the Sabbath Sacrifice and Related Manuscripts*. Review of Biblical Literature [http://bookreviews.org] (2008).

———. "Goodenough, E. R." In *Dictionary of Early Judaism*. Edited by John J. Collins and Daniel Harlow. Grand Rapids, Mich.: Eerdmans, forthcoming.

———. "Judaism: Mystery Religion as." In *Dictionary of Early Judaism*. Edited by John J. Collins and Daniel Harlow. Grand Rapids, Mich.: Eerdmans, forthcoming.

———. "'Riddled' with Guilt: The Mysteries of Transgression, the Sealed Vision, and the Art of Interpretation in 4Q300 and Related Texts." *Dead Sea Discoveries* 15 (2008): 155–71.

Thompson, Leonard L. "Mapping an Apocalyptic World." Pages 115–27 in *Sacred Places and Profane Spaces: Essays in the Geographics of Judaism, Christianity, and Islam*. Edited by Jamie Scott and Paul Simpson-Housley. Contributions to the Study of Religion 30. New York: Greenwood, 1991.

Tigchelaar, Eibert J. C. "The Addressees of 4QInstruction." Pages 62–75 in *Sapiential, Liturgical, and Poetical Texts from Qumran: Proceedings of the Third Meeting of the International Organization for Qumran Studies, Oslo 1998*. Edited by D. Falk. Studies on the Texts of the Desert of Judah 35. Leiden: Brill, 2000.

———. "The Imaginal Context and the Visionary of the Aramaic *New Jerusalem*." Pages 257–70 in *Flores Florentino: Dead Sea Scrolls and Other Early Jewish*

Studies in Honor of Florentino García Martínez. Edited by Anthony Hilhorst, Émile Puech, and Eibert J. C. Tigchelaar. Journal for the Study of Judaism: Supplement Series 122. Leiden: Brill, 2007.

———. *To Increase Learning for the Understanding Ones: Reading and Reconstructing the Fragmentary Early Jewish Sapiential Text 4QInstruction.* Studies on the Texts of the Desert of Judah 44. Leiden: Brill, 2001.

———. *Prophets of Old and the Day of the End: Zecharia, the Book of the Watchers and Apocalyptic.* Oudtestamentische Studiën 35. Leiden: Brill, 1996.

———. "Your Wisdom and Your Folly: The Case of 1–4QMysteries." Pages 69–88 in *Wisdom and Apocalypticism in the Dead Sea Scrolls and in the Biblical Tradition.* Edited by F. G. Martínez; Bibliotheca ephemeridum theologicarum lovaniensium 168. Leuven: Leuven University Press, 2003.

Tiller, Patrick. "The 'Eternal Planting' in the Dead Sea Scrolls." *Dead Sea Discoveries* 4 (1997): 312–35.

Tillich, Paul. *Systematic Theology, Vol. 1.* Chicago: University of Chicago Press, 1951.

Tiryakian, Edward. "Toward the Sociology of Esoteric Culture." *American Journal of Sociology* 78 (1972): 491–512.

Toepel, Alexander. "Planetary Demons in Early Jewish Literature." *Journal for the Study of the Pseudepigrapha* 14 (2005): 231–38.

Toorn, Karel van der. *Scribal Culture and the Making of the Hebrew Bible.* Cambridge: Harvard University Press, 2007.

Tov, Emanuel. *Scribal Practices and Approaches Reflected in the Texts Found in the Judean Desert.* Studies on the Texts of the Desert of Judah 54. Leiden: Brill, 2004.

———. "The Text of Isaiah at Qumran." Pages 477–80 in *Writing and Reading the Scroll of Isaiah: Studies of an Interpretive Tradition. Volume 2.* Edited by C. C. Broyles and C. A. Evans. Supplements to Vetus Testamentum 70.2. Leiden: Brill, 1997.

———. *The Texts from the Judaean Desert: Indices and an Introduction to the Discoveries in the Judaean Desert Series.* Discoveries in the Judaean Desert 39. Oxford: Clarendon Press, 2002.

Troxel, Ronald. *LXX-Isaiah as Translation and Interpretation: The Strategies of the Translator of the Septuagint of Isaiah.* Journal for the Study of Judaism: Supplement Series 124. Leiden: Brill, 2008.

Ulrich, Eugene. "The Dead Sea Scrolls and the Hebrew Scriptural Texts." Pages 77–99 in *Scripture and the Scrolls.* Edited by James H. Charlesworth. Vol. 1 of *The Bible and the Dead Sea Scrolls: The Princeton Symposium on the Dead Sea Scrolls.* Edited by James H. Charlesworth. Waco, Tex.: Baylor University Press, 2006.

———. *The Dead Sea Scrolls and the Origins of the Bible.* Studies in the Dead Sea Scrolls and Related Literature. Grand Rapids: Eerdmans, 1999.

———. "The Developmental Composition of the Book of Isaiah: Light from 1QIsaa on Additions in the MT." *Dead Sea Discoveries* 8 (2001): 288–305.

———. "The Qumran Scrolls and the Biblical Text." Pages 51–59 in *The Dead Sea Scrolls Fifty Years after Their Discover: Proceedings of the Jerusalem Congress, July*

20–25, 1997. Edited by Lawrence H. Schiffman, Emanuel Tov and James C. VanderKam. Jerusalem: Israel Exploration Society in Cooperation with the Shrine of the Book Museum, 2000.

———. *The Qumran Text of Samuel and Josephus*. Harvard Semitic Monographs 19. Cambridge: Harvard University Press, 1978.

Urbach, Ephraim. "When Did Prophecy Cease?" *Tarbiz* 17 (1955): 1–11. Hebrew.

Urban, Hugh. "The Torment of Secrecy: Ethical and Epistemological Problems in the Study of Esoteric Traditions." *History of Religions* 37 (1998): 209–48.

Unnik, W. C. van. "Flavius Josephus and the Mysteries." Pages 244–79 in *Studies in Hellenistic Religions*. Edited by M. J. Vermaseren. Leiden: Brill, 1979.

VanderKam, James C. "The Angel of the Presence in the Book of Jubilees." *Dead Sea Discoveries* 7 (2000): 378–93.

———. "Apocalyptic Tradition in the Dead Sea Scrolls and the Religion of Qumran." Pages 113–34 in *Religion in the Dead Sea Scrolls*. Edited by John J. Collins and Robert A. Kugler. Studies in the Dead Sea Scrolls and Related Literature. Grand Rapids: Eerdmans, 2000.

———. "Authoritative Literature in the Dead Sea Scrolls." *Dead Sea Discoveries* 5 (1998): 382–402.

———. "The Birth of Noah." Pages 213–31 in *Intertestamental Essays in Honor of Jósef Tadeusz Milik*. Edited by Z. J. Kapera. Kraków: The Enigma Press, 1992.

———. *Calendars in the Dead Sea Scrolls: Measuring Time*. London: Routledge, 1998.

———. *The Dead Sea Scrolls Today*. Grand Rapids, Mich.: Eerdmans, 1994.

———. *Enoch and the Growth of an Apocalyptic Tradition*. Catholic Biblical Quarterly Monograph Series 16. Washington, D.C.: The Catholic Biblical Association of America, 1984.

———. "Greek at Qumran." Pages 175–81 in *Hellenism in the Land of Israel*. Edited by John J. Collins and Gregory E. Sterling. Christianity and Judaism in Antiquity Series 13. Notre Dame, Ind.: University of Notre Dame Press, 2001.

———. "Identity and History of the Community." Pages 487–533 in *The Dead Sea Scrolls After Fifty Years, Volume 2*. Edited by Peter Flint and James C. VanderKam. Leiden: Brill, 1999.

———. "The Judean Desert and the Community of the Dead Sea Scrolls." Pages 159–71 in *Antikes Judentum und Frühes Christentum: Festschrift für Hartmut Stegemann zum 65. Geburtstag*. Edited by B. Kollmann, W. Reinbold, and A. Steudel. Berlin: de Gruyter, 1999.

———. "Mantic Wisdom in the Dead Sea Scrolls." *Dead Sea Discoveries* 4 (1997): 336–53.

———. "Mapping Second Temple Judaism." Pages 1–20 in *The Early Enoch Literature*. Edited by Gabriele Boccaccini and John J. Collins. Journal for the Study of Judaism: Supplement Series 121. Leiden: Brill, 2007.

———. "Messianism in the Scrolls." Pages 211–34 in *The Community of the Renewed Covenant: The Notre Dame Symposium on the Dead Sea Scrolls*. Edited by E. Ulrich and J. C. VanderKam. Christianity and Judaism in Antiquity Series 10. Notre Dame, Ind.: University of Notre Dame Press, 1994.

————. "The Prophetic–Sapiential Origins of Apocalyptic Thought." Pages 163–76 in *A Word in Season: Essays in Honour of William McKane*. Edited by James D. Martin and Philip R. Davies. Journal for the Study of the Old Testament: Supplement Series 42. Sheffield: JSOT Press, 1986.

————. "Revealed Literature in the Second Temple Period." Pages 1–30 in *From Revelation to Canon: Studies in the Hebrew Bible and Second Temple Literature*. Leiden: Brill, 2002.

————. "The Righteousness of Noah." Pages 13–32 in *Ideal Figures in Ancient Judaism: Profiles and Paradigms*. Edited by John J. Collins and George W. E. Nickelsburg. Society of Biblical Literature Septuagint and Cognate Studies 12. Chico, Calif.: Scholars Press, 1980.

————. "Shavuʿot." Pages 871–72 in vol. 2 of *Encyclopedia of the Dead Sea Scrolls*. Edited by James C. VanderKam and Lawrence Schiffman. 2 vols. Oxford: Oxford University Press, 2000.

————. "The Wording of Biblical Citations in Some Rewritten Scriptural Works." Pages 41–56 in *The Bible as Book: The Hebrew Bible and the Judaean Desert Discoveries*. Edited by Edward D. Herbert and Emanuel Tov. London: The British Library and Oak Knoll Press in association with The Scriptorium: Center for Christian Antiquities, 2002.

————. Review of M. Goff, *The Worldly and Heavenly Wisdom of 4QInstruction*. *Catholic Biblical Quarterly* 67 (2005): 117–18.

———— and Peter Flint. *The Meaning of the Dead Sea Scrolls: Their Significance for Understanding the Bible, Judaism, Jesus and Christianity*. San Francisco: HarperSanFrancisco, 2002.

Vaux, Roland de. "La Grotte des manuscrits hébreux," *Revue Biblique* 66 (1949): 589–610.

Vermes, Geza. "Bible Interpretation at Qumran." Pages 184–91 in *Yigael Yadin Memorial Volume*. Edited by A. Ben–Tor, Jonas C. Greenfield, and A. Malamat. Jerusalem: Israel Exploration Society, 1989.

————. *Scripture and Tradition in Judaism: Haggadic Studies*. Studia post-biblica 4. Leiden: Brill, 1974.

Vogt, E., S.J. "'Mysteria' in Textibus Qumrân." *Biblica* 37 (1956): 247–57.

Wacholder, Ben Zion. "The 'Sealed' Torah Versus the 'Revealed' Torah: An Exegesis of the Damascus Covenant V, 1–6 and Jeremiah 32:10–14." *Revue de Qumran* 12 (1986): 351–68.

Walker-Ramisch, S. "Graeco-Roman Voluntary Associations and the Damascus Document: A Sociological Analysis." Pages 128–45 in *Voluntary Associations in the Graeco-Roman World*. Edited by John S. Kloppenborg and S. G. Wilson. London: Routledge, 1996.

Wallis, Roy, ed. *Sectarianism: Analyses of Religious and Non-Religious Sects*. New York: Wiley, 1975.

Weber, Max. *The Sociology of Religion*. Translated by E. Fischoff. Boston: Beacon, 1963.

Weinfeld, Moshe. *Normative and Sectarian Judaism in the Second Temple Period*. Library of Second Temple Studies 54. London: T&T Clark, 2005.

——. *The Organizational Pattern and the Penal Code of the Qumran Sect: A Comparison with Guilds and Religious Associations of the Hellenistic-Roman Period*. Göttingen: Vandenhoeck & Ruprecht, 1986.

Weissenberg, Hanne von. *4QMMT: Reevaluating the Text, the Function, and the Meaning of the Epilogue*. Studies on the Texts of the Desert of Judah 82. Leiden: Brill, 2008.

Weitzman, Steven. "Why Did the Qumran Community Write in Hebrew?" *Journal of the American Oriental Society* 119 (1999): 35–45.

Werman, Cana. "'The תורה and תעודה Engraved on the Tablets." *Dead Sea Discoveries* 9 (2002): 75–103.

——. "What is the Book of *Hagu*?" Pages 125–40 in *Sapiential Perspectives: Wisdom Literature in Light of the Dead Sea Scrolls. Proceedings of the Sixth International Symposium of the Orion Center for the Study of the Dead Sea Scrolls, 20–22 May, 2001*. Edited by J. J. Collins, G. E. Sterling and R. Clements. Studies on the Texts of the Desert of Judah 51. Leiden: Brill, 2004.

Wernberg-Moeller, P. *The Manual of Discipline Translated and Annotated with an Introduction*. Studies on the Texts of the Desert of Judah 1. Leiden: Brill, 1957.

Westenholz, J. G. "Thoughts on Esoteric Knowledge and Secret Lore." Pages 451–62 in *Intellectual Life of the Ancient Near East: Papers Presented at the 43rd Rencontre assyriologique internationale; Prague, July 1–5, 1996*. Edited by J. Prosecky. Prague: Academy of Sciences of the Czech Republic Oriental Institute, 1998.

Whybray, R. Norman. *The Heavenly Counsellor in Isaiah xl 13–14: A Study of the Sources of the Theology of Deutero-Isaiah*. Cambridge: Cambridge University Press, 1971.

Widengren, Geo. "Les quatre Âges du monde." Pages 23–62 in *Apocalyptique iranienne et dualisme qoumrânien*. Edited by Geo Widengren, Marc Philonenko and Anders Hultgård. Paris: Maisonneuve, 1995.

Widengren, Geo, Anders Hultgård and Marc Philonenko. *Apocalyptique iranienne et dualisme qoumrânien*. Recherches Intertestamentaires 2. Paris: Adrien Maisonneuve, 1995.

Willi–Plein, I. "Das Geheimnis der Apokalyptik." *Vetus Testamentum* 27 (1977): 62–81.

——. *Vorformen der Schriftexegese innerhalb des Alten Testaments: Untersuchungen zum literarischen Werden der auf Amos, Hosea und Micha zurückgehenden Bücher im hebräischen Zwölfprophetenbuch*. Beihefte zur Zeitschrift für die alttestamentliche Wissenschaft 123. Berlin: de Gruyter, 1971.

Wills, Lawrence M. *The Jew in the Court of the Foreign King*. Harvard Dissertations in Religion 26. Minneapolis: Fortress, 1990.

Wilson, Bryan R. *Magic and the Millennium: A Sociological Study of Religious Movements of Protest among Tribal and Third-World Peoples*. London: Heinemann, 1973.

——. *Religion in Sociological Perspective*. Oxford: Oxford University Press, 1982.

——. *The Social Dimensions of Sectarianism*. Oxford: Oxford University Press, 1990.

————, ed. *Patterns of Sectarianism: Organization and Ideology in Social and Religious Movements*. London: Heinemann, 1967.

Wilson, Robert R. "Prophecy and Ecstasy: A Reexamination." *Journal of Biblical Literature* 98 (1979): 321–37.

————. "From Prophecy to Apocalyptic: Reflections on the Shape of Israelite Religion." *Semeia* 21 (1981): 79–95.

————. *Prophecy and Society in Ancient Israel*. Philadelphia: Fortress, 1980.

Winston, David. "The Iranian Component in the Bible, Apocrypha, and Qumran: A Review of the Evidence." *History of Religions* 5 (1966): 183–216.

Wise, Michael O. "מי כמוני באלים: A Study of 4Q491c, 4Q471b, 4Q427 7 and 1QHa 25:35–26:10." *Dead Sea Discoveries* 7 (2000): 173–219.

Wold, Benjamin G. *Women, Men, and Angels: The Qumran Wisdom Document 'Musar leMevin' and Its Allusions to Genesis Creation Traditions*. Wissenschaftliche Untersuchungen zum Neuen Testament 2/201. Tübingen: Mohr Siebeck, 2005.

Wolff, H. W. *Amos the Prophet: The Man and His Background*. Translated by F. R. McCurley. Philadelphia: Fortress, 1973.

————. *Joel and Amos: A Commentary on the Books of the Prophets Joel and Amos*. Translated by W. Janzen et al. Hermeneia; Philadelphia: Fortress, 1977.

Wolfson, Elliot. "The Hermeneutics of Visionary Experience: Revelation and Interpretation in the Zohar." *Religion* 18 (1988): 311–45.

————. "Introduction." Pages 1–10 in *Rending the Veil: Concealment and Secrecy in the History of Religions*. New York University Annual Conference in Comparative Religions. New York: Seven Bridges Press, 1999.

————. "Mysticism and the Poetic-Liturgical Compositions from Qumran." *Jewish Quarterly Review* 85 (1994): 185–202.

————. "The Seven Mysteries of Knowledge: Qumran E/Sotericism Recovered." Pages 177–213 in *The Idea of Biblical Interpretation: Essays in Honor of James L. Kugel*. Edited by Hindy Najman and Judith H. Newman. Journal for the Study of Judaism: Supplement Series 83. Leiden: Brill, 2003.

————. *Through a Speculum That Shines: Vision and Imagination in Medieval Jewish Mysticism*. Princeton, N.J.: Princeton University Press, 1994.

————, ed. *Rending the Veil: Concealment and Secrecy in the History of Religions*. New York University Annual Conference in Comparative Religions. New York: Seven Bridges, 1999.

Wright, Benjamin G. III. "From Generation to Generation: The Sage as Father in Early Jewish Literature." Pages 309–332 in *Biblical Traditions in Transmission: Essays in Honour of Michael A. Knibb*. Edited by C. Hempel and J. M. Lieu. Journal for the Study of Judaism: Supplement Series 111. Leiden: Brill, 2006.

————. "Putting the Puzzle Together: Some Suggestions Concerning the Social Location of the Wisdom of Ben Sira." Pages 133–49 in *SBL Seminar Papers, 1996*. Society of Biblical Literature Seminar Papers 35. Atlanta: Scholars Press, 1996.

Wright, Benjamin G. III, and Lawrence M. Wills, eds. *Conflicted Boundaries in Wisdom and Apocalypticism*. Soceity of Biblical Literature Symposium Series 35. Atlanta: Society of Biblical Literature, 2005.

Wright, George E. *The Old Testament Against Its Environment.* Studies in Biblical Theology 2. Naperville, Ill.: Allenson, 1957.

Yadin, A. "Samson's *HÎDÂ.*" *Vetus Testamentum* 52 (2002): 407–26.

Yadin, Yigael. "Excavations at Masada: 1963–64. Preliminary Report." *Israel Exploration Journal* 15 (1965): 105–108.

———. *The Temple Scroll.* 3 vols. Jerusalem: Israel Exploration Society and The Shrine of the Book, 1977–83.

Yamauchi, E. M. *Persia and the Bible.* Grand Rapids, Mich.: Baker Book House, 1990.

Zangenberg, Jürgen. "Wildnis unter Palmen? Khirbet Qumran im regionalen Kontext des Toten Meeres." Pages 129–64 in *Jericho und Qumran.* Edited by B. Mayer. Regensburg: Freidrich Pustet, 2000.

Zellner, William and Mark Petrowski, eds. *Sects, Cults and Spiritual Communities: A Sociological Analysis.* Westport, Conn.: Praeger, 1998.

BIBLICAL AND APOCRYPHAL BOOKS

DEAD SEA SCROLLS AND RELATED TEXTS

OTHER ANCIENT LITERATURE

MODERN AUTHORS

Abegg Jr., Martin G., 129, 204
Adams, Samuel, 73
Albright, William F., 197
Alexander, Philip S., 14–15, 30, 31, 54, 60, 101, 123, 124, 175, 218, 220, 239
Anderson, Francis I., 88–89
Argall, Randall, 37, 95, 154, 224
Arnold, Russell C. D., 68–69, 167
Aune, David, 188, 192–93

Bainbridge, W. S., 3, 65–66
Bakhtin, Mikhail, 72
Bar-Ilan, Meir, 77
Barkun, Michael, 39, 40, 53
Barr, James, 16–17, 245
Barton, John, 188
Baumgarten, Albert, 18, 29, 61, 62, 64–65
Beale, Todd S., 192
Bedenbender, Andreas, 39
Ben Dov, Jonathan, 26, 30, 53, 59, 60–61, 235
Bernstein, Moshe, 120, 198, 199, 246
Berrin, Shani, 199
Betz, Otto, 199, 205
Beaulieu, Paul-Alain, 36, 56, 58
Bietenhard, Hans, 114
Blanchot, Maurice, 35
Blenkinsopp, Joseph, 61, 107, 110, 141, 142, 190–91, 194, 201, 203, 229–230
Bloom, Maureen, 81
Boccaccini, Gabriele, 29, 53, 63–64
Böck, Barbara, 60
Bockmuehl, Markus, 9–10, 145, 175
Bohak, Gideon, 30
Bok, Sisela, 39
Bolle, Kees, 36, 40
Botterweck, G. J., 83, 161

Bourdieu, Pierre, 77
Boustan, Ra'anan, 30
Boyce, Mary, 245, 247–48
Brayer, Menachem, 59
Bremmer, Jan, 1, 31
Brooke, George, 22, 148, 192, 194, 195–96, 198, 199, 202–203, 207, 220, 221
Brown, Raymond, 6–7, 89, 175
Brownlee, William, 199, 207
Bruce, F. F., 169
Burkes, Shannon, 178
Burns, Joshua Ezra, 12
Burrows, Millar, 192
Burstein, Stanley, 97

Callendar, Dexter, 93, 96–98
Cansdale, Lena, 27
Carmignac, J., 8–9
Chalcraft, David, 61, 69
Charlesworth, James H., 30,
Clifford, Richard J., 82
Clines, David, 82, 94
Cohen, Chaim, 37
Cohen, Naomi, 189, 194
Cohen, Shaye D., 62
Cohn, Norman, 245
Collins, Adela Yarbro, 8–9
Collins, John J., 8, 9, 12, 18, 25, 28, 38, 49, 53, 63, 64, 66, 67, 73, 91, 115, 140, 141, 151, 153, 171, 178, 195, 218, 224, 226, 251
Cooke, G., 82, 87
Corbin, Henry, 13
Corley, Jeremy, 158
Cotton, Hannah, 18
Cowley, A. E., 250
Crawford, Sidney White, 198

CPSIA information can be obtained
at www.ICGtesting.com
Printed in the USA
BVHW031514110620
581230BV00002B/38

9 781589 834132